CONTEMPORARY POLITICAL IDEOLOGIES

Second Edition

Edited by

Roger Eatwell and Anthony Wright

CONTINUUM
London and New York

Continuum
The Tower Building, 11 York Road, London SE1 7NX
370 Lexington Avenue, New York, NY 10017–6503
www.continuumbooks.com

First published 1993. Reprinted 1994, 1996
Second edition published 1999. Reprinted 1999, 2000, 2001

British Library Cataloguing in Publication Data
A catalogue record for this book is available from the British Library
ISBN 1 85567 605 2 (Hardback)
0 8264 5173 X (Paperback)

Library of Congress Cataloging-in-Publication Data
Contemporary political ideologies/edited by Roger Eatwell and
Anthony Wright.—2nd ed.
   p. cm.
Includes bibliographical references and index.
ISBN 1–85567–605–2.—ISBN 0–8264–5173–X (pbk.)
1. Political science. 2. Right and Left (Political science).
3. Ideology. I. Eatwell, Roger. II. Wright, Anthony, 1948– .
JA83.C637 1999
320.5—DC21   98–30981
                                               CIP

Typeset by York House Typographic Ltd
Printed and bound in Great Britain by Biddles Ltd, *www.biddles.co.uk*

CONTENTS

NOTES ON CONTRIBUTORS

Richard Bellamy is Professor of Politics at the University of Reading. Among his publications are *Modern Italian Social Theory* (1987), *Liberalism and Modern Society* (1992) and (as co-author) *Gramsci and the Italian State* (1993). He is editor of *Victorian Liberalism* (1990), *Constitutionalism in Transformation: European Theoretical Perspectives* (1996) and *Liberalism and Pluralism* (1999).

Valerie Bryson is Principal Lecturer in Politics at Huddersfield University. Her publications include *Feminist Political Theory* (1992) and *Feminist Debates. Issues of Theory and Political Practice* (1999). Among her recent articles are various ones on the role of women in Israel, and on feminist theory.

Youssef Choueiri is Reader in Arab and Islamic Studies at the University of Exeter. Born in Lebanon, Dr Choueiri studied at the American University in Beirut and the University of Cambridge. A fellow of the Royal Historical Society, his publications include *Arab History and the Nation-State, 1820–1980* (1989) and *Islamic Fundamentalism* (new edn, 1997).

Andrew Dobson is Professor of Politics at Keele University. Among his publications are *An Introduction to the Politics and Philosophy of José Ortega y Gasset* (1989), *Jean-Paul Sartre and the Politics of Reason* (1993), *Green Political Thought* (second edn, 1995) and *Justice and the Environment* (1998). He is the editor of *The Green Reader* (1991) and of *Fairness and Futurity* (1999), and the co-editor (with Paul Lucardie) of *The Politics of Nature* (1993).

Roger Eatwell is Professor of European Politics at the University of Bath. His books include (as co-editor) *The Nature of the Right* (1989), *Fascism: A History* (1995), and (as editor) *European Political Cultures* (1997) and *Un* *nuovo modello di fascismo generico* (1999). He has also published numerous articles and chapters, especially on aspects of fascism and contemporary extremism.

Joseph V. Femia is Reader in Politics at the University of Liverpool. His publications include *Gramsci's Political Thought* (1981), *Marxism and Democracy* (1993) and *The Machiavellian Legacy* (1998). He is also the author of numerous articles and chapters, particularly on Marxism, most notably Gramsci's thought, and aspects of democratic theory.

Roger Griffin is Professor of Modern History at Oxford Brookes University. Among his main publications are *The Nature of Fascism* (1991) and the edited readers *Fascism* (1995) and *International Fascism: Theories, Causes and the New Consensus* (1998). He is also the author of numerous chapters and articles on aspects of twentieth-century nationalism.

Jeremy Jennings is Professor of Political Theory at the University of Birmingham. He is author of *Georges Sorel* (1985) and *Syndicalism in France* (1990), and editor of *Intellectuals in Twentieth-Century France* (1993) and *Intellectuals and Politics* (1997). He has recently edited a new translation of Georges Sorel's *Reflections on Violence* for Cambridge University Press and is currently completing a history of political thought in France.

Noël O'Sullivan is Professor of Politics at the University of Hull. His publications include *Conservatism* (1976), *Fascism* (1983), *Political Obligation* (1986) and *Santayana* (1992). He is editor of *Revolutionary Theory and Political Reality* (1983), *Terrorism, Ideology and Revolution* (1986) and *The Structure of Modern Ideology* (1989), and co-editor of *The Corporate State* (1988) and *The Nature of the Right* (1989).

Anthony Wright was Reader in Politics at the University of Birmingham before becoming MP for what is now the Cannock Chase constituency in 1992. His many publications include *G.D.H. Cole and Socialist Democracy* (1989), (as editor) *British Socialism: Socialist Thought from the 1880s to 1960s* (1983), *Citizens and Subjects* (1994) and *Socialisms: Old and New* (new edn, 1996).

PREFACE

In everyday usage, 'ideology' tends to be a pejorative term, synonymous with deceitful and fanatical. As such, it is often contrasted with pragmatism and truth. This is *not* the primary sense in which the term is used in this book. Nor does this book adopt the instrumental approach to 'ideology' commonly employed by Marxists and social scientists, who seek to trace how 'ideology' is socially determined, especially by dominant groups. Similarly, this book is not primarily concerned with the alleged role 'ideologies' play for individuals and groups in terms of finding their place in a complex world. This is a book about political thought rather than anthropology, sociology, psychology, and so on. It is about political ideologies understood as a relatively coherent set of values – a set of 'isms' which have been, and in most cases remain, central to the language of post-Enlightenment politics. As such they have a variety of more concrete effects, including both inspiring and constraining behaviour and policy.

This is not to deny that there are interesting questions to be asked about the social origins and role of ideologies understood more broadly – problems which the following chapters often touch upon. However, to do these questions full justice would require a separate book – or rather a series, for they raise cosmic issues about individuals, society, history and change. Even then, it is not necessarily clear that we would be much the wiser. All too frequently books on 'ideology' understood in a sweeping sense produce obfuscation more than clear thinking – a tendency encouraged by the pretentious and often obscure language which sometimes characterizes attempts to demystify power relations in society. Indeed, such books on 'ideology' are sometimes themselves ideological in the common pejorative sense: many of their authors have firm political convictions, and write with a strong normative flavour. They seek to exert influence by unmasking allegedly dominant power relationships.

The belief that objective intellectuals can exercise neutral judgement has been frequently criticized. Even with the best will in the world, it is impossible completely to break free from the prejudices of our backgrounds and times. Nevertheless, it is important not to jump from an Enlightenment belief in the power of rationality and science to a 'post-modern' belief that all is relative, that there are no truths or standards against which political ideologies can be judged. The contributors to this book – all leading experts in their fields – come from a variety of political points of view, but they all seek to analyse 'their' ideology as rationally as possible (it is important to underline that whilst some contributors write about bodies of thought which they basically admire, others do not). They also seek to write as clearly as possible, trying to avoid unnecessary jargon. This book is, therefore, suitable for those who seek a balanced introductory text, although the expertise of its contributors and their willingness to make controversial judgements at times, means that it will also be of interest to the more expert reader.

This book's focus on ideologies as thought is not simply an attempt to limit the field of study. It also reflects the belief that ideologies understood in this sense are major motive forces in history. However, the editorial brief to contributors was *not* one which sought to elucidate this point about the power of ideas compared to material, institutional, mythical, symbolic and other forces. Rather, contributors were asked to help the reader to understand political ideologies more in their own terms – analysing their key tenets, tensions and contradictions, and demonstrating how difficult it can be at times to draw neat lines between key 'isms'. 'Liberal-conservatism' or 'feminist-socialism', for instance, are not necessarily contradictions in terms, or a rag bag of ideas. A key task for the analyst of ideologies is to identify the core from the periphery, to tease out meanings and to chart the dynamics of changed conceptions and beliefs. One thing which certainly emerges from this book is the difficulty of pinning the common tags 'left' and 'right' on many ideologies.

The terms 'left' and right' in a political context came into common usage in Europe after the French Revolution, especially during the nineteenth century (the terms stemmed from the fact that the defenders of the old order took their place on the right of the National Assembly which met in France in 1789).[1] This was the period when most of the great political 'isms' first began to emerge in clearly articulated forms. Although the main focus of this book is on the twentieth century, contributors were asked to offer overviews of developments before 1900 in order to help underline both the origins of ideologies, and how they have adapted to changing historical contexts. At the end of each chapter, contributors peer forward into the new millennium. However, this is not essentially a work of futurology, especially at the world level. It is primarily a book about Western ideologies, although the inclusion of a chapter on Islam and Fundamentalism underlines the existence of other (often poorly understood in the West) belief systems. At the turn of the 1990s, Francis Fukuyama caught the mood of the hour when he proclaimed the 'end of history' – the triumph of liberalism and capitalism at the world level over communism and other 'totalitarian' forces.[2] But at the turn of the new millennium, many Western commentators have become much less sanguine.

The first edition of this book was jointly planned at the turn of the 1990s by the two editors whose names appear on the cover, and first appeared in 1993. But the fact that Anthony Wright was elected to parliament in 1992 meant that the editorial work fell largely on Roger Eatwell, who alone has undertaken the work for this revised and expanded edition. Hence whilst two names have been left on the cover to avoid confusion in the market-place, this new Preface is signed by just one person, whose views it represents.

All that remains is to express the usual caveats and thanks. In particular, I am grateful to the original contributors for once again fulfilling the editorial brief and providing such excellent revised chapters, and to Youssef Choueiri for providing a new chapter on Islam. I would also like to thank Cassell's Commissioning Editor for Social Sciences, Petra Recter, for suggesting a new edition in the belief – reflected in the reviews of the first edition – that this is the most authoritative work of its type available.

Roger Eatwell
Bath, July 1998

NOTES

1. This book does not specifically discuss the nature of the terms 'left' and 'right'. On this see N. Bobbio, *Left and Right*, Polity Press, Oxford, 1996, who focuses on equality as the core distinguishing principle. For a discussion of the problems of understanding the left–right spectrum in terms of a specific core principle see R. Eatwell and N. O'Sullivan (eds), *The Nature of the Right*, Pinter, London, 1989. Eatwell identifies five 'rights': the 'reactionary'; the 'moderate'; the 'radical'; the 'extreme'; and the 'new'. Note: some writers distinguish between an old and a new left–right spectrum, with the old focusing on (left) issues such as support for the big state and high taxation, and the new (left) issues centring more on feminism, ecologism, etc.
2. F. Fukuyama, *The End of History and the Last Man*, Hamish Hamilton, London, 1992.

1
INTRODUCTION: WHAT ARE POLITICAL IDEOLOGIES?

Roger Eatwell

INTRODUCTION

The opening chapter of this book is atypical of what follows: it is about approaches and definitions to the elusive concept of 'ideology'. It will probably be the least read section. Many – probably most – readers will pick up this volume in order to study one or more of its ten chapters on a particular political ideology.

A student might seek help to write an essay on questions relating to a particular 'ism'. For instance:

1. Will we all become liberals during the twenty-first century? Certainly the language of 'rights' and 'markets' have become central to the vocabulary of all the mainstream Western ideologies.
2. Or has a new form of socialism, epitomized by Tony Blair's post-1997 government, emerged at the turn of the twenty-first century – a 'Third Way' between the old left and right?
3. What have been the main historic forms of nationalist ideology, and do these doctrines still have a relevance in a world supposedly characterized by 'globalization'?
4. Is feminist ideology losing its force after the early successes of the women's movement? Are differences among the many strands of feminism greater than their similarities?
5. Is Islamic fundamentalism a fanatical creed which poses a danger to world peace?; or have its key ideological tenets been travestied by Western critics?

The more advanced reader might be interested in detailed points of interpretation, or on the exact focus of the contributions – especially as this book is unique among competing surveys of political 'isms' in the sense that the author of each central chapter is a noted expert in his/her field. For instance:

1. Why does the chapter on conservatism hold that since the 1970s conservatism has been too influenced by the technocratic-efficiency oriented themes of the neo-liberal New Right?
2. Why does the Marxism chapter hold that the collapse of communism does not offer the chance for a new start, in which Marxism can divorce itself from dictatorship?
3. Why does the chapter on anarchism hold that so-called contemporary 'anarcho-capitalism' is really a form of liberal rather than classic anarchist thought?
4. Why does the chapter on fascism stress the serious nature of its ideology, rather than organization and style, which are typically seen as its main defining characteristic?
5. Why does the chapter on ecologism note the totalitarian dangers of an ideology often associated with the slogan 'small is beautiful'?

Many students, and even some academics, shy away from the problems of conceptual and methodological analysis – especially when opinions vary notably. And they certainly do over 'ideology'. Indeed, an introductory text on the subject by David McLellan begins by claiming, 'Ideology is the most elusive concept in the whole of social science'.[1] So why bother with this conundrum, especially as it may put someone off studying the following chapters? The main reason lies in the importance of delineating both the strengths and weaknesses of this book's conception of 'ideology'.

In everyday usage, 'ideology' tends to be a pejorative term, used especially to characterize ideas which seem biased and/or extreme. Thus opponents have ideologies, whereas 'we' are characterized by principles, pragmatism or common sense. Even some academic usage echoes this sense, though, in general, academic approaches are more characterized by their remarkable diversity. A recent major monograph on ideology, by the eminent political theorist Michael Freeden, opens by noting:

> Over the past half-century the concept of ideology has emerged as one of the most complex and debatable political ideas. It is remarkable for being discussed on levels that seemingly do not intersect, for attempting to organize phenomena that appear unrelated, and for causing confusion among scholars and political commentators. Political theorists, historians, philosophers, linguists, cultural anthropologists, sociologists, and psychologists have all grappled with the notion of ideology.[2]

At the risk of oversimplifying so broad a set of approaches ('debates' would be a misleading word, as much of the literature is a 'dialogue' of the blind and the deaf), they can be divided into:

1. ideology as political thought
2. ideology as beliefs and norms
3. ideology as language, symbols and myths
4. ideology as élite power.

It is important to stress that these approaches are not entirely exclusive: there is a strong tendency especially among approaches 2 and 3 to be interested in the exercise of power too. However, the above four categories point to different areas of primary study. The first relates especially to the great 'isms', like liberalism and its key thinkers such as John Stuart Mill (1806–73) or F.A. Hayek (1899–1992). It tends to focus on questions such as: what are the limits of freedom – should we tolerate the intolerant? Is there a contradiction between liberalism's emphasis on individual autonomy and rationality and the constraints of the capitalist market? The second relates to the body of views held by ordinary people, thoughts which tend to be much less systematic. For instance, many people in Western societies believe that it is only common sense that we need relatively high income differentials, though they could not articulate a full liberal-capitalist ideology. The third approach looks more at discourse and iconography (semiotics). For instance, in the West we have a 'free' market (a term which diverts attention from constraints such as advertising); our coins often bear the symbols of continuity, like a monarch, or the apparent principles of democracy ('Liberty, Equality and Fraternity'). The fourth approach relates more to the way in which élites seek to ensure conformity and support. In the past this may have focused on physical repression, but now media moguls, or the very state education system, are more typically seen as the basis of conformity.

What follows in this opening chapter is a highly selective introduction to the main approaches to the nature of 'ideology', presented in terms of brief overviews of a wide variety of key individuals or schools of thought. To anticipate the linking theme of this chapter, I will argue that there are dangers in inflating the term 'ideology' to cover what might better be termed 'propaganda', 'socialization' and 'culture'. This book, therefore, treats ideologies as a major branch in the study of political thought, though one which needs to be situated in specific historical contexts, for ideas – and especially their popular resonance – are very much related to other factors. This is not to claim that approaches based on other disciplines, or transdisciplinary studies fail to reveal insights in the workings of society, or the thinking of individuals. The point is more that ideas are important in their own right, and they need studying as such. Understood in this sense, ideologies are combinations of political concepts organized in a particular way. They acquire specific meaning through discourse and context. However, what Freeden calls their 'morphological' aspects are also crucial – namely, 'what does an ideology look like? How does it behave?'[3]

THE ORIGINS OF THE TERM 'IDEOLOGY'

The French philosopher Antoine Destutt de Tracy (1754–1836) coined the term '*idéologie*' in 1796. De Tracy was an aristocrat, sympathetic to the French Revolution (1789), but was imprisoned during the subsequent Jacobin Terror. On release, he turned his attention to what had caused such barbarities, to how a brutal intolerance could have emerged in the name of progress and the people. More generally, he posed the question of the way in which the values of epochs and societies differed significantly.

De Tracy was a rationalistic heir to the eighteenth-century movement known as the Enlightenment – critical of traditional authority and the mystification of religious thought – but also deeply concerned by the fanatical perversion of the Enlightenment by Robespierre and other Jacobins. De Tracy saw 'ideology' as a science of the human mind (like biology and zoology were sciences of species), capable of pointing the true way forward. Like many other members of the Institut National, which replaced the royal academies after the revolution, de Tracy believed that his task was not simply explanatory. He wanted, in true Enlightenment fashion, to further 'progress' by improving people – to show which ideas were false, and to develop a system of secular education which could produce better people (the nineteenth century was to see a great extension of public education in the West).

The association of 'ideology' with science and objective study was short lived. Indeed, the term 'ideology' quickly degenerated into a pejorative term, referring to the object rather than the form of study and often contrasted with scientific approaches. The first major figure to use the term in this pejorative way was Napoleon Bonaparte (1769–1821). Napoleon had initially been sympathetic to de Tracy's work, not least because he was highly interested in the power of ideas and symbols to mould people, and to reinforce support for regimes which lacked traditional legitimacy. However, after becoming emperor, he caricatured the Enlightenment and de Tracy's group as 'ideologues' (partly influenced by a desire to court favour with traditional groups, especially the Catholic church). Napoleon thus began a long line of critics who were to associate 'ideology' with traits such as an *a priori* desire to overturn old ways and 'improve' people's lives, and/or to advocate beliefs which suited the interests of those proclaiming them (de Tracy was a liberal republican, who envisaged a new world in which intellectuals like himself would have a significant role to play).

MARX AND HIS FOLLOWERS ON 'IDEOLOGY'

Ideology as a pejorative concept was particularly important in the work of Karl Marx (1818–83). Indeed, a leading political philosopher, John Plamenatz, has written that it was Marx 'more than anyone, who introduced the word into social and political theory, and he used it in all its important senses without troubling to make clear how they differ'.[4] Subsequently, Marxist approaches have had a dominant influence on the methodological debates about 'ideology' (see also Chapter 5).

Arguably the best known Marxist statement on ideology appears in *The German Ideology*, which Marx wrote with Friedrich Engels (1820–95) in the 1840s:

> The ideas of the ruling class are in every epoch the ruling ideas, i.e. the class which is the material force of society, is at the same time its ruling intellectual force. The class which has the means of material production at its disposal, has control at the same time over the means of mental production, so that thereby, generally speaking, the ideas of those who lack the means of mental production are subject to it.[5]

Marx was critical of those who held that the role of ideas was crucial in history and in social life. He believed that social existence determined consciousness, and not the other way round. He thus adopted a materialist view of history, in which economic forces rather than great leaders or ideas led to 'progress'. Marx made a distinction in capitalist society between a 'base' and 'superstructure'. The former referred to the basic organization of the means of production, and resulting class system. The superstructure referred more to individuals, to ideologies. These ideologies were not simply 'isms', but were reflected in any feature of society which served to defend the ruling class. Thus ideologies were the 'legal, political, religious, aesthetic or philosophic' principles which reinforced capitalist society.[6]

Marx did not believe that his own views were 'ideology', seeing them as based on a scientific understanding of history and the inevitable triumph of the working class and socialism. However, it was Engels who sought to popularize the term 'scientific socialism' for Marx's work. It was also Engels who dismissed 'ideology' as 'false consciousness', a phrase not used by Marx, although it subsequently became central to Marxist work.[7] False consciousness refers to socially or time-bound views, which help support a particular system. A good example of this would be the belief that the liberal democratic state is 'neutral': in other words, holding the view that individuals and groups have equality before the law, that the civil service does not pursue class-interest, and so on. For Marx and Engels, the law was ultimately a defence of capitalism and property, as were other key features of the liberal democratic state.

Marx was not the first to notice that groups tend to have systems of outlooks, which can be implicit more than explicit. Nor was he the first to stress that these views both limit the questions which can be asked, and the answers reached. Marx was especially indebted here to the German philosopher G.W.F. Hegel (1770–1831). (Note: in other ways his work was a critique of Hegel.) However, it was Marx who first attributed the term 'ideology' to such belief systems, though as with much of Marx, there was some notable variation in his usage. In particular, there was a tension between the pejorative sense of ideology as something which masked the interests of capitalist society, and a more general sense in which ideologies were seen as a necessary part of the belief systems of all societies – something which provided shorthand rules for behaviour, and which helped people perceive their place and role in society.

V.I. Lenin (1870–1924), too, identified Marxism as a science, but he effectively accepted that 'ideology' was a term which should not be restricted to capitalist, or pre-capitalist, society (the 'revisionist' Marxist Eduard Bernstein (1850–1932) had shortly before also associated socialism with ideology). In *What Is To Be Done?* (1902) Lenin argued for a socialist ideology which could help develop working-class consciousness beyond the 'economism' of immediate concerns (though this was secondary to his emphasis on revolutionary organization). Lenin especially believed such an ideology was important to prevent the working class from falling into trade union consciousness. He saw unions as premised on the existence of capitalism, particularly in the sense that their demands for better wages and conditions could, in the short run, best be achieved through a healthy capitalism. Moreover, unions threatened to divide the working class into a relatively well-paid unionized group, and an impoverished proletariat, lacking the leadership of those who had been attracted by unions. In Lenin's words:

> All those who talk about 'overrating the importance of ideology', about exaggerating the role of the conscious element, etc., imagine that the labour movement pure and simple can elaborate, and will elaborate, an independent ideology for itself ... But this is a profound mistake ... Since there can be no talk of an independent ideology formulated by the working masses themselves in the process of their movement, the only choice is – either bourgeois or socialist ideology.[8]

This socialist ideology was largely to be developed by an intelligentsia, which clearly must have broken free from the power of capitalist conditioning. Exactly where this left the materialist conception of history, and especially the primacy of base over superstructure, was never made fully clear. However, it reflected a challenge to those Marxists who sought to delineate rigid materialist laws of history.

This development was taken even further in the works of the Italian communist Antonio Gramsci (1891–1937). Gramsci rejected the crudest forms of Marxist materialism which reduced the 'superstructure' solely to 'base' factors. In his later writings, he also became increasingly critical of Leninism, believing that it did not pay sufficient attention to the strength of 'civil society' in liberal democracies – namely, non-governmental institutions and forms of social conditioning, such as education or the mass media. Gramsci believed that the rule of one class over another was not simply an economic one, backed by a coercive state apparatus. It depended on 'hegemony' – on cultural and ideological forces as well (the concept of hegemony was drawn in part from the important works of the Hungarian Marxist, Georg Lukács [1885–1971]).[9] In its ultimate form, ideology became a kind of common sense, something which was simply not challenged. To counter this ideological power, Gramsci was especially interested in the role of intellectuals, whom he divided into 'traditional' and 'organic'. The former considered themselves to be free of classes, and rational: people like university academics and ecclesiastics. Gramsci held that in practice such intellectuals were normally imbued with the hegemonic culture, or were incapable of offering any serious challenge to dominant values. Organic intellectuals, on the other hand, were closely connected organizationally with the class structure. They were people like members of the communist party and/or unions. For Gramsci, these were the intellectuals most likely to help create a counter-hegemony, through their writings, or their role in key institutions which could challenge capitalist hegemony.

Gramsci's ideas became especially important during the 1960s as the prospect of violent revolution in the West seemed to recede. They often meshed closely with work which stemmed from the so-called Frankfurt critical theory school, which attacked the more dogmatic economic determinism of Soviet and much other Marxism. A notable member of this group was the American-resident German social theorist Herbert Marcuse (1898–1979). He wrote, in his 1960s bestseller, *One Dimensional Man*, of a 'totalitarian' West in which the powers of social conditioning and the growth of welfare had all but removed dissent.[10] Marcuse looked to blacks, students and others for a revolutionary lead, a call which found an echo among a radical fringe of students, especially in France, Germany and the USA, during the late 1960s. Jurgen Habermas (1929–) similarly attacked the more crude Marxist positions, arguing that the capitalist ethic had become more technocratic, legitimating itself through science and technology, or consumerism, which in a sense depoliticized society.[11] Habermas's appeal proved more enduring, especially among left-inclined academics.

Gramsci's work also had an influence on a cult figure in French thought in the 1960s and 1970s, Louis Althusser (1918–90).[12] Althusser, in keeping with the later Marx, held that there was no rigid relation between base and superstructure, developing the idea of the 'relative autonomy' of the superstructure. However, whereas Marx had recognized the importance of institutions such as the family, or religion, he had not seen them as part of the state. Althusser held that the state, and its influential tentacles, was now much more diverse. Power was now exercised in a more diffuse fashion through a variety of structures (Althusser was also influenced by structuralism, which grew out of both linguistics and anthropology, and which sought to understand society in terms of deep-lying patterns of authority and rules). He included within this 'ideological state apparatus' (to be distinguished from the repressive state apparatus) 'spheres' such as education and trade unions, and argued that ideology worked largely sub-consciously on people.

More generally, these approaches helped spawn schools of media and cultural studies. An early pioneer in this new academic boom industry was the Glasgow University Media Group, which sought to show that trade union activities were presented in a hostile manner, whereas the working of markets was largely unchallenged. Often the bias was subtle, for instance smart and apparently reasonable managers were interviewed at their desks whereas unions were interviewed on the picket line.[13] Mass rather than high culture became the new totem. Goethe and Shakespeare were out, and popular soap operas like *Dallas*, or *Coronation Street* moved centre stage. The glossy lifestyles of the former were seen as a powerful symbolic cultural influence; the working-class life of the latter was seen as a sanitized charade, divorced from major real-life concerns such as class or race.

Some Marxists remained committed to a more rigid analysis of the relationship between base and superstructure. Abercrombie, Hill and Turner, for example, viewed ideology as mainly useful for uniting élites; subordinate groups were seen as divided (an important feature of élite control), and influenced more by the material power of economics than ideology.[14] However, increasingly in recent decades Marxists, and those highly influenced by Marxist work (a much larger group of academics), have used superstructural factors to explain why 'contradictions' in the base had not produced the much heralded downfall of capitalism. Power in capitalist societies – to adopt the terms of a leading social theorist, Steven Lukes – was not seen as one-dimensional, and based on observable conflict. Nor was it two-dimensional, in which the strength of capitalism and its state led people to see dissent as futile. Rather, it was three-dimensional, based on a broad ability to produce hegemony – a society in which most did not perceive the way in which they were controlled.[15] The argument contained many insights, though like Marxism in general it was replete with hidden assumptions about human nature, historical progress and what society would be like but for capitalism. Put another way, the counter-factual question 'What would society x be like but for ideological conditioning?' can only be answered at the level of broad assertion. For instance, the fact that some 'primitive' societies have existed which were not based on private property, or on inegalitarian relations, does not prove that a large contemporary society could be organized in this way.

NON-MARXIST INTERPRETATIONS OF 'IDEOLOGY'

Non-Marxist approaches have been more diverse. Some have been overtly anti-Marxist, both in method and in targeting Marxism as an especially dangerous form of thinking. But others have borrowed from Marxism, and/ or have focused on similar basic questions, especially concerning the nature of power in society – typically extending the study, rather like Althusser, to a broad variety of structural and symbolic forms.

The first major – some would argue the only sweeping[16] – non-Marxist attempt to discuss 'ideology' after de Tracy came from Karl Mannheim (1883–1947), a Hungarian intellectual who in many ways sought to return to de Tracy's quest for a science of ideas, designed to make a better world. Mannheim's key book, *Ideology and Utopia*, was first published in 1929 (1936, English translation).[17] Like Marx, Mannheim's use of terminology was not always clear or consistent, but central to his thought were two distinctions. First, he distinguished between the 'particular' and 'total' conception of ideology. The former remains at the level of more or less conscious manipulation, even deceipt; the latter refers more to the mind of era or of a major socio-economic group, a *Weltanschauung*. Second, he distinguished between 'ideology' and 'Utopia': the former tends to protect the *status quo*, whereas the latter can be subversive of it (though he saw that 'ideologies' could have Utopian elements).

Mannheim, who had worked with Lukács, accepted Marx and Engels's view that ideological thought was distorted, but he argued that the reductionist use of 'ideology' could be turned against Marxism. If the 'dominant ideology' was the ideology of the ruling class, why was not the ideology of other social groups also a body of self-interested thought? Put simply, was not socialism a reflection of the interests of the working class, possibly not all of the working class? The point was telling. However, Mannheim's quest for what he termed a 'sociology of knowledge' was plagued by the problem of whether there can be objective knowledge and truth. Mannheim tried to get round this by distinguishing, somewhat unclearly, between 'relativism' and 'relationism'. The former holds that all knowledge is relative to the group, place and time. The latter accepts that there is a strong relationship between ideas and their context, but holds that a certain type of intellectual is capable of rational debate about such ideas and developments. Critics have identified this as a crucial flaw in Mannheim's approach, arguing – often following Gramsci – that intellectuals themselves are very much a product of the society in which they live.

Mannheim's concern with the integrative functions of 'ideology' were increasingly picked up from the 1940s onwards by the growing school of academic social science, although this did not produce an entirely homogenous body of thought on the subject. Some work – especially in the USA – relied heavily on the new sociological and psychological techniques of in-depth interviewing, or the large-scale opinion survey. This work seemed to

point towards the way in which ideology serves a dual function: it binds
societies together and helps structure and mould the personalities of people
as they mature from childhood through adulthood. A second approach
adopted a more anthropological approach, typified by Clifford Geertz
(1926–   ), which focused on mythical and symbolic life, and imaginative
interpretation. But the general import was often similar: ideology provided
an ordered system of symbols which helped people understand life in terms
of meaningful patterns, and helped give their behaviour purpose.[18]

This work was open to a variety of methodological objections. For
instance, some – epitomized in the political context by the classic Almond
and Verba study, *The Civic Culture* - tended to ignore the question of how
dominant ideologies were formed.[19] Some anthropological works seemed
ultimately untestable, more akin to literary criticism. However, they pointed
to the importance of values, symbolism and myths in society, and the cultural
approach stressed the dangers of understanding influence simply in terms of
ideologies understood as 'isms'. Subsequently, many social scientists – like
the British psychologist Michael Billig – have made a clear distinction
between 'lived' and 'intellectual' ideologies, seeing the former as less systematic but a more important object of study.[20]

A parallel development, again largely emanating from American social
science – though it was reinforced by British philosophical thought – sought
to make a distinction between loosely organized values which structured life,
and 'ideologies', which were understood more specifically. The latter
approach accepts only certain types of belief system as an 'ideology', usually
limiting the term to radical/extremist forms like communism and fascism.
Key early writers in this vein included Karl Popper (1902–94) and Hannah
Arendt (1906–75).[21] The argument here often focuses on whether a set of
beliefs is 'historicist' or 'monist': namely, the extent to which it is held that
there is a single fundamental truth, depending on 'rationalist' knowledge
(Marxism as science, the biological basis of race, etc.). Such ideologies
involve a rejection of pluralism, tolerance and discriminatory forms of
arguments. This analysis was reinforced by the writing of philosophers, such
as Michael Oakeshott (1901–90), who drew a distinction between a tradi-
tionalist and an ideological stance in politics. Ideology represented a
simplification, an abstraction; tradition exalted practical, pragmatic knowledge, which could not be acquired *a priori* or formulated in grand
propositions. Thus conservatism, at least of the traditional mainstream
British type, was not an ideology – a claim which has frequently been made
by many leading members of the Conservative Party.

These last approaches were an important influence in the development of
what became known as the 'end of ideology' thesis (see Chapter 12 for a
fuller discussion, including its more recent post-1989 manifestation). In his
much discussed book, *The End of Ideology* (1960), the American sociologist
Daniel Bell (1919–   ) celebrated the demise of radical ideologies, notably
fascism and communism. He argued:

Few serious minds believe any longer that one can set down 'blueprints' and through 'social engineering' bring about a new utopia of social harmony. At the same time, the older 'counter-beliefs' have lost their intellectual force as well. Few 'classic' liberals insist that the state should play no role in the economy, and few serious conservatives, at least in England and on the continent, believe that the Welfare State is 'the road to serfdom'. In the Western world, therefore, there is today a rough consensus among intellectuals on political issues . . . the ideological age has ended.[22]

This approach held that the great social strains which had allegedly produced radical ideologies had diminished in the face of the post-1945 boom. Moreover, there was a greater philosophical awareness of the dangers of 'totalitarianism'.

Critics pointed out that Bell and other 'endists', like Seymour Martin Lipset (1922–),[23] were really American propagandists, using apparently objective social science and philosophical methodology to legitimize their own beliefs and political system. Others pointed out that whilst belief systems like liberalism and Marxism varied in content, they were far more similar in form. Both were heirs to the Enlightenment, envisaging a particular type of historical development which, in different ways, involved a universalist form of rationality. The final nail in the coffin of turn-of-the-1960s end of ideology thesis seemed to come from the real world of politics. At the international level, communism continued to grow; at the same time new forces – most notably Islamic fundamentalism – broke on to the scene. Domestically in the West, there was also a flowering of radical movements, including a New Left, a new wave of feminism, and the emergence of an ecology movement.

Yet this apparent revival of ideological movements contained within it the intellectual seeds of what was to become during the 1970s, and especially the 1980s, another notable approach to 'ideology'. This can be termed the 'postmodern' thesis (the term first emerged in this context among American literary critics in the 1960s), although it is important to stress that there are variations within this school. In some ways this is a new form of end of ideology thesis, though it is one very much divorced from the celebration of a specific set of beliefs. The great ideologies of the Enlightenment, of modernity, were universal in scope. Even the most pragmatic and unsystematic forms of conservatism assumed that it was a doctrine which had lessons for everyone. According to one of the great exponents of postmodernist thinking, the French academic J.-F. Lyotard (1924–) the current world is characterized by a crisis of 'metanarratives', a loss of faith in the grand sweep of ideology.[24] Instead, post-modernism celebrates pluralism; it rejects monocausalism and stresses different possibilities. It supports the politics of personal identity over those of class, nation, and so on.

This is sometimes related to sociological analysis of change, and breakdown of old identities. But at times the argument is essentially normative, criticizing the old 'metanarratives' for seeking to eliminate difference, for involving – albeit different – totalitarian assumptions. At this point, some of the approach's problems begin to become more clear. First, is not the celebration of pluralism in itself an ideology? Besides, are there not dangers in excessive pluralism: nationalism, for instance, may have sought to obliterate many differences, but it could also facilitate what many would see as desirable goals, e.g. redistributing tax from rich to poor. Running throughout post-modernism there is also a denial of objective reality in favour of an emphasis on who is assessing that reality and how. As has already been noted, this is an important perspective, but pure relativism makes it impossible to say anything significant about different lifestyles, etc. What reason does post-modernism give us for choosing, say, to believe in human rights rather than a system where persecuting religious heretics is seen as legitimate?

This point further emerges if we turn to the last of the non-Marxist approaches to 'ideology' surveyed in this section. This could be termed structuralist-discourse analysis, which once again should not be seen as a single, rigidly coherent school. Discourse analysis is typically a term given to studies which have sought to relate the language of 'ideology' (understood usually in terms of everyday life) to underlying structures. One of the most prominent examples of this approach is the French academic, Michel Foucault (1926–84).[25] Foucault, who was a student of Althusser, has studied various forms of social exclusion, such as madness and criminality. He sees them as the result of the social domination which relates to the power of language, myths and symbols. Foucault accords these great power, and rejects the idea of the conscious individual, able to chose between ideological alternatives.

Foucault, whose language can be especially obscure, has aroused very divergent opinions. Undoubtedly he points to the power of language and symbols, including everyday ones, to condition thought and action. But there are dangers of according discourses magical powers. How can the critic think outside them? Is there an assumption, following Mannheim, that a certain type of intellectual can break free of conditioning? The argument seems rather like the worst forms of Marxism, where the power of capitalism seems to make dissent impossible. Yet the fact is that in liberal democracies, different forms of political view are expressed, and at times they have the power to attract notable support. There is also an epistemological relativism which is equally misleading. For instance, Darwin's theory of natural selection was developed in a Britain which had previously spawned Malthusian doctrines of the struggle for food supplies, and *laissez-faire* doctrines of competition. But whilst social context and the dominant ideology helped shape Darwinist thought, it was also essentially true. It is interesting to compare this case with the former USSR, where the official view under Stalin was that Darwin was wrong. Instead, it was held that selection was determined by environmental factors (Lysenkoism). Marxist ideology drove science, but in a wrong direction – which had disastrous effects on Soviet policy in areas such as plant breeding. Clearly there are not the same truths relating to 'isms' as there are in relation to some areas of science, but it is vital not to reject an Enlightenment view in the possibilities of some form of rational debate and discussion of normative issues – for instance, in relation to political ideologies.

HOW POLITICAL IDEOLOGIES ARE UNDERSTOOD IN THIS BOOK

In order to understand the approach adopted in this book, it is helpful to begin by considering why there is not a chapter on what many would consider the key contemporary ideology in the West: namely, democracy. The simple answer is that this is more a governmental system, which can be conceived in notably different ways. A major distinction concerns the more holistic and participatory forms envisaged by 'direct democracy' and the pluralist-representative 'liberal democracy'. Is extensive popular participation necessary to 'true' democracy? Or are the 'masses' a threat to the freedom and tolerance which are crucial to democracy – a danger which means that stable democracy requires relatively low interest and participation in political affairs? Clearly, the term 'democracy' can encompass almost polar opposites. Indeed, in some ways the twentieth century – especially the period since 1945 – has seen a competition amongst almost all the main ideologies to monopolize the term 'democracy'. Thus the pre-1989 Eastern European communist systems called themselves 'Peoples' Democracies', and mocked the West's pretensions to democracy.

The Oakeshott-influenced political philosopher, Noël O'Sullivan, holds that ideologies always involve a programmatic element.[26] 'Formal' politics, in other words the maintenance of procedural conditions (especially laws), are not seen as 'programmatic'. Democracy could thus be ruled out as an ideology, using this approach. There are important points here, especially the highlighting of the action and goal-orientation of ideology. Nevertheless, there are dangers in necessarily associating an ideology with a specific, clear programme. Lenin was fond of the Napoleonic maxim: '*on s'engage, et puis on voit*' (we enter the struggle, and see how the situation develops). Early Italian fascism managed to adopt contradictory programmes in quick succession; more generally, fascism often played down the need for programme, stressing instead the need for leadership and action. Where, exactly, does this leave the relationship between an ideology and a seriously-taken programme? Moreover, a commitment to formal political procedural rules could be an important part of a programme – in, say, post-communist states or states which are becoming democracies in the developing world. Perhaps the crucial point is that it is hard to imagine someone supporting such a set of formal arrangements without, implicitly, or overtly, holding related arguments. Concepts such as the 'rule of law' or 'checks and balances' are clearly related either to a view of human nature and/or to some knowledge of history. There would be something strange about a person who believed that mankind was universally and inherently good, and that no abuses of power had ever taken place, who also held that formal rules were required to prevent political exploitation.

This points to a way of envisaging ideologies which can include all the main 'isms', but which does not involve accepting that democracy is an ideology. An 'ideology' must possess a certain set of attributes. In particular, an ideology has an overt or implicit set of empirical and normative views which are goal-oriented about: 1) human nature; 2) the process of history; 3) the socio-political structure. This is not to argue that there is necessarily a single view of each aspect, or that views are held with rigid logical consistency. For example, socialists could disagree over whether human nature was inherently good, or something which was socially determined (and thus changeable). However, a socialist could not hold that human beings were inherently and irretrievably greedy and aggressive. Or take another example: Marxists could disagree over the extent to which 'great' individuals and ideas mattered in determining the course of history, but they could not adopt a purely 'high politics' approach which saw such forces as the main motor of history.

This approach also helps explain why democracy is not an ideology, but nationalism is (thus meriting inclusion in the following chapters). Some might find this separation perplexing. Is not nationalism consistent with a broad variety of forms of government, both dictatorial and democratic? Have there not been liberal nationalists, fascist nationalists, Marxist nationalists, and so on – indicating that nationalism, like democracy, is compatible with many ideologies? However, there are crucial differences compared to democracy. These do not simply stem from the fact that recent years have seen a contest among the main ideologies to monopolize the term 'democracy', whereas nationalism has been more a pariah term (although the growth since the 1980s of micro-nationalisms, like Flemish separatism, and new nationalist parties, like the French Front National, reflects that a change is taking place here, including a growing realization that nationalism encompasses a serious body of thought).[27] Nor is the main point that some ideologies have adopted nationalism for instrumental rather than fundamental reasons. Thus Marxists who have been sympathetic to nationalism have seen it in terms of a wider view of 'progress': nationalism was seen as a stage some societies needed to go through, rather than as an underlying principle of political organization. The central point relates more to the basic threefold framework of an ideology, outlined above. There is no fundamental democratic view on issues such as human nature, or the process of history (compare the implicit or overt views of those who see democracy as necessarily involving continual popular participation, with those who believe that the masses are a threat to the values of rationalism and toleration on which democracy is based). On the other hand, nationalists hold that there is something universally natural about people wanting to group into national units. They see history as the process of successful, and unsuccessful, nation-building and rivalry. And they hold that the socio-political system should favour the national interest, for example in judging the benefits and disadvantages of economic policies. Nationalists can differ about the implications of these views: for instance, an autarchic economy may not be in the long-run interests of the nation. But there is a core set of values around which disputes centre.

It also helps to set out what a political ideology is not by comparing it with 'propaganda', 'socialization' and 'culture'. This risks raising a series of massive new issues. In particular, Raymond Williams has argued that 'culture is one of the two or three most complicated words in the English language'[28] (McLellan 'only' claims that 'ideology' is the most elusive word in the social sciences!). However, pointing to the existence of other concepts underlines the fact that it is helpful to restrict the concept of 'political ideologies' as much as possible. A basic problem with the generic use of the word 'ideology', in the way in which it was generally used in the two previous sections of this chapter, is that it all too quickly degenerates into a study of virtually any aspect of social activity. This is not to deny that we need to study a myriad of factors in order to understand the workings of society, and the nature of power relationships. The point is more that it is helpful to have a conceptual language which highlights different areas of study.

Propaganda

A political ideology should not be confused with propaganda, although the distinction is not always clear. 'Propaganda' is another concept which is rarely clearly defined. Within communist systems, it has sometimes been used in a positive way to refer to rational political education, whereas 'agitation' was the term used to refer to simplistic appeals. On the other hand, 'propaganda' tends to have pejorative connotations in the West, often being associated with deception and manipulation. It therefore seems best to limit the term to deliberate attempts to gain political influence by focusing on a relatively limited and simple set of issues. These do not necessarily involve deceit, although they do involve putting forward only a limited range of relevant arguments and facts. Propaganda cannot be distinguished from ideology on the grounds simply that it is action oriented. All ideologies, in different ways, seek to influence behaviour – although in the case of dominant ideologies, this can involve non-action rather than change.

Socialization

Political ideology, and propaganda, should not be confused with social-ization although, again, the distinction is not always clear. Socialization refers to the process by which values are transmitted to members of society, especially the young, in particular with a view to integrating them within the dominant value-system. Studies of socialization could look at a variety of social and political phenomena, such as the family, schools or the media. For example, the way women are portrayed in advertisements as objects of sexual lust, is part of sexual stereotyping. However, this is not political ideology, as it is only a partial world-view. It may also not be propaganda, as some of it is probably not deliberate, reflecting more the norms which socialization can produce. Nevertheless, even in democracies, educational systems can be designed both to produce narrow perspectives (the medium is the message: the less able should not challenge authority), and to transmit dominant values (for instance, encouraging teenage children to compete in games relating to success on the stock exchange).

Culture

'Culture' could be used as a synonym in many books for 'ideology', although academics who use the word 'culture' in this sense tend to be less interested in issues of power. Culture can refer to various things, and should not be limited to its common twentieth-century sense of 'high' culture (opera, great works of art, etc.). Sometimes it refers to actual values, rather than the process by which these are disseminated. Since Gottfried Herder (1784–91) in particular, there has been a tendency to use 'culture' to refer to the value structure of a society, or subgroups within a society. This includes attitudes and opinions which are not necessarily conscious, or systematic, and which stem from many sources. Thus it is possible to talk of an American political culture, or a Mid-West subculture, but these are not ideologies. They are essentially mass based, though there is of course a relationship to political ideology. 'The American way of life', 'log cabin to White House', and so on are very much part of individualistic, entrepreneurial liberalism. However, culture is also closely linked to socialization, and to a wider symbolic universe which helps condition behaviour from virtually cradle to grave. Culture can also be linked to the production of values, especially in relation to education and the media. Culture is thus the better generic word for a broad field of study than 'ideology'.

POLITICAL IDEOLOGIES

All three of these areas – propaganda, socialization, culture – are legitimate areas of study. However, this book is about political ideologies *qua* political thought. This raises another potential pitfall. Even among those within universities who term themselves 'political theorists', there has often been a tendency to look down on ideologies as an inferior form of thinking, and/or as necessarily involving a normative approach which is not held to be present in the study of 'political philosophy'. The stock in trade of the normal academic of this ilk has been great thinkers (Marx, Mill, etc.), or key concepts (rights, justice, etc.). However, to cite Freeden:

> ideologies are forms of political thought that provide important direct access to comprehending the formation and nature of political theory, its richness, varieties, and subtlety. The academic investigation of ideologies ... must be accorded equal rank with the study of political philosophy.[29]

The study of political ideology in this sense is interested in questions such as: who have been the key thinkers and what have been the main propositions of an ideology? To what extent are there contradictions or tensions within an ideology? Why have different aspects of an ideology been stressed at different times and why have different syntheses been formed?

For those who like brief definitions, the following forms the working basis of this book:

> **Political ideology.** A political ideology is a relatively coherent set of empirical and normative beliefs and thought, focusing on the problems of human nature, the process of history, and socio-political arrangements. It is usually related to a programme of specific short run concerns. Depending on its relationship to the dominant value structure, an ideology can act as either a stabilizing or radical force. Single thinkers may embody the core of an ideology, but to call a single person an 'ideologist', or 'ideologue', would normally be seen as pejorative. The term 'political philosopher' or 'political theorist', therefore, seems more appropriate for a thinker capable of developing a sophisticated level of debate. Political ideologies are essentially the product of collective thought. They are 'ideal types', not to be confused with specific movements, parties or regimes which may bear their name.

This last point highlights a final problem. If a political ideology involves the study of many thinkers, movements, parties and regimes, is there not a problem concerning the very construction of an ideology? Fascism and ecologism serve as a good examples here, as they are the ideologies which arguably raise the most fundamental issues about construction.

One key problem in constructing fascist ideology is whether the focus should be mainly on individual fascists (writings and speeches), or should the emphasis be on movements and regime policies – the types of problem studied more by historians. Some individuals (usually not leaders) can provide a high level of thought, of interest to the academic political theorist, but it is not clear how, indeed whether, these influenced movements and regimes. Moreover, Italian Fascism and German Nazism had very different movement and regime phases. Fascism in its pre-power phase tended to be radical, for example it was highly critical of religion and capitalism. In power, it was more accommodating to these interests. Many would, therefore, consider a model of fascism which was not based primarily on concrete regime practice as totally missing the point.

Marxists would see no problem here. Fascism would be viewed as an example of false consciousness, largely to be understood in terms of base influences.[30] Such an analysis sees fascism as a product of capitalist crisis, as the form of 'dictatorship of capital' necessary when economic crisis means it is no longer possible to preserve 'bourgeois freedoms'. It should be added that it is not necessary to be a Marxist to hold that fascist ideology should be seen mainly in terms of its social role. Functionalists, too, have seen it largely in terms of the attempt to end anomie, or to prepare societies such as Germany, Italy and Japan for the strains which élites believed would stem from the wars necessary to ensure national greatness (an attempt to create what Durkheim called 'mechanical solidarity).

Many of these points recur, and others emerge, if we consider how to construct 'ecologism'. Should we study major individual thinkers, or actual green parties and movements? The latter are clearly very much an ideological *mélange*, and to some extent likely to make compromises to attract support. This would probably be even more true if a Green movement ever gained a mass following. Or, should ecologism be understood primarily in terms of its social base? An extensive sociological literature shows that the membership of Green movements tends to be young, educated and employed in the non-productive sector of the economy. But does this mean we should call ecologism a middle-class ideology (as fascism is often termed, although in fascism's case, the emphasis is on its alleged 'petit bourgeoisie' rather than professional middle-class base)? Such class issues are a perfectly legitimate concern within sociology, but the futility of using them to understand ideology *per se* can be seen by considering the hypothetical case of a Green Party which became a major national party. This would inevitably have to attract a broad class and age base: would ecologism therefore then become an 'all-class' ideology? It is worth adding that recent historiography shows that Nazism, far from being a middle-class party, attracted notable all-class support. So much for reducing ideologies to their class base in terms of support!

These points raise important questions which cannot be answered simply. Indeed, they threaten to lead on to ever more methodological debates. Nevertheless, it is worth making two points related to fascism in conclusion here. First, studying 'practice' should not necessarily be seen as providing a truer insight than studying political ideas. Whilst what fascism actually did should never be forgotten (especially in view of its bestialities), the main fascist regimes were short-lived, and went through turbulent times. Even the movements tended to exist for only short periods of time. Studies which focus primarily on movements and regimes should therefore not be seen as necessarily providing the key to 'real' fascism. (Compare arguing that Marxism should be understood solely by the record of Soviet communism in the ten or twenty years after 1917; or that ecologism should be understood by looking at the programmes of Green parties, or speeches of their leaders.) Secondly, most recent historiography has shown that the relationship between fascism and business was complex, but that on balance fascism influenced business more than vice versa. Even among Marxists there are now major debates about the extent to which ideology can be reduced to interests, and about the 'relative autonomy' of the state – issues touched upon near the beginning of this chapter.

The discussion of approaches has thus come full circle. Readers who have acquired a taste for further conceptual and methodological analysis of 'ideology' should turn to the 'Guide to further reading' which follows. Those more concerned with the 'real thing' please read on. For 'real thing', understand mainly political thought, combined with the insights provided to a lesser extent by practice. Thus the 'Marxism and Communism' chapter has little to say about communist regimes; the 'Social Democracy and Democratic Socialism' chapter says little about the governments of Tony Blair or Lionel Jospin or Gerhard Schröder. As the Preface points out, this book is mainly concerned with political ideas, rather than history, sociology or public policy. Or rather, as feminists would probably argue, this is a book mainly about the ideas of DWEMs – dead, white, European males (or soon-to-be DWEMs). But then, this is yet another methodological issue (is 'yet another' male chauvinist?).

NOTES

1. D. McLellan, *Ideology*, Open University Press, Buckingham, 1995, p.1.
2. M. Freeden, *Ideologies and Political Theory: A Conceptual Approach*, Clarendon Press, Oxford, 1996, p.13.
3. M. Freeden, 'Political Concepts and Ideological Morphology', *Journal of Political Philosophy*, 2, 1994, p.140.
4. John Plamenatz, *Ideology*, Pall Mall, London, 1970, p.11.
5. Lawrence and Wishart, London, 1974, p.64. Although this work was finished in the 1840s, a full text did not appear until the 1930s.

6. Karl Marx and Friedrich Engels, *Selected Works in One Volume*, London, Lawrence and Wishart, 1984, p.183.
7. T. Carver, *Marx's Social Theory*, Oxford University Press, Oxford, 1982, p.44.
8. V.I. Lenin, *What Is To Be Done?*, Progress, Moscow, 1973, pp.39–40.
9. For example, *History and Class Consciousness*, Merlin Press, London, 1971.
10. H. Marcuse, *One Dimensional Man*, Routledge and Kegan Paul, London, 1964.
11. See, for instance, J. Habermas, *Theory and Practice*, Heinemann, London, 1974.
12. See especially L. Althusser, *Lenin and Philosophy*, New Left Books, London, 1971.
13. Their first book was *Bad News*, Macmillan, London, 1976.
14. N. Abercrombie, S. Hill and B.S. Turner, *The Dominant Ideology Thesis*, Allen and Unwin, London, 1980.
15. S. Lukes, *Power*, Macmillan, London, 1974.
16. M. Seliger, *Ideology and Politics*, Allen and Unwin, London, 1976, p.13.
17. K. Mannheim, *Ideology and Utopia*, Routledge and Kegan Paul, London, 1936.
18. For instance, C. Geertz, 'Ideology as a Cultural System', in D.E. Apter (ed.), *Ideology and Discontent*, Free Press, New York, 1964.
19. G. Almond and S. Verba, *The Civic Culture*, Princeton University Press, Princeton, 1963.
20. M. Billig, *Ideological Dilemmas*, Sage, London, 1988, pp.25ff. Others have made similar distinctions, though not always prioritizing the 'lived' – for example Plamenatz's separation of 'sophisticated' from 'unsophisticated' ideologies. Plamenatz, op. cit., p.18.
21. H. Arendt, *The Origins of Totalitarianism*, Doubleday, New York, 1951; K. Popper, *The Open Society and Its Enemies*, 2 vols, Routledge and Kegan Paul, London, 1945.
22. D. Bell, *The End of Ideology*, The Free Press, New York, 1962, pp.402–3.
23. See especially S.M. Lipset, *Political Man*, Heinemann, London, 1961.
24. J.-F. Lyotard, *The Postmodern Condition*, Manchester University Press, Manchester, 1984.
25. For instance, M. Foucault, *Power/Knowledge*, Routledge, London, 1980.
26. N. O'Sullivan (ed.), *The Structure of Modern Ideology*, Elgar, Aldershot, 1989, p.188ff.
27. See especially D. Miller, *On Nationality*, Clarendon Press, Oxford, 1995; cf. the excellent M. Canovan, *Nationhood and Political Theory*, Elgar, Cheltenham, 1996.
28. R. Williams, *Keywords*, Fontana, London, 1976, p.76.
29. Freeden, *Ideologies and Political Theory*, p.1.
30. It is important to underline that there have been many forms of Marxist analysis of fascism, even in the inter-war era. For example, see D. Beetham, *Marxists in Face of Fascism*, Manchester University Press, Manchester, 1983.

GUIDE TO FURTHER READING

Surveys of the debate about 'ideology'

Freeden, Michael, *Ideologies and Political Theory: A Conceptual Approach*, Clarendon Press, Oxford, 1996. Excellent book on ideology as political philosophy/theory, best read after covering the basics.

Hamilton, B., 'The Elements of the Concept of Ideology', *Political Studies*, 35, 1987. Good, brief survey, but best read after other reading.

McLellan, David, *Ideology*, Open University Press, Milton Keynes, 2nd edn, 1995. Best student starting-point to ideology as a concept.

Seliger, Martin, *Ideology and Politics*, Allen and Unwin, London, 1976. Clear, though in some ways more a monograph than an introduction.

Thompson, J.B., *Ideology and Modern Culture*, Polity Press, Cambridge, 1990. Frankfurt School influenced stress on the need to consider the power of the media.

Williams, Howard L., *Concepts of Ideology*, Harvester, Brighton, 1988. Useful brief comparison especially of Marx, Mannheim and Oakeshott.

Major Marxist works on ideology and works on Marxism

Althusser, L., *Lenin and Philosophy*, New Left Books, London, 1971.

Carver, Terrell, *Marx's Social Theory*, Oxford University Press, Oxford, 1982.

Eagleton, Terry, *Ideology*, Verso, London, 1991. Reflects fashionable Marxist/structuralist influences.

Femia, J., *Gramsci's Political Thought*, Oxford University Press, Oxford, 1981.

Gramsci, Antonio, *Selections from the Prison Notebooks*, Lawrence and Wishart, London, 1971.

Harding, Neil, *Lenin's Political Thought*, 2 vols, Macmillan, London, 1977 and 1981.

Larrain, J., *The Concept of Ideology*, Hutchinson, London, 1979. A good, Marxist, survey.

Lenin, V.I., *What Is To Be Done?*, Penguin, London, 1988.

McLellan, D., *Karl Marx: Selected Writings*, Oxford University Press, Oxford, 1977.

McLellan, D., The *Thought of Karl Marx*, Macmillan, London, 1980.

Marcuse, H., *One Dimensional Man*, Routledge and Kegan Paul, London, 1964. Cult student book of the 1960s.

Marx, K. and Engels, F., *The German Ideology*, Lawrence and Wishart, London, 1974. The first Marxist attempt, completed in the 1840s, to link ways of thinking with social structure.

Parekh, Bhikhu, *Marx's Theory of Ideology*, Croom Helm, London, 1982. Good survey.

Rossi-Landi, Ferruccio, *Marxism and Ideology*, Clarendon Press, Oxford, 1990.

Other works

Bell, D., *The End of Ideology*, Free Press, New York, 1962.

Billig, M., *Ideological Dilemmas*, Sage, London, 1988. Prolific psychology writer on ideology.

van Dijk, T.A., *Ideology: A Multidisciplinary Approach*, Sage, London, 1998. Focuses on cognition and discourse.

Foucault, M., *Power/Knowledge*, Routledge, London, 1980.

Lyotard, J.-F., *The Post-Modern Condition*, Manchester University Press, Manchester, 1984.

Mannheim, Karl, *Ideology and Utopia*, Routledge and Kegan Paul, London, 1936.

Minogue, Kenneth, *Alien Powers: The Pure Theory of Ideology*, Weidenfeld and Nicolson, London, 1985. Sweeping anti-Marxist work.

Oakeshott, M., *Rationalism in Politics*, Methuen, London, 1967. Conservative defence of pragmatism and practical knowledge over 'rationalistic' ideology.

O'Sullivan, Noël (ed.), *The Structure of Modern Ideology*, Elgar, Aldershot, 1989.

2
LIBERALISM
Richard Bellamy

—

The triumph of the West, of the Western *idea*, is evident first of all in the total exhaustion of viable systematic alternatives to Western liberalism.

Francis Fukuyama[1]

Twentieth-century liberalism has suffered the curious fate of steadily declining in most countries as an electoral force exclusive to a particular party, whilst prevailing and even growing as a background theory or set of presuppositions and sentiments of a supposedly neutral and universal kind which dominates political thinking across the ideological spectrum. In the West, and increasingly elsewhere, most major political groupings now generally employ the liberal language of rights, democracy and the market to legitimize their views. From New Right conservatives to democratic socialists, it seems we are all liberals now. This chapter will examine liberalism's transformation from ideology to a supposedly neutral meta-ideology, capable of providing the ground rules for all legitimate ideological disputes, and critically evaluate its suitability for this role.

LIBERALISM DEFINED

'the end of man, or that which is prescribed by the eternal or immutable dictates of reason, and not suggested by vague and transient desires, is the highest and most harmonious development of his powers to a complete and consistent whole'; that, therefore, the object 'towards which every human being must ceaselessly direct his efforts ... is the individuality of power and development'; that for this there are two requisites, 'freedom and variety of situation'; and that from the union of these arise an 'individual vigour and manifold diversity', which combine themselves in originality.

J.S. Mill[2]

The all-pervasiveness of liberalism results from the fact that liberal values both shaped and reflect the character of the modern states and the other social and economic systems of Western Europe. However as the other ideologies examined in this book show, it is possible to take a different perspective on the political institutions and socio-economic processes of the contemporary world to the liberal one. The distinctiveness of liberalism consists in its being the dominant ideology rather than unideological. For analytical purposes, we can separate out three interrelated components of liberal ideology: one philosophical, another social, and a third political deriving from the first two. We shall examine each in turn.

Liberal philosophy

At the philosophical level, liberals have affirmed a commitment to the concepts of equality, liberty, individuality and rationality. They have been egalitarians in the sense of denying that anyone is naturally the subordinate of anyone else. This view does not entail regarding everyone as the same, merely that all human beings are of equal moral worth. Rather than seeking to guarantee an equality of outcome in the manner of some socialists, liberals desire that everyone should have an equal opportunity to deploy what talents they do possess on the same basis as everyone else. Their attachment to liberty goes together with this interpretation of equality, for liberals have traditionally attempted to achieve the most extensive individual liberty compatible with the assertion of an equal degree of liberty for all other members of society. Similarly, their egalitarianism also informs their insistence on the moral primacy of the individual against any social collectivity. Finally, as rationalists they contend that views in the public domain at least have to be open to critical scrutiny and amendment so that their validity can be tested and affirmed.

As the above exposition indicates, liberals see these four concepts as hanging together in a particular way. The coherence of this interpretation does not lie in any special affinity between the concepts themselves, however. Not only have adherents of other ideologies understood this particular conceptual complex in very different ways, there are also profound differences of opinion even amongst liberals as to why at a philosophical level these concepts fit together as they do, and what political consequences follow from them. Philosophically, the liberal canon includes methodological individualists and holists, materialists and idealists, determinists and voluntarists, utilitarians and adherents of natural rights, whilst politically it extends from libertarian upholders of the free market to defenders of the welfare state.

For example, there has been considerable disagreement amongst liberals as to what individual liberty involves and how it might be expanded equally for all. Some, such as Herbert Spencer (1820–1903) and F.A. Hayek (1899–1992) have advocated a predominately negative view of liberty.[3] They have maintained that enhancing liberty simply involves keeping to a minimum the interferences of the state and others in our lives. We should only be prevented from directly and intentionally inflicting physical harm. For these liberals, almost the only legitimate role of government is the maintenance of law and order so as to secure our person and property. Others, such as L.T. Hobhouse (1864–1929) and William Beveridge (1879–1963), have adopted a more positive view of liberty. They have argued that our activities can impose upon and adversely affect other people's lives in a variety of foreseeable and controllable, even if unintentional, ways. Certain liberals have even argued that the state has a duty to guarantee the availability of certain options, through measures such as public education, health care and welfare schemes.

Nevertheless, liberals have by and large shared a moral and social ethos, and their differences reflect in part alternative views of how well particular social arrangements realize its ideals. At the core of this ethos lies a concern that societies reflect as much as possible the effort and talents of individuals and a resulting distaste of all unearned privileges and unexamined traditions which might provide particular groups with illegitimate advantages. Thus, liberals like Spencer and Hayek, who see the market as a neutral mechanism that responds to countless individual demands and initiatives in a totally unpredictable but essentially fair way, have generally not been impressed by arguments calling for welfare support for the unemployed. By contrast, liberals like Hobhouse and Beveridge, who believe that markets can often be distorted by differences in wealth and organization in ways that unfairly, directly and predictably mar the life chances of certain individuals, have supported welfarism. The differences among liberals, involve variations on a common theme stressing the moral significance of the individual within any social order. This central notion can be traced to the social forces which it both reflects and helped to shape.

Liberal society

Historically, the most important social influences on the formation of liberal individualism were the wars of religion and the rise of modern science in the sixteenth and seventeenth centuries, and the passage from feudalism to capitalism from the same period through to the nineteenth century. The first fuelled the demand for religious toleration which lies behind much of the liberal commitment to rationalism and the equality of individuals. Liberalism's general concern with protecting each individual's ability to pursue his or her own conception of the good to the extent that this does not illegitimately interfere with a similar pursuit by others, can in large part be traced to this source. Hence, the traditional liberal defence of those civil and personal liberties necessary to individuals to live in accordance with their own beliefs without being penalized or imprisoned for unorthodox religious, political or sexual views and practices. The second went hand-in-hand with the liberal attack on ascribed status and its commitment to equality of opportunity. The closed feudal order of inherited rights, with its hierarchical system of aristocratic privileges, was to give way to an open and egalitarian capitalist order, in which an individual's social position and success supposedly mirrors his or her ability and effort – a way of life they felt was best realized in a free-market economy.[4]

Some contemporary liberals and many of liberalism's critics regard the ethos resulting from such social origins as essentially sceptical, subjectivist, materialistic and egoistic.[5] Traditionally, however, liberals have been extremely wary of such attitudes and have sought to avoid them. Although liberals insist on the individual's right to pursue his or her own conception of the good, this does not mean that they treat all beliefs or ways of life as equally valuable. Drawing on the experimental method in modern science and the Protestant defence of freedom of conscience, they merely contend that we have a right to find out the worth (or worthlessness) of our opinions for ourselves – indeed, this is the only way for truth and morality to emerge. According to this thesis, the validity of ideas and practices can only be asserted if individuals are allowed to experiment, calling into question accepted doctrines and trying out new and occasionally eccentric or potentially offensive pursuits. A way of life or belief that cannot withstand the light of public scrutiny is not worth saving in the first place. Similarly, they maintain that personal virtue only really comes from us taking responsibility for our lives. For the state or any group to paternalistically impose its views on the rest of society risks falling into dogmatic error, demoralizes the population and produces stagnation. Individuals must be able to make mistakes so that they can learn from them.

Much the same mixture of ethical and instrumental reasoning lies behind the liberal adherence to the economic individualism of the market. This aspect of the liberal social vision emerged from the experiences of the entrepreneurs, traders, shopkeepers and artisans of early capitalism, and invokes the image of an idealized market order in which rewards are closely linked to effort and desert. This linkage was codified in the labour theory of value and, in British and American culture at least, it drew additional force from the religious beliefs of certain Protestant sects which encouraged industriousness as a mark of salvation. As we noted earlier, liberals have tended to praise the market to the extent that it acts as a stimulus to individual initiative and discovery which brings about the progress of society. In this respect, the virtues of a free market in labour and commodities parallel those of a free market in ideas – they promote the good and weed out the bad. When these advantages are missing, liberals have often proved less enthusiastic about *laissez-faire*.

Liberal politics

The political face of liberalism follows on from the philosophical and social elements outlined above, for the demand to construct the state on liberal principles grew out of the political struggles caused by the wars of religion and the erosion of feudalism. As the social structures based on status gave way to contractual relationships between civil equals, so the feudal hierarchical political structures were undermined. The state, like society as a whole, came to be seen as a voluntary association held together by the mutual consent of its members rather than the ties of deference to social superiors – a conception of the political order summed up in the theory of the social contract.

At the heart of liberal politics is a strict distinction between the state and civil society. The purpose of the state is solely to regulate and facilitate social interaction in all its forms, rather than to substitute for individual initiative through the state management of social institutions. Liberalism is opposed, for example, to the way former fascist and communist regimes sought to organize the individual's whole life, from direct state control of the workplace and trade unions to state-run newspapers and leisure clubs. Nevertheless, in some forms of social liberalism (examined in the next section) the state's tasks are held to involve considerable economic intervention and social provision of an enabling nature. Such activities might range from a publicly funded transport system to state schools and welfare schemes. However, unlike the superficially similar programmes of certain fascist and communist states, their purpose is the liberal one of providing a framework for individuals to pursue projects of their own choosing. Social liberals merely contend that the public provision of certain resources frequently forms a necessary precondition for such free individual action. The basic components of the liberal political settlement were established in the aftermath of the British, American and French revolutions of 1688, 1776 and 1789 respectively. Of primary importance was the principle of the rule of law which informed the various bills of rights and constitutions which were drafted in order to establish the new political order resulting from these events. Two criteria guided the framing of these documents. First, laws were to be applied impartially and universally. There were to be no special exemptions for particular groups, such as nobles or clerics, as there had been in the past. Second, the laws were to guarantee to the greatest extent possible the equal right of each individual to pursue his or her own plan of life. For the majority of liberals, the most basic rights in this respect were traditionally the rights to private property and freedom of belief. These rights were essential to their understanding of the virtues of toleration and the market mechanism, which they regarded as the embodiment of the new ethos. As we shall see, both of these commitments have been modified, though not the general reasoning that underlies them.

Liberals have been more ambivalent about the benefits of democracy. They have tended to see government as having the essentially negative purpose of preserving the openness of society rather than as pursuing positive courses of action. The state is supposed to operate within the bounds of the rule of law as inscribed in the written constitution and bill of rights. Its function is limited to formulating, interpreting and applying the law so as to meet the specific circumstances of a given society at a particular time and place. As a result, many liberals have assigned democratic institutions the purely protective function of controlling the actions of government, especially in the areas of taxation and warfare. In this role, it supplements the division of powers between the legislature, the executive, and the judiciary. A further device designed to uphold the rule of law, the aim of this division, was to ensure that the making of laws was separated from their implementation and interpretation respectively. This method was supposed to preserve the law's impartiality and universality by preventing governments devising legislation biased in favour of its own or its supporters' interests.[6]

Other liberals have viewed democracy more positively though, as a means for deliberating on the common good. Seen in this light, democracy offers a public sphere where ideas and policies might be rationally debated. It provides the cultural conditions conducive to the examination and critical development of our beliefs and goes together with the traditional liberal rights to freedom of the press, freedom of expression, freedom of association, etc. Moreover, liberals generally have appreciated that the enjoyment of their private lives entails a certain degree of public involvement to ensure the fair and efficient enactment and administration of government policies.[7]

In the past, all liberals believed that political citizenship should be limited to those possessing the educational and propertied preconditions necessary for making independent decisions. According to this line of thinking, those lacking a certain level of intellectual and economic independence were unable to appreciate the liberal attachment to rational enquiry and the pursuit of the good – they depended literally on others for their opinions and livelihood. As such, they had no interest in the liberal way of life with its emphasis on individual autonomy. Workers and women formed the main categories of the excluded. Although liberals usually hoped that universal education and the discipline of the market would enable them eventually to enfranchise all adults, this was not achieved in practice in any European country until after the First World War, and even then not everywhere. Indeed, liberals have continued to fear the danger of a vulgar and shortsighted tyrannical majority imposing its wishes on the enlightened and innovative few, and have remained as haunted by the prospect of a populist mob in the twentieth century as they were in the eighteenth. Consequently, liberals still emphasize the importance of constraining government decisions within a constitutional framework which reflects the basic principles of the liberal social order by upholding the rights of individuals.[8]

Liberalism and modern society

The conceptual, socio-economic and political elements of liberal doctrine are inextricably interconnected, forming part of a single historical process. Liberalism corresponds in large part to the self-image and aspirations of the emergent middle classes, and operated in the eighteenth and nineteenth centuries as a creed whereby they sought to oust the aristocratic and agrarian élite and fashion a new environment suited to the needs of commerce, industry and the professions. This was clear to the contemporary theorists of what is sometimes called 'classical' liberalism, who wrote during this period. They saw British society, which had been the first to experience the industrial and political revolutions, as offering a model which they sought to emulate. Whilst the relationship between the liberal ethos and British social and political development was often perceived only very incompletely by the main exponents of the English liberal tradition, such as John Locke (1632–1704), J.S. Mill (1806–73) and Herbert Spencer, the Scots – notably Adam Smith (1723–90) and David Hume (1711–76) – were more aware of its historical contingency. Continental liberals appreciated this to an even greater extent, and there is far more sociological sophistication in writers such as Montesquieu (1689–1755), Benjamin Constant (1767–1830), Alex de Tocqueville (1805–59), François Guizot (1787–1874) and Carlo Cattaneo (1801–69) than in their admired English counterparts.[9]

In the twentieth century, the social basis of liberalism has become an issue that no liberal theorist has been able to ignore. In a mass industrial society dominated by large-scale corporations and other administrative organizations, on the one hand, and increased functional differentiation, on the other, the type of free individual agency assumed by classical liberalism seemed to many liberals writing at the turn of the century to be in jeopardy. The first process had gradually enveloped individuals into the rule-bound and hierarchical structures of bureaucratic agencies, replacing the entrepreneur with the administrator and professional director, and deskilling a large portion of the workforce. The second had so enhanced the complexity of industrial societies that our ability to encompass in a rational way the resulting social diversity within a single moral and cognitive framework had been considerably reduced. The more individuals became trapped in the logic of their various and occasionally conflicting social roles and functions, and bombarded by a growing mass of often contradictory information and sources of persuasion, the more their capacity for autonomous orientation in the world became undermined. These developments had distorted the liberal ideal of the market and added to liberal worries about democracy. Moreover, they

were inextricably linked to the rise of organized labour, which in threatening
the socio-economic and political domination of the middle classes potentially
posed the greatest challenge to liberal hegemony.

In classical liberal eyes the free market did not produce social conflict, it
resolved it. The invisible-hand mechanism of the laws of supply and demand
promoted the harmonization of individual life plans. For analogous reasons
they advocated free trade between states as the best means for achieving
international peace. From this perspective, the liberal ideal consisted not of a
society of self-interested egoists, but of an association of self-reliant and
responsible citizens, co-operating together in pursuit of individual, social,
material and moral improvement. However, perfect competition and the
smooth operation of the price mechanism assumes both that consumers are
fully informed about their needs and the services on offer to meet them, and
that they are equally able to make their demands felt. But in reality, the size
of markets, the inequitable division of wealth, the control exercised by large
corporations and labour organizations over the supply of goods, services and
information in a particular area, all mean that individuals rarely possess such
knowledge and can only very imperfectly influence the economy even when
they do. Such factors have meant that in practice the market economy has
given rise not to a co-operative society of mutually improving individuals,
but to a world of conflicting group interests.

The same causes have radically altered the nature of democracy. Universal
suffrage destroyed the power of local notables and made the main democratic actors the mass political parties. The influence exercised by such
organizations has rendered many of the traditional concepts of liberal
democracy obsolete. Talk of popular sovereignty and representation has
only a limited, if any, value when the choice of candidates, the setting of the
electoral agenda and the recruitment of votes rests almost wholly in the
hands of the various party machines. This development has also undermined
the conventional liberal view of the division of powers, with the executive
usually commanding a passive majority in the legislature. In any case, the
tendency of modern mass parties to be bound by ties of interest rather than
conviction has altered the nature of liberal politics from a process of rational
debate to a means of bargaining and conciliating between self-interested
groups and individuals. Political debate is no longer concerned with the
quality and truth of rival arguments so much as the manipulation of passions
and interests in order to build a majority with which to govern.

From the mid-nineteenth century onwards, liberals watched these changes
in modern societies with great trepidation. An ambivalence to the new
industrial age runs right through the writings of J.S. Mill, for example. His
essay *On Liberty* (1859) has achieved the status of one of the classic
statements of liberalism, yet it originated as a desperate plea for liberal values
in a world in which Mill thought 'individuals are lost in a crowd' and the
dangers of bureaucracy and the pressures to conform to the 'collective
mediocrity' of the masses seemed overwhelming. His defence of *laissez-faire*

in the essay, as elsewhere in his writings, is on practical rather than principled grounds and admitted of numerous exceptions. Though an early enthusiast for universal suffrage, he feared the 'tyranny of the majority'. By the end of his life he had become an extremely cautious democrat and an advocate of Charles Fourier's brand of socialism.

In the sections that follow, we shall trace the liberals' responses to this assault on their moral and social vision. As we shall see, all have involved an attempt not just to adapt liberal principles to this new social context, but to a certain extent to reshape society in a more liberal direction as well. In spite of numerous innovations in liberal theory, the continuity with the traditional liberal ethos remains discernible in all of them, however, so that the prime questions confronting us are whether liberal values are either plausible or desirable today.

LIBERALISM TRANSFORMED: SOCIAL LIBERALISM AND NEO-CLASSICAL LIBERALISM

the subject matter of Liberalism is changing ... Now, this change ... is partly a result of the victory of democracy, and of the new self-consciousness and the new organisation of the wage-earning classes. But it is not entirely psychological in its origins. It is due also, as I believe, to the arrival of a new industrial revolution, a new economic transition which we have to meet with new expedients and new solutions.

John Maynard Keynes[10]

During the period of c.1870–1930 two main liberal strategies emerged to cope with the changed circumstances of modern societies, which I shall call social liberalism and neo-classical liberalism. Significantly, the former predominated in Britain, France and the USA, where liberal democracy seemed relatively secure, whereas the latter was largely formulated in Italy, Germany and Austria, where democracy either barely existed or if it did was severely distrusted by liberals. The first was associated with a more positive view of liberty and greater state intervention, particularly in the regulation of the economy and social reform. The second stuck to a predominately negative view of liberty and stressed the self-sufficiency of the market. Both movements can plausibly claim to have developed certain core aspects of the liberal ethos.

Social liberalism

with the growth of experience a more matured opinion has come to recognize that Liberty (in a political sense) is not only a negative but a

positive conception. Freedom cannot be predicated, in its true meaning, either of a man or of a society, merely because they are no longer
under the compulsion of restraints which have the sanction of positive
law. To be really free, they must be able to make the best use of faculty,
opportunity, energy, life. It is in this fuller view of the true significance
of Liberty that we find the governing impulse in the later developments
of Liberalism in the direction of education, temperance, better dwell-
ings, an improved social and industrial environment; everything, in
short, that tends to national, communal and personal efficiency.

H.H. Asquith[11]

In Britain, social liberalism was associated with the so-called 'new liberalism'
of figures such as T.H. Green (1836–82), L.T. Hobhouse, J.A. Hobson
(1858–1940), J.M. Keynes (1883–1946) and William Beveridge and the two
prominent liberal politicians of the period, H.H. Asquith (1852–1928) and
David Lloyd George (1863–1945). The downturn in economic growth
brought on by a general depression at the turn of the century and increased
competition from other states; a growing perception of the unprecedented
levels of poverty, unemployment and relative deprivation present within
modern industrial cities; the rise of corporate capital and organized labour –
all these factors highlighted the challenge posed by the evolution of modern
societies to the principles of classical liberalism considered at the end of the
last section. The ideal of the self-made individual, who through hard work
and talent could make his or her place in the world, seemed increasingly
implausible. The new liberals sought to adapt the old language of liberalism
to meet these altered circumstances. They defended a broader and more
interventionist conception of the role of the state through, to quote Hobson,
'a fuller appreciation of individual liberty contained in the provision of equal
opportunities for self-development'.[12] An equal right to liberty, they now
believed, could not be established merely by ensuring that individuals did not
physically interfere with each other and that the laws were impartially
formulated and applied. More positive measures were required to ensure
that each individual had an equal chance of success.

Classical liberal political economists had always accepted that there were
certain basic public goods and services essential to the working of a society
which were best provided by the state. Some of these individuals either could
not or would not provide, others were natural monopolies lacking the normal
market incentives deriving from economic competition. They cited light-
houses and health and safety legislation as examples of the first, and gas and
water as typical instances of the second. They also saw the need to regulate
individual behaviour when the rational pursuit of an individual good risked
producing a public bad which would adversely affect the quality of life of
others. Mill advocated strict birth control measures, for example, to prevent
overpopulation, and there was a great deal of legislation throughout the
nineteenth century on matters such as working hours, housing conditions,

sewage disposal and the like. Moreover, they recognized the need to ensure at least a minimal degree of poor relief, health care and education. Admittedly their reasons tended to be highly moralistic. They believed charity in such areas was often haphazard, failing to offer the desired stimulus to individuals to become more prudent and self-reliant. The Poor Law amendment of 1834, with its criterion of making conditions in workhouses 'less eligible' than even the humblest forms of employment elsewhere, was a notorious instance of this sort of thinking. Nevertheless, a public responsibility was accepted. Far from being a period of *laissez-faire*, therefore, the Victorian age saw a veritable explosion of government activity and public works.

Thus, the new liberalism was not as dramatic a break with what had gone before as is sometimes made out. The central issue remained the extent to which individuals could be held responsible for their success or failure. The new pension and unemployment schemes, for instance, retained an important contributory element and continued to be aimed at the 'deserving' poor. The new liberals merely acknowledged that in a complex economy individuals were sometimes thrown out of work for reasons beyond their control, that sickness was often unexpected, and that those who had served society throughout a long working life deserved some security in their old age in recompense. They may have thought the worker had a right to 'the means of a living livelihood' but this brought the correlative duty 'to make the best use of his opportunity' so that 'if he fails he may fairly suffer the penalty of being treated as a pauper or even, in an extreme case, as a criminal'. 'Punitive discipline' remained the appropriate course of action against the 'morally unfit', such as alcoholics.[13] Eugenic and Social Darwinist theories often mixed somewhat unfortunately with these arguments. William Beveridge, for example, was not above advocating 'loss of independence by entering a public institution, emigration, or immediate starvation' as the only humane alternatives that could be offered to those unable, either through personal defects or as a result of being 'in excess' to society's requirements, 'to fill ... a "whole" place in industry'.[14] Even his wartime reports on *Social Insurance and the Allied Services* (1942) and *Full Employment in a Free Society* (1944), which are generally regarded as laying the intellectual foundations for the welfare state, were motivated not by the socialist desire for raising material conditions and securing economic equality but to ensure 'freedom from Idleness' by providing individuals an 'opportunity of service and earning in accordance with their powers'.[15]

The arguments justifying the progressive taxation needed to pay for these policies similarly echoed old liberal doctrines. They argued that all activity was to some degree co-operative in nature. Inventors built on the ideas and inventions of others, for instance, as did entrepreneurs who relied additionally on the skill of their workforce and the whole range of public services – from the education of their employees to the roads necessary to obtain their supplies and distribute their goods. Even favourable trading conditions were mainly socially created, and depended on processes, such as demographic movements, which were often fortuitous and in any case totally out of their hands. As Hobhouse topically remarked of the property speculators of his time, 'the value of a site in London is something essentially due to London, not the landlord'.[16] On this argument, a successful business person who happened to be the right individual in the right place no more deserved a reward than someone standing at a street corner deserved to be knocked over by a bus that accidentally swerved on to the pavement. As a result, they argued that a large proportion of profits constituted an 'unearned surplus' that rightfully belonged to society as a whole. Hobhouse, whose *Liberalism* (1911) is generally regarded as the key text of the movement, set 'the limit of the industrial value of the individual' at £5000 – the figure at which Lloyd George just happened to have introduced super-tax in his 1909 budget!

Certain dogmas of classical political economy were called into question, but once again only in order to preserve liberal values. The idea of a self-regulating free market, reflecting natural law and embodying a just social order, was eroded by the economic ills of recurrent economic crises with their mass unemployment. Hobson in the wake of the pre-First World War depression, and most influentially Keynes in his *General Theory of Employment, Interest and Money* (1936) written in response to the great depression that followed it, became increasingly convinced of the often counter-productive effects of *laissez-faire* economics and the need for state intervention in certain sectors of the economy. As we saw, classical political economy had provided grounds for state control of certain public services basic to the welfare of the population or the economic infrastructure, either through nationalization or some other means. Although the new liberals accepted such measures, unlike collective socialists they saw no need for the state to become directly involved in the planning and management of production throughout the economy, and even in those sectors where this was thought necessary urged that state control be as decentralized as possible. For Keynes, the worst effects of the free market arose from leaving saving and investment to the chance of private judgement and profit, particularly when there existed gross inequalities in the distribution of wealth. Consequently, he advocated greater state management of consumption and investment in order to boost demand to a level at which full employment could be achieved, with progressive taxation being used to regulate the former and fund the latter. However, he contended that economic activities should remain in the hands of private capital. State ownership of the means of production would prove inefficient, bureaucratic and authoritarian.

Although Beveridge's welfare proposals and Keynes' economic theories were taken up after 1945 by the Labour Party, both were firm supporters of the Liberal Party and profoundly influenced its policies – most notably in the 'Yellow Book' of 1928. For them, the reasoning behind the mixed economy remained the traditional liberal one of combating the unjustified privileges of particular groups and classes to achieve a proper balance between the individual and the social, leaving up to the former all matters that could properly be said to be within his or her competence so long as they did not have deleterious effects on others. In their eyes, the Labour and Conservative parties were too strongly associated with the sectional interests of workers and capitalists respectively. Liberalism, by contrast, offered a middle way. At one level, the attempts by the British new liberals to maintain a consensus around liberal values ultimately proved a failure. Although the Liberal Party was in power for most of the first quarter of the twentieth century, its electoral fortunes gradually waned and it has never achieved office again after 1922. The Liberals failed to prevent either the working or the middle classes deserting them to the Labour and Conservative parties respectively. At another level, however, much of their programme did come to form the core of the social democratic consensus that developed between these two parties in the two decades after the war.

None the less, it would be wrong to give the impression that all British liberals were new liberals. Herbert Spencer's long life allowed him to both witness and rail against what he regarded as the 'New Toryism'. Linking liberal arguments for the market with a vulgar form of Social Darwinism, he contended that the economic intervention and welfarism of the new liberals saved people 'from the natural penalties of dissolute living' and warned ominously that national economic survival would eventually necessitate 'the infliction of artificial penalties in solitary cells, on treadwheels, and by the lash'.[17] Such views were in a minority, however, and, not totally justified in any case given the new liberals' anxiety that the naturally 'unfit' should receive their just deserts. Even those, like Sir Ernest Benn (1875–1954), who continued to bemoan the decline of liberty and called for a return to the old liberalism of the mid-nineteenth century, did so in a self-consciously elegiac manner, as belonging to a world that was lost.[18] Appropriately enough, they found refuge at the extreme right of the Conservative Party and such sentiments only rejoined the mainstream of British politics with the rise of New Right thinking in the 1970s (see Chapter 3).

Similar policies to the new liberals were developed and pursued during the same period in France by solidarist thinkers such as Alfred Fouillée (1838–1912) and Emile Durkheim (1858–1917), and radical politicians influenced by their ideas such as Léon Bourgeois (1851–1925). Like their British counterparts, they justified a number of important social and economic reforms on the ground of an enhanced understanding of the dependence of individual liberty on a favourable social environment. However, this theme was given a particularly extended examination by the French theorists, many of whom played an important role in the development of modern sociology.[19] Indeed, sociology became the official philosophy of the Third Republic, supposedly showing the ideals of solidarist liberalism to be inherent to the proper functioning of contemporary societies.

The solidarists argued that the massive extension of the division of labour entailed by an advanced industrial economy had meant that paradoxically the greater opportunities and individualism of modern societies went hand in hand with greater and more complex interdependence among individuals. As a result, they contended that the individual was to a large extent 'in debt' to society for all that he or she is or could become. We had a duty, therefore, to offer a fair exchange for the services rendered us by our fellow citizens and to renew the common legacy for the use of future generations in return for the benefits we had received from the efforts of our predecessors.

Adopting much the same line of reasoning as the British new liberals, they drew from this argument a justification for progressive taxation to fund certain public works and welfare schemes. Their preferred form of organizing the latter, however, was through various forms of co-operative insurance schemes, whereby they sought to encourage all members of society to club together to share the burden of the 'social risks' as well as the profits accruing from the 'social capital' arising out of their collaboration. Some even went so far as to see all property as inherently 'social property', to be held by the state and leased out to individuals or various co-operative business ventures. Nevertheless, they limited the state's role to one of co-ordination rather than direct management. Its function was to facilitate the practice of mutual aid among individuals through institutions that developed an awareness of their interdependence, not to substitute for their activity through state provision and planning. For example, comparatively little was done in the way of developing a welfare state with pensions, unemployment and sickness benefits etc., whereas there was a great deal of legislation to encourage the setting up of mutual benefit societies for these purposes.

Whilst sympathetic to the socialist movement, they remained critical of it. Like the new liberals, they were meritocrats rather than egalitarians. They saw class struggle as the product of unequal opportunities due to the unfair advantages of particular groups. Remove these barriers to social mobility and make everyone aware of their relationship and dependence on all other members of society, and class conflict would give way to co-operation and harmony. Their sociological cast of mind led them to delineate the social assumptions of the liberal ethic far more clearly than the new liberals – notably the belief that in a healthy and open society each individual would discover the place he or she deserved and that their competition would prove mutually beneficial and improving rather than divisive and counter-productive.

In common with the new liberals, they were ambiguous about the fate of individuals who might not find a particularly fulfilling place or any place at all, and tended to stigmatize such misfits as moral or social degenerates. Radical politicians, for example, were not averse to the brutal repression of the revolutionary syndicalists, whose ranks were largely filled by skilled craftsmen rendered unemployed by new factory technology.

Like France and unlike Britain, there has never been a national Liberal party in the USA. However, liberal ideas form an intrinsic part of the national heritage. Refugees from religious persecution in Europe, the Puritan Pilgrim Fathers brought the liberal doctrines of freedom of conscience, limited government and the economic values associated with the Protestant work ethic to the new continent. The constitutionalism of John Locke and Montesquieu combined to a lesser extent with the more democratic and egalitarian sentiments of J.-J. Rousseau (1712–78) informed both the American Revolution and the resulting constitutional settlement. Both elements are present within the writing of the leading American liberal thinker of this period, Thomas Jefferson (1743–1826), for example. As elsewhere, however, liberalism split into a right-wing libertarian camp and a left-of-centre social liberal camp.

The libertarian camp was greatly influenced by Herbert Spencer's brand of Social Darwinism, which it mixed with a Lockean style natural-rights jurisprudence. Writers in this school, such as William Graham Sumner (1840–1910), advocated an extreme form of *laissez-faire* in which the government's sole role was to secure each individual's freedom to compete in the market-place. Not only state welfare but even private charity was condemned as detrimental to the health of society. As Sumner argued, 'A drunkard in the gutter is just where he ought to be, according to the fitness and tendency of things. Nature has set up on him the process of decline and dissolution by which she removes things which have [outlived] their usefulness'.[20] Such thinking remained marginalized, however, until the rise of neo-liberal economic thought after the Second World War under the influence of the Austrian neo-classical school, examined in the next section. The dominant form of American liberalism was that of the social liberal camp, who even succeeded in appropriating the term 'liberal' so that in the USA it became synonymous with someone who holds left-of-centre views. Thus, the literary critic Lionel Trilling, writing in 1946, went so far as to define liberalism as 'a ready if mild suspiciousness of the profit motive, a belief in progress, science, social legislation, planning and international cooperation'.[21] Progressive intellectuals such as Walter Lippmann (1899–1974) and John Dewey (1859–1952) essentially rethought liberalism along the lines of the French and British theorists examined above, and the New Deal initiatives undertaken by the Democratic administration of President Roosevelt from 1932 to 1940 have much in common with the economic and social programme put forward in the British Liberal Party's 'Yellow Book'. As in Britain and France, the steady pace of industrial growth and the presence of democratic institutions had enabled liberal hegemony to be well enough established to adapt to the altered circumstances of a complex mass industrial society. Elsewhere social liberal arguments found less fertile soil, however. Italy and Germany provide an instructive contrast in this respect.

Neo-classical liberalism

Today the tenets of [the] nineteenth century philosophy of liberalism are almost forgotten. In continental Europe it is remembered only by a few. In England the term 'liberal' is mostly used to signify a programme that only in details differs from the totalitarianism of the socialists. In the United States 'liberal' means today a set of ideas and political postulates that in every regard are the opposite of all that liberalism meant to the preceding generations ... The few upright citizens who dare to criticize this trend towards administrative despotism are branded as extremists, reactionaries, economic royalists and fascists.

Ludwig von Mises[22]

Although certain thinkers, such as Guido de Ruggiero (1888–1948) and to a lesser extent Benedetto Croce (1866–1952) in Italy and Lujo Brentano (1844–1931) in Germany, sought to develop a form of new liberalism on the British model, they had no great influence on either liberal thought or practice. Liberals either feared the working classes too much to attempt such a *rapprochement*, or – in the case of those theorists critical existing liberal politics – viewed such policies as a paternalistic strengthening of the power of the state. From this latter perspective, social liberalism far from being a progressive expression of modern social relations, was a regressive attempt to impose an outmoded morality on an intransigent social reality. I shall briefly examine three broadly neo-classical attempts to develop this point and to rethink liberalism in a quite different manner to the social liberals: that of the Italian theorist Vilfredo Pareto (1848–1923), the Austrian economists and the German sociologist Max Weber (1864–1920).

Pareto began as a devoted follower of Mill and Spencer, critical of the illiberal practices of the Italian state and sympathetic to the grievances of socialists. However, the failure of any liberal movement to emerge and the continued corruption (in his view) of the main liberal politician of his time – Giovanni Giolitti – led him to become cynical about the humanitarian and ethical claims of liberalism. Mass democracy, he believed, was simply a mechanism whereby various élite groups sought legitimation for their control of the state. Whatever their professed beliefs, the governing class always used this power for their own ends and those of their supporters, and employed the state to enrich themselves at everyone else's expense. Moreover, to stay in office, governments were always tempted either to employ coercion or to manipulate support through granting various benefits to particular groups of people – both of which involved undue interferences with individual liberty. He therefore advocated a drastic reduction in the role of the state to that of maintaining a free market in goods and labour. However, he divested the market mechanism of most of the moral advantages earlier liberals attributed to it. For Pareto it was merely a practical device for allowing individuals to maximize whatever their interests and desires happened to be, regardless of their worth. Unlike the classical liberals, he regarded judgements of value as inherently subjective and all attempts to place them on a rational or objective basis as inherently illiberal. The advantage of the market lay in its being a less corruptible and more neutral mechanism than democracy for revealing individuals' preferences and achieving the optimal degree of satisfaction. Indeed, he even ended up welcoming Mussolini's seizure of power, believing at least a temporary break with democracy was necessary to implement the free-market system he desired. Had he lived, however, he would undoubtedly have withdrawn his support owing to Mussolini's economic policies.

The 'subjective' theory of value is at the heart of the economic liberalism of the Austrian school of Carl Menger (1840–1921), Ludwig von Mises (1881–1973) and F.A. Hayek, and had a common source in the work of W.S. Jevons and Léon Walras – Pareto's predecessor as Professor of Political Economy at the University of Lausanne. They argued that human beings are purposeful creatures whose free actions and choices are the sole source of meaning and value. A free market is the only mechanism capable of responding to human choices in this way. In their view, the socialist ideal of a planned economy was doubly flawed in being both impractical and necessarily coercive. It assumed the existence of an objective standard for the just allocation of burdens and benefits and the distribution of resources. By contrast, they argued that it was impossible efficiently or rationally to decide on the relative value of different and incommensurable goods and wants. Only a market system responding through the price mechanism to the forces of supply and demand was capable of setting a fair rate of exchange between products and services in a calculable manner, and of providing through the profit motive an incentive for individuals to innovate and improve their performance. A planned economy necessarily entailed an arbitrary dictatorial regulation which enforced particular patterns of consumption and production. Such a system would not only greatly enhance the power of the state over people's lives, it would ultimately collapse through bureaucratic stagnation and the impossibility of its task within an economy of any size and complexity. The Austrian school insisted on the analytical priority of microeconomic theory and denied the validity of much macro-economic thinking, questioning all governmental attempts to interfere in the economy. State action was not only an illegitimate interference with the individual's freedom to express his or her preferences, it also disturbed the discovery process whereby new products and methods of production were explored and tested. Although their ideas found little favour at the time, the emigration of leading members of the school during the 1930s meant that they retained a significant, if minor, place in the academic world and continued to develop their views. Their theories were also spread through the international Mont Pelérin Society founded by von Mises, Hayek and others in 1947. It was only in the late 1970s, however, that their ideas began to gain widespread public recognition, influencing the economic thinking of the libertarian New Right and the rhetoric, if not always the policies, of Margaret Thatcher and Ronald Reagan (see Chapter 3).

Max Weber agreed with those of the Austrian school, such as his former doctoral student von Mises, that the core of liberalism resided in our capacity through our activities to endow our lives with a worth and meaning that was otherwise lacking in a world which, without the solace of religious faith, we could no longer plausibly regard as intrinsically meaningful. As a result, he shared their antipathy to any attempt to substitute state action for that capacity. But he was rather less sanguine about the possibility of returning to the economic policies of the early nineteenth century in the very different social and political conditions of the twentieth. He believed that the values and practices of classical liberalism were historically contingent, corresponding to the early phase of capitalism. Countries such as Germany, Italy or Russia which industrialized later and went immediately to an advanced stage of capitalism were unlikely to develop this ethos. The structural power of the large-scale organizations of the modern world, as manifested for example by the influence of mass parties and industrial corporations on individual choices, rendered liberalism's traditional individualist, entrepreneurial and rationalist spirit anachronistic in any case.

More honestly or realistically than either Pareto or the Austrians, he believed that within modern societies only the captains of industry and political leaders were in a position to act with anything like the responsibility and creativity demanded by the liberal ethos. He sought to rethink liberal institutions of the market and democracy as mechanisms for sustaining a certain degree of competition between the élites and interest groups in society. By this means, he hoped to create at least some space for certain individuals battling against the pressures to conform within a bureaucratic and technological society. However, in contrast to earlier liberals, he believed such instances of individuality were more likely to generate conflict than harmony, and could in no sense be regarded as furthering moral and social progress. Individual self-expression was valuable in itself, but it often had adverse effects on the lives of others. Such clashes could only be resolved procedurally and politically rather than philosophically – through compromise rather than principled consent.

Like Pareto and the Austrians, therefore, he defended the liberal credentials of the market as a purely procedural device capable of distributing resources in a manner that reflected individual choices. He also thought that democracy could be reconceived in these terms, and hence was less cynical about democratic politics than his Italian contemporary. He argued that the selection and rational debate of policies were indirect results of a competition between party leaders for the people's vote, rather than something ordinary electors did or even could do themselves. Genuine mass political participation could only generate a confused mess of ill-informed and differing half-baked opinions, with most people all too inclined to follow the first demagogue to promise them the moon. A competitive party system, by contrast, constrained debate and disagreement within manageable limits, pushing capable individuals to the fore.

COLD WAR LIBERALISM

The opposite of liberalism is totalitarianism.

F.A. Hayek[23]

The rise of fascism and communism in the 1920s and 1930s appeared to confirm the pessimism of Weber concerning the demise of liberal values in the modern world. Yet if for many contemporaries the rival authoritarianisms of left and right made liberalism seem outmoded or inadequate, for others liberal ideas attained a new urgency. In the period after the Second World War, liberalism became redefined in contradistinction to the supposed totalitarianism of communist and fascist regimes. Books such as F.A. Hayek's *The Road to Serfdom* (1944), Karl Popper's (1902–94) *The Open Society and its Enemies* (1945), Albert Camus's (1913–40) *The Rebel* (1951), J.L. Talmon's (1916–80) *Origins of Totalitarian Democracy* (1952) and Isaiah Berlin's (1909–97) *Four Essays on Liberty* (1969)[24] all developed this theme. They argued that whereas totalitarian doctrines were ideological, Utopian, historicist and holistic, liberalism was empirical and pluralistic and aimed not at the construction of an ideal state but at a form of government which allowed for the peaceful expression of the diversity of human values and interests. In place of what they regarded as the totalitarian's fanatical desire to rebuild society anew on the basis of some abstract schema, these liberals advocated piecemeal reform and adaptation in the light of the revealed preferences of individuals. Like the last group of thinkers examined above, they regarded the market and democracy as essentially procedural devices for achieving this goal. Unlike them, they were rather more complacent about the adequacy of existing institutions to perform this role. However, they were far from being a homogeneous group. For example, certain of them – notably F.A. Hayek – viewed the welfare state as a dangerous piece of socialist Utopianism, whilst others, such as Isaiah Berlin, saw it as a liberal reform.

This period may have witnessed the further decline of avowedly liberal parties, but liberal theorists confidently declared that in all developed industrial societies in the West ideological conflict had given way to a general consensus around the values and practices of liberalism. During the 1950s and early 1960s this view was sustained by the general prosperity generated by the post-war boom. Both the West German Social Democratic Party and the British Labour Party, for example, began to argue that the traditional aims of socialism had been achieved and that class had ceased to be an issue as the proletariat was gradually absorbed into the bourgeoisie. However, this complacency proved short-lived. During the late 1960s the black civil rights movement in the USA and the similar campaigns – such as that of Catholics in Northern Ireland – that it inspired; liberation movements in the Third World and most especially the débâcle of the Vietnam War and the deep political divisions it aroused; the world depression of the 1970s and 1980s with the accompanying return of high inflation and mass unemployment to developed capitalist states – these and other events made it clear that ideological divisions still gripped modern societies, and that various sources of deprivation and injustice both at home and abroad persisted to fuel them. In these circumstances, one would expect the coherence of contemporary liberalism's claim to be a non-ideological meta-ideology to have been seriously weakened. However, this same period has seen a remarkable revival of liberal theorizing all of which seeks to portray liberalism as offering a neutral framework for resolving the divisions of the modern world.

LIBERALISM AT THE TURN OF THE TWENTY-FIRST CENTURY

A liberal is someone who cannot take his own side in an argument.
Robert Frost[25]

Recent liberal philosophers share the belief that the prime virtue of pluralism lies in its being neutral between rival conceptions of the good. They argue that the chief advantage of liberal theories of the market, democracy and justice resides in letting people holding different moral and material priorities and preferences live peaceably and profitably together. Unlike most earlier liberals, therefore, they seek to divorce liberal principles from controversial ethical, epistemological and ontological viewpoints. In spite of this agreed approach, however, these theorists split along the main ideological divisions of the contemporary world. The gradual electoral drift of liberals to social democracy on the one hand and conservatism on the other has been reflected in a parallel division in contemporary liberal philosophy between social democratic and New Right thinkers. I shall briefly examine an example of liberal thinking from each of these main camps.

The major exponent of contemporary social democratic liberalism is John Rawls (1921–), whose *A Theory of Justice* (1972) is probably the most important work of political philosophy written in English since the Second World War. Rawls uses the classical liberal device of a social contract to arrive at two principles of justice which he believes will serve to regulate the relations between individuals within modern societies. He asks us to imagine what principles we would choose to adopt if we knew neither what sort of person we were – whether we were lazy or hard working, intelligent or stupid, able bodied or not, male or female etc. – nor what position we might come to hold in society, or the precise circumstances of that society – whether it was rich or poor, for example. All we know are certain general facts about human psychology, sociology, economics and politics.

Rawls believes that this thought experiment, which he elaborates in great detail, will produce a theory of justice that everyone will accept as legitimate because it is untainted by any preconceptions about the worth or lack of it, of particular beliefs or ways of life. Rather, we shall be drawn to appreciate the value of showing equal concern and respect to all people, regardless of their views. For, faced with the radical uncertainty of what Rawls calls the 'original position', we will seek to arrive at principles of justice that are as fair as possible to all persons whatever their talents or ideals might be. Indeed fairness, rather than truth or goodness, is the only acceptable criterion of modern justice for Rawls.

What then are Rawls's two principles, and what kind of policies do they require for their realization? According to the first principle, the state must provide the most extensive system of equal liberties possible. All individuals must enjoy the greatest degree of liberty consistent with the enjoyment of a like liberty by everyone else. According to the second principle, there must be equal opportunity to obtain positions and status in society, regardless of colour, gender, creed, etc. To help achieve this, each person is to have an equal share of wealth *except* when an unequal distribution would improve the welfare of the least well off in society, by providing incentives that encourage people to work harder and produce more in ways that raise the living standards of everyone. Even so, a progressive taxation policy would be necessary if the trickle-down effect failed to produce any benefits from this greater affluence for those at the bottom of society.

Like the social liberals, therefore, Rawls's theory tries to combine the liberal values of liberty and equality with a concern for social justice tempered, in characteristic social-liberal fashion, by the requirements of efficiency. Unlike the social liberals, however, he has sought to dissociate his argument for these policies from the traditional liberal ethos and meta-physics.

Three years after Rawls's book appeared, Robert Nozick (1938–) published *Anarchy, State and Utopia* (1974) defending the market and a minimal state and criticizing any form of welfarist policy on libertarian grounds. He argues that any attempt to redistribute resources or to intervene in the economy involves an illegitimate attempt to use people to further some social purpose with which they may not agree. In his view, the advantage of the market is that it reflects no particular conception of the good, the resulting distributions being merely the unplanned consequence of numerous exchanges among individuals. So long as nobody is deliberately and phys-ically coerced into exchanging goods or selling his or her labour to another and there are no legal barriers discriminating against who can apply for jobs or what can be sold, then the liberal criteria of liberty and equality have been satisfied and the market system can be judged as fair. The inequalities that result from its operation follow no strict pattern. Those who do well cannot be said in any absolute sense necessarily to deserve or merit their success – they have merely been fortunate to be born to rich rather than poor parents, or to have had talents that proved to be marketable. Their entitlement to their wealth rests simply on the right not to be interfered with by others, for what we have obtained through transactions which honour the right of each and every individual not to be coerced is rightfully ours. As he puts it, governments have no legitimate grounds for meddling with capitalistic acts between consenting adults.

Just as Rawlsean social liberalism has been taken up by social democrats, so New Right theories such as Nozick's, which offer a neo-classical liberal defence of the free market, have been taken up by conservatives. Indeed, his argument does contain a strong conservative bias, since it rests on an explicitly historical view of justice based on the pattern of distribution that evolves through market exchanges over time. However, Nozick never claims to be a conservative and others with similar views, such as Hayek, explicitly reject the label.[26] As Roger Scruton has pointed out in his book *The Meaning of Conservatism,* Nozick's right-based argument is in direct opposition to the Old Right emphasis on 'the web of obligations by which citizens are bound to each other and the state'.[27] Moreover, although his theory accords best with *laissez-faire* capitalist society, he draws on the anarchist and Utopian traditions to suggest that it could be compatible with any form of social organisation provided it was voluntarily entered into (see Chapters 3 and 6). In common with other contemporary liberal thinkers, therefore, the central commitment of his theory is to a pluralist framework which provides scope for people to live according to diverse conceptions of the good.

How convincing are these two versions of liberalism? Do either of them manage to sustain their claim to neutrality? Why, in any case, should we find neutrality appealing? Once we leave the Rawlsean 'original position', for example, and discover who and where we are, what would motivate us to adhere to the two principles if they appeared to conflict with our most important ideals or interests? Surely, only someone who had already swallowed a good dose of liberal neutrality in the first place would feel at all inclined to distance themselves from their cherished beliefs and social and material attachments in the way Rawls's theory requires. Similarly, Nozick offers no reasons for why we have certain rights rather than others. His theory appears to assume that we share his moral intuitions as to what liberty and equality involve. If we do not, then his whole argument fails. A more 'positive' understanding of liberty and equality, for instance, will yield a quite different perception of coercion to the one Nozick relies on to characterize the market as 'free'.

Rawls has recently reworked his theory in *Political Liberalism* (1993) to meet some of these sorts of objections. He now insists his conception of liberalism is 'political not metaphysical', a response to the 'fact of pluralism' within modern societies. Such pluralism arises from what he terms 'the burdens of judgement'. These concern the difficulties of identifying, weighing up and evaluating the evidence in any moral dispute, of reconciling different sorts of moral claim, or even of being sure which set of values or sorts of consideration are relevant. Thus, people may disagree over fundamental values, or agree yet differ on how they ought to be ranked or about exactly how they should be applied to the given case; they may employ different modes of reasoning, or argue from the perspective of different experiences or traditions of thought. Debates over welfare, for example, typically exhibit these features. Utilitarians, libertarians and social liberals, say, hold divergent views of what values are most important – utility, property rights or needs, diverge on whether the beneficiary's responsibility for his or her plight is relevant or not to his or her receipt of aid, and how, and so on. Rawls believes that once we acknowledge such questions are intractable, we should accept the necessity for certain constitutional ground rules to ensure their resolution is free and fair. 'Reasonable' people will appreciate that they cannot publicly justify the single minded rational pursuit of their own ideals and interests to the exclusion of the equally valued, but perhaps conflicting, activities of others. Only dogmatists will seek to impose their beliefs on everyone else. In consequence, citizens will embrace a common set of political principles – essentially the liberties enumerated in his first principle of justice. These entail avoiding reference to their own comprehensive conceptions of the good when discussing collective arrangements and respecting the equal rights to liberty of other members of society.

Rawls may have recast his theory, but in essence it remains much as before and suffers from the same problems we noted above. Far from resolving discord, the 'method of avoidance' has the curious upshot of requiring disputants to put to one side the very source of their disagreement. Yet that will prove both mutually unsatisfactory and inconclusive. Opponents of abortion, for example, are hardly likely to accept that just because the moral status of the foetus is disputed it should not be discussed at all. As Joseph Raz had observed, such 'epistemic abstinence' makes little sense for liberals either. Faced with a challenge to their ideals, they will wish to defend liberalism in much more robust terms. The liberal core, Raz insists, lies in *The Morality of Freedom* (1986) and the value of autonomy. Prudence combined with a respect for the rights of others suggests that liberals should avoid imposing their beliefs on others if they can avoid it. But when forced to, they must stick to their guns. Luckily the problem is a temporary one. Since the only way to get on in modern societies is to be autonomous, then the ways of life that shun it can be expected to simply wither away.

Raz advocates a straightforward return to the campaigning ethos of earlier versions of liberalism. To this extent his theory is more upfront about its assumptions than that of Rawls or Nozick. Yet this may not be an advantage if Rawls is right that such metaphysical liberalism is even less plausible today than in the nineteenth century. If pluralism is endemic to complex social systems, then multiculturalism and value conflict can not be attributed to premodern, pre-liberal societies and modes of thought alone that are destined to disappear. Nor can we be sanguine about the prospects for autonomous agency in a world increasingly characterized by the multiplication of unaccountable private (non-state) sources of power, from the media to corporate capital, with an ever greater capacity to shape individual lives.

For all their philosophical sophistication, contemporary liberal theories seem politically and sociologically naïve, greatly exaggerating the possible independence and opportunities available to individuals within complex societies. The division of labour; international markets; the organizational structures of modern economies – from large-scale bureaucratic states to multinational corporations and financial and political institutions such as the International Monetary Fund (IMF) and the European Union (EU) – these and other factors make theories which take as their starting-point the autonomous individual agent, capable of making his or her way in the world through talent, effort and voluntary agreements with other individuals, blatantly ridiculous. They ignore the forces shaping our choices and the limits of our ability rationally to control or harmonize them. In sum, liberals must either idealize present social conditions to fit their views or deliberately abstract from them in an unsuccessful attempt to arrive at neutral principles unsullied by any particular ideological prejudice. Either way, they end up being largely irrelevant to the lives people actually lead.

The collapse of the Soviet bloc and the decisive victory of the combined Western military might in the Gulf War, made it fashionable to talk of an end of ideology and the inevitable triumph of liberal values and practices.[28] The weaknesses of such views are threefold. First, either they ignore the significant pockets of dissent from liberal values by nationalist and religious groups or they overestimate the capacity of liberalism to encompass them within a common framework. Liberal incomprehension at the continued appeal of fundamentalist religion is a good case in point. Second, they overlook the continuing sources of social tension from deprivation and inequalities arising from a number of structural factors both within and between states. Finally, and most importantly, liberalism retains an archaic image of social relations. The continued validity of liberal concepts such as autonomy, consent, representation and popular sovereignty, remain highly dubious within the advanced capitalist systems of the contemporary world. The application of this political vocabulary of the eighteenth and early nineteenth centuries to the problems of the twenty-first has become an increasingly academic exercise. In the rapidly changing circumstances of the contemporary world, the need to go beyond the assumptions of liberalism has become an urgent task.

NOTES

1. 'The End of History', *The National Interest*, Summer, 1989, p.3.
2. Quoting Wilhelm von Humboldt's *The Sphere and Duties of Government* (1792) in *On Liberty* (1859), in *On Liberty and Other Essays*, Oxford University Press, Oxford, 1991, p.64.

3. For a classic contemporary statement of the negative/positive liberty distinction, as freedom from intentionally imposed external constraints as opposed to freedom to pursue certain worthwhile goals, see I. Berlin's essay 'Two Concepts of Liberty', in his *Four Essays on Liberty*, Oxford University Press, Oxford, 1969. Berlin claimed that the negative concept accorded best with the liberal tradition, although he accepted that many liberals had employed the positive view. Later scholarship has tended to dispute both the conceptual distinctiveness of the two accounts of liberty and pointed out that most liberals have adopted a more positive version than Berlin thought. See Z.A. Pelczynski and J. Gray (eds), *Conceptions of Liberty in Political Philosophy*, Athlone Press, London, 1984 which contains useful chapters on Locke, Mill and Berlin himself elaborating this thesis. Indeed, in the 'Introduction' to the 1969 collection of his essays on liberty, Berlin himself modifies his argument in this direction.

4. The following overview is meant as a characterization of perhaps the three most systematic of early liberal philosophers, John Locke, J.S. Mill and Adam Smith, although of course they differ on many points.

5. E.g. C.B. Macpherson, *The Political Theory of Possessive Individualism: Hobbes to Locke*, Clarendon Press, Oxford, 1962.

6. The classic statement of this view of politics is John Locke's *Second Treatise of Government* (first published 1689, although largely written much earlier). This argument was further elaborated by Charles-Louis de Secondat, Baron de Montesquieu in Volume 1, Book XI, Chapter 6 on the English constitution of his book *The Spirit of the Laws* (1748). The American constitution, which was heavily influenced by the writings of Montesquieu and Locke, is the most famous attempt to implement this theory.

7. The role of political participation was best appreciated by French liberals such as Benjamin Constant, François Guizot and above all Alex de Tocqueville, whose two-volume study of *Democracy in America* (1835 and 1840) provides the classic statement of this point of view. J.S. Mill, who greatly admired the French liberals, combines both the Lockean protective approach and the more participatory arguments for democracy in his *Considerations on Representative Government* (1861).

8. This ambivalence about democracy is discussed in C.B. Macpherson, *The Life and Times of Liberal Democracy*, Oxford University Press, Oxford, 1977.

9. This difference is usefully explored by Larry Siedentop in his article, 'Two Liberal Traditions', in A. Ryan (ed.), *The Idea of Freedom*, Clarendon Press, Oxford, 1979.

10. 'Liberalism and Industry', in H.L. Nathan and H. Heathcote Williams (eds), *Liberal Points of View*, Ernest Benn, London, 1927, p.205.

11. 'Introduction' to H.L. Samuel, *Liberalism: An Attempt to State the Principles and Proposals of Contemporary Liberalism in England*, Grant Richards, London, 1902, p.x.

12. J.A. Hobson, *The Crisis of Liberalism: New Issues of Democracy*, P.S. King and Son, London, 1909, p.xi.

13. The quotes come from L.T. Hobhouse, *Liberalism* (1911), Oxford University Press, Oxford, 1964, pp.83, 86, 106.

14. W.H. Beveridge, 'The Problem of the Unemployed', *Sociological Papers*, 3, 1906, p.327.

15. W.H. Beveridge, *Why I am a Liberal*, Herbert Williams, London, 1945, p.16.

16. Hobhouse, *Liberalism*, p.100.

17. H. Spencer, *The Man versus the State* (1884), ed. D. MacRae, Penguin, Harmondsworth, 1964, p.83.

18. Sir Ernest Benn, *Happier Days: Recollections and Reflections*, Benn, London, 1949.

19. See W. Logue, *From Philosophy to Sociology: The Evolution of French Liberalism 1870–1914*, University of Illinois Press, Urbana, 1983.

20. W.G. Sumner, *What Social Classes Owe to Each Other*, Caldwell, Caxton, ID, 1970, p.88.

21. L. Trilling, *The Liberal Imagination: Essays on Literature and Society*, Penguin, Harmondsworth, 1970, p.106.

22. 'Preface' to the English edition of *Liberalism in the Classical Tradition* (1927), Cobden Press, San Francisco, 1985, pp.xvi–xvii.

23. *The Constitution of Liberty*, University of Chicago Press, Chicago, 1960, p.103.

24. The four essays in this collection were written between 1949 and 1959.

25. Quoted by T. Nagel, 'Moral Conflict and Political Legitimacy', *Philosophy and Public Affairs*, 16, 1987, p.218.

26. Hayek added as a postscript to his *Constitution of Liberty* (1960) an appendix entitled 'Why I am not a Conservative'.

27. R. Scruton, *The Meaning of Conservatism*, Macmillan, London, 1984, p.106. This tension between the liberal-inspired New Right and the conservative Old Right is further explored by D. King, *The New Right: Politics, Markets and Citizenship*, Methuen, London, 1987.

28. See F. Fukuyama, The *End of History and the Last Man*, Hamish Hamilton, London, 1992.

GUIDE TO FURTHER READING

Primary source anthologies

Bramstead, E.K. and Melhuish, K.J. (eds), *Western Liberalism: A History of Documents from Locke to Croce*, Longman, London, 1978.

Eccleshall, Robert, *British Liberalism: Liberal Thought from the 1640s to 1980s*, Longman, Harlow, 1986.

Sandel, M. (ed.), *Liberalism and its Critics*, Blackwell, Oxford, 1986.

Primary sources: twentieth-century classics

Berlin, I., *Four Essays on Liberty*, Oxford University Press, Oxford, 1969.

Durkheim, E., 'Individualism and the Intellectuals' (1898), trans. S. and J. Lukes, *Political Studies*, 27, 1969.

Hayek, F.A., *The Constitution of Liberty*, University of Chicago, Chicago, 1960.

Hobhouse, L.T., *Liberalism* (1911), Oxford University Press, Oxford, 1964.

Nozick, R., *Anarchy, State and Utopia*, Blackwell, Oxford, 1974.

Pareto, V., *The Other Pareto*, trans. and ed. P. Bucolo, Scolar Press, London, 1980.

Rawls, J., *A Theory of Justice*, Clarendon Press, Oxford, 1972.

Rawls, J., *Political Liberalism*, Columbia University Press, New York, 1993.

Weber, Max, *From Max Weber: Essays in Sociology*, eds H.H. Gerth and C. Wright Mills, RKP, London, 1948.

General

Arblaster, Anthony, *The Rise and Decline of Western Liberalism*, Basil Blackwell, Oxford, 1984.

Bellamy, Richard, *Liberalism and Modern Society*, Polity Press, Cambridge, 1992.

Bellamy, Richard, *Rethinking Liberalism*, Cassell, London, 1999.

De Ruggiero, Guido, *The History of European Liberalism*, Oxford University Press, Oxford, 1927.

Gray, John, *Liberalism*, Open University Press, Milton Keynes, 1986.

Hall, John A., *Liberalism: Politics, Technology and the Market*, Paladin, London, 1987.

Laski, Harold I., *The Rise of European Liberalism*, Allen and Unwin, London, 1936.

Manet, P., *An Intellectual History of Liberalism*, Princeton University Press, Princeton, 1994.

Manning, D.J., *Liberalism*, Dent, London, 1976.

Liberalism defined

Bellamy, Richard (ed.), *Victorian Liberalism: Nineteenth Century Political Thought and Practice*, Routledge, London, 1991.

Holmes, Stephen, *Benjamin Constant and the Making of Modern Liberalism*, Yale University Press, New Haven, 1985.

Macpherson, C.B., *The Political Theory of Possessive Individualism*, Oxford University Press, Oxford, 1962.

Parry, Geraint, *John Locke*, Allen and Unwin, London, 1978.

Sheehan, I.I., *German Liberalism in the Nineteenth Century*, Chicago University Press, Chicago, 1978.

Siedentop, L., 'Two Liberal Traditions', in A. Ryan (ed.), *The Idea of Freedom*, Clarendon Press, Oxford, 1979.

Simon, W.M. (ed.), *French Liberalism 1789–1848*, Wiley, London, 1972.

Tully, J., *An Approach to Political Philosophy: Locke in Contexts*, Cambridge University Press, Cambridge, 1993.

Winch, Donald, *Adam Smith's Politics*, Cambridge University Press, Cambridge, 1978.

Liberalism transformed

Beetham, David, *Max Weber and the Theory of Modern Politics* (2nd edn), Polity Press, Cambridge, 1985.

Beetham, David, 'Max Weber and the Liberal Political Tradition', *European Journal of Sociology*, 30, 1989, pp.311–23.

Bellamy, Richard, 'From Ethical to Economic Liberalism: The Sociology of Pareto's Politics', *Economy and Society*, 19, 1990, pp.431–55.

Freeden, Michael, *The New Liberalism: An Ideology of Social Reform*, Clarendon Press, Oxford, 1978.

Freeden, Michael, *Liberalism Divided: A Study in British Political Thought 1914–39*, Clarendon Press, Oxford, 1986.

Kloppenberg, J.T., *Uncertain Victory: Social Democracy and Progressivism in European and American Thought 1870–1920*, Clarendon Press, Oxford, 1986.

Logue, W., *From Philosophy to Sociology: The Evolution of French Liberalism, 1870–1914*, University of Illinois Press, Urbana, 1983.
Meadowcroft, J., *Conceptualizing the State: Innovation and Dispute in British Political Thought, 1880–1914*, Oxford University Press, Oxford, 1995.

Contemporary liberalism

Barry, B., *The Liberal Theory of Justice*, Clarendon Press, Oxford, 1973.
Bellamy, R., *Liberalism and Pluralism*, Routledge, London, 1999.
Gray, J., *Liberalisms: Essays in Politcal Philosophy*, Routledge, London, 1989.
Gray, J., *Enlightenment's Wake*, Routledge, London, 1995.
King, D., *The New Right: Politics, Markets and Citizenship*, Methuen, London, 1987.
Meadowcroft, J. (ed.), *The Liberal Political Tradition: Contemporary Reappraisals*, Edward Elgar, Cheltenham, 1996.
Newman, S., *Liberalism at Wit's End*, Cornell University Press, Ithaca, NY, 1984.
Raz, J., *Ethics in the Public Domain*, Clarendon Press, Oxford, 1994.
Sandel, M., *Liberalism and the Limits of Justice*, Cambridge University Press, Cambridge, 1982.

3
CONSERVATISM
Noël O'Sullivan
—

INTRODUCTION

Although conservatism became more intellectually respectable during the 1980s than it had been at any time since the Second World War, there is still widespread uncertainty about its precise moral status. Putting the matter bluntly, the suspicion remains that it is ultimately no more than a veil for the selfishness of the possessing classes. Barely concealed behind the veil, in this view, lie the unpalatable realities of inequality and economic exploitation. Such are the grounds, for example, that recently led an eminent radical philosopher, Ted Honderich, to conclude an ambitious study of conservative philosophy with the sweeping assertion that 'Conservatism ... has, in the end, nothing to say for itself'.[1] Since Honderich wrote, the widening social division which characterizes both Britain and the USA following a period of conservative rule seems to add still more weight to his indictment.

Nevertheless, in what follows a more sympathetic view will be taken. It will be suggested, more precisely, that far from merely being a veil for selfishness, conservative philosophy at its best – the qualification is important – offers a more profound response to the human condition than is to be found in the progressive orthodoxy which has dominated the Western world for the past two centuries. The essence of this orthodoxy, conservatism maintains, is ideology, which involves an attempt to construct alternative realities that make no concession to the limitations inherent in the human condition. Conservatism is not opposed to change, as is sometimes thought, or even to radical change, in some situations: what it *is* opposed to is change that is advocated on preconceived ideological grounds.

THE FRENCH REVOLUTION AND THE NEW IDEOLOGICAL STYLE OF POLITICS

The term 'conservative' was first used in its distinctively modern sense in this context – i.e. to indicate a political position opposed to ideological politics – when Chateaubriand (1768–1848) gave the name *Conservateur* to a journal he issued in order to resist the spread of the new politics, and especially the democratic ideas which were its main manifestation. The name was soon taken up by many other groups that opposed the progress of democracy, in its more radical forms at least. In the USA, for example, the American national republicans were calling themselves 'conservatives' by 1830, and this term was used to describe the British Tory party in 1832.

The conservative critique of the new ideological style of politics inspired by the French Revolution centred on the optimistic belief underlying it, according to which human reason and will are sufficiently powerful for us to be able to shape history in accordance with whatever ideals we may feel inspired to adopt.

During the nineteenth century, the most influential vehicle for revolutionary optimism was liberalism, and conservative doctrine was consequently shaped primarily by the need to meet the challenge posed by liberal defenders of the democratic ideal. During the twentieth century, however, socialism replaced liberalism as the principal vehicle of radicalism, and it is in opposition to this new enemy that conservative doctrine has therefore mainly been defined in our own age.

Although the enemy of conservatism is easy to identify, it must immediately be noticed that the conservative doctrine opposed to it has never been homogenous. On the contrary, ever since the French Revolution it has always included very different, and ultimately conflicting, strands of thought. Nevertheless, it is possible to detect a unifying conservative intellectual aspiration, even though it is worked out from entirely different philosophical standpoints, and is subject to entirely different practical interpretations. This intellectual aspiration consists of a quest for a theory of political order which views people and society in a way that is wholly untinged by Utopian ideas and aspirations. Conservatism seeks, more precisely, to develop a theory of limits which will not only enable it to cut through the various ideological systems that characterize the modern world, but will also provide a principled defence of political realism.

BEYOND IDEOLOGY: THE CONSERVATIVE QUEST FOR LIMITS

Realism in politics all too easily becomes the cynical doctrine that might is right, or the Machiavellian proposition that the end justifies the means. In the more thoughtful forms of conservatism, however, realism is not a doctrine of mere power, but a doctrine of limits. What this means is that any viable concept of order must begin from a clear recognition of the main feature of the human condition, which is the existence of objective limits that subject the core of our lives to inescapable tension. This tension arises because we are creatures inevitably divided between a multiplicity of conflicting dualities: dualities such as those between spirit and matter; between us and nature; between the individual and society; between governors and governed; between free enterprise and state regulation; between different groups within society; and between different states. These dualities or oppositions may indeed be partially harmonized, but never wholly eliminated. For conservatism, to dream of eliminating them from human existence is the hallmark of all Utopian conceptions of order.

Before proceeding further, and at the risk of overemphasizing the obvious, it may be noted that tension in the sense discussed here does not refer to subjective feelings of stress and anxiety, but to objective features of existence. That is, it is ontological and not psychological tension which is at issue. An eloquent statement of the meaning and central place of ontological tension in the conservative philosophy of order was provided not long ago by the German-American thinker, Eric Voegelin (1901–85). If anything is constant in the history of mankind, he wrote:

> it is the language of tension between life and death, immortality and mortality, perfection and imperfection, truth and untruth, sense and senselessness of existence; between *amor Dei* and *amor sui, l'âme ouverte* and *l'âme close*; between the virtues of openness toward the ground of being such as faith, hope and love and the vices of unfolding closure such as hubris and revolt; between the moods of joy and despair; and between alienation in its double meaning of alienation from the world and alienation from God. If we split these pairs of symbols, and hypostatize the poles of the tension as independent entities, we destroy the reality of existence – ... we deform our humanity and reduce ourselves to a state of quiet despair or activist conformity to the 'age'.[2]

The unifying theme of conservatism, then, is the quest for a realistic concept of order which acknowledges the ineliminable tension at the heart of the human condition. It is the principled nature of conservative realism which provides the answer to cynics who dismiss the doctrine as nothing more than a commitment to pure pragmatism, power, and success.

THE THREE MAIN KINDS OF CONSERVATIVE
REALISM

It is now necessary to examine more closely the very different ways of interpreting realism to be found within conservative philosophy. Taking the twentieth century as a whole, three different interpretations may be distinguished, each of which involves a distinct response to the age of mass democracy, and in particular to socialism.

The first response consists of a more or less outright rejection of the radical heritage. This is the response of the reactionary school of thought, which relies upon a static vision of tension. The essence of this vision is the conception of the universe as an ordered whole in which everything, including ourselves, has a specific position assigned to it. To leave that position (as we are prone to do) is a formula for anarchy. Although this vision has a long history in Western theology, it is also capable of being stated in purely secular terms. In both its theological and secular versions it has been particularly influential in France. What gives the reactionary school a continuing relevance that extends beyond national frontiers, however, is its powerful analysis of the sources of instability within the modern democratic state.

According to the reactionary critique, democracy is inevitably doomed to be destroyed by the very ideals it sets out to realize, namely liberty, equality, and humanitarian concern. Ironically, however, the alternative proposed by the reactionary school is more unsatisfactory. This alternative takes the form of a vision of an organic, largely static and hierarchical state which enjoys perfect harmony. The vision is unsatisfactory because it involves, as we shall see, precisely the same inability to come to terms with the reality of ineliminable tension as the reactionary school attributes to its democratic foe. In a word, the reactionary position is itself imbued with Utopian propensities.

The second interpretation of realism is represented by the revolutionary school of conservatism, and is diametrically opposed to the first. Whereas the reactionary school relies on a static theory of tension, the revolutionary one regards tension as a dynamic condition of permanent flux. In practice what this means is that the reactionary ideal of the organic state is replaced in radical conservatism by the ideal of the total state, in which all of life is continuously involved in vindicating and reconstituting the unity of individual and group identity. In practice, the revolutionary school insists on the need to embrace what are regarded as the inescapable revolutionary tendencies of the century and to build a new, dynamic kind of conservatism upon them, instead of engaging in a futile attempt to suppress them. For reasons which will be considered later, this second school of conservatism has found its most impressive advocates in Germany.

Finally, a third interpretation of realism is marked principally by sympathetic acceptance of the sheer diversity of existence, and by a commitment to accommodating it within the framework of the limited state. The political ideals stressed by this third school are balance, compromise and moderation, and it has accordingly struggled hard to come to terms with democracy and socialism. Since the degree of compromise envisaged varies greatly, however, and assumes very different forms, there is obviously room for a considerable mixture of types of doctrine within the third school, which may be termed the school of moderate conservatism. This third school has been particularly influential in Britain, although it has also enjoyed varying degrees of influence in European conservatism at large. In the USA, it may be added, a significant number of thinkers has contributed to this moderate tradition, despite the fact that the difference between American and European historical experience has led some scholars to question the propriety of speaking of an American conservative tradition at all. This third school has some claim to be the most viable, endeavouring as it does to translate the idea of ineliminable tension into a defence of the limited state by means of the rule of law, a dislike of the doctrinaire and dogmatic, and, more generally, a defence of what a notable twentieth-century conservative philosopher, George Santayana (1863–1952), termed a pious regard for 'the human scale' in politics.

THE RELATION OF CONSERVATISM TO 'THE RIGHT' AT LARGE

Before proceeding further, it is necessary to indicate why it has not seemed appropriate to begin by relating the analysis of conservatism to the left-right spectrum which is commonly regarded as the most basic way of classifying the various ideas and groups in the modern European political tradition. The answer is that the precise nature of the spectrum in question is too vague for this kind of approach to be illuminating.

Although the original distinction between left and right referred to the seating arrangements in the new French National Assembly of 1789, it has come in the meantime to be conceived of in a way which owes more to intellectual prejudice than to historical insight. More precisely, the concept of the left was until recently associated with everything believed to contribute to progress, while the concept of the right was associated with the forces of darkness. The spectrum, in consequence, sheds more light on the demonology of modern European thought than it does on the precise character of conservative intellectual concerns.

It has been necessary to dwell on the vagueness of the spectrum approach because various political phenomena which are commonly felt to be connected with 'the right' are on that account deemed to be in some way connected with conservatism. The unsatisfactory nature of this loose line of thinking becomes apparent, however, as soon as it is recalled that conservatism is an attempt to achieve a realistic political balance of the complex tensions which characterize the human condition. The concept of 'the right', by contrast, is so vague that it includes doctrines which reject the ideal of balance altogether. This is most obviously true in the case of fascism, which abandons the complex concept of balance in favour of a blind, simplistic faith in the will of a leader.

It must immediately be added, however, that the two extreme forms of conservatism – that is, the reactionary and radical schools – can act as bridges over which it is possible to pass into the fascist camp. Why that is so will become clear shortly. For the moment, it is sufficient to have noticed that the concept of the right is too vague and unfocused to be of any assistance in the present context.

REACTIONARY CONSERVATISM

The twentieth century prides itself on the progressive character of its opinions and therefore tends to dismiss the reactionary tradition as a purely negative, and hence unilluminating, response to the democratic world. This attitude, however, is far too complacent. Although the reactionary position is indeed in many respects a negative one, it exposes with ruthless clarity some of the principal weaknesses of modern democracy, and it is therefore well worth listening carefully to what it has to say.

The essence of the reactionary position is the claim that no political order can be stable unless it rests on a consensus about true spiritual values. It asserts that political unity requires spiritual unity. In this perspective democracy is doomed to self-destruction because it encourages unlimited freedom, and accordingly fosters spiritual division and fragmentation. Instead of acknowledging the basic tensions inherent in the human condition, and the kind of spiritual consensus necessary to accommodate them, modern democracy takes off into a world of ideological fantasies in which all contact with political reality rapidly begins to disappear.

What are these ideological fantasies that the reactionary tradition regards as so disastrous? According to Joseph de Maistre (1753–1821), the most fundamental is a false optimism about the possibility of perfecting human nature by political and social change. The French Revolution, which was inspired by this impious aim, would not have occurred, were it not for the fact that the Enlightenment foisted on the world a new theory of evil. The traditional theory came from Christianity, which has always insisted that evil is an inherent part of the human condition. This was the meaning of the Christian story of man's fall, and of the burden of original sin which he has been doomed to bear ever since. Following in the footsteps of Rousseau, however, the modern world has come to believe the new theory, which teaches that man is naturally good, and infers that the main source of human unhappiness is the social order under which we live. This modern belief in human perfectibility is the first object of de Maistre's scorn.

Closely linked to the perfectibility fantasy is another, which is the belief that the human will is powerful enough to reshape the whole of the social order in a way which would eliminate all the supposed sources of misery. In reality, de Maistre insists, we are impotent creatures, condemned to live in a world not of our making, and faced by largely unpredictable results, even when we do manage to assert ourselves.

Yet another fantasy is the democratic ideal of self-government. This is an intrinsic absurdity: all government involves the rule of some over others, and therefore excludes the possibility of taking popular self-government seriously. No less absurd is the modern idea that democracy is the only legitimate form of government, since it alone derives power from the consent of the governed. If this means anything, de Maistre says, it must mean that every individual consents to every measure the government adopts. This, however, is a manifest impossibility. Indeed, it is not a formula for government of any kind, but for anarchy. The subsequent history of reactionary thought saw this critique extended and revised in various respects. During the first part of the twentieth century, for example, Maurice Barrès (1862–1923) argued that modern democracy was not merely a threat to political stability, but to civilization itself. This is because the extreme individualism and aimless liberty it encourages destroy the overriding sense of national tradition which is the source of our true identity and spiritual inspiration. The result is that the modern world increasingly tends to produce *Les Déracinés*, or rootless ones, after the title of an influential book Barrès published in 1897. A similar prospect was conjured up by Charles Maurras (1868–1952), who founded the Action Française movement to pursue the cause of restoring the monarchy. In Maurras's work, however, the reactionary critique was extended in particular to the industrial structure of modern society. In this context, Maurras maintained, all that the democratic dream of creating liberty and equality for the common man does in practice is open the door for rule by financiers, businessmen and bureaucrats. That is, liberty turns out to be only freedom for exploitation by capitalism, and equality proves to mean only the creation of a new, entirely self-seeking hierarchy.

The limitations of the reactionary critique of democratic modernity begin to emerge as soon as the alternative which this kind of conservatism offers is examined. Specifically, the problem is that the reactionary conception of spiritual unity is so pure that it eliminates tension from the ideal society, which means that the reactionary position is as Utopian as the one it rejects. There is no middle ground, and no room for compromise, which is always regarded as a symptom of decadence: the choice offered is always the unreal one between the purely black world of democracy on the one hand and the purely white one of the reactionary ideal on the other. This means that in practice reactionaries are usually only able to envisage extra-constitutional political measures, and inevitably discredit themselves and their cause in the process. Thus Maurras, for example, used the Camelots du Roi to destroy socialist property and engage in street fights, with the result that his support was eventually rejected by those whose interest he sought to promote, namely the Church and the Pretender. This extremist tendency explains how the reactionary school plays into the hands of fascism. Although reactionaries insist that their position is clearly distinct from fascism, on the ground that they hold a static concept of order and have no intention of instilling the masses with activist fervour, their complete alienation from the *status quo* and their willingness to countenance extra-constitutional violence mean that in practice they are open to the charge of maintaining a distinction without a difference.

CONSERVATIVE REVOLUTIONARY THOUGHT

At the opposite extreme to reactionary conservatism is the school of conservative revolutionary thought. In this school, the idea of tension as the heart of existence is embraced with such enthusiasm that it results in the rejection of all stability as a form of degeneracy. Claiming to be the most realistic of all conservatives, the conservative revolutionaries insist that what realism means is acceptance of the intrinsic value of conflict and struggle as the essence of life itself. Whereas the reactionary school conceives of order as static and largely beyond the control of human will, the conservative revolutionary adopts a Darwinian dynamism which takes the stress on will so far that conservatism tends to disintegrate into a cult of irrational activism, in the service of a nationalist ideal which extols total absorption in the community and total obedience to a great leader. What is it, one must ask, that radicalizes conservatism in this extraordinary way? The answer was given by Moeller van den Bruck (1876–1925), when he declared that the only relevant form of conservatism today is one which faces the fact of revolution and does not flinch from working through it, instead of against it. Conservatism and revolution would merely destroy each other, he added, 'if the conservative had not the political wisdom to recognize that conservative goals may be attained even with revolutionary postulates and by revolutionary means'. The essence of revolutionary conservatism, then, is that it 'seizes directly on the revolution, and by it, through it and beyond it saves the life of Europe and of Germany'.[3]

Since it was in Germany that the revolutionary school originally appeared, to look briefly at the special circumstances which accompanied its rise there will help to make the nature of this form of conservatism clearer. It emerged in the Weimar Republic, following the German defeat in the First World War. It was developed, more precisely, by those who had found in the war experience itself a model for true morality and true community, and found it hard to accept the German defeat. This was made more bearable by their insistence that true morality is essentially heroic, since what matters to the hero is not so much the success or failure of his actions as the spirit in which he faces death: that is, morality is an essentially inward matter for which the outward vicissitudes of fortune are a largely incidental affair. In particular, they believed, what mattered was to keep alive the camaraderie of the trenches. This transcended class, and therefore seemed to point to a kind of socialism which would unify the nation instead of dividing it, as Marxism threatened to do.

For those who thought in this way, the main response to the post-war world was one of complete alienation. Everything seemed to suggest decadence, fragmentation and disunity, and nothing seemed worth conserving. The multiparty parliamentary system, in particular, was rejected as a foreign imposition by the Allies which ensured that the nation's need for a strong leader was not met. Above all, they held, what the parliamentary system fostered was the ruinous delusion that politics are a matter of talking and formulating programmes, when the only thing which really counted was action.

This mode of thought found one of its most dramatic expressions in Ernst Jünger's (1895–1998) *Der Arbeiter*, a work which fused socialism with nationalist sentiment in a vision of total mobilization as the supreme end of the modern state. Jünger's aim was thereby to recapture in peacetime the heroic, highly collectivist ethos of the wartime experience.

Needless to say, this combination of nationalism and socialism bears a resemblance to Nazi teaching, although conservative revolutionaries themselves were generally anxious to distinguish their position from it. They did not rely on anti-semitism, for example. Thus one of the leading theorists, Carl Schmitt (1888–1985), emphasized that the political bond was based on the existential hostility of friend and foe, but insisted that there was no reason to assume that the nature of the foe had to be defined in racial terms. Indeed, he explained, the foe might be an entirely imaginary one, provided that fear of it was real and served to unite the friends. Conservative revolutionaries also despised Hitler for his willingness to pursue his ends by a parliamentary strategy: this seemed to them to be a quite unacceptable compromise with the forces of decadence. They also tended to take their version of socialism more seriously than Nazism took its own socialist professions, to the point where some of them even envisaged co-operation with communism. Finally, the conservative revolutionaries often tended to despise the Nazis as mere rabble-rousers. Thus Moeller van den Bruck, for example, who was one of the most influential, and was greatly admired by Hitler himself for his book *Das Dritte Reich*, wanted nothing to do with Hitler's proposals for starting a mass movement. Similarly, although the Nazis insisted that they were merely implementing Jünger's ideal of total mobilization, Jünger always dissociated himself from them. All Hitler had achieved, he subsequently remarked, was the 'metaphysical solution, the purely technical execution of Total Mobilization'.[4]

Even when all allowances have been made, however, the fact remains that the nationalism, militarism, anti-constitutionalism and dynamic activism of the conservative revolutionaries played into Nazi hands. Jünger, for example, openly proclaimed his indifference to truth or falsity on moral and political matters; the important thing, he said, is 'to sacrifice oneself for a faith, regardless of whether that faith embraces truth or error'. Fanaticism of this kind meant that, like reactionary conservatism, the conservative revolutionary school tended to give unwitting support to causes from which it tried to distance, or at least distinguish itself.

Far from disappearing at the end of the Second World War, the themes of the revolutionary school acquired a new lease of life during the 1960s and 1970s. Widespread concern about the advent of the 'counterculture' and the New Left during those decades led liberal thinkers to sympathize with the revolutionary conservative belief that modern democracy is a breeding ground for extreme subjectivist and Utopian tendencies that are incompatible with the survival of institutions of any kind. This revival of conservative revolutionary themes was facilitated by the fact that the original proponents had meanwhile made their position more respectable by insisting that Nazism had been a perversion of their ideas. They were careful, in particular, to reject the former sympathy they had shown for the total state as the answer to the modern experience of alienation. Arnold Gehlen (1904–76), for example, who was prominent among those who now enjoyed renewed influence, insisted that the appropriate response was one of ironic resignation, rather than the activist fervour with which he had formerly sympathized.[5] For Hans Zehrer (1899–66), by contrast, the solution was found in religion. Fascism and communism, he maintained, had occurred because the modern world is bent upon putting man in the place of God as the ultimate source of authority. As a result, the secular culture of the democratic state leaves it prone to totalitarianism and will continue to do so until man, recognizing his inability to provide his own answer to the meaning and purpose of his life, once more becomes open to divine revelation.[6] In their different ways, members of the inter-war generation of conservative revolutionary thinkers had thus finally discovered a truth which has always been fundamental to moderate conservatism, which is that the good for man cannot be found in politics. Having discovered this, they also discovered the merits of compromise, and were at length able to come to terms with mass industrial democracy.

The story of revolutionary conservatism does not, however, quite end on that relatively happy note of moderation rediscovered. During the 1970s and 1980s, the movement acquired a new lease of life outside Germany, in the form of the Nuova Destra in Italy and, more influentially, the movement inspired by Alain de Benoist (1943–) in France. By means of books and, in particular, through three journals which he edits – Eléments, Nouvelle Ecole and Krisis – de Benoist propagated his conviction that the modern West has fallen into a condition of extreme decadence, of which the obsession with money and material values is the most obvious symptom. From this position, he went on to break with the ideas of the more traditional French right in four fundamental respects (see Chapter 8).

In the first place, he rejected the Christian heritage as the ultimate source of one of the most disastrous symptoms of modern decadence, which is the egalitarianism that inspires socialism and democracy. To counter this he sought to foster a 'new paganism', for which the thought of Nietzsche (1844–1900) is the guiding light. Basic to the new paganism is a view of human nature as something which is not fixed or given, but is in constant process of recreation. It is from this view that there arose the stress on action and heroism which links the ideas of the French school with those of the German thinkers just considered. A second theme of de Benoist's school, however, breaks not only with the old French right, but also with the radical German one, by advocating the establishment of a transnational identity as the only effective means of countering the threat from world superpowers. This transnational identity is usually theorized in racial terms, with primary emphasis laid upon Indo-European characteristics. The third feature of the French school is support for what it deems to be the oppressed peoples of the Third World. This is not inspired by the sense of guilt for an imperial past which troubles liberals, however. The motive is rather a desire to enlist the help of Third World opponents of capitalism (especially in its American ramifications) in destroying the mutual enemy.

Finally, the French school is notable for its vehement denunciation of violence as a method of pursuing power. This does not mean that it is committed to moderation or constitutionalism. It is, on the contrary, merely part of a revolutionary strategy which owes much to the left-wing publicist Antonio Gramsci (1891–1937). This strategy consists of concentrating upon cultural indoctrination as a necessary prelude to successful political revolution.

Like the reactionary school then, the revolutionary conservative school offers a powerful critique of the failure of modern democratic politics and culture to place the idea of ineliminable tension at the heart of the human condition. Like the reactionary school, again, the remedies it proposes merely exacerbate matters, instead of alleviating them. It is to the tradition of moderate conservatism that we must therefore now turn, in the hope of finding a more satisfactory basis for the conservative claim to realism.

MODERATE CONSERVATISM

The core of moderate conservatism is the commitment to the maintenance of the limited state. This commitment has been a particularly pronounced feature of the British conservative tradition, which shares with liberalism a regard for the rule of law, the maintenance of a distinction between state and society, a constitutional opposition, and an independent judiciary. The overlap with liberalism does not, however, mean that moderate conservatism has simply taken over liberal values in an unmodified form. The relationship is more complex and can best be understood by considering briefly the form which it originally assumed in the thought of Edmund Burke (1729–97), whose response to the ideas of the French revolutionary democrats marks the beginning of the British conservative tradition.

On the one hand, Burke rejected the abstract, universalist conception of rationality upon which the revolutionaries relied when they invoked the rights of man. This sceptical side of Burke's thought was inherited by the British conservative tradition, and distinguishes its view of the individual and society from the rationalist one that liberalism shares with the radical tradition at large. On the other hand, Burke was an eighteenth-century Whig – the term 'conservative', it will be recalled, had not yet entered the political vocabulary – who supported the English revolution of 1688, and was therefore committed, like his fellow Whigs, to defending the balanced constitution which it had created. The Whig roots of British conservatism, in a word, explain the commitment to limited politics which it shares with liberalism.

During the nineteenth century, British conservatives rarely abandoned the commitment to the balanced constitution which they inherited from Burke. Long before the beginning of the twentieth century, however, it was becoming obvious that the new problems created by an industrial society could not be dealt with without major changes in the role of government which might conflict with the tradition of limited politics. The possibility of such a conflict had in fact already emerged during the first half of the nineteenth century, when Thomas Carlyle (1759–1881) declared that the parliamentary system which Britain had inherited from the medieval world was outmoded and must be replaced by a new system of government based on strong leadership. This, he maintained, was the only way of coping with the difficulties of the new age.[7]

Although the parliamentary system remained in place, Carlyle's demand for strong leadership was nevertheless met, in some degree at least, by the constant increase in the power of the executive which marked the British system of government from the last decades of the nineteenth century down to the present day. What contributed most to the stabilization of the parliamentary system, however, as well as to the creation of a national basis of support for conservatism in the democratic era, was Disraeli's (1804–81) introduction of mass suffrage, on which he gambled as the most effective means of uniting the two nations into which he saw England being divided by the progress of industrialism. Disraeli's gamble paid off, in so far as many of the extended electorate proved to be more willing to vote conservative than had generally been expected, and have continued to be so. Other conservatives, however, were much less willing than Disraeli to put their trust in democracy. Foremost among them was Lord Salisbury (1830–1903), whose thought is indicative of the misgivings which troubled conservatives as the twentieth century began.

Salisbury argued that the advent of mass politics and the demand for welfare measures which inevitably accompanied them would create three almost insuperable threats to the preservation of the balanced constitution. The first threat consisted of the triumph of the doctrine of popular sovereignty, which meant that the House of Commons would increasingly dominate over the monarchy and the House of Lords within the constitution. The second threat came from the need of every government to win the support of the newly enfranchised electorate by the formation of mass political parties. This was likely to mean, Salisbury observed, that considerations of party advantage would regularly be placed above the national interest. The third threat identified by Salisbury echoed de Tocqueville's misgivings about the future of democracy, arising from the tendency of democracy to value equality more than liberty. The democratic dream of an egalitarian, classless society, de Tocqueville had forecast, will not be the automatic guarantee of harmony which its radical defenders assume. It is more likely to mean, instead, the creation of an atomized social order presided over by a benign but despotic state, and troubled by the conflict which destroyed the democracies of antiquity – the conflict, that is, between haves and have-nots.[8]

In the event, Salisbury's misgivings about the future of democracy proved to have been somewhat exaggerated. His concern about the balanced constitution, however, was well founded. What did most to undermine it, in the event, was not so much the progress of democracy that Salisbury had feared, as two world wars. These required total mobilization, thereby giving an enormous impetus to the centralization and collectivization of European economies at large. After the First World War, this process was given moral respectability in the eyes of many conservatives by the recession of the 1930s, which seemed to demonstrate the inability of unplanned capitalist societies to ensure adequate levels of employment, growth and prosperity. In order to deal with the recession, they accepted the need to adopt many of the interventionist techniques of government originally designed as exceptional wartime measures, and associated with peacetime use only when they were taken over by the socialist enemy. The shift towards a more managerial and pragmatic kind of conservatism culminated in the post-war acceptance by conservatives of the welfare state, along with a commitment to maintaining full employment through the use of Keynesian methods of demand management.

It would be a mistake, however, to conclude that the new managerialism was universally adopted by conservatives. Not only the reactionary and radical conservatives rejected it, but throughout the inter-war and post-war years many other conservative thinkers responded in a different way. These critics, however, did not succeed in formulating a credible alternative.

Consider, for example, T.S. Eliot (1888–1965) and Ortega y Gasset

(1883–1955). Eliot saw the principal problem of the age as the decline of religion and culture, echoing the continental reactionary tradition in his vision of mass democracy as a spiritual wasteland and, somewhat perversely, proceeding to sympathize with totalitarian regimes, on the ground that they at least set out to be more spiritual than the materialistic democracies he despised.[9] Unfortunately, the only remedy Eliot could suggest was the creation of an organic form of society based on the parish and structured on hierarchical lines. In practice his conservatism tended to collapse into nostalgia for a lost Victorian golden age.

Sharing Eliot's cultural and aesthetic perspective, although not his Christian religiosity, the Spanish philosopher Ortega y Gasset condemned *The Revolt of the Masses*, but was careful to stress that the mass is not to be identified with the working class. What defines the member of modern mass society is not social position, which may be an elevated one, but a mentality marked above all by sheer complacency, and manifested in total opposition to individualistic values. What Ortega sought to defend in the mass age was not:

> the petulant person who thinks himself superior to the rest, but the man who demands more of himself than the rest, even though he may not fulfil in his person those higher exigencies ... – This reminds me that orthodox Buddhism is composed of two distinct religions: one, more rigorous and difficult, the other easier and more trivial: the Mahayana – 'great vehicle' or 'great path' – and the Hinayana – 'lesser vehicle' or 'lesser path'. The decisive matter is whether we attach our life to one or the other vehicle, to a maximum or a minimum of demands upon ourselves.[10]

As in Eliot's case, it was difficult to see what could be done, since what was being called into question was the very nature of modernity.

In so far as conservative thinkers have devised a practical alternative to managerialism, it is to the ideal of Christian democracy that one must turn. The most suggestive thinker is Jacques Maritain (1882–1973), whose philosophy embodies the spirit of compromise which was to become influential on the continent after the Second World War. Maritain identified the main problem of modern mass society as an 'anthropocentric humanism' which has cut us off from God and is the source of totalitarianism. His combination of mild socialist sympathies, on the one hand, with a conservative stress on authority and the need to preserve such traditional values of European civilization as the church and the family, on the other, is an eloquent expression of the kind of conservative compromise which has achieved widespread support on the Continent.

Although this compromise lost ground during the 1960s and 1970s, as memories of the war receded and ideological polarities no longer seemed as threatening as they had in the immediate post-war years, the 1970s and

1980s brought Christian democracy a new lease of life. Indeed, by the mid-1980s the Christian democrats had become the leading party of government in Germany, Italy, Belgium, The Netherlands and Luxembourg, while in Austria they became the main opposition party. Voting statistics for the 1984 elections to the European parliament illustrate the extent of this success: the Christian Democrats polled more votes than any other group, with an average poll throughout the community (excluding the UK, which has no Christian Democratic party) of about 32 per cent.[11] By the end of the 1980s, however, the revival of national sentiment was subjecting Christian Democratic principles to increased pressure. Whether those principles can be reconciled with nationalism has become a central problem for Germany in particular, as leading Christian Democratic politicians have enthusiastically embraced the cause of reunification.

It is from the post-war course of British conservatism, however, that most is to be learned about the kind of difficulties to which a politics of compromise is prone. For three decades after the war, British conservatives were generally quite happy with the middle way ideal formulated by Macmillan (1894–1986). Above all, the ideal was so effective as a means of winning electoral support that important criticisms which had been made of the middle way from the very beginning were largely ignored. Thus Friedrich Hayek's (1899–1992) repeated warnings about the inflationary pressure that would inevitably be created by the new managerial politics were greeted with complacency, as was his warning that managerial politics were likely to mean the constant growth of an administrative state with arbitrary powers which were wholly at odds with the requirements of limited politics. Hayek no doubt exaggerated when he maintained, in *The Road to Serfdom* (1944), that the end result of managerialism would inevitably be totalitarianism, since this was simply not the means by which totalitarianism had been brought into existence in the USSR and Nazi Germany (see Chapter 2). Nevertheless, what remained true was that conservatism was open to the charge of now having nothing better with which to underpin its traditional concern for limited politics than an act of faith in the benign effects of managerial paternalism. This complacency had been strikingly evident in, for example, Macmillan's original outline of the middle way. 'From my own knowledge of the managerial class in industry', he wrote, 'I am confident that in the overwhelming majority of cases they have a sense of social responsibility and that their interest, like most of us, is to do their job efficiently and well.'[12] Macmillan's faith in planning and managers was to become the most remarkable feature of the post-war consensus upon which British conservatism was built.

By the 1960s, criticisms of the middle way finally began to get a hearing. They did so when it became clear that conservatism had moved so far in a collectivist direction that voters were finding it increasingly difficult to decide whether any distinct conservative identity was still possessed by the party of that name. By 1973, the problem of identity had become so acute that a leading British Labour Party politician, Anthony Wedgwood Benn, could hail the policies of the Conservative Prime Minister of the day, Edward Heath, who held office from 1970 to 1974, as having created 'the most comprehensive armoury of government controls that has ever been assembled for use over private industry, far exceeding all the powers thought to be necessary by the last Labour Government'.[13] The result of the middle way compromise, it was suggested, would be the gradual creation of a corporatist state. Some commentators played on the fascist overtones of that concept, suggesting that Britain was already advanced on the path to fascism, although it was added that this was 'fascism with a human face'.[14]

Even if vague and emotive language of this sort is ignored, it was none the less clear that the ideal of limited politics which had been the basis of the British tradition of parliamentary government was being replaced by a new system of government in which old institutions still remained alive, but in name only, since their functions were being completely changed. In England, one well-known conservative publicist, Samuel Brittan, made the nature of the change clear in an article entitled 'Dangers of the Corporate State'.[15] The article, which attacked the system of government by informal tripartite meetings between government, the Trade Union Congress (TUC) and the Confederation of British Industry (CBI) which was emerging in Britain, asked: 'Is it really the job of trade unions to restrain wages, or of employers to keep down prices? This is the job of trade unions in the Soviet bloc ... '. It is against the background of this increasing dissatisfaction with the middle way that a determined search for a new conservative identity developed during the 1970s.

THE CRITIQUE OF THE MIDDLE WAY AND THE CONSERVATIVE SEARCH FOR A NEW IDENTITY

The chief inspiration for this search came from a broad body of liberal and libertarian philosophy with very disparate strands of thought within it, but with an especial emphasis on economic issues and perspectives. The sources of this philosophy were international, and included such bodies as the Chicago group of political economists led by Milton Friedman (1912–   ); the Mont Pelérin Society in Switzerland, of which Friedrich Hayek (a leading representative of the Austrian school and especially important in British political life) is a past president; and the Virginia school of public choice theory. The principal themes of the critique may be formulated under ten headings (see Chapter 2).

First, there was general agreement that post-war democratic governments had fostered the illusion that every evil has a political cause, and therefore, by implication, a political remedy. The result was said to be that the modern state was becoming ungovernable, since the populace was being encouraged to develop wholly unrealistic expectations about what lay in the power of governments. This contention must be viewed with some suspicion, since there was at least as much evidence to suggest that modern citizens tend towards excessive stoicism in the face of their politicians' schemes and demands. What could not be doubted, however, was that belief in the efficacy of political remedies was sufficiently deep-seated to have created pressure for the constant expansion of the state sector, with little awareness of the erosion of liberty which that might entail.

Second, it was claimed that the post-war collectivist consensus had rested on the naïve assumption that economic growth would henceforth be an automatic feature of modern life, so that only problems of just distribution remained to be dealt with. What socialism had caused us to forget, it was said, was the possibility that the quest for social justice might unwittingly kill the goose that laid the golden eggs.

Third, it was argued that this naïve optimism about economic growth had been accompanied by an equally naïve conviction that general prosperity would automatically guarantee general happiness. The possibility that prosperity might instead bring with it boredom, a drug cult, a rising divorce and illegitimacy rate, pornography, and violence, was not foreseen.

Fourth, the critics maintained that the post-war period had seen the triumph of a totally groundless belief in the intrinsic superiority of state planning. This faith was attacked on the ground that it rested upon a complete misunderstanding of the nature of the market. To the crude collectivist mind, the market appears to be a wholly irrational and chaotic way of conducting economic life. In reality, thinkers like Hayek and Polanyi sought to show that the market is a highly sophisticated means of co-ordinating the infinitely complex practical knowledge required to match supply and demand in an efficient way.

It was not only at the level of first principles, however, that the attack on planning was conducted. A fifth line of attack occurred at the empirical level, where a large body of social research sought to demonstrate that even the best-intentioned welfare plans often turned out in practice to be counter-productive. Evidence was produced which showed, for example, that welfare policies which were intended to create a spirit of individual initiative and personal responsibility were instead fostering a spirit of dependency. The outcome was said to be the formation of a new underclass, characterized by the prospect of permanent unemployment.

The most dramatic empirical work on the counter-productive nature of welfare measures was done in the USA, in response to growing dissatisfaction with the results of the 'War on Poverty' launched by President Johnson in the 1960s, under the ideological banner of creating the Great Society. Two works in particular exercised an important influence on conservative opinion. One was George Gilder's *Wealth and Poverty* (1981); the other was Charles Murray's *Losing Ground* (1984). Murray's book was found especially persuasive. During the 1970s, he showed government efforts to increase job opportunities had been accompanied by a rise in unemployment, especially among young blacks. In addition, welfare measures appeared to have contributed to the destruction of the family, as a result of their tendency to encourage illegitimate births among young women who would automatically receive benefits as a result of their situation. In 1989 Murray extended his analysis to Britain, observing that the result was likely to be the creation during the 1990s of an underclass larger (in proportional terms) than that in the USA:

> I am not talking here about an unemployment problem that can be solved by more jobs, nor about a poverty problem that can be solved by higher benefits. Britain has a growing population of working-aged, healthy people who live in a different world from other Britons, who are raising their children to live in it, and whose values are now contaminating the life of entire communities.[16]

The great weakness in the literature on the underclass was the assumption that the class had been created by government policy. Seizing on this assumption, defenders of interventionism responded by plausibly maintaining that some at least of the responsibility lay with causes quite independent of politics. Of these, the one usually stressed was the decline of the work ethic in modern Western societies at large. If the difficulty of pinning responsibility for the underclass on interventionist governments is ignored, however, then the question still remained of what was to be done.

On this matter the theorists of the underclass were divided. Three possibilities were canvassed. The first, somewhat unrealistic, possibility was adopted by Murray, who took the radical step of advocating the demolition of the welfare state in its present centralized form and its replacement by the local community as the basis of welfare provision.[17] A second remedy, advocated by Milton Friedman in particular, was a negative income tax, but experiments with this remedy have proved disappointing. The third remedy was in effect a return to Victorian attitudes, with a stigma once more being attached to the receipt of welfare benefits. This was advocated by Gilder, for example. Whatever the ethics of the matter, it does not seem likely that any government would regard such a policy as electorally feasible, for the time being at least.

Sixth, critics of the middle way dismissed the idea that it could ever be a stable half-way house between capitalism and socialism. Hayek in particular argued that planning cannot be terminated at some notional halfway stage but must constantly be extended, in order to secure the implementation of the existing range of plans.[18] The middle way is thus not a stable plateau, but is rather a raging river which forces anyone who enters it even further downstream (to use an analogy from a leading article on 'The Middle Way or Muddle Way' in *The Times*).[19]

Seventh, the conservative critique stressed that the origins of inflation are moral and political, rather than economic. A democratic electoral system, it was pointed out, inevitably creates a preference among politicians for 'soft' rather than 'hard' finance: once they have control over the money supply they almost inevitably succumb to the temptation to manipulate economic policy in the interests of winning electors by 'free' offers. The only remedy for inflation is, therefore, to find a way of taking money out of politics. This was, of course, easier said than done. In a wild moment, Hayek even envisaged the possibility of privatizing the currency, so that governments would no longer be able to expand the money supply with impunity.

An eighth line of conservative attack on the interventionist consensus of post-war politics derived support from the Virginia school of public choice theory. Interpreting political calculations by analogy with economic ones, public choice theory undermined the optimistic faith which had been placed in the altruism and disinterestedness of the public officials who were entrusted with the task of administering the providential state. Defenders of the middle way tended to regard these officials as impartial interpreters of Keynesian economic theory, making no allowance for the fact that many of them were in reality politicians. As politicians, they did not live in a world of pure economic rationality, but in one where power and advantage were the very stuff of every calculation. In consequence, public choice theory concluded, attempts to apply Keynesian theory were almost inevitably doomed to failure in the context of democratic party politics, since it is wholly predictable that democratic politicians who are given control of the budget will use their power for short-term party gain. To imagine they will confine themselves to detached 'fine tuning' of the economy in the interests of evening out the ups and downs of the trade cycle, as Keynesian theory assumes they will, is to enter a world of fantasy.

The same sceptical mood that is manifested in public choice theory led to a ninth, closely related, assault on another vital prop which had underpinned post-war complacency. This was the belief that the needs of limited government are adequately met by a pluralist social system in which more or less unrestrained competition between many small interest groups ensures that no dictatorship of the majority, of the sort feared by the classical liberal thinkers of the nineteenth century, can emerge in the modern democratic state.[20]

It was once again the application of economic modes of thought to politics that discredited pluralist optimism. Just because majority despotism might be unlikely, a leading economist pointed out, it did not follow that the possibility of *minority* despotism, created by the pressure groups themselves, could be discounted. As Mancur Olson indicated in *The Logic of Collective Action*,[21] larger pressure groups in particular could only deal with the 'free-rider' problem by direct sanctions against their members, best illustrated by the endeavour of trade unions to use the 'closed shop' to maintain discipline among their members. More generally, Olson went on to argue, the very success of pluralism in promoting prosperity and stability would in due course ensure economic decline. This occurs because the growth of state intervention brings about the progressive politicization of the economy. Responding to this, pressure groups turn away from the market and look instead to the exercise of political influence over government as the best means of securing their ends.[22] The result is that economic momentum is reduced, and the existing economic structure ossifies.

Finally, a tenth line of attack on the collectivist consensus was inspired by a more philosophic and normative interest. This consisted of the revival of the old Lockean tradition of individualistic rights theory in order to defend the minimal state. Thus Robert Nozick (1938–), for example, began *Anarchy, the State and Utopia* by declaring that:

> Individuals have rights, and there are things no person or group may do to them (without violating their rights). So strong and far-reaching are these rights that they raise the question of what, if anything, the state and its officials may do ... Our main conclusions about the state are that a minimal state, limited to the narrow functions of protection against force, theft, fraud, enforcement of contracts, and so on, is justified; and that the minimal state is inspiring as well as right.[23]

As was also the case with public choice theory, the result was to reawaken concern for constitutional guarantees for limited government (see Chapters 2 and 6).

These, in outline, are the main themes of the critique which destroyed the post-war collectivist orthodoxy. It is against this background that the general swing, from the late 1970s, of most Western societies towards more conservative politics must be seen. Although this resurgent conservatism has naturally reflected the different traditions and circumstances of different states, a common pattern is discernible in hostility to interventionism and a preference for neo-liberal economic policies which combine monetarist and supply-side measures.

It will be useful at this point to consider briefly the ideas of the New Right, since these did most to fashion the neo-liberal orthodoxy which superseded the middle way orthodoxy. Attention will be concentrated on Britain and the USA, since it was in these countries that the New Right made the going, so to speak, in the conservative swing of the 1980s.

THE NEW RIGHT

Within the New Right there exist at least two distinct (and ultimately incompatible) schools of thought, which for present purposes may be termed the economic and the political schools.

Since the economic school draws heavily on the liberal arguments already discussed, little needs to be added. Its thesis is that a free society requires a free market, and that the legitimacy of the state derives in large part from its contribution to the creation and maintenance of such a market. In the course of maintaining this thesis, the great merit of the economic New Right has been to restore rationality to unplanned institutions (most notably the market) in an age which has tended to equate rationality with planning. Unfortunately, by tying the defence of limited politics to the defence of capitalism the school has also displayed a defect which it has found no way of remedying. The problem is that if capitalism fails to deliver the goods, then the case for limited government is automatically jeopardized. The school, in other words, lacks any firm ethical basis for the political ideals to which it is committed.

The political school sympathizes with the free-market ideology, but qualifies it by adding a concern for moral and communal factors, as well as a greater emphasis on nationalism and the authority of the state. The aim of the political school, whose members are predominantly British and American, was formulated by a leading British academic representative, Maurice Cowling,[24] as the creation of a type of conservatism at once 'less liberal and more populist' than the middle way, and 'less liberal and more political' than the economic liberalism associated with the Thatcher government. The best known representative of this school, however, is Roger Scruton (1944–), the editor of *The Salisbury Review*.

In *The Meaning of Conservatism* Scruton identified the task of the New Right as the creation of an organic society which would end the alienation of modern man. Throughout his writings a neo-Hegelian yearning for 'wholeness' and community is combined with a nationalist commitment on the one hand, and an affirmation of the value of a pluralist civil order based on autonomous institutions on the other. Unfortunately, Scruton has never resolved an underlying tension in his thought between constitutional sentiments and anti-parliamentary leanings. This tension is heightened by his insistence that civil society rests on a prepolitical unity in which racial identity plays a vital part. There is, moreover, a potentially anti-constitutional undercurrent in Scruton's claim that Parliament is merely a vehicle for 'the opportunistic aims of the small professional class – the class of politicians',[25] with the implication that the underlying social unity of the nation might best be identified by spokespersons with no position or responsibility within the established political order. In practice, however, Scruton is deeply committed to such conditions of limited politics as the rule of law and autonomous social institutions.

The difficulties created by attempts to implement New Right economic doctrines are well brought out by the intellectual career of John Gray (1948–), a contemporary British thinker who initially sympathized with the New Right but who has gradually become completely disillusioned with the free-market ideal. Gray's reason for changing ground was his growing conviction that a doctrinaire free-market commitment gradually destroys the moral conditions which make the free market itself possible in the first place. Gray's disillusion, it may be noted in passing, created common ground with the American neo-conservative thinker Irving Kristol (1920–   ). What is especially interesting about Gray's retreat from free-market dogma is his attempt not to end up by merely travelling full circle back to the middle way interventionism which the New Right had demolished. Gray's alternative position endeavours to fuse three ingredients which had frequently been regarded as incompatible with one another.

The first involves a revised version of the classical ideal of civil association originally developed by Hobbes:

> It is in the works of Hobbes, who wrote for an age of religious wars and barbarous movements much like ours, that we glimpse the outlines of a form of government suited to our circumstances. It is a form of government devoted to securing the peace, and that first of all, thereby leaving the largest space for liberty of thought and action ... all or most of the activities not essential to the primary peacemaking task of the state are left to private initiative ... What it suggests is the salience to our present condition of a state which is strong but small ... This is a form of government devoted not to truth, or to abstract rights, and still less to any conception of progress or general welfare, but instead one which by securing a non-instrumental peace creates the possibility of civil association.[26]

This commitment to civil association gives Gray common ground with the late Michael Oakeshott (1901–90), a member of an older generation but extremely influential amongst the more profound theorists of the New Right. Unlike Oakeshott, however, Gray insists upon the need for a broad range of state welfare activity. This leads to the second part of his project.

The aim of this part is to supplement the ideal of civil association with a non-ideological concept of the welfare state. For this, Gray has drawn upon the concept of objective, satiable 'basic needs' introduced by Raz.[27] The result is an ideal of the enabling state, and of welfare rights, which constitutes Gray's alternative to the non-interventionist libertarian New Right, to the romantic high Tory politics of Scruton, and to the benign managerial pragmatism of William Hague and his supporters.

The third part of Gray's project is to undergird the revised theory of limited politics with a historically derived philosophic anthropology which abandons the abstract, universalistic type of theorizing upon which liberal defenders of limited politics have tended to rely ever since the Enlightenment. The result is not so much relativism as a recognition of the *conditionality* of political values. Whilst denying that reason can provide foundations for a liberal order, Gray recognizes that liberal institutions are nevertheless uniquely appropriate for Western peoples, in view of the emphasis those peoples place on choice and individuality.

At first sight, it might be felt that the outcome of Gray's retreat from the New Right is indeed little more than a sceptical 'social market' variant of the very middle-way ideal which the New Right originally set out to discredit. Unlike the middle way, however, Gray's position is not a purely pragmatic construct with a built-in propensity to slide leftwards. The core concept of civil association gives it a principled, non-pragmatic foundation, while the concept of 'basic needs' aims to confine government to specific and restricted objectives. If the 'enabling state' which Gray has in mind seems nevertheless hard to distinguish decisively from social democratic conceptions, then Gray has at least a provocative reply, which is that his ideal, unlike social democratic ones, is not harnessed to ideological goals such as equality. Its basis, he maintains, is the moral ideal of autonomy, which he wishes to substitute for what he takes to be the arid liberal ideal of negative liberty. In the interest of promoting autonomy the state must foster the family, independent private associations at large, a free-market system and a culture which has room for intrinsically valuable activities.

Much of this is of course problematic, both in theory and in practice. Not surprisingly, Gray has been accused of opening the door to the creation of a state at least as *socially* interventionist as that which the more libertarian New Right set out to discredit in the sphere of *economic* intervention. In particular, his belief in objective basic needs, and his reliance upon a problematic ideal of 'positive' autonomy, have also been the target of attack. What is of interest here, however, is the range and moderation of Gray's programme, offering as it does a suggestive alternative to New Right theorizing.

CONSERVATISM IN THE USA

One of the most remarkable features of the contemporary quest for a viable conservative doctrine is the contribution made by American thinkers. Indeed, to some of their critics, the very idea of an American conservatism has appeared to be a contradiction in terms since, as one scholar put it, all efforts to 'locate a conservative tradition ran up against the blank wall of the American past, which offered men no heritage but that of change'.[28] What is certainly true is that attempts to create an American conservatism by importing European concepts and perspectives have not taken root. At one extreme, for example, Russel Kirk (1918–94) and Robert Nisbet (1913–) have tried to graft ideas of hierarchy, class and corporate social structure drawn from the European aristocratic and feudal past on to American experience, inevitably alienating themselves from the egalitarian and rationalistic nature of American tradition in the process. At the other extreme, Ayn Rand has promulgated a Nietzschean cult of the heroic which is necessarily at odds with a society that celebrates the consumer and the common man.

More interesting, because more relevant to the problem of preserving limited politics in contemporary Western industrial democracies at large, has been the attempt to develop a conservatism which takes account of actual American experience – a conservatism, that is, which seeks to come to terms with mass democracy, industrialization and the culture of the common man. From this point of view, much is to be learnt from two groups of thinkers. One consists of the 'economic' critics of state intervention, such as Milton Friedman and James Buchanan, whose attack on the collectivist ideal of the Great Society has already been touched upon. A second consists of neo-conservatives like Irving Kristol,[29] Daniel Bell (1919–), and Nathan Glazer (1923–), whose perspective is moral rather than economic. Inspired by the American ideal of self-reliance, and committed to the family, school and local community, the latter are less concerned with wasteful and inefficient government than with (as Kristol dramatically expressed it) the prospect of nihilism engendered by the destruction of spiritual values through the working of a morally indifferent market system.[30] Thinkers like these have qualified their sense of the limitations of interventionism with an equally deep sense of the limitations of market ideology as an integrating device.

It is, however, from the American institution of a written constitution that many British conservatives with liberal sympathies have felt that they had most to learn, after a decade in which the most notable feature was the growth of the power of central government. Unfortunately, as one thoughtful scholar sceptically observed:

> they can take little comfort from the experience of America, for despite an apparently 'rigid' Constitution, the typical consensus policies have been pursued there with little formal restraint. That they have not proceeded as far as in Britain is [more] a tribute to the temper of the American people, which is still broadly sympathetic to the free market, ... than to the presence of a significant institutional constraint.[31]

Of especial interest in this connection is the critique developed by the black economist, Thomas Sowell, of attempts made by the Supreme Court to interpret the constitution with a view to ending racial discrimination. Supreme Court rulings in this sphere, he maintains, have not only tended to put the rule of law in jeopardy, but have also proved far less efficacious than leaving the fate of minorities to be determined by the market.[32]

CONSERVATISM AT THE TURN OF THE TWENTY-FIRST CENTURY

Conservatism was defined at the outset as a principled attempt to come to terms with the ineliminable tension which characterizes the human condition. From this point of view it became clear that neither reactionary nor radical conservatism succeeded in presenting very coherent forms of conservative doctrine. Roughly speaking, the former tried to transcend all tension in an ideal which was too static, while the latter sought to embrace it in an ideal which was too completely fluid and dynamic. Not surprisingly, it was moderate conservatism that went furthest towards coming to terms with ineliminable tension.

It will be evident from what has been said, however, that not every form of moderate conservatism offers a *principled* accommodation of tension, and that even those which try to do so have difficulty in dealing with the problems of mass industrial democracies. It will therefore be appropriate to end by glancing back at the conservative resurgence of the 1980s, and considering briefly what progress has been made in working out a viable doctrine.

One thing at least is clear. Regardless of its limitations as a conservative doctrine, credit must immediately be given to the New Right for its contribution to the most striking feature of the decade, which has been a change in the framework of political debate. Socialism no longer holds a monopoly of orthodoxy, and socialist parties themselves have had to incorporate a positive provision into their programmes for the sympathetic re-evaluation of market processes which the economic New Right helped bring about. The emergence of New Labour in Britain is an excellent illustration of the impact of the New Right in this respect.

There would have been relatively little gain, however, if the post-war faith in state economic planning had merely been inverted, to be replaced by an equally dogmatic faith in the universal and automatic efficacy of free markets. Fortunately, that has not happened: there is no evidence of the widespread spiritual conversion of Western populations to the individualistic, pro-enterprise and anti-welfare ideology that many New Right propagandists would like to foster. Instead, the 1990s reveals something more encouraging – at least potentially. This is a mood of disillusion with the foolish idea that *any* universal remedy exists for human ills.

Disillusion is the most reliable foundation for modern conservatism, in which religion can no longer play a significant role. It remains a treacherous ally, however, unless it becomes the progenitor of principled commitment. It is just here that the current neo-liberalism fails to give adequate guidance. Its revolt against planning, as well as against the more dogmatic forms of egalitarianism and cradle-to-grave welfarism, appears to have been motivated in considerable part by a concern for efficient modernization, rather than for the ideal of limited politics which formerly gave ethical significance to the tradition of moderate conservatism. The rhetoric of limited politics was indeed invoked during the past decade; but the reality was often more centralization, along with an increasingly ubiquitous managerial outlook. The danger, in consequence, is that the conservatism of the twenty-first century may abandon the more dogmatic and missionary aspects of the economic New Right, only to settle for a benign but unprincipled pragmatism.

It would be unduly complacent to regard such a development as merely a return to the post-war middle way, mainly because the state is now much more centralized (which is not to say that it is any stronger, of course), and the older traditions and practices which helped to secure the autonomy of intermediate institutions are extinct. It may indeed be that benign pragmatism is what electorates want, and in theory at least such a form of paternalism is quite compatible with the creation of happy societies. Whether the politics of happiness are ultimately compatible with the politics of dignity, however, is another matter. If it is asked what a politics of dignity means in this connection, then the most suggestive answer has already been touched upon: it can only be (in Gray's words) 'the reassertion of a limited government with positive tasks', since this alone can protect us from the spectacle 'of a *dirigiste* Behemoth, in whose wake nothing is left but a litter of ephemeral corporatist projects and the ruins of civil society'.[33] To combine the ideal of civil association with a non-ideological concept of welfare is, therefore, the most important task confronting a viable form of moderate conservatism today.

NOTES

1. *Conservatism*, Hamish Hamilton, London, 1990, p.239.
2. *From Enlightenment to Revolution*, Duke University Press, Durham, North Carolina, 1975.
3. *Germany's Third Empire*, Fertig, New York, 1971, p.193.
4. J.P. Stem, *Ernst Jünger*, Cambridge University Press, Cambridge, 1953, p.12.
5. See *Urmensch und Spätkultur*, 1956; also Peter L. Berger's introduction to Gehlen's *Man in the Age of Technology*, Columbia University Press, New York, 1980.
6. See J.Z. Muller, *The Other God that Failed*, Princeton University Press, Princeton, 1987, pp.213–14, 399–402.
7. See *Heroes and Hero-Worship*, 1840, and *Latter-Day Pamphlets*, 1850.
8. See Paul Smith (ed.), *Lord Salisbury on Politics*, Cambridge University Press, Cambridge and New York, 1972.
9. See *The Idea of a Christian Society*, Faber and Faber, London, 1939.
10. *The Revolt of the Masses*, Allen and Unwin, London, 1932.
11. R.E.M. Irving, *The Christian Democratic Parties of Western Europe*, Allen and Unwin, London, 1979; D.L. Hanley (ed.), *Christian Democracy in Europe*, Pinter, London, 1994.
12. *The Middle Way*, Macmillan, London, 1938.
13. *The Sunday Times*, 25 March 1973.

14. R.E. Pahl and J.T. Winkler, 'The Coming Corporatism', *New Society*, 10 October 1974.
15. *Financial Times*, 19 October 1972.
16. *The Sunday Times*, 26 November 1989, colour supplement.
17. C. Murray, 'The Prospects for Muddling Through', *The Critical Review*, 4, p.503; see also his books *In Pursuit of Happiness and Good Government* and *Losing Ground*, especially ch. 11.
18. *The Road to Serfdom*, Routledge and Kegan Paul, London, 1976.
19. 10 July 1985.
20. See, for example, B. Crick, *In Defence of Politics*, Penguin, Harmondsworth, 1964; and R. Dahl, *A Preface to Democratic Theory*, University of Chicago Press, Chicago, 1956.
21. Yale University Press, New Haven, 1965.
22. See *The Rise and Decline of Nations*, Yale University Press, New Haven, 1982.
23. Basil Blackwell, Oxford, 1984, p.ix.
24. See *Conservative Essays*, Cassell, London, 1978.
25. *The Meaning of Conservatism*, Penguin, Harmondsworth, 1980.
26. *The Salisbury Review*, 7, p.44.
27. Joseph Raz, *The Morality of Freedom*, Clarendon Press, Oxford, 1986.
28. O. Handlin, *The American People*, Penguin, Harmondsworth, 1963, p.446.
29. *On the Democratic Idea in America*, Harper Row, New York, 1972.
30. See I. Kristol, 'When Virtue Loses All her Loveliness', *The Public Interest*, 21, 1970.
31. N.P. Barry, *The New Right*, Croom Helm, London, 1987, p.165.
32. See T. Sowell, *Markets and Minorities*, Basic Books, New York, 1981.
33. *Limited Government: A Positive Agenda*, IEA, London, 1989, p.78.

GUIDE TO FURTHER READING

Books on British and European conservatism

Eatwell, R. and O'Sullivan, N. (eds), *The Nature of the Right*, Pinter, London, 1989.

Freeden, M., 'The Adaptability of Conservatism', *Ideologies and Political Theory*, Clarendon Press, Oxford, 1996.

Hanley, D. (ed.), *Christian Democracy in Europe*, Pinter, London, 1994.

Herf, J., *Reactionary Modernism*, Cambridge University Press, Cambridge, 1984. A good account of the considerations which produced revolutionary conservatism in inter-war Germany.

Honderich, Ted, *Conservatism*, Penguin, Harmondsworth, 1992.

Mannheim, K., 'Conservative Thought', in *Essays on Sociology and Social Psychology*, Routledge and Kegan Paul, London, 1971.

Nisbet, R., *Conservatism*, Open University Press, Milton Keynes, 1986. A useful short review of the Anglo-American conservative tradition.

O'Gorman, F., *British Conservatism*, Longman, Harlow, 1986. A convenient collection of documents, with comments.

O'Sullivan, N., *Conservatism*, Dent, London, 1976. A critical survey of the main

European conservative traditions, in terms of the light they shed on the requirements of limited politics.

Peacock, A. and Willgerodt, J. (eds), *German Neo-Liberals and the Social Market Economy*, Macmillan, London, 1989.

Quinton, A., *The Politics of Imperfection*, Faber and Faber, London, 1978.

Rogger, H. and Weber, F. (eds), *The European Right*, Weidenfeld and Nicolson, London, 1965.

Scruton, R. (ed.), *Conservative Thinkers: Essays from the Salisbury Review*, Claridge, London, 1988.

Tannsjo, T., *Conservatism for Our Time*, Routledge, London, 1991.

Willetts, D., *Modern Conservatism*, Penguin, Harmondsworth, 1992.

American conservatism

Dunn, C.W. and Woodward, J.G., *The Conservative Tradition in America*, Rowland and Littlefield, Lanham, MD, 1996.

Nash, G.H., *The Conservative Intellectual Movement in America since 1945*, Basic Books, New York, 1976.

On recent American conservatism, see also J. David Hoeveler Jr, *Watch on the Right: Conservative Intellectuals in the Reagan Era*, University of Wisconsin Press, Madison, 1991 and Jerome L. Himmelstein, *To the Right: The Transformation of American Conservatism*, California University Press, Berkeley, 1990. The journal *The Public Interest*, founded by Daniel Bell and Irving Kristol, is an interesting source of moderate American conservative thought. See also the incisive chapter by A. Aughey in R. Eatwell and N. O'Sullivan (eds), *The Nature of the Right*, Pinter, London, 1989.

The New Right

Barry, N.P., *The New Right*, Croom Helm, London, 1987. An excellent, very comprehensive survey of New Right doctrine in *all* the principal countries in which it has been influential.

In addition to the writings of Scruton, Gray, Hayek and Oakeshott mentioned elsewhere in this bibliography, see Levitas, R., *The Ideology of the New Right*, Polity Press, Cambridge, 1986; Gamble, A., *The Free Economy and the Strong State: The Politics of Thatcherism*, Macmillan, London, 1994; Green, D.G., *The New Right*, Wheatsheaf, Brighton, 1987. Note also Murray, C., *The Emerging British Underclass*, IEA, London, 1990.

A representative selection of conservative thinkers

de Benoist, Alain, *Les Idées a l'endroit*, Hallier, Paris, 1979.

Burke, E., *An Appeal from the New to the Old Whigs*, Bobbs-Merrill, New York, 1962. An eloquent defence of conservatism by the first thinker to recognize clearly the dangers presented by the new ideological politics brought into the world by the French Revolution.

Carlyle, Thomas, *Past and Present*, London, 1843. Carlyle provides a classic statement of anti-parliamentary paternalistic conservatism.

Eliot, T.S., *The Idea of a Christian Society*, Faber and Faber, London, 1939.

Gasset, Ortega y, *The Dehumanization of Art*, Princeton University Press, Princeton, 1968. For Ortega's aristocratic conservatism, aesthetics and a sense of play were more fundamental than religion. On the vital importance of play, see also the superb study by J. Huizinga, *Homo Ludens, A Study of the Play-Element in Culture*, Routledge and Kegan Paul, London, 1949.

Gray, J., *Limited Government: A Positive Agenda*, IEA, London, 1989. See also his *The Moral Foundations of Market Institutions*, IEA, London, 1992.

Hayek, F.A., *The Road to Serfdom*, Routledge, London, 1944. One of the earliest identifications of the problems which were to be created by the post-war middle-way policy. Still well worth pondering over.

Macmillan, H., *The Middle Way*, Macmillan, London, 1938.

Maistre, Joseph de, *The Works of Joseph de Maistre*, ed. and trans. J. Lively, Allen and Unwin, London 1965. See also J.S. McClelland (ed.), *The French Right*, Jonathan Cape, London, 1970.

Maritain, J., *True Humanism*, Centenary Press, London, 1938.

Oakeshott, M., *Rationalism in Politics*, Liberty Press, Indianapolis, 1991. The most subtle critique of ideological politics to have appeared in the twentieth century.

Röpke, W., *A Humane Economy*, Regnery, Chicago, 1971.

Scruton, R., *The Meaning of Conservatism*, Macmillan, London, 1980.

Smith, P. (ed.), *Lord Salisbury on Politics*, Cambridge University Press, Cambridge, 1971.

Spengler, O., *The Decline of the West*, Allen and Unwin, London, 1961.

de Tocqueville, A., *Democracy in America*, ed. J.P. Mayer and M. Lerner, Fontana, London, 1968. A sceptical vision of the fate of liberty in mass democracy which constantly grows, rather than declines, in relevance.

4
SOCIAL DEMOCRACY AND DEMOCRATIC SOCIALISM

Anthony Wright

—

> One can have democracy without socialism, and vice versa. Whether the two can be effectively combined is the prime question of our age.
> George Lichtheim[1]

At first glance it may seem odd, or at least unnecessary, that a book on contemporary political ideologies should have separate chapters devoted to different aspects of the socialist tradition. On one side, Marxism and communism; on the other side, social democracy and democratic socialism. Certainly a word of explanation – and of justification – is required.

It would not have been necessary to tell the story in this way for much of the nineteenth century and will not be necessary as we move further into the new millennium, but for the twentieth century (and it is this experience which is the central focus of the book) this division has marked out the critical faultline within socialism. This has been true both organizationally, in terms of movements and parties, and intellectually, as a body of ideas and doctrines. In many respects it is misleading. It obscures the extent of the common ground, but it also disguises the fact that socialism has always been distinguished by a much more variegated plurality of traditions.[2] Even the language misleads: a century ago 'social democracy' denoted organized Marxism, whereas it has come to mean organized reformism. So too with 'democratic socialism', a term coined by its adherents as an act of disassociation from the twentieth-century realities of undemocratic socialism (an illegitimate, indeed impossible, coupling in terms of classical doctrine, including Marxist doctrine), but also, at least in some modes, intended to reaffirm a commitment to system transformation rather than a merely meliorist social democracy. In much of Europe though, if not in Britain, the terms have been interchangeable and 'social democracy' carries the whole weight of this complex history.

It stands as the dominant twentieth-century form of socialism in the West, where (apart from North America) it provided the chief opposition to political conservatism and to the political organization of capitalism. Not the only opposition though, even in socialist terms, for if it found an antagonist on one side in the defenders of the *status quo*, it found another antagonist in a Marxist tradition (organized, more or less strongly in different places, in a politics of communism) which disputed its socialist credentials and claimed to offer a more theoretically sophisticated and politically vigorous alternative. Indeed, one of the questions to be considered about social democracy is whether it should properly be seen as a 'revision' of Marxism, in terms of its ancestry and political trajectory, or whether it is more accurately to be regarded as a political tradition in its own right. For the moment, though, it is enough to record that the fissure within socialism into Marxist and social democratic traditions has been the fundamental characteristic of much of its twentieth-century history, although not of its contemporary condition as that century ends and a new millennium begins.

HISTORIES AND TRADITIONS

The focus here is on social democracy, but it is useful first to get some general bearings. In one sense the history of socialism is as long as history itself. It is to be found whenever and wherever people have sought to raise, whether speculatively or actively, issues about the proper basis of social organization and have sought solutions in the direction of equality and co-operation. Thus some socialists have wanted to anchor their doctrine in the social application of Christianity, others to echo the profoundly simple affirmation of Robert Burns that 'a man's a man for a' that', yet others to find the heart of the matter in Rainborough's declaration in the famous Putney debate of the 1640s that 'the poorest he that is in England has a life to live as the greatest'.[3] But if socialist ideas, in some form, have a long and various history, the fact remains that socialism is irredeemably modern, part and parcel of the modern world itself.

As a doctrine (and as a movement) it was a product of the modern world and defined itself in relation to it. This was the world created by what Hobsbawm has described as the 'dual revolution', a French Revolution which overturned not just monarchies but whole ways of thinking (as Burke [1729–97] famously observed) and an industrial revolution which transformed the material upon which both thought and action had to operate. A political revolution met an economic and social revolution. Rousseau (1712–78) had kicked over the traces of liberal individualism and offered the tantalizing (if enigmatic) prospect of a communitarian democracy, while the philosophers of rationalism had invented a world in which humanity was firmly in the driving seat armed with an ability to steer it in the progressive directions mapped out by their own first principles. The 'left wing' of the French Revolution (as with Babeuf [1760–97] and his 'conspiracy of equals') was soon engaged on the task of extending political revolution into social and economic revolution; a group of economic thinkers in Britain were to be found exploring an early version of a labour theory of value; while in Germany philosophical debate provided the setting in which Hegelian idealism was eventually transmuted into Marxian materialism. In shorthand terms, it is in this trinity of French politics, English economics and German philosophy that George Lichtheim locates the essential origins of socialism.[4]

It is in the first decades of the nineteenth century, then, that 'socialism' makes its appearance (the term appeared in Britain in the 1820s, in France in the 1830s). It denoted the attempts being made from a number directions and in a number of places to impose a 'social' organization on the new economic order that was coming into existence. There was Robert Owen (1771–1858) and his new models of factory life; the technocratic industrialism of Saint-Simon (1760–1825); the idiosyncratic communitarianism of Fourier (1772–1837) and the decentralist mutualism of Proudhon (1809–65). When Marx swept all these together under the label 'Utopian', the name stuck, just as he mobilized a 'communism' against these prevailing versions of 'socialism' which were to be seen as merely speculative constructs. When the liberal John Stuart Mill (1806–73) wrote, approvingly, about socialism in the middle of the nineteenth century, he also understood the term to mean associations of producers of the kind the Utopian socialists had described.

In some ways, it is possible to see the faultlines of socialism being laid down not in the dramatic fractures of the early twentieth century, but in these points of departure in the first half of the nineteenth century. Indeed, if we add in Louis Blanc's (1811–82) labour reformism, with its focus on a right to work, there are already the beginnings of a conspicuously social democratic tradition. One of the misleading achievements of the ascendancy of Marxism within European socialism during the second half of the nineteenth century was to suggest that 'scientific' socialism represented the historical transcendence of earlier and other traditions, rather than particular political and theoretical victories. Indeed, as has frequently been pointed out, Marxism was a typically nineteenth-century ideology in believing not only that there were laws of motion of human history but also that it had discovered them. In fact, as organized labour movements drew from this well of ideas, socialism did not lose its diversity, although it could seem so. It is only necessary to recall the running battle within the international labour movement between the Marxists and the anarchists, or the constant struggle of the Germans to control the wayward tendencies of French socialism, or the opprobrium heaped upon British reformist socialism by the continental movement, for it to be clear that, even at its moment of supreme political and theoretical coherence under Marxist auspices (during the period of the Second International at the end of the nineteenth century), socialism remained a mansion with many rooms. It was only a short distance from this to the separate – and often warring – houses of the twentieth century.

Before turning to that crucial turn-of-the-century moment of disjuncture, it is useful to register some of the underlying terrain upon which socialist argument has been conducted throughout its modern history. This reveals both the common ground and the disputed areas of territory. In a basic sense socialism defined itself by what it was against. It was framed as the ideological expression of the workers' movement that arose in resistance and opposition to the depredations of industrial capitalism. If 'labourism' sought to protect and defend the interests of labour in relation to this system, 'socialism' sought to change the system itself. It was the voice of a class in a society divided by classes. It analysed and exposed the nature and consequences of capitalism, while offering the prospect of something different and better, crucially through the replacement of private by public ownership of the means of production. Moreover, it linked its critique of capitalism with a critique of the ideology of capitalism, of a liberal individualism that was held to be fraudulent in its claimed universalism but which, by excluding social and economic relationships from the account, was in fact class-bound and partial. In this sense socialism sought to 'socialize' and integrate the *liberté*, *égalité* and *fraternité* launched upon the modern world by the ideas of 1789 as these met the material reality of the other part of the dual revolution. Democracy entailed a social democracy.

So far, so good. However, the actual history of socialism (illustrated equally by its organizational fragmentation and its doctrinal diversity) reveals that both within and beyond the common ground there were always many different traditions in evidence. Some of these were marshalled, eventually, into the larger currents of Marxism or social democracy, where they served to define the separate identity of these currents, but others were not so easily marshalled and continued to make their separate waves. Consider some of the questions at issue. Was socialism the necessary future or just one possible future? Was it a science of society or an ethical choice? Was it a class doctrine or something broader? Was its mission to organize society or to liberate it? Was the state to be deployed or destroyed? Was its method that of revolution or of reform? On these and other questions of analysis, strategy and prescription, socialists found ample scope for vigorous and continuing disagreement.

It is easier to see this now than it was a century ago, when the great 'synthesis' of Marxism seemed not only to have established a political dominance within Western socialism but to have established an intellectual dominance that had firmly dispatched such unsettling questions to the footnotes of history. It was a period not for questions but for answers, the apotheosis of scientific socialism, as evidenced by the Erfurt Programme (1891) of German social democracy and the theoretical sweep of Kautsky

(1854–1938) and Bebel (1840–1913), with the course of economic development shown to be moving inexorably in the direction of the imminent historical victory of a revolutionary proletariat. However, within two decades both the political and intellectual picture was transformed. The failure of the Western working class to put 'class' before 'nation' in 1914, followed by the victory of Bolshevism in 1917, produced a rupture within the socialist camp that shaped everything that followed. On one side, 'Marxism' was appropriated as the official ideology of communist parties and regimes; on the other side, 'social democracy' disengaged itself from its ancestral Marxism (except in Britain, where there had been no serious engagement) and launched out on its own path of reformist politics.

However, the rupture had really begun much earlier, at least intellectually. As already suggested, its origins are to be found in the diversity that had always characterized socialism, notwithstanding claims to the contrary on the part of those who believed they were in possession of the true and singular article. If this was the case in the nineteenth century, it became manifestly so in the twentieth. Socialism was a product of the most developed economies of the West and of the class structure spawned by such economies. Indeed, it was basic to socialist doctrine that these societies were the indispensable site of socialism – economically, socially, culturally and politically. In twentieth-century terms, this has remained the case with social democracy, although there was a marked shift of site towards those places (such as Scandinavia and Britain) where reformism was firmly established; but at the same time, from 1917 onwards, the active site of revolutionary socialism moved east and south, not merely confounding traditional analysis but feeding back into the politics of socialism in the West. The plurality of socialism was intimated in the nineteenth century; it was acted out in the twentieth.

It is against this background that the character of twentieth-century social democracy has to be understood. If it remained as the culturally specific form of socialism in the West, it now had to define itself explicitly both in relation to other forms of socialism and in relation to the wider traditions of the societies in which it lived and in which it sought to find an effective political voice. As we shall see, what this involved brought with it a process of ideological adjustment and adaptation in relation to the changing circumstances with which it was confronted. In significant respects, what social democrats had to say was different at the beginning of the twentieth century, at mid-century and towards the end of the century; just as the political fortunes of social democracy have differed too. Put starkly, it might be said that at the beginning of the century social democracy believed it was the future, while at the end of the century the question became whether it had a future at all. It will be necessary to return to that question, but only after identifying some of the main features and staging posts of social democratic thought in the intervening period.

THE FOUNDATIONS OF SOCIAL DEMOCRACY

There is a convenient starting-point, neatly located at the close of the nineteenth century and setting the framework for the social democratic tradition in the twentieth. Before the political rupture within socialism in the second decade of the twentieth century, there had already occurred an intellectual rupture that prefigured this fissure into revolutionary Marxism and reformist social democracy. In the debate about 'revisionism' which divided the socialist movement at the end of the nineteenth century, with Eduard Bernstein (1850–1932) as the leading protagonist of the revisionist case against the orthodox Marxists of German social democracy, it is possible to identify the terrain upon which subsequent Western socialism was to assemble its social democratic position. The word 'revisionism' is both revealing and misleading here. What it reveals is that it was out of the internal debates within Marxism that modern Western social democracy was developed (and Bernstein himself had his home in orthodox Marxism); and the form of the debate was entirely in that mode. Where it is misleading is in the inference that what emerged was simply a revised version of the original.

In questioning some of the central tenets of 'scientific' socialism (the theory of value, the concentration of capital, the pauperization of the workers, economic crisis), Bernstein hoped to educate the socialist movement in the possibilities of practical reformism in the context of democratic politics. Socialism was not to be seen as a culminating and catastrophic historical event, but as a gradual democratic process. In an article in 1898 Bernstein summarized this position:

> If by the realization of socialism we understand the establishment of a society organized in all respects along strictly communist lines, then indeed I do not hesitate to say that this seems to me to be a long way off yet. On the other hand, it is my firm conviction that even the present generation will see the realization of a good deal of socialism, if not in the patented form, then at least in *fact*. The steady expansion of the sphere of social obligations (i.e. the obligations of the individual towards society, his corresponding rights, and the obligations of society towards individuals), the extension of the right of society, as organized in the nation or the state, to regulate economic life; the growth of democratic self-government in municipality, district and province, and the extended responsibilities of these bodies – for me all these things mean development towards socialism or, if you will, piecemeal realization of socialism ... However, it is also true that as soon as the community makes proper use of its right to control economic conditions, the actual transfer of economic enterprises to public management ceases to have the fundamental importance commonly ascribed to it. There can be more socialism in a good factory act

than in the nationalization of a whole group of factories.

I frankly admit that I have extraordinarily little feeling for, or interest in, what is usually termed 'the final goal of socialism'. This goal, whatever it may be, is nothing to me, the movement is everything.

According to this view, Social Democracy should neither expect nor desire the imminent collapse of the existing economic system, if this is to be envisaged as the product of a great and catastrophic trade crisis. What Social Democracy should be doing, and doing for a long time to come, is organize the working class politically, train it for democracy, and fight for any and all reforms in the state which are designed to raise the working class and make the state more democratic.[5]

The form of Bernstein's argument was an engagement with Marxism. It was an empirical challenge, disputing the evidence and trends on which the certitudes of Second International orthodoxy were built, and a strategic challenge, arguing for a new approach to fit the new facts. However, it was also more than that, for what was really being challenged was the *kind* of theorizing that Marxism was (or, more accurately perhaps, had become). It is at this point, in advocating a more open and flexible theory, that it becomes misleading to see modern social democracy simply as a revised version of orthodox Marxism (notwithstanding the fact that its actual course of development, even in a country like Sweden, was typically hammered out on that anvil). For what Bernstein was doing, and what social democracy became, was not an exercise in the revision of Marxism, but the development of a quite different kind of ideology.

This was an ideology which, at bottom, was grounded not in materialism but in morals. Thus Bernstein summoned up Kant to point the way towards a politics of ethical choices, while arguing that 'the point of economic development attained today leaves the ideological, and especially the ethical, factors greater space for independent activity than was formerly the case'.[6] More generally, socialism was now not to be seen as standing apart, either theoretically or practically, from 'bourgeois' society, but as an integral part of a common process of development, expressing its best self and drawing from the reservoir of Western humanism. Thus Jaurès (1859–1914), whose influence dominated French socialism in the two decades prior to his assassination in 1914, was fundamentally an idealist, for whom socialism was grounded more in the general republican tradition than in the prevailing categories of historical materialism. Democracy was not just a means but an end, a value in itself. This also implied a revised attitude to liberalism, no longer to be seen by socialists as merely the ideological wing of capitalism but as the predecessor and precursor of socialism, through a process in which the restricted liberal view of freedom was expanded and socialized. 'There is actually no really liberal thought which does not also belong to the elements of the ideas of socialism,' argued Bernstein; and 'in this sense one might call socialism "organizing liberalism"'.[7]

It is clear from all this that what may have taken the form of a 'revision' of Marxism was, in fact, laying the foundations for a different socialist tradition. Themes from this period (for example, the ethical emphasis and the socialization of the idea of freedom) were to become central to modern social democratic thought. So too, of course, was the embrace of practical reformism as the appropriate strategy for socialists and the rejection of a politics of impending crisis and revolutionary transformation. Indeed, the nub of the revisionist case was that German social democracy, notwithstanding its doctrinal Marxism, had in practice already become a party of reform ('Is social democracy today anything beyond a party that strives after the socialist transformation of society by the means of democratic and economic reforms?'[8]) and should therefore bring its theory in line with its practice. The fact that it resolutely refused to do anything of the kind meant, as Peter Gay puts it, that 'the SPD continued to behave as a Revisionist party and, at the same time, to condemn Revisionism; it continued to preach revolution and to practice reform'.[9] The closing of that particular gap is central to the twentieth-century history of social democracy.

Rosa Luxemburg (1871–1919) expressed a general view in describing Bernstein as having 'constructed his theory upon relationships obtaining in England – he sees the world through English spectacles'[10] but, irrespective of personal biography, this serves as a useful reminder that in Britain a reformist socialism was already firmly in place when the revisionist debates were taking place within the continental movement and, although outside these debates because of its lack of a significant Marxist tradition, was to come into its own as a major source of twentieth-century social democratic ideology. In part, this was because of its explicit moralism, but also because it managed to combine this with its own confident belief in the historical processes at work favourable to a reformist socialism. This is an important point, since it links the continental revisionists and the British Fabian socialists, united not in a pessimism about the revolutionary prospectus of Marxism, but in an evolutionary optimism about the prospects for socialist reform.

This is a crucial ingredient of early twentieth-century social democracy, the more so since it contrasts so sharply with the later anxieties of the tradition. Indeed, orthodox Marxism and revisionist social democracy were at one in this respect: both believed that history was on their side. When the Fabians urged the 'inevitability of gradualness', the inevitability was as significant as the gradualness. It was possible to point to the ever expanding role of the state (both national and local) in social and economic regulation as evidence that modern societies were set firmly on the path of collective organization, while the impact of democratic politics would mean an irresistible momentum in the direction of policies to secure the interests of the working-class majority. Presenting socialism as the 'outcome of a gradual change of thought in economics, ethics and politics', Sidney Webb (1859–1947) could portray a contemporary history in which 'Society is reforming itself on Collectivist, not on Individualist principles, and although the advocates of each particular change intend no further alteration, the result is nevertheless an increasing social momentum in the same general direction'.[11]

This serves to establish the essential character of the modern social democratic project. The state was to be deployed by democratic politics to reform capitalism into socialism, a process rooted both in moral development and in the logic of economic development. Socialism was not therefore to be seen as a rupture with existing society and its cultural traditions, but as an enterprise of extension and growth. It was a project of persuasion, but in a context where the political, economic, social and cultural conditions were conducive to such persuasion. In answer to the question (which runs through all socialist thought) about whether capitalism was held to be defective on the grounds of injustice or of inefficiency, social democrats could safely reply that it was both. On one side, it could be assaulted by the values of equality, justice and solidarity; on the other side, it could be confronted with the merits of economic planning and social organization. Programmatically, for social democratic parties, this entailed an electoral politics in which they offered a mixture of socialization, planning, welfare and redistribution, with the state envisaged as a massive public service organization (with dissenting voices from those, such as the English guild socialists, for whom this was an excessively bureaucratic and insufficiently democratic prospect[12]).

Two figures whose thought may be seen as encapsulating the spirit and basis of social democracy in the inter-war period are R.H. Tawney (1880–1962) and Ernst Wigforss (1881–1977), the former an outstanding voice of British socialism and the latter the leading exponent of Swedish social democracy. In *The Acquisitive Society* (1921) and *Equality* (1931), Tawney assembled a powerful moral case against competitive individualism and contrasted it with the benefits to be enjoyed in a solidaristic community rooted in a practical equality and a common culture. The root principle was clear: 'because men are men, social institutions, property rights, and the organisation of industry, and the system of public health and education – should be planned, as far as is possible, to emphasise and strengthen, not the class differences which divide, but the common humanity which unites, them'.[13] Here was an ethical socialism which combined a dogmatism about values with a flexibility about the techniques of implementation, a combination also characteristic of social democratic politics. Here, too, was a sustained attempt to apply the belief that social change was located in the realm of ideas and values, rather than in the iron grip of historical determinants, and Tawney marshalled the resources of a culture for his enterprise of moral persuasion in which a freedom worthy of the name required a heavy dose of practical equality. At bottom, Tawney's socialism (like Orwell's) rested on a view of what constituted decency; and on a challenge to think of society as a purposive moral association.

Unlike Tawney, Wigforss did not ground his values in the Christian tradition but, having played a key role in the disengagement of Swedish socialism from Marxist determinism, he was equally emphatic about the need to articulate a distinctive set of social democratic values as the basis for a politics of reform, so much so that it has been claimed that 'his exposition of a Social Democratic politics that rests on the ideals of freedom, equality, democracy, security, solidarity and economic efficiency comprises the heart of Swedish Social Democratic ideology'.[14] Like Tawney, Wigforss identified the centrality of equality (not a mathematical equality, but the removal of class inequality) for the development of a solidaristic society in which people were in fraternal reach of each other through common access to the material and spiritual culture. In a similar vein, another Swedish socialist, Per Albin Hansson (1885–1946), used the metaphor of the 'people's home' to describe his vision of a good society. Like Bernstein, Wigforss presented socialism not as the antagonist of liberalism but as its natural extension:

> Social democracy has never denied, but on the contrary considered it an honour to have its roots in the same intellectual soil that nourished the old liberal ideas of freedom. But it never saw the way to realise these ideas as being competition between individuals, regulated only by the free market and with the state's and the society's tasks reduced to a minimum.[15]

Although the values of social democracy were fixed and enduring, their application was seen by Wigforss as a matter of constant exploration and experimentation (hence his refusal to make socialization the primary component of the shift from capital to labour). He coined the term 'provisional Utopia' to describe the nature of this link between principle and policy in the social democratic politics of permanent reform.

PRINCIPLES AND PRACTICE

It was easier, though, to define that link conceptually than to apply it in practice. Yet this was necessarily the focus of the social democratic project. Having established the theoretical credentials of a reformist socialism, the task then became to put it to work. This is why 'social democrats have taken *programme* writing extraordinarily seriously'.[16] It was necessary to show how, in ever changing circumstances, social democratic values could be operationalized through programmes of economic planning, public ownership and social welfare. This became the stuff of social democratic politics everywhere, to which relentless intellectual and political energy was applied. Although the activities of social democratic parties are not the chief concern here, their ability to give practical expression to the ideology of socialist reformism cannot be disassociated from the ideology itself. Nor has it been, for practice has constantly fed back into theory, and theory into practice. At its simplest level, a reformist theory entailed a viable reformist practice.

It was not long before the twentieth century gave notice that this was not an unproblematical relationship, nor that the kind of historical optimism exhibited by Bernstein and Webb was itself a revisionism in need of revision. The manner in which the German social democrats after 1918 proved quite unable to run the new German state, formulate an effective socialist reformism or prevent the collapse of Weimar democracy, was an early indication of things to come. Elsewhere, during the long years of capitalist recession, social democrats found themselves confronted not with the task of making steady incremental incursions into a functioning capitalism until one system had changed into another, but of what to do when charged with the responsibility for a capitalism in crisis. As one German trade unionist described this dilemma, socialism did not know whether it was the doctor at the sickbed of capitalism or whether it was the heir waiting to inherit.[17] The immobilism of the British Labour government in 1931 in the face of financial crisis seemed to exemplify the general dilemma of social democracy.

This is not entirely fair. Socialists did attempt to grapple with an economics of recovery. The Belgian socialist Hendrik de Man (1885–1953), whose reputation is tainted by his collaboration with the Nazis, advocated a planning strategy for full employment. The Swedish Social Democratic Government put in hand a successful counter-cyclical policy based on deficit budgeting. A group of young British socialist economists (such as Jay, Durbin and Gaitskell) were putting together the basis for a new economics of stabilization.[18] Yet the point remains that there was much in the first half of the twentieth century to test and question the basis of socialist reformism, unsettling many of its own earlier assumptions. On one side, socialism had been liquidated by fascism; on another side, Marxism had acquired a new lease of life by its seeming ability to explain a world racked by capitalist crisis and to offer a functioning alternative in the full employment planning of the first communist state. By contrast, reformist socialism seemed to have had the ground kicked from beneath it, leaving it intellectually marooned and politically enfeebled. Voices within its ranks were to be found asking, with Harold Laski (1893–1950),[19] whether it was really possible after all to accomplish the democratic reform of capitalism into socialism. In fact, from mid-century social democracy experienced a remarkable renaissance, accompanied by a new process of ideological revision. The Keynesian revolution in economics is usually cited as decisive here. Keynes (1883–1946) was a liberal, but a social liberal and, like Beveridge, was part of the co-mingling of socialism and liberalism which helped to shape modern social democracy. More specifically, Keynesian economics provided a new understanding of how capitalist economies worked and how, through demand management, they could be made to work by an intelligent state (with Roosevelt's New Deal in America as its untheorized example). It is important not to make Keynes too pivotal to social democratic development for, as already suggested, there were independent initiatives already in place. In Michael Harrington's (1928–89) words, 'John Maynard Keynes was not a *deus ex machina* who saved European socialism from its own sterility, but one influence among many'.[20] Nevertheless, it is more than convenient shorthand to use the label 'Keynesian social democracy' to describe the post-war social democratic project, for it undoubtedly put reformism back on the track.

If the key problem for inter-war social democracy was to find a way to save and replace capitalism at the same time (especially when called upon to govern), then the key contribution of the new economics was to provide it with a set of tools. The particular usefulness of these tools was that their field of action was not the rival terrains of 'capitalism' and 'socialism' but the no man's land of practical reformism which had proved so trouble-some, yet so critical, to inter-war social democracy. In this sense, intellectual breakthrough prefigured political breakthrough. A philosophy of reform depended upon there being a viable strategy of reform. The experience of the inter-war years had raised serious questions about this; but now Keynesian social democracy seemed to have answered them. An active interventionist state would be able to overcome the cyclical instabilities of capitalism through energetic and intelligent demand management, thereby securing full employment and providing the basis for the progressive extension of welfare provision and measures designed to bring about an equality of social citizenship.

But was this 'socialism'? In the immediate post-war situation, there seemed no need to frame the question in this way, for the world that emerged from war was busily preparing to deploy the instruments of wartime col-lectivism and the spirit of anti-fascism for the task of social and economic reconstruction. More generally, rather like an earlier social democracy, it was again plausible to believe that socialism was the necessary product of a process of economic and political development. Indeed, it was plausible to believe this even if, like Joseph Schumpeter (1883–1950), you did not also welcome it.[21] In socialist terms, history was back on course, as the future. The French socialist leader, Léon Blum (1872–1950), could describe socialism as having arrived at its 'triumphant period' when:

Socialist assumptions and axioms have been taken over by men and parties who have waged the most ferocious of wars against socialist organisations. It is on the foundation of socialist principles that societ-ies, whether consciously or not are everywhere being reconstituted.[22]

THE SOCIAL DEMOCRATIC COMPROMISE

However, this kind of historical triumphalism scarcely endured beyond the end of the 1940s. Its ending inaugurated a further period of social democratic revisionism, as significant as that half a century earlier when social democracy first defined itself, extending (albeit unevenly, because of different domestic traditions) right across the parties of the West and setting the ideological course for at least a generation. At its heart was a developing conviction that a reformed capitalism might not just be the route to socialism but the socialist destination itself. What had formerly been regarded as the 'transition' found itself elevated to the status of 'settlement'. The chief casualty of this process of ideological revision was the doctrine of public ownership of the means of production, the traditional hallmark of socialism and of its critique of capitalism. Instead of the antinomies of 'capitalism' and 'socialism', the post-war world could be seen as having opened up the prospect of a mixed arrangement of economy and society, neither state nor market, not public or private, but a new kind of hybrid. This provided the setting for what became known as the 'social democratic compromise', the arena in which the Keynesian techniques of economic management and the instruments of social engineering could be utilized in the service of traditional socialist objectives by non-traditional means.

This bald summary compresses a more complex story, in which arguments raged between fundamentalists (some of whom now deliberately emphasized their attachment to a 'democratic socialism' as distinct from a purely reforming 'social democracy') and the new revisionists, and in which some social democratic traditions (as in Germany) embraced the new tendencies more readily and explicitly than others (notably Britain), some met stout resistance from older tendencies (as in Austria), while in the most successful social democratic movement (Sweden, where the social democrats were in office for over 40 years) public ownership had long since ceased to be the central constituent of social democratic ideology. Nevertheless, the summary tells the essentials of the story, in which post-war social democracy undertook a protracted process of ideological readjustment (and, in traditional terms, of deradicalization) in the face of what it took to be both the opportunities and the obstacles presented to it by post-war society.

The Bad Godesberg programme (1959) of the German Social Democrats (SPD) is usually regarded as the landmark expression of the new revisionism. Inspired by the electoral need to distance itself from the heritage of Marxism, the tyranny of Soviet communism and the doctrine of public ownership, the SPD declared that the basis of democratic socialism was to be found in 'Christian ethics, humanism and classical philosophy'. In an accommodation to the CDU-inspired (Christian Democrats) social market economy, the new programme produced the celebrated formulation designed to effect a conciliation between economic planning and markets: 'as much competition as possible, as much planning as necessary'. A class-based politics was also rejected, with the Social Democrats now declaring themselves to be a broadly based people's party. The distance from Erfurt to Bad Godesberg provides a dramatic measure of the ideological journey of social democracy in the twentieth century.

Another significant text from this same period, also making the case for a new social democratic revisionism, is Anthony Crosland's (1918–77) *The Future of Socialism* (1956). The core of his argument was that the world had changed and that socialist doctrine had therefore also to change to fit the 'new reality' if it was to retain its relevance:

> The need for a restatement of doctrine is hardly surprising. The old doctrine did not spring from a vacuum, or from acts of pure cerebration in a monastery cell. Each was the product of a particular kind of society, and of minds reacting to that society. Since this external factor was not constant and unchanging, the doctrines changed through time. And as society has changed again since before the war, so again a restatement of objectives is called for. The matter can be put quite simply. Traditional socialism was largely concerned with the evils of traditional capitalism, and with the need for its overthrow. But today traditional capitalism has been reformed and modified almost out of existence, and it is with a quite different form of society that socialists must now concern themselves. Pre-war anti-capitalism will give us very little help.[23]

The full-employment welfare state was a secure achievement and the task was to redefine the socialist project in relation to it. For Crosland this meant a reaffirmation of socialism as an ethical doctrine, rooted in a belief in social equality, which provided the basis for a contemporary politics of classlessness and welfare. Thus a revisionist socialism was not required to give up anything of its essence, merely to recognize that new means (social policy rather than public ownership) were required in the service of traditional ends. A new kind of capitalism needed a new kind of socialism.

In its own way, this revisionism was as confident in its analysis as an earlier social democracy had also been, different in their programmatic conclusions but sharing a belief in their understanding of the developing nature of Western societies and economies. It soon became clear that post-war social democracy had been altogether too confident in its analysis, as gains which were thought to be permanent turned out to be conditional and as the reservoir of capitalist growth showed signs of drying up. Yet the fact remains that the period of post-war boom (stretching into the 1970s) was also the period when social democracy was most buoyant. Stripped of its ancestral ideological commitments, it could offer itself as the progressive, modernizing wing of the post-war consensus, employing the techniques of economic management and social engineering to ensure that welfare capitalism delivered on its promises. J.K. Galbraith (1908–   ), American liberal but European social democrat, demonstrated that there was much for a busy state to do if 'private affluence and public squalor' was not to be the order of the day and that, faced with corporate power in the new industrial state, a range of public interventions was required to ensure 'that the monopoly of the industrial system on social purpose be broken'.[24] In this period it was possible to see social democracy as fulfilling its promise to be the extension and successor of liberalism, as it sought to universalize the benefits of Western societies to all their citizens and to make their economies work in the public interest.

FROM COMPROMISE TO CRISIS

However, this turned out to be a far from straightforward enterprise. The 'post-war' world effectively ended in the 1970s, as Western economies were hit by inflationary pressures which outstripped the capabilities of Keynesian demand management. This also outstripped the capabilities of Western social democracy and opened up a new period of ideological disorientation, as the turbulent history of social democratic parties in this period testifies.[25] Those revisionists who had anchored their analysis to the permanency of the post-war settlement were left stranded as that settlement disintegrated. This in turn provided an opportunity for those socialists who rejected the social democratic 'compromise' to argue the case for a new radicalism. On this view it was necessary to travel 'beyond' social democracy and to renew a mission for socialism not as the humanization of capitalism (which anyway had proved impossible to accomplish, with gains now being reversed) but as its replacement.

The context in which this turn to the left took place was of a conjunction between the difficulties of social democratic revisionism in the face of economic downturn and the impact of a neo-Marxist New Left which was critical both of Soviet-style communism and reformist social democracy. There was a renewed emphasis on the importance of ownership, with attention to issues of industrial democracy. It was the period of 'autogestion' in French socialism, the impact of the 'new movements' such as ecology on German socialism, the Meidener plan for wage-earner funds as a way of transferring ownership in Sweden, and the factional chaos of the British left. In one sense this was a period of great political and intellectual vitality on the part of Western socialism (when social science and socialism were virtually synonymous); but in another it was an illusory interlude sustained only by its own misconceptions. One of these was that the task of going 'beyond' traditional social democracy was an unproblematical one, while another was that this task was the central contemporary challenge for socialists.

These illusions were soon exploded and, as they were, socialist parties reverted to the path of deradicalization, except that this was no longer (as it had been in the 1950s) an expression of an ideological confidence but of a profound ideological disorientation. At root was an uneasy sense that the world had changed in ways which raised fundamental questions about the whole socialist project. The collapse of Mitterrand's socialist experiment in France in the early 1980s could be seen as carrying with it larger lessons about the vulnerability of any 'socialism in one country'. More generally (and not unlike the unpreparedness of the left, especially the Marxist left, for the development of fascism at an earlier period, contrary to all ideological expectations), what actually turned out to be 'beyond' social democracy was not a more muscular socialism but a vigorous revival of market liberalism, not a new left but a new right. Even in Sweden, the heartland of social democracy, power was lost for the first time in half a century. The new sites for socialist political success were in the new Mediterranean democracies, but here (notably in Spain and Portugal) ideological pragmatism in the cause of capitalist modernization was the order of the day. Elsewhere, socialist parties (including, as in Italy, communist parties) moved relentlessly in social democratic directions, casting off old ideological baggage in the search for a secure political and electoral anchorage in conspicuously difficult times.

A further decisive development was the collapse of Soviet communism (and of its appendages) at the end of the 1980s, thereby bringing to an end the institutional and ideological polarization of 'socialism' that constituted its twentieth-century history since the triumph of Bolshevism in 1917. In one sense this extraordinary historical moment could be seen as a victory and vindication for the reformist social democracy that had carved out its own ideological path at the turn of the century. Indeed, one of former Soviet president Gorbachev's last acts was to abandon Marxism for social democracy, citing Sweden as the model for emulation and declaring that 'socialism and the market are not just compatible but essentially inseparable'.[26] It was possible to see a new opportunity for socialism here, as the dissolution of communist regimes not only ended the contaminating influence of communist tyranny on the socialist idea in the West but also opened up the prospect of a new kind of 'third way' socialism (combining social ownership with markets and democracy), thereby heralding a revitalization of the social democratic tradition. It was even possible to provide a plausible sketch of how such a system would work.[27] In the event, it soon became apparent that such a prospect was a chimera, a hopeful invention of Western socialists who had not understood how 'actually existing socialism' had totally discredited *any* version of socialism among those who had lived under it.

SOCIALISM AT THE TURN OF THE TWENTY-FIRST CENTURY

It is against this background that the attempt to take stock of the ideological condition of the socialist tradition at the turn of the new millennium has to be made. Is it the case, as one commentator (echoing many others) has put it, that 'the "ism" has become a "wasm"'?[28] Certainly a comparison with its early-century ideological condition is instructive. Then it had a secure analysis, showing clearly that socialism was the coming thing, a secure understanding of what socialism involved (the replacement of capitalism) and a secure strategy – whether reformist or revolutionary – whereby it would be achieved. Orthodox Marxists and social democratic revisionists were alike in their different securities. By the end of the century, all this had changed. Elements of socialism might have become part of the 'common sense' of Western societies, socialism could be seen as 'reunified' following the collapse of communism and the eventual integration of Marxism into mainstream thought, socialism might have coalesced around its social democratic variant, but none of this could gainsay the fact that in the closing decade of the twentieth century the socialist tradition in the West was in a condition of considerable intellectual bewilderment. In Perry Anderson's words: 'There is no guaranteed position or assured direction for Social Democracy at the end of the century. Its contours are in flux as never before.'[29] It might have the socialist field to itself now, but the terrain looked distinctly inhospitable.

From a number of directions the socialist project seemed to have run into trouble, even to the extent that its contemporary condition could be interpreted as a terminal malady. Changing class patterns and forms of production ('post-Fordism') could be seen to have eroded much of its original social and industrial basis. A new individualism was corroding the foundations of a traditional collectivism. The process of globalization was undermining the scope for socialist initiatives at the level of the national state. A reaction against statism was necessarily also a reaction against the central instrument of socialist social engineering. Perhaps the social democratic 'compromise' between capital and labour, the regulated welfare capitalism that had come to be seen as a historic achievement of social democracy, was therefore not to be seen as a secure achievement but as a conditional product of a particular time and place:

> Developments since the Seventies have prompted the question as to how far we are dealing with a compromise which by its nature is tied to an era (perhaps geographically tied as well), and whether social democracy as such appears to have been a political movement tied to a particular time and location. It is not merely the political opponents of social democracy who ask this question. Doubt has even crept into our own circle: is social democracy, given its original drives and ideals,

perhaps finished, and can it therefore be relegated to history with thanks for services rendered?[30]

Perhaps it was the case that there were inescapable contradictions in being 'for' and 'against' capitalism at the same time, and that such contradictions would necessarily surface whenever socialists were called upon to do something other than distribute the fruits of economic growth.

Indeed, always excepting those ideological groupuscules for whom socialism was necessarily still on its original unsullied course (but for the endless betrayal of social democratic leaderships), there had developed a general recognition that new thinking had to be called in aid of the old. This applied as much to social democrats who were faced with the collapse of the post-war compromise as to those democratic socialists who wanted to travel beyond that compromise but found the route increasingly elusive and a shortage of passengers willing to embark on the journey in the 'culture of contentment' (J.K. Galbraith's phrase)[31] which characterized the possessive individualism of increasingly privatized societies.

New analysis was clearly required, capable of understanding the nature of contemporary societies and economies and finding a coherent socialist perspective. In some respects this was a gloomy perspective. It meant abandoning the clear ideological antinomies of 'capitalism' and 'socialism' which had sustained socialist politics for so long. It meant an acceptance that in crucial respects socialist reformism had been a dependent strategy, depending upon the capacity of a functioning capitalism to deliver growth-based reforms to the working class but undercutting socialist politics when these conditions could not be met. Indeed, in such circumstances, socialist politics could be immobilized, its extractive ambitions seemingly at odds with the very conditions for their success. It could neither fulfil the expectations of its adherents nor embrace the conditions for its own resumption. The Keynesian economic magic had ceased to work its macro-economic spell and some socialists were to be found looking for a 'supply-side socialism' to fill the gap.

In other respects, though, a contemporary socialist perspective could be made to seem much less gloomy and much more positive. On this view the old capitalism/socialism antinomy had indeed broken down, but its breakdown was to be seen much less in terms of capitalist triumphalism than in terms of the centrality of an energetic state in securing the successful development of post-Keynesian economies. Thus Marquand was able to point to a 'developmental state', rather than market liberalism, as the contemporary route to economic success.[32] In analysis of this kind, what distinguished developed economies was the interconnection of state and market, the interpenetration of public and private, with the crucial issue becoming the terms on which these relationships were conducted. One analysis from the left described the position thus:

at root, the counterposition of public and private sectors delayed a recognition of the complex interdependence between the two. This recognition of the interdependence of politics and markets – embodied in public institutions and rules that govern private activity – was and is the distinguishing characteristic of what, in simple terms, can broadly be conceived as an alternative economic and political model to that which has been dominant in Britain (and North America). This 'European' model is essentially a dynamic model of economic and social change – a model whose own capacity for change allows it to keep pace with shifting political, economic and social demands. Its dual focus is the framework for market competititon, and the changes prompted by and within it. In its social democratic guise, the model fuses socialist concern for equality with the dynamism of markets through pro-active state intervention.[33]

The task (described in this text as 'collective reregulation') was to make this state/market order work in the public interest, both in terms of its ability to achieve economic efficiency and to fulfil criteria of social justice. There were many policy tools available for this purpose and much for busy socialists still to do. The real political choice concerned the kind of capitalism that was on offer and this was the contemporary challenge for socialists.

Even if this analysis was plausible, though, there remained the task of converting it into an ideological discourse that could command some resonance (as successful ideologies necessarily must). This was the task of finding a public language to describe the distinctive purpose of socialist politics in new conditions; and a theoretical anchorage firm enough to combine old values with new structures and strategies. If these were the challenges at the end of the twentieth century, socialists were responding to them with increasing intellectual energy. Indeed, the erosion of old certainties (whether Marxist or social democratic) and of the traditional boundary lines within which they were organized had prompted a new theoretical openness, unconcerned with familiar orthodoxies and following arguments where they lead. There was not a new orthodoxy, but there were a number of approaches in evidence.[34] What they had in common was an attempt to find a new basis for socialism in the light of those developments that have proved so problematical for its old basis. They could be seen as the attempt to restate core socialist values in ways that might find a contemporary resonance, coupled with a renewed revisionism in relation to means and structures.

Thus there was a widespread recognition that a politics of class had to be expanded to incorporate other dimensions of inequality (such as gender) and other arenas of exploitation (notably of the environment), involving a broader-based kind of politics than traditionally engaged in by socialists – 'a broad reform alliance with as many groups and forces as possible' in the words of the most recent programme of the German Social Democrats.[35] There was a dissatisfaction with a traditional socialist statism and an embrace of more pluralistic and decentralized organizational forms. The emphasis on a directing state had given way to perceptions of an enabling and empowering state. A focus on the national state had been replaced by an attention to the transnational organization of power. Models of 'market socialism' (of different kinds) were advanced to describe ways in which the reconciliation could be effected between market dynamics and socialist objectives in the ordering of advanced economies. Theorists of 'citizenship' sought to restate the basis for an integrated conception of social, economic and political rights, and for an active engagement in the public good.

From such assorted sources it was possible to envisage the development of a new kind of socialism, still rooted in its longer tradition but reformulated for contemporary tasks. Michael Harrington described this as a 'socialist republicanism' in which 'the political, social and economic development of modern society points socialism toward an ethical, multiclass and decen-tralized conception of its goal based on ... the creation of new forms of community, both within the nation and throughout the world'.[36] It could scarcely be denied that the contemporary world had ample and urgent need of new forms of community. However, this did not mean that they would be structured, nor that (even if they were) they would have anything to do with 'socialism' as traditionally understood. As ever, it was easier to see where a political tradition had come from than where it might still be going.

This is certainly true of the new revisionism (or neo-revisionism) that has become the common currency of social democratic parties at the turn of the twenty-first century. 'By the 1990s', writes Sassoon, concluding his vast survey of a hundred years of socialism, 'socialists and social democrats throughout Europe were converging upon neo-revisionist positions.'[37] Such neo-revisionism had a number of distinguishing characteristics:

> It implies that markets should be regulated by legislation and not through state ownership. It means accepting that the object of social-ism is not the abolition of capitalism, but its coexistence with social justice; that regulation of the market will increasingly be a goal already achieved by supra-national means; that national – hence parliamentary – sovereignty is a limited concept; that the concept of national roads to socialism should be abandoned. It means that the historic link with the working class, however, defined, is no longer of primary importance, and that the trade unions are to be regarded as representing workers' interests with no *a priori* claim to have a greater say in politics than other interest groups. It means giving a far greater priority than in the past to the concern of consumers. Neo-revisionism entails accepting important aspects of the conservative critique of socialism – including the association between collective provision and bureaucratic iner-tia.[38]

If this is what social democracy has come to mean by the end of the twentieth century, it might be asked if it has any residual connection with the socialist tradition at all. In the course of a century it seemed to have abandoned its distinctive political and intellectual territory. The new revisionism takes this process even further than the mid-century revisionism that preceded it. In that version, the repudiation of public ownership as the essential mark of socialism was accompanied by the substitution of a fiscal socialism of taxing and spending. Yet in the new version of revisionism, 'taxing and spending' finds itself rejected as the hallmark of social democracy and replaced by the activism of a clever state in opening up pathways of opportunity. Equality gives way to inclusion. The new 'mixed economy' no longer denotes the coexistence of public and private ownership but the harnessing of market and state in pursuit of public interest goals.

All this represents a striking development of a political tradition. Yet the charge that it marks the abandonment, or even betrayal, of social democracy is unhistorical and misconceived. The whole history of social democracy has been shaped by its response to the changing nature and fortunes of capitalism, and the present period is no exception. It has also been shaped by the changing nature and behaviour of electorates whose support it has had to compete for, and this remains conspicuously the case today. Nor is it true to say that the new revisionism is distinctive in having finally abandoned the socialist project of abolishing capitalism, for this ceased to be the social democratic project (in practice if not always in theory) much earlier in the twentieth century. The real project has long been to advance social democratic values in the context of a capitalist market economy.

In this sense, the new revisionism can be seen as an attempt to bring clarity to social democratic politics and to remove the burden of a history in which socialism has struggled to free itself from meanings and associations that have been damaging (a struggle that produced both 'democratic socialism' and 'social democracy'). Western socialism, in its dominant social democratic forms, has been preoccupied with the task of applying its values to an ever changing economic and social environment. This has involved a permanent revisionism, of which its contemporary version is merely the latest twist. Yet there are claims that it represents something more than this, even perhaps the basis for a new ideological settlement in Western societies that is neither market liberalism nor welfare collectivism.

This is an unexpected development in the light of recent history. The late twentieth century revival of market liberalism had seemed to carry all before it, buttressed by the collapse of communism, sustained by imperatives of globalization, and dancing on the grave of social democracy. Yet no sooner was the final triumph of market socialism confidently announced than it found itself in trouble among electorates increasingly alarmed at some of its consequences. The landslide return to power of Labour in Britain in 1997 after nearly two decades in the wilderness – with similar, if less spectacular victories for social democrats elsewhere – seemed to mark the end of one historical period and the beginning of another.

But of what kind? It is clearly much too soon to write with confidence about this. What is clear, though, is that there is an explicit attempt to reformulate social democracy in such a way that it becomes the new 'common sense' defined in terms of the ambition to combine a dynamic market economy with the requirements of a decent and cohesive society, and to construct a broad political coalition on this basis. It involves a rejection of both new right and old left, of market individualism and state collectivism. Tony Blair describes it as a 'third way' that represents a new kind of politics. The question is whether such a political synthesis can prove durable – and whether it represents the epic renewal of social democracy (as its opponents claim) or its final retreat (as its critics allege). At least the new revisionists have put the question on the table.

NOTES

1. *A Short History of Socialism*, Weidenfeld and Nicolson, London, 1970, p.281.
2. The plurality is discussed in A. Wright, *Socialisms: Theories and Practices*, Oxford University Press, Oxford, 1987.
3. These socialist 'preconditions' are explored in B. Crick, *Socialism*, Open University Press, Milton Keynes, 1987, pp.1–13.
4. G. Lichtheim, *The Origins of Socialism*, Weidenfield and Nicolson, London, 1969.
5. E. Bernstein, 'The Struggle of Social Democracy and the Social Revolution: 2. The Theory of Collapse and Colonial Policy', *Neue Zeit*, 19 January 1898, in H. and J.M. Tudor (eds), *Marxism and Social Democracy: The Revisionist Debate 1896–1898*, Cambridge University Press, Cambridge, 1988, pp.168–9.
6. E. Bernstein, *Evolutionary Socialism* (trans. F. Harvey, 1899), New Schocken, New York, 1961, p.15.
7. Ibid., pp.153–4.
8. Ibid., p.197.
9. P. Gay, *The Dilemma of Democratic Socialism: Eduard Bernstein's Challenge to Marx*, Columbia University Press, New York, 1952, p.266.
10. Quoted in D. McLellan, *Marxism After Marx*, Macmillan, London, 1980, p.23.
11. Quoted in A. Wright, *British Socialism: Socialist Thought from the 1880s to the 1960s*, Longman, London, 1983, p.62.
12. Discussed in A. Wright, *G.D.H. Cole and Socialist Democracy*, Oxford University Press, Oxford, 1979.
13. R.H. Tawney, *Equality* (1931), Allen and Unwin, London, 1964, p.49. Tawney's thought is discussed in A. Wright, *R.H. Tawney*, Manchester University Press, Manchester, 1987.
14. T. Tilton, *The Political Theory of Swedish Social Democracy*, Oxford University Press, Oxford, 1990, p.69.
15. F. Wigforss, quoted in Tilton, op. cit., p.52.
16. S. Padgett and W. Paterson, *A History of Social Democracy in Post-war Europe*, Longman, London, 1991, p.11.
17. Fritz Tarnow, quoted in H. James, 'The SPD and the Economic Depression', in R. Fletcher (ed.), *Bernstein to Brandt*, Edward Arnold, London, 1987, p.143.

18. Discussed in F. Durbin, *New Jerusalems: The Labour Party and the Economics of Democratic Socialism*, Routledge, London, 1985.
19. H. Laski, *Democracy in Crisis*, Allen and Unwin, London, 1933.
20. M. Harrington, *Socialism: Past and Future*, Arcade, New York, 1989, p.97.
21. J. Schumpeter, *Capitalism, Socialism and Democracy*, Allen and Unwin, London, 1943.
22. Quoted in B. Graham, *The French Socialists and Tripartisme 1944–1947*, Weidenfeld and Nicolson, London, 1965, p.61.
23. A. Crosland, *The Future of Socialism* (1956), quoted in Wright, *British Socialism*, p.146.
24. J.K. Gaibraith, *The New Industrial State*, Signet, New York, 1968, p.387.
25. The period is chronicled and discussed in Padgett and Paterson, *A History of Social Democracy*.
26. 'Marxism No Longer Party's Life and Soul', *The Times*, 26 July 1991.
27. A. Nove, *The Economics of Feasible Socialism*, Allen and Unwin, London, 1983.
28. P. Kellner, 'State Socialism: An "ism" that Became a "wasm" ', *Independent*, 16 August 1991.
29. P. Anderson, 'The Light of Europe', in his *English Questions*, Verso, London, 1992, p.325.
30. *The Future of Democratic-Socialism in Europe*, Socialist Group of European Parliament, Wiardi Beckman Foundation, Amsterdam, 1988, p.142.
31. J.K. Galbraith, *The Contented Society*, Sinclair-Stevenson, London, 1992.
32. D. Marquand, *The Unprincipled Society*, Cape, London, 1988.
33. *Next Left*, Institute for Public Policy Research, London, 1992, p.6.
34. A useful survey is L. Martell, 'New Ideas of Socialism', *Economy and Society*, 21, 1992, pp.152–72.
35. *Basic Programme and Berlin Declaration of the Social Democratic Party of Germany*, Friedrich Ebert Stiftung, Bonn, 1990, p.45.
36. M. Harrington, *Socialism: Past and Future*, p.277.
37. D. Sassoon, *One Hundred Years of Socialism*, I.B. Tauris, London, 1996.
38. Ibid., pp.734–5.

GUIDE TO FURTHER READING

General surveys and discussions include R. Berki, *Socialism* (Dent, London, 1975), B. Crick, *Socialism* (Open University, Milton Keynes, 1987) and A. Wright, *Socialisms: Old and New* (Routledge, London, 1996). Good general histories include G. Lichtheim, *A Short History of Socialism* (Fontana, London, 1975) and A.S. Lindemann, *A History of European Socialism* (Yale, New Haven, 1983). G.D.H. Cole's five-volume *A History of Socialist Thought* (Macmillan, London, 1953–60) remains an indispensable survey. D. Caute, *The Left in Europe Since 1789* (Weidenfeld, London, 1966) is an excellent popular illustrated history of ideas and movements. D. Sassoon, *One Hundred Years of Socialism* (I.B. Tauris, London, 1996) is a magisterial history of West European socialist parties and their ideological development. Anthologies provide an easy access to some of the key texts. Useful ones are I. Howe (ed.), *A Handbook of Socialist Thought* (Gollancz, London, 1972), A. Fried and R. Sanders (eds), *Socialist Thought: A Documentary History* (Edinburgh University Press, Edinburgh, 1964) and A. Wright, *British Socialism: Socialist Thought from the 1880s to 1960s* (Longman, London, 1983).

The 'revisionist' controversy within German social democracy is a critical moment. Bernstein's *Evolutionary Socialism* (1899) is the key English text (Schocken, New York, 1961), but the arguments can be followed in detail in H. and J.M. Tudor (eds), *Marxism and Social Democracy: The Revisionist Debate 1896–1898* (Cambridge University Press, Cambridge, 1988). P. Gay, *The Dilemma of Democratic Socialism: Eduard Bernstein's Challenge to Marx* (Columbia University Press, New York, 1952) remains an important commentary. Important texts for the study of British socialism include the original *Fabian Essays* (1889), R.H. Tawney, *Equality* (Allen and Unwin, London, 1931), G.D.H. Cole, *Self-Government in Industry* (Bell, London, 1917), C.A.R. Crosland, *The Future of Socialism* (Cape, London, 1956) and D. Marquand, *The Unprincipled Society* (Cape, London, 1988). The outstanding study of Swedish socialism is T. Tilton, *The Political Theory of Swedish Social Democracy* (Oxford University Press, Oxford, 1991). Useful studies of other countries include W.L. Guttsman, *The German Social Democratic Party, 1875–1933: Ghetto to Government* (Allen and Unwin, London, 1981), S. Miller and H. Ponhof, *A History of German Social Democracy* (Berg, Oxford, 1986), R. Fletcher (ed.), *Bernstein to Brandt* (Edward Arnold, London, 1987), D. Bell and B. Criddle, *The French Socialist Party* (2nd edn, Oxford University Press, Oxford, 1988), T. Gallagher and A. Williams, *Southern European Socialism* (Manchester University Press, Manchester, 1989).

The relationship between social democratic thought and practice is variously explored in G. Esping-Andersen, *Politics Against Markets: The Social Democratic Road to Power* (Princeton University Press, Princeton, 1985), A. Przeworski and J. Sprague, *Paper Stones: A History of Electoral Socialism* (Cambridge University Press, New York, 1986) and F. Scharpf, *Crisis and Choice in European Social Democracy* (Cornell University Press, Ithaca, 1991). Good sources for wide-ranging discussion of recent social democratic politics (and ideological developments) are W. Paterson and A. Thomas (eds), *The Future of Social Democracy* (Oxford University Press, Oxford, 1986) and S. Padgett and W. Paterson, *A History of Social Democracy in Postwar Europe* (Longman, London, 1991). P. Beilharz, *Labour's Utopias: Bolshevism, Fabianism and Social Democracy* (Routledge, London, 1991) discusses social democratic ideology and has a good bibliography. Other works in the 1980s/1990s include A. Nove, *The Economics of Feasible Socialism* (Allen and Unwin, London, 1983), J. Dunn, *The Politics of Socialism* (Cambridge University Press, Cambridge, 1984), M. Rustin, *For a Pluralist Socialism* (Verso, London, 1985), P. Hirst, *Law, Socialism and Democracy* (Allen and Unwin, London, 1986), N. Bobbio, *Which Socialism?* (Polity Press, Cambridge, 1988), M. Harrington, *Socialism: Past and Future* (Arcade, New York, 1989), J. Le Grand and S. Estrin (eds), *Market Socialism* (Oxford University Press, Oxford, 1989), B. Hindess (ed.) *Reactions to the Right* (Routledge, London, 1990), A. Giddens, *Beyond Left and Right* (Polity Press, Cambridge, 1994), D. Miliband (ed.), *Reinventing the Left* (Polity Press, Cambridge, 1994), J. Gray, *After Social Democracy* (Demos, London, 1996), D. Marquand, 'After Socialism', in his *The New Reckoning* (Polity Press, Cambridge, 1997).

5
MARXISM AND COMMUNISM
Joseph V. Femia

——

Marxism and communism almost defy definition. It might be said that Marxism is the theory and communism the practice – or else that both are perplexing mixtures of theory and practice. There is no easy way to dispel the uncertainty and confusion, for Marxist/communist ideologists have been many and various. Examining their collective output is akin to entering the Tower of Babel. Yet, like Christian theologians, they have always sought to square their thoughts with the sacred texts that originally defined their creed. In order, therefore, to impose order on a vast and sprawling topic, let us begin at the beginning.

THE FOUNDER

Karl Marx (1818–83) left an ambiguous legacy – a permanent source of conflict amongst his ideological descendants. We may distinguish two principal, and possibly contradictory, motifs in his thought. The first, the romantic or moralistic motif, condemns capitalism for its destruction of human creativity and for its dissolution of 'organic' ties and loyalties. These objections are epitomized in Marx's famous and multifaceted concept of 'alienation', which, for all its complexity, can be reduced to one simple idea; that in all spheres of life human beings have forfeited what is essential to their nature – to be in control of their activities – to 'external' forces of their own making: vengeful gods, pitiless economic 'laws', repressive and fraudulent states. The subjugation of the collectivity to its own products also entails the mutual isolation of individuals. 'Man', having alienated himself from his creative essence, loses all sense of what it means to be human. Spiritual values disappear as social relations are transformed into purely instrumental or contractual relations. Legal fictions provide a veneer of civility to what is little more than the law of the (capitalist) jungle.

Marx inherited his notion of alienation from Hegel (1770–1831), the German idealist philosopher, for whom history was the progressive unfolding of the collective human spirit or mind, searching for reconciliation with itself and with the world. This goal is achieved when mind/spirit, after passing through the travails of history, finally comes to understand the world as an exteriorization of itself, thus divesting reality of its objective, hostile character. Alienation therefore ceases as 'man', abstractly conceived, assimilates and ratifies the world as his own truth.

According to Marx, Hegel asked the right questions but arrived at the wrong answers. For he mistakenly assumed that human existence is centred in the head, thereby reducing history to a process of thought. Marx instead focused on 'earthly reality'. In his estimation, man is a practical being whose thought processes are governed by material needs: if he feels his life to be empty and meaningless, the origins of his distress must be sought in objective reality rather than in any false conceptions he might have about his existential condition. The transcendence of alienation is brought about by communism – the goal of history, a total transformation of human existence, the recovery by man of his natural 'essence'. Communism does away with private property in the means of production, as well as all the evils that flow from it: religion, crime, inequality, class conflict and state repression. Men and women, living under a system of communal property, will no longer feel estranged from their fellow citizens or from anonymous sources of power. Voluntary solidarity, not compulsion, will ensure the smooth harmony of social relations. But this collective liberation will not mean the destruction of individuality – on the contrary. Hitherto repressed individuals, treated as mere objects in the capitalist order, will be encouraged to realize their full creative potential.

The ideas outlined above were all advanced in Marx's early writings, in particular the *Paris Manuscripts* of 1844, which remained unpublished until the 1930s. Before long, however, he developed the second motif in his *oeuvre*, that of scientific determinism. Marx often spoke of the 'laws' of social life, operating in the same way as the laws of nature. By this he meant that they impose themselves on people with the same inexorable necessity as an earthquake or a typhoon. It is for objective scientific thought to study these laws as a naturalist does, without sentiment or prejudice. In Marx's well-known words, 'Marxism does not preach morality at all'. The normative concepts of alienation, freedom and self-realization faded from view as Marx increasingly portrayed himself as a scientific analyst of socio-historical processes, 'working with iron necessity towards inevitable results'. While he never repudiated his early ideas in so many words, and while a case can be made for the thesis that these ideas remained implicit in his later works, the

humanistic concerns of his youth sit uneasily alongside the kind of determinism that sees individuals as 'personifications of economic categories' and
historical evolution 'as a process of natural history'.[1]

Marx's explanation of social change and development accorded privilege
to the economic factor over other factors. 'In direct contrast to German
philosophy,' we are told, 'here one ascends from earth to heaven.'[2] That is to
say, mankind's struggle to master nature and satisfy our ever developing
material needs is somehow more 'real' than our mental activity. Specifically,
Marx gave prime importance to the forces of production (the tools and
instruments) and the relations of production (the way in which human beings
organize themselves in order to use the productive forces). For him, in all
societies where the productive forces, or means of production, are owned by
a minority, the relations of production are exploitative, as the majority will
be forced to work for subsistence pay, while the parasitic minority uses its
economic power to appropriate the surplus. Classes are therefore defined
with reference to ownership (capitalists, feudal lords) or non-ownership
(industrial proletarians, serfs) of the means of production. According to the
theory, the expansion of the productive forces determines society's relations
of production (e.g. 'The windmill gives you society with the feudal lord; the
steam mill, society with the industrial capitalist'[3]), since human beings will
always, in the long run, change their way of producing to facilitate the
efficient functioning and continued advance of their productive power. The
relations of production, though, do influence the pace and direction of
economic development. They also comprise the 'real foundation' of society,
'on which rise legal and political superstructures and to which correspond
definite forms of social consciousness'. Systems of law, political institutions
and policies – these merely serve to perpetuate existing class relations.
Likewise, the general consciousness of society – its ideas, its values – will be
shaped by the nature of its production: 'It is not the consciousness of men
that determines their existence, but, on the contrary, their social existence
determines their consciousness.'[4] Hence there are no universal or trans-
historical truths; so-called, truths, no less than 'legal and political
superstructures', are relative to particular forms of economic interaction.

It can be seen that, in Marx's scheme, nothing is permanent. As society's
productive forces develop, they clash with existing production, or property,
relations, which now fetter their growth. 'Then comes the period of social
revolution',[5] as this 'contradiction' (to use the Marxist jargon) engenders a
class war between those who want to preserve the old relations and those
who seek a new order. This conflict is resolved in favour of progress, as new
relations of production emerge which better accommodate the continued
development of society's material capacity. Appropriate legal and political
relationships, together with corresponding forms of consciousness, then
establish themselves in response to the changed material situation. Essential
to the theory is the idea that progressive economic systems eventually (and
inevitably) become regressive and fall by the wayside. Capitalism for exam-

ple, raised society to a productive level undreamt of in past ages. Now, however, this highly developed form of commodity production and exchange is beset by 'internal contradictions' that make it a barrier to the efficient employment of society's productive capabilities.

The main problems, says Marx, are falling profits and underconsumption. His economic analysis rests upon the labour theory of value, which holds that the ratio of exchange between commodities is proportional to the hours of labour that went to produce them. Physical labour, working upon the gift of nature, is the only source of value. Machines or tools do not create fresh value, but only transfer to the product part of the value crystallized in them – for they themselves are products of human labour. But since capitalism is founded upon the competitive search for profit, technological improvement is a major weapon of each capitalist in the battle for survival in the market, for it enables him to produce at a cheaper rate than his competitors.

This, however, only encourages other capitalists to follow suit by introducing similar technology, so that the initial capitalist's profit advantage disappears. In the meantime, each capitalist has increased his expenditure on machinery or new technology, which – unlike human labour – generates no additional value. The rate of profit on total investment therefore declines. Although this tendency can be counterbalanced by increasing productivity or exploitation (i.e. extracting even more surplus from the workers), such remedies are only temporary and cannot deal with the underlying, insoluble contradiction.

Depressed profits invariably lead to depressed wage levels, one of the main causes of 'underconsumption', a situation where the mass of workers cannot afford to purchase all the goods that a dynamic capitalist system is able to produce. The result is periodic and ever worsening 'crises of overproduction'. In Marx's estimation, capitalism can neither avoid nor forever endure these endemic crises. Eventually the proletariat, racked by poverty and reduced to either chronic unemployment or chronic insecurity, will rise up and destroy the rotten system. In Marx's memorable phrase, the bourgeoisie 'creates its own gravediggers'. Capitalism, in common with all previous 'antagonistic' forms of economic organization, succumbs to its 'internal laws of motion'. After the burial the victorious proletariat sets up a dictatorship to expropriate the expropriators and pave the way for communism.

For Marx, 'all history is the history of class struggles', but it also charts the rise and fall of economic systems. He put forward a model of historical development through five stages, or methods of production: the Asiatic, the ancient, the feudal, the bourgeois (capitalist) and, finally, the communist stage. In places, he refers to these as 'successive phases' of 'normal development' from which no society is exempt;[6] but elsewhere he suggests that certain countries may lag behind or even skip stages. Either way, he was a historical determinist, describing an inexorable process, 'independent of human will, consciousness, and intelligence'.[7] The most plausible interpretation is that Marx's proposed 'law' of evolution applied to humanity as a whole, not to individual countries, none of which was preordained to follow any particular path.

In the remainder of this chapter, we shall see how the uneasy coexistence of moralistic and scientific themes in Marx's own thinking lies behind the bewildering variety of Marxist thought in this century.

ORTHODOX MARXISM

Marx*ism*, as a systematic and comprehensive world-view, came into being after Marx's death and was the work, primarily, of three men: Friederich Engels (1820–95), Marx's close friend Karl Kautsky (1854–1938), the 'Pope' of German socialism and Georgi Plekhanov (1856–1918), the chief theoretician of the Russian Marxist movement. As a thinker, Engels was very much the leading figure and the others worked within the framework he erected. His contribution to the development of Marxism is a cause of some controversy. He collaborated with Marx on a number of works (notably the *Communist Manifesto*) and orthodox Marxists simply regarded him as Marx's loyal ally, who helped to propagate the master's ideas. But many observers detect a clear intellectual difference – Engels supposedly being more deterministic. At any rate, no one disputes the historical fact that his philosophical writings, rather than those of Marx, elaborated and systematized the distinctive *Weltanschauung* known as dialectical materialism.

An authoritative formulation of this doctrine can be found in the polemical *Anti-Dühring*, written by Engels in 1876, while his mentor was still alive. There has been much debate over whether or not Marx actually sanctioned the ideas expressed in this work. He certainly read parts of it and made some approving comments, though at the time he was quite ill. There is no doubt, however, that *Anti-Dühring* defended a form of materialism that never surfaced in his own writings.

Engels, along with Kautsky and Plekhanov, wanted to reduce all psychological facts to physical facts. In their scheme, there was no qualitative distinction between mind and matter: mind was nothing more than matter. Mental events – values, purposes, ideas, feelings – were reducible to chemical secretions within the brain, to physiological processes which, in turn, merely reflected external stimuli. On this view, the mind was a passive receptacle of sense impressions, not an active creative agent.

However, dialectical materialism is not to be confused with what Marxists called 'bourgeois' materialism, which also reduced 'mind' to 'matter'. *This* type of materialism, found in the writings of Hobbes (1588–1679) and Voltaire (1694–1778) amongst others, saw the universe as an unchanging mechanism, locked in a perpetual cycle of the same processes. All development in nature was denied. For example, the celestial bodies were stable and eternal; the planets, once set in motion, circled on and on in their predestined way for all eternity; the stars remained forever fixed and immovable in their places, and so on. But for the *dialectical* materialists, the universe was not static. Darwin had taught them that it was *dynamic* – in continuous evolution; and the driving force of this development was provided by the internal contradictions that operate in every natural process.

In other words, natural development proceeds *dialectically*, through the struggle of the mutually opposing tendencies or forces in all phenomena. The idea of an evolutionary dialectic originally came from Hegel, who believed that mind (and therefore humanity) progressed through a series of conflicts between abstract principles. Marx, aiming to turn his idealist predecessor 'right side up',[8] claimed to discover an economic 'dialectic' or clash – between forces and relations of production, between dominant and oppressed classes – that propelled history from one stage to another. It was Engels's unique contribution to locate the dialectic in the natural world. For him, the dialectical motion of matter comprehended all changes and processes in the universe, including thinking – for, to repeat, mind was viewed as nothing more than matter organized in a certain way.

Human history was therefore an extension of natural history, and the movement of social and economic life was presumed to follow laws of the same character as those of the natural sciences. If human beings are objects in nature – no more, no less – then their behaviour, just like that of a falling stone, can be accounted for by verifiable physical hypotheses. Free will is but an illusion: our actions, as much as our biological processes, are subject to physical laws. It follows that society (and history) can be described in the language of the natural sciences, in terms of mechanical causality. There was no need to consider the explanatory role of human intentions or purposes, for these were themselves objects to be explained by underlying material causes. And so the links between the different spheres of human life, as well as the progression from one historical phase to the next, were seen as matters of natural necessity, independent of human will.

In Marx's own writings, historical materialism never encompassed nature as such. The material Marx referred to was economic material, human technology. Nowhere did he argue that historical evolution obeyed *the same* laws as natural evolution. With or without his approval, Engels certainly did shift the doctrine on to a new path. Marxism, as he (and, later, Kautsky and Plekhanov) conceived it, was a cosmic synthesis which purported to explain *everything*, from the most elementary biological level right up to the level of human history. It would be superficial, however, to condemn dialectical materialism as a heretical deviation from the teachings of Marx. For, as we have seen, his thought was bedevilled by an unresolved tension between evolutionary determinism and a libertarian belief in (potential) human autonomy. This apparent inconsistency remained to plague his followers, and divide them. If Engels and like-minded thinkers developed the deterministic theme, while ignoring the other, it is because they were typical products of their scientistic era, inspired by Darwin and the advance of physics and chemistry. But the strictly causal and 'objective' interpretation of social phenomena could hardly be reconciled with Marx's humanistic aims. If, as Plekhanov maintained, we are governed by a 'necessity' that is 'irresistible and utterly invincible', if 'mind' is only another perspective on brain matter, if freedom is merely submission to natural necessity, then our liberation from objective and anonymous forces is, strictly speaking, impossible.[9]

The belief in 'iron laws' of history induced a kind of political passivity in that it always made sense to wait for the preconditions for revolution to ripen still further rather than risk all in premature revolutionary activity. Why endanger life and limb for a cause whose victory is predetermined and inevitable? For the orthodox Marxist, salvation comes not through works but through grace. Nevertheless, the consolidation of Marxism as a distinctive, all-embracing world-view coincided with a golden age of socialist politics, spanning the period from about 1890 to the outbreak of world war in 1914.

This was the era of the Second International, a loose, multinational federation of parties and trade unions, working separately though united by their belief in socialism. Despite its ideological and organizational diversity, the International seemed to be the first true embodiment of Marx's dream of a marriage between class struggle and the theoretical analysis of social processes. Although non-Marxist traditions of socialism still exerted influence (anarchism in France and Italy, utilitarianism in Great Britain – see Chapter 6), it was Marxism that stood out as the reigning creed of the movement. Throughout its existence, the Second International was dominated by German socialists, whose party (the SPD) was eventually to become the largest party in their native land. The thinking of the SPD was epitomized by the Erfurt Programme of 1891.

This document, drafted by Kautsky and Eduard Bernstein (1850–1932) (later to become the leading revisionist critic of Marxist orthodoxy), came to be seen as a classic but accessible statement of scientific socialism. Reaffirming all the theoretical points made by Marx in his master-work, *Capital*, it dwelt upon the self-destructive nature of capitalism and looked forward to the socialization of the means of production. In Kautsky's memorable words: 'Irresistible economic forces lead with the certainty of doom to the shipwreck of capitalist production.'[10] The final victory of the proletariat was guaranteed. A second section set out immediate, practical objectives: universal suffrage, secret ballot, proportional representation, free education, equal rights for women, free medical care, eight-hour working day, etc. But no explicitly revolutionary plan of action was put forward; the programme conveyed the impression that socialism would simply emerge, as if it were an organic product of the parliamentary struggle for limited reforms.

Taken as a whole, the Erfurt Programme combined doctrinal intransigence with tactical/strategic caution, and this peculiar combination came to be the hallmark of the Second International. It also appeared to be a recipe for success, given the remarkable electoral gains of the SPD. But the discrepancy between theory and practice was too glaring to be ignored. Kautsky, for his part, dealt with the problem by ostentatiously pretending that it did not exist. Contrary to appearances, he claimed, parliamentary democracy was not *inherently* an instrument of the capitalist class; its procedures and institutions could be used by the proletariat for socialist purposes. This was of dubious orthodoxy. Marx certainly admitted the *possibility* of revolution through the ballot box, but Kautsky elevated this approach to an article of faith. It is also unlikely that Marx envisaged, as did Kautsky, a permanent place for parliamentary democracy in the socialist future. Though never dwelling on the subject, Marx plainly saw communism as a radically new mode of social organization, free of bureaucrats and professional politicians, devoid of all distinctions between rulers and ruled. To scientific Marxists of Kautsky's ilk, this splendid vision smacked of Utopianism.

Kautsky came under fire from two directions. From the right, Bernstein (by 1899) argued that his colleague had not gone far enough in revising Marx's ideas. It was impossible to defend, at one and the same time, both class war *and* liberal democratic values. In fact, *all* of Marx's doctrines had been rendered obsolete by economic developments: capitalism was *not* lurching from crisis to crisis, class polarization was *not* occurring, living standards were *not* declining, the middle classes were *not* disappearing. Marx's economic analysis, no less than his political prescriptions, had to be jettisoned. From the left, however, thinkers like Rosa Luxemburg (1871–1919) and V.I. Lenin (1870–1924) maintained that the only way to close the gap between theory and practice was to change the practice, to abandon the commitment to electoral politics. For Luxemburg 'parliamentary cretinism' had only served to dampen the naturally revolutionary instincts of the proletariat. Parliaments were mere 'talking shops'. If bourgeois democracy ever became a threat to the ruling classes, they would order their agents in the army and police to overthrow said democracy. Instead of urging workers to vote or join trade unions or read turgid pamphlets, Marxist activists should encourage them to rise up against their oppressors. Revolution will come not through the ballot box but through mass action – strikes, riots, factory takeovers, etc.

While Lenin was equally hostile to 'parliamentary cretinism', he did not share Rosa's faith in the spontaneous revolutionary inclinations of the workers. In his famous work entitled *What Is To Be Done?*, published in 1902, he advanced a ground-breaking theory of revolution, which possessed three key features: (i) that the working class, exclusively by its own efforts, could develop only 'trade union consciousness' – essentially a form of bourgeois consciousness, for (in defining the workers as a commodity) it could not transcend the logic of the present system; (ii) that socialist consciousness, being alien to the everyday experience of the proletariat, must be developed by bourgeois intellectuals and then brought, like a gift, to the benighted masses; and (iii) that the party should not be *of* the working class but *for* the working class, a self-appointed vanguard drawn from all social backgrounds and subject to the disciplined control of a party centre. This conception of 'revolution from above', deemed heretical at the time, was later accepted as gospel by the world-wide communist movement.

In their different ways, Lenin and Luxemburg understood that parliamentary electioneering could insidiously lead a revolutionary party to accept the 'rules of the game' and renounce, or at least forget, the ultimate goal. The day-to-day pressure of attracting votes could easily become an end in itself, resulting in a dilution of revolutionary energy and a fixation on organizational imperatives. Both Lenin and Luxemburg accused their more orthodox opponents of betraying the movement, but the former, a less doctrinaire thinker, was willing to concede that the 'traitors' were burdened by shortcomings in the classical Marxist analysis.

In this connection, he developed his theory of imperialism after the outbreak of the First World War. The theory was basically a mixture of ideas culled from other Marxists – especially Rudolf Hilferding (1877–1941) – but the result was both innovative and influential. Imperialism, to Lenin, referred to developments *within* capitalism, as well as to relations between advanced and backward countries. It was another name for the final stage of capitalism – a stage characterized by (i) the growth of monopolies, (ii) the increasing control of financial institutions over industry, (iii) the export of capital to underdeveloped parts of the globe, in order to exploit cheap labour and raw materials, and (iv) direct or indirect (neo-colonial) political control of less developed countries by the capitalist powers. Lenin admitted that exploitation of backward areas brought super-profits to the big cartels, which enabled them to counteract the internal contradictions of capitalism and to 'buy off' an aristocracy of skilled labour at home. Yet the mad scramble for overseas territories was bound to cause international tension and (eventually) war. Moreover, by becoming parasitic upon colonial and neo-colonial exploitation, capitalism had universalized its own contradictions, generating conflict between foreign capital and native labour. Since modern capitalism was like a global chain, tethering diverse peoples and cultures to a monstrous system, it was now possible to attack it at its weakest links – Russia, for example. The implication – which later became a sacred Marxist truth – was that the collapse of the capitalist world system would begin in backward countries, whose liberation struggles would then spark off revolution in the war-weary West. This meant, *pace* people like Plekhanov, that it was possible to leap over stages of 'normal' historical evolution in those countries where the strains endemic to capitalism were exaggerated by under, or uneven, development.

The success of the Bolshevik Revolution in 1917 appeared to sound the death knell for the brand of orthodoxy espoused by the Kautskys and Plekhanovs of the movement. Lenin, unwilling to be bound by rigid (and often misleading) interpretations of Marx's message, demonstrated that Marxism could adapt to circumstances without losing sight of its revolutionary objectives. By 1919, he had set up a Third (Communist) International, committed to his own views on world revolution. Yet, despite his modifications to the theory of historical materialism, he never questioned the deep philosophical assumptions of orthodox Marxism. On this score, the challenge came from the so-called 'Hegelian Marxists', the most prominent of whom were Georg Lukács and Antonio Gramsci.

HEGELIAN MARXISM

Hegel must not be treated as a 'dead dog', but even so we must demolish the 'dead' architecture of the system in its historical form and release the extremely relevant and modern sides of his thought and help them once again become a vital and effective force in the present.

G. Lukács.[11]

Writing in the aftermath of the Russian Revolution, both Lukács and Gramsci concluded that the realization of Marxism's revolutionary 'essence' required abandonment of the fatalistic determinism that had encouraged Marxists to view socialism as manna from heaven or, more accurately, 'history', in no way dependent on free human choice. The attack on this 'passive' Marxism involved a rediscovery of Hegelian idealism, with its emphasis on consciousness or subjectivity. But neither Gramsci nor Lukács wanted to repeat the Hegelian error of interpreting human action solely in terms of mind or spirit. For them, the great contribution of Marx's philosophy lay in its perfect fusion of human creativity and socio-economic materiality. Though men and women operate within structurally determined limits, they retain a capacity for autonomy.

Lukács (1885–1971) and Gramsci (1891–1937) were almost exact contemporaries, but the former was the first to make a philosophical impact, with the publication of *History and Class Consciousness* in 1921. At this time Gramsci was an active politician in his native Italy. His philosophical themes were not really developed until the early 1930s, when – surveying the world from a Fascist prison cell – he composed his *Prison Notebooks*, which remained unpublished until after the war. Lukács, for all his acclaimed philosophical sophistication, also had political pretensions and actually became Commissar of Education during the ill-fated Hungarian Soviet Republic of 1919. Like Gramsci he was influenced by the general revival of idealist philosophy in the early years of this century, and by the consequences of Einstein's theory of relativity, which threw doubt upon the principle of scientific objectivity, the cornerstone of orthodox Marxism.

Given their shared stress on 'man the creator', the acting subject, both thinkers rejected naturalistic materialism. 'Man' was not simply an object in nature; nor – on their reading – did Marx ever conceive him as such. Marx's materialism did predicate the priority of 'being' over 'thought', but 'being' was, in his view, not synonymous with matter. Rather, 'being' referred to the productive organization of society, which, needless to say, embodied human subjectivity. Gramsci and Lukács therefore thought it erroneous to interpret Marxism as a precise science, discovering immutable laws similar to those of the natural world. Concepts or techniques derived from physics or chemistry had no place in social/historical analysis. To pretend otherwise was not only false; it was a form of culpable self-deception, by means of which Marxists evaded their historical responsibilities. One cannot forecast revolution in the way that one forecasts the weather, as if human intervention were irrelevant. Accordingly, both thinkers saw consciousness, not material developments, as decisive in history. The 'vulgar materialists', with their one-way causal sequences, with their tendency to move directly from economic cause to political or cultural effect, were, once again, distorting Marx's intentions. Gramsci and Lukács alike, in keeping with their emphasis on human creativity, saw Marxism as a humanistic philosophy, aiming for a cultural renaissance where freedom and self-development would be the birthright of all. Man could never achieve this noble status if he were encouraged to view himself as a passive plaything of material forces.

Notwithstanding these shared ideas, the two great proponents of Hegelian Marxism differed in crucial respects. Lukács, while rejecting mechanical determinism, did not see the future as open-ended. For he followed Hegel in arguing that history manifested an 'inner logic' which would propel the human race towards its 'essential', predetermined goal of (for Lukács) the victory of communism. Because of the intrinsic needs and propensities of the human spirit, history was fated to have a happy ending. Gramsci, in contrast, rejected Hegelian teleology and denied that all events – past, present and future – fit into some foreordained pattern. The social world, according to him, was a fluid process, characterized by infinite variety and multiplicity. History possessed no inherent meaning, immanent in human nature, and nothing was guaranteed.

Another difference between Gramsci and Lukács concerned their vision of the future society. In common with the orthodox Marxists, the Italian was a 'productivist', who wanted to order the factors of production in accordance with the principle of optimality, where this meant the rationalization and mechanization of the productive process. He had no opportunity to read Marx's (posthumously published) *Manuscripts* of 1844, and some of the ideas expressed there might have struck him as unacceptably heterodox. For he never used the language of 'alienation' or 'human essence', language he associated with conventional idealism, and he therefore focused on improved industrial output as the key to human emancipation. Self-expression at the workplace would be achieved through democratic participation, not through a transformation or 'humanization' of bourgeois productive techniques.

On this issue, he and Lukács could not have disagreed more. The latter's hostility to the capitalist labour process and its detrimental effects on the wider society is summed up in his concept of 'reification', whose similarity to Marx's doctrine of alienation is remarkable, given that the 1844 *Manuscripts* did not become available until a decade after the publication of *History and Class Consciousness*. Put simply, 'reification' denotes a process whereby men and women become passive spectators of the social forces that structure their lives. The origins of this passivity lie in capitalism's dehumanization of the worker, who is reduced to a marketable commodity, a 'thing', to be bought in the market, just like any other instrument of production or consumption. Since, in the quest for profit, technical efficiency is all that matters, work is fragmented in order to achieve maximum output. Workers are consequently confined to narrow, repetitive tasks, which transform them from spiritual beings, with individual talents and ideas, to mere appendages of the productive machine, robbed of initiative and geared to the maximization of profit. Eventually, the principles of factory organization spread to other spheres of life: the factory becomes a microcosm of the whole structure of capitalist society. All aspects of social interaction are specialized, standardized and subsumed under formal, calculable rules. In every domain, human beings are spiritually crippled, confined to a narrow range of skills and subjected to the deadening effects of instrumental rationality. The quality of imagination gradually disappears as everyone, not just manual workers, sinks into a state of mechanical passivity. The world around us – the product of our own creativity – comes to be experienced as alien and hostile, a system of independent 'things', ruling us through apparently unbreakable laws. Capitalism thus persists because it (temporarily) succeeds in subduing the essential humanity of those who might oppose it.

Gramsci's explanation for the persistence of a system so rife with internal contradictions was rather different. For him, Marx's epigones, by reducing thought to a 'reflex' of the productive process, had underestimated the power of myths and ideas. It was common for Marxists (Lukács excepted) to assume that bourgeois society was held together by pure force, or at least the threat of it. Even the Hungarian, by pinpointing the passivity of the masses, denied that they might *actively embrace* bourgeois ideology. According to Gramsci, however, the cohesion of the modem capitalist order stemmed primarily from the 'hegemony', the spiritual and cultural supremacy, of the ruling classes, who – through manipulation of the mechanisms of socialization, such as the media, the churches, the schools – had managed to foist their own values and beliefs on an unsuspecting populace. In such a setting, revolution *presupposed* a transformation of mass consciousness, effected through a protracted 'battle of ideas', or 'war of position' (Gramsci was fond of military metaphors). With its stress on gradual subversion, on persuasion and consent, his proposed strategy undoubtedly differed from the straightforward insurrectionary approach advocated by Lenin. To Gramsci, this approach would only work in backward societies, where consent counted for little. Yet he opposed the 'parliamentary road' to socialism, and saw the 'war of position' as a prelude to, rather than a substitute for, a paramilitary assault on the state. His novel analysis and prescriptions struck a responsive chord in the 1960s and 1970s, when the traditional communist shibboleths no longer seemed to make contact with reality. Depressed by the bureaucratic degeneration of Soviet communism, and by the stubborn refusal of Western workers to see the light, many Marxists exalted Gramsci as a prophet of 'alternative' communism.

MARXISM IN PRACTICE

> (T)he course taken by history holds nasty surprises, and is ruled ... not so much by the cunning of reason which guarantees that bad causes have a good outcome, as by the malice of unreason which perverts even the most well-intentioned acts.
>
> Norberto Bobbio.[12]

Since Marxists are communists, in the sense that they envisage an ideal future of communal bliss, the revolutionary regimes installed in Russia and elsewhere came to be known as 'communist' regimes – even though communism, strictly speaking, was their long-term goal, not a description of actual reality. Thus communism, in conventional parlance, usually refers to the institutionalization of Marxism – or the Leninist variant thereof – as an instrument of despotic power. The gap between communism (in practice) and communism (Marx's splendid vision of universal emancipation) is/was so great as to move many Marxists to absolve Marx from any responsibility for the former. They point out that all 'communist' revolutions occurred in countries that had no traditions of tolerance or participation or political liberty. These lands, moreover, were economically underdeveloped and therefore unprepared for a genuinely proletarian revolution of the kind forecast by Marx, a revolution carried out by literate industrial workers, who would constitute the 'immense majority' of society, a revolution designed to spread *existing* wealth, not to modernize a primitive productive base. Many orthodox Marxists, we are reminded, warned Lenin about the dangers of a premature revolution in what later became the USSR. In addition, they predicted that his élitist approach – which assumed that the Marxist intelligentsia understood the interests of the workers better than the workers themselves – would lead to dictatorship *over* the proletariat, not *of* the proletariat.

While all this is true, it is also the case that Marx's vague generalities about the proletarian revolution and the ensuing dictatorship provided little ground for specific political conclusions. The most contradictory aims could be and were deduced with equal logic from the same theoretical formulations. If, as Marx said, history followed a 'normal' sequence of stages, did this mean that Russia itself had to pass through the phase of advanced capitalism or was it enough for global capitalism to do so? And when Marx referred to communists as 'the most advanced and resolute section of the working class', who – unlike 'the great mass of the proletariat' – have 'the advantage of clearly understanding the line of march, the conditions, and the ultimate general results of the proletarian movement', was he attempting to justify 'revolution from above' or was he simply extolling the merits of his own historical analysis?[13]

To be fair to Lenin and later 'communists', the distinction Marx drew between his own ideas (scientific truth) and those of his opponents (bourgeois distortion) was hardly indicative of a democratic mentality. Likewise, his economic reductionism might be said to have laid the theoretical groundwork for the repressive excesses of the Bolshevik and other communist regimes. If law is nothing but the instrument whereby one class oppresses another, there is clearly no essential difference between the rule of law and rule by direct compulsion; all that matters is which class has the upper hand. Similarly, if Marxism exposes the falseness of universalistic moral claims, then Lenin might be excused for concluding that everything which serves or injures Soviet rule is 'morally' good or bad respectively. He assumed that the end justified the means, and Marx himself offered no reason to assume otherwise.

Lenin, it can be argued, was Marx *in actu*. When the Bolshevik hero terrorized opposition parties (even socialist parties, like the Mensheviks and the Social Revolutionaries), when he suppressed the autonomy of the universities, when he extinguished press freedom (a 'bourgeois deceit'), when he deprived vast swathes of the population of their right to vote, when he expelled intellectuals and introduced purges in every walk of life – when he carried out all these harsh policies, he thought he was removing obstacles to the future communist paradise.

Lenin's notorious successor, Josef Stalin (1879–1953), using the repressive machinery Lenin had bequeathed, took these policies to absurd and pathological extremes: the massacre of perhaps millions of peasants, the liquidation of thousands of party officials suspected of disloyalty, the vilification and eventual murder of many eminent Bolsheviks, including Leon Trotsky (1879–1940), one of the revolution's chief architects. Though Lenin, who died in 1924, would probably have condemned these terrible deeds, they could all be plausibly justified in terms of some dictum or principle enunciated in his speeches and writings. It is doubtful, however, whether Stalin actually believed in the communist goal. In his regime, brutality was exacerbated by cynicism and a bizarre campaign of falsification where white would become black or vice versa according to the mood of the infallible leader. In this unreal world, universal fiction took on the guise of truth. Show-trial defendants, not to mention lesser victims of Stalin's mass purges, were invariably forced to confess to imaginary 'crimes' before being executed. History was constantly rewritten, eliminating inconvenient personalities and events as if by magic. General elections were (literally) staged, so that the Communist Party could confidently expect 99 per cent support from the 'electorate'. The strengthening of state power was hailed as 'dialectical' proof that the state was in fact withering away, since life is 'full of contradictions'.

Grotesque though his tyranny was, Stalin was careful to give it a spurious scientific justification. He not only ignored but actively suppressed Marx's humanistic themes and writings. Doctrine was absolutely subordinated to the purpose of legitimizing and glorifying the regime. Whereas Hegelian Marxists stressed 'man the creator', what Stalin christened 'Marxism-Leninism' interpreted man as the helpless victim of uncontrollable social forces. Strict determinism suited the aims of the supreme leader. Since choices, alternatives, the whole panoply of mental freedom, were dismissed as childish fictions, Stalin could present himself as an instrument of the historical dialectic, entrusted with the regrettable but necessary task of eliminating whoever or whatever blocked the path of scientific progress. And since human beings, like all phenomena, were seen as nothing but matter in motion, it was possible to treat human material as one would treat, say, trees – as objects to be manipulated and consumed in the course of social development.

Nevertheless, Stalin sometimes found it opportune to set aside the canons of dialectical materialism. For example, once his revolutionary changes (e.g. collectivization of agriculture) and personal rule were established beyond question, Soviet historians were forced to acknowledge the crucial role of 'great' individuals like himself, to whom the anonymous masses owed a tremendous debt of gratitude. The exaltation of heroes was hardly compatible with historical determinism. Nor was it easy to reconcile official doctrine with the moralistic language used to describe purge victims: 'insects', 'fiends', 'traitorous hirelings', 'dregs of humanity'. But Stalin remained untroubled by contradictions in his thinking or pronouncements. To him, the needs of the regime, as he perceived them at any given time, transcended the rules of 'bourgeois logic'.

Stalin's reign of terror came to an end with his death in 1953. Three years later, the new leader of the Soviet Union, Nikita Khrushchev, denounced Stalin's crimes before the Twentieth Party Congress. From that point on, communist leaders in the USSR and the East European satellite states (with the possible exception of Romania) tried to avoid the worst excesses of Stalinism: the 'cult of personality' and overt terror as a weapon of social control.

Asian communism, which still manages to survive, by and large rejected this moderate path. The short-lived Pol Pot regime in Cambodia during the mid-1970s actually managed to out-Stalin Stalin in its campaign of mass murder. But from a historical point of view, the People's Republic of China, especially during the years of Mao Zedong (1893–1976), was (and remains) much more significant. Here party dictatorship and an exaggerated cult of personality were reinforced by Confucianism, a body of doctrine deeply embedded in Chinese tradition and drawn from the teachings of Confucius, the ancient philosopher, who stressed order, hierarchy, and rule by a learned élite, the Mandarins. The communists became the new Mandarins, so to speak.

On the theoretical level, Mao made three amendments to Marxism-Leninism. First, he played down the importance of the urban proletariat, claiming that revolution – at least in countries like China that were victims of Western imperialism – would begin in the countryside and be spearheaded by the peasantry. A second significant amendment was to place 'consciousness' or political 'will' above material or objective conditions. The third distinctive contribution was Mao's extension of the concept of class to cover the concept of nation. Building on Lenin's theory of imperialism, he denied that revolution in China was a purely internal struggle. China was a poor and oppressed 'proletarian' nation that needed to throw off the yoke of the wealthy 'bourgeois' oppressor nations. The class struggle was shifted to an international plane: nations became its protagonists.

By the mid-1960s, Mao's cult of personality was building towards a disastrous conclusion: the so-called Cultural Revolution. As Mao thought that China was increasingly dominated by experts whose commitment to ideological purity was suspect, he called for a 'revolution' against those who were technically qualified. Workers were encouraged to humiliate managers and engineers, and students to humble their professors. Many thousands of educated people were killed or imprisoned or removed from their posts and sent to work in the fields. When industrial and agricultural production fell drastically, Mao finally agreed to call in the army to restore order. But the damage was done. His power diminished; and, after his death in 1976, the radicals were officially discredited. Since then China has reintroduced some features of a free-market economy and now enjoys a fair degree of prosperity. Some steps towards freedom of expression were taken, but progress was abruptly halted when tanks crushed the Tiananmen Square rebellion in June 1989.

The fate of Asian communism remains unclear. It appears that the existing structure can be maintained only through simultaneous doses of political repression and market economics – an unstable combination at best. Mikhail Gorbachev's failed efforts to revivify communism by means of *glasnost* (openness) and *perestroika* (restructuring) do not bode well for surviving communist states. It is hard to resist the conclusion that one can retreat only so far from Stalinism without undermining the communist system itself. Let us now, after our brief historical survey, set out the essential features of this system.

The first is the merger of party and state, so that loyalty to one entails loyalty to the other. Only the Communist Party is allowed to exercise power, and that party is itself hierarchically organized, with authority flowing from the top downwards. The party, moreover, permeates every nook and cranny of the state apparatus, and advancement in the latter normally depends on party membership.

The second essential feature of the system – obviously related to the first – is its totalitarian ambition to harness all national energies in the pursuit of goals embodied in the official doctrine and defined by the party-state. An ideological impetus for total control distinguishes communism from the old-style authoritarianism of, say, Louis XIV of France. On the totalitarian conception, the party-state is not only absolute in its exercise of power, but also unlimited in its field of operations. Nothing lies outside its scope: industry, family life, education at every level, the press and other forms of communication, trade unions along with other voluntary associations – all must submit to political direction. No area of privacy remains that an individual can call his or her own. Marx himself was a fierce collectivist who wished to see an end to the liberal distinction between 'public' and 'private', and his communist disciples interpreted this as a justification for silencing dissenters and discouraging independent thought.

Finally, the communist model involves public ownership of the means of production (though in practice, all communist regimes, save Albania and Cambodia, have allowed varying degrees of private enterprise, particularly in agriculture) as well as all-embracing central planning of economic activity (though, again, market mechanisms, at least on the margins of production, have always been tolerated to a certain extent).

The communist or (more accurately) Soviet model was openly challenged in the 1970s by the largest Western European communist parties – those of Italy, Spain and France – which felt that neither violent insurrection nor single-party dictatorship could attract sufficient support in a democratic political arena. So-called 'Eurocommunism' harked back to Kautsky's 'parliamentary path' and Gramsci's 'war of position', but its immediate progenitor was Palmiro Togliatti (1893–1964), the Italian communist leader who speculated about 'polycentrism' in the late 1950s and early 1960s. In opposition to the old Stalinist (and indeed Trotskyist) line, he argued that roads to socialism must correspond to the conditions and circumstances specific to each country. In advanced capitalist countries, it was necessary to recruit adherents from non-proletarian social strata – peasants, intellectuals, professionals, civil servants, even small businessmen – who might have cause to dislike monopoly cap-italism. Also, alliances should be sought with Catholic and other parties in pursuit of structural reforms. All this required ideological and tactical flex-ibility on the part of the communist party. Eventually a socialist hegemony (in Gramsci's sense) would develop, and society could be radically transformed through peaceful, constitutional means. Change would be evolutionary, not revolutionary. And since bourgeois power structures could be dismantled through existing state institutions, there would be no need to destroy these liberal institutions. Suitably reformed, they could remain as integral com-ponents of the socialist future.

While Togliatti was always guarded in his criticisms of the Soviet Union, his ideological offspring were more forthright. Santiago Carrillo (1915–) and Enrico Berlinguer (1922–84), the two most important spokesmen for Eurocommunism, openly attacked Soviet 'monism' and embraced Western 'pluralism'.[14] Abandoning even the pretence of Leninist rhetoric, these supposed Marxists portrayed themselves as champions of human rights and multiparty politics. As for the vanguard theory of the party, it was dismissed as an embarrassing relic of the past. Still more surprising, free enterprise was no longer viewed as a plague to be banished from the planet; so long as the 'commanding heights' of the economy were nationalized, small businesses and worker co-operatives could be allowed to survive and thrive.

In domestic politics, Eurocommunist parties increasingly identified themselves with the governing process, becoming serious contenders for parliamentary power through electoral competition. True to Togliatti's legacy, they sought alliances or common platforms with non-Marxist socialist parties, from which, however, they took pains to distinguish themselves. These efforts at coalition-building were generally unfruitful; although when President Mitterrand appointed his first government in 1981, four minor posts went to communists.

In Italy, where Eurocommunism enjoyed its greatest electoral success, Berlinguer's party, in 1977, actually signed a formal parliamentary accord with the coalition government led by the Christian Democrats. Bursting with confidence after winning a third of the popular vote in the general election of the previous year, the communists showed their 'responsibility' by agreeing to support austerity and public order measures. Indeed, the party joined the parliamentary majority, though not the cabinet, and kept up this anomalous stance until 1979.

But the willingness of Italian and French communists to prop up non-Marxist governments did not succeed in attracting new voters to the cause. Support for Eurocommunism declined throughout the 1980s, and the fall of communism in Eastern Europe and the USSR was a devastating blow to all those with the temerity to call themselves 'communists', Euro or otherwise. The great majority of Italian communists, having rechristened themselves as the 'Party of the Democratic Left', no longer even pretend to be Marxist revolutionaries. A breakaway group, still loyal to the old Leninist pieties, formed a separate party but managed to attract only 6 per cent of the vote in the 1996 general election.

In retrospect, the Eurocommunist model represented not the regeneration of communism but its last dying gasp. It was impossible, in the end, to save communism by taming it. If people wanted a liberal brand of socialism, they could turn to the reformist or social democratic parties, which did not suffer from any Leninist stigma. Hampered by its Kremlin ancestry, and bereft of a *raison d'être*, Eurocommunism became an irrelevance. In former East Germany and elsewhere, ex-communist parties have in the late 1990s shown signs of revival. However, they should be seen mainly as catch-all protest parties rather than a reflection of the continuing appeal of Marxism.[15]

RECENT THEORETICAL DEVELOPMENTS

Among Western Marxists, dissatisfaction with Kremlin political orthodoxy was matched by disenchantment with its theoretical orthodoxy. Intellectual innovation was especially pronounced after the Second World War, as Marxism was forced into strange alliances with apparently antithetical philosophies, including Freudianism, existentialism and structuralism. Perhaps the most influential Western Marxist was Herbert Marcuse (1898–1979), guru of the 'New Left' and founder member – together with Max Horkheimer (1895–1973) and Theodor Adorno (1903–69) – of the Frankfurt school of 'critical theory'.

Continuing the tradition of Lukács and Gramsci, these thinkers showed little interest in the scientific claims advanced by Marx. He was, in their eyes, essentially a philosopher of human freedom, condemning the alienation of bourgeois society. Their main theme was the threat posed by technological progress and its indifference to spiritual needs. Whereas conventional Marxists condemned capitalism for producing poverty, the principal grievance of the Frankfurt theorists was that capitalism engendered abundance and satisfied a multiplicity of artificial wants. In contradistinction to orthodox Marxism, with its stress on efficient material production, Marcuse and his colleagues gave pride of place to the *quality* of life, to the liberation of our distinctively human potentialities. Furthermore, the Frankfurt thinkers believed that Marxists, focusing as they did on social and economic forces as determinants of human behaviour, tended to ignore questions of individual psychology. Borrowing from Freud's analysis while rejecting his conclusions, the Frankfurt school insisted that a distorted society produced a distorted psyche, a deeply rooted malaise, whose eradication required more than simple economic changes.

All these themes were memorably developed in Marcuse's modern classic, *One Dimensional Man*, published in 1964. The book's fundamental thesis was that modern technology, by satisfying all reasonable material desires, had removed the obvious motives for dissent or protest in advanced capitalist societies. Under the impact of sustained and expanding affluence, the working classes had been transmuted into passive, acquiescent instruments of the established order.

Marx, as Marcuse pointed out, expected a proletarian revolution because the labouring masses, in their misery, represented the absolute negation of bourgeois society. But in a world where workers own cars, houses, televisions, household appliances, etc., the standard Marxist doctrine of class conflict is inapplicable. An all-embracing consumer fetishism unites all classes: the inhabitants of the affluent society come to identify with their material possessions. They find their 'souls' in their cars, in their hi-fi equipment, not in their own qualities. The very instinctual structure of individuals is moulded to suit the requirements of the system.

It is not simply that people's *ideas* are distorted by consumerism; their *personalities* are transformed, as they become sheep-like creatures, without minds of their own. One-dimensional thought and behaviour is reinforced, according to Marcuse, by the triumph of scientific and technological rationality in all spheres of life. Such rationality reduces everything to observable and measurable quantities. Since questions of value do not admit of quantification or calculation, they are ignored or else dismissed as inconsequential. The victory of the scientific method thus spells the defeat of critical imagination. What is more, this method, because it involves a manipulative and instrumental attitude towards the world of nature, encourages a manipulative and instrumental attitude towards the human world. People come to be viewed as 'things', pushed hither and thither in the interests of 'rational' organization.

Marcuse offered Marxism without the proletariat – and without much hope. Given that capitalism had solved its 'internal contradictions' one could not count on its ultimate collapse or on the proletariat's will to kill the goose that lays the golden egg. It was possible, he conceded, that society's marginalized groups – the ethnic or racial minorities, drop-outs, the long-term unemployed – might take to the streets and shake the system at its foundations. But pessimism remained his keynote: 'The critical theory of society possesses no concepts which could bridge the gap between the present and its future; holding no promise and showing no success, it remains negative.'[16]

A different kind of pessimism was expressed by Jean-Paul Sartre (1905–80), who tried to combine Marxism with existentialism's awareness of the pain and uncertainty endemic to the human condition. A playwright and novelist as well as a philosopher, the Frenchman found it difficult to confine his imagination within the rigid categories of orthodox Marxism. Central to Sartre's existentialism is the conviction that man is 'condemned to be free'. Freedom, in this sense, comprises three elements. First, unlike inert nature, human behaviour is not governed by causal laws. Why? Because in contrast to stones or trees, human beings possess imagination, an ability to perceive alternatives, to see the world around us in different lights; that is to say, we can transcend our immediate situation in unpredictable ways. The second element of existential freedom is that there are no universal traits of human nature, no innate dispositions to adopt certain attitudes and conduct rather than others. Thirdly, freedom, according to Sartre, means that there are no absolute moral laws, binding on all human beings and dictated by some infallible source – be it scripture or abstract 'reason' or 'history'. We are free to choose our own values, because the universe is inherently meaningless or – in Sartre's terminology – 'absurd'.

Since there are no universal ethical norms, no unbreakable social or historical laws, no fixed traits of human nature, each individual is totally responsible for everything he or she does. The result is angst, anxiety, dread. Brought face to face with their own freedom, men and women wilt under so vast a burden of responsibility. Small wonder, then, that we try to avoid this anguish by seeking refuge in 'bad faith' or self-deception, whereby we pretend that things are inevitable or self-evidently true when they are not. Most people lead unauthentic lives, forever making excuses or hiding behind 'infallible' guides (God, history, social convention), in order to deny the void at the centre of human existence.

Existentialism, it can be seen, insists on free will, individuality and the essential meaninglessness of life. Marxism, by contrast, preaches determinism and collectivism, and attributes an intrinsic coherence and purpose to history. How could Sartre integrate these two, opposing philosophies? He begins by distinguishing Marx from later 'lazy Marxists', with their mechanical modes of analysis and their vulgar reduction of human beings to the status of material objects. Orthodox Marxists, we are told by Sartre, forget Marx's own contention that 'man makes his own history', that human beings are capable of choice and autonomy: they are not the passive tools of some irresistible dialectic.

Contrary to Marx's intentions, historical materialism has become a dogmatic, *a priori* formula, forcing everything that happens into a preconceived mould. Existentialism, by encouraging Marxists to recognize free will, as well as the uniqueness of particular individuals and particular situations, could therefore revive Marxism – or so Sartre and his numerous admirers said.

If we confine our gaze to the humanistic strain in Marxist thought, there are indeed similarities between the two philosophies. Both believe that humans have surrendered individual freedom to false idols of their own making; both pour scorn on capitalist oppression and bourgeois hypocrisy. Yet it is hard to see how a *consistent* Marxist could agree with existentialism's gloomy diagnosis of the human condition. Conversely, it is equally hard to see how an existentialist could plausibly abdicate his individual judgement in the name of history or collective solidarity, for such 'bad faith' would surely detract from the 'authenticity' of his life. Curiously, however, Sartre came to adopt a strikingly authoritarian political stance, championing 'Maoism' and defending terror as the only way of preserving communal commitment in the face of individual subjectivity. His contempt for the cowardly majority who led inauthentic lives caused him to concur with Rousseau's paradoxical conclusion: the people must be 'forced to be free', i.e. forced to shed the bourgeois falsehoods that prevent the attainment of 'authenticity'. In Sartre we see a perfect illustration of how Marxism's concern for human liberation degenerated into a demand for political conformity.

In the 1960s orthodox Marxist materialism came under attack from another maverick French philosopher, Louis Althusser (1918–90), who offered an intriguing, and temporarily influential, synthesis of Marxism and structuralism. The latter had its origins in the linguistic studies of Ferdinand de Saussure (1857–1913), which investigated the universal structure underlying language in general rather than specific human languages. Years later, Claude Lévi-Strauss (1908–   ) used the concept of structure to illuminate primitive myths and kinship systems. By 'decoding' these, he found that the activities of diverse tribal communities followed invariant logical patterns or structures, of which participants were unaware. His conclusion was that all societies unconsciously adopt a combination of timeless structural components, independent of human intentions.

Structuralism enabled Althusser to develop a theoretical perspective equidistant from humanistic Marxism, on the one hand, and orthodox Marxism, on the other. Against thinkers like Gramsci and Sartre, he insisted that history is a 'process without subjects', which must be analysed in terms of objective and autonomous structures. Our behaviour, in other words, is reactive, not active or freely chosen; it is subject to deep structural determinants. But if human purposes and choices are themselves explicable in terms of objective forces, then notions dear to the hearts of Marxist humanists – authenticity, self-realization, self-determination – are so much idealistic gibberish. Humanists, said Althusser, paid too much attention to Marx's early writings, which were still heavily indebted to Hegelian categories and assumptions. There is an 'epistemological break', no continuity whatsoever, between the young, 'pre-Marxist' Marx, and the older, 'true' Marx, who inaugurated a scientific revolution in social thought. That is to say, he moved from myth to reality, illusion to truth.

Althusser, despite his desire to restore the scientific rigour of Marxism, strongly objected to the mechanistic materialism of the orthodox Marxists. For one thing, he rejected their simplistic model of base and superstructure. The economy, he maintained, is just one structure among others: the political, the scientific, and the ideological. Society is best described as a 'structure of structures', a 'decentred totality' of four autonomous structures interacting one with another. Each structure determines, and is determined by, the global structure, as well as all the others.

Social determination is therefore complex. This is what Althusser labels the 'law of overdetermination'. At first glance, this 'law' might seem a radical deviation from the principles of historical materialism, but he preserves his Marxist credentials by saying that the autonomy of so-called superstructures is relative as opposed to absolute; economic practice is determinant 'in the last instance', because it determines the respective degrees of autonomy of the other practices, or structures. On this model, causality is understood in structural rather than linear or mechanical terms. It is not that A *causes* B, where A and B are isolated phenomena, but that A and B require each other. The focus is on coexistential regularities, not on causal laws in the classical Marxist sense. Because social change is the result of interacting structures, exerting a multitude of reciprocal influences and burdened by a bewildering variety of contradictions, there is no logical or inevitable dynamic to the process, and historical prediction – even historical generalization – becomes impossible. In so far as Marx himself and subsequent Marxists attempted to impose a grand design on history, they fell victim, Althusser argued, to the insidious influence of Hegelian teleology, with its mystical premise that human behaviour expressed some 'higher', 'rational' purpose.

For a time, the French thinker was an honoured prophet. His avoidance of reductive generalizations inspired a number of disciples, most notably Nicos Poulantzas,[17] to refine and develop the Marxist theory of the state, hitherto confined, in orthodox circles, to a few simpleminded propositions (e.g. 'The state is a tool of the capitalist class'). But Althusser's Marxism was ultimately sterile and unappealing. His emphasis on the irreducible complexity of social causation rendered his scientific pretensions otiose, while his conception of the self as a passive bearer of impersonal forces undermined the moral case for communism.

MARXISM AND COMMUNISM AT THE TURN OF THE TWENTY-FIRST CENTURY

The question whether objective [*gegenständliche*] truth can be attributed to human thinking is not a question of theory, but is a *practical* question. In practice man must prove the truth, that is, the reality and power, the this-sidedness [*Diesseitigkeit*] of his thinking.

Karl Marx[18]

By his own criterion (practice), the doctrine founded by Marx must be judged harshly. The dramatic death of world communism (though aspects linger on in China), and the attendant emergence of ethnic hatreds and capitalist greed in the former 'workers' paradises', have shattered any lingering hopes for the global realization of his dream. As a blueprint for the future, Marxism is totally discredited.

Despite the protests of scattered academic apologists, few people would now wish to dissociate Marx from the dreadful practices his ideas inspired. Of course, he would have been horrified by the brutality and economic incompetence of communist regimes, but this depressing reality was the probable, if not logical, outcome of a deeply flawed theory. In his criticisms of bourgeois society – of its economic injustice, of its fraudulent political claims – Marx made some valid points. Moreover, as an analyst of historical development, he was enormously influential. Before the impact of his theories, it was common to view history as if it were dancing to the tune of ideas, orchestrated by 'Great Men'. Marxist materialism directed our attention, instead, to the vital role played by economic interests in shaping human behaviour. If the need to take account of (often hidden) economic factors is now universally recognized by historians and social analysts, this is largely because of Marx. But, alas, he did not simply argue that we should give economics its due. Notwithstanding occasional equivocations, his claims were much stronger. What Marx bequeathed to his disciples was a facile economic *reductionism*, and it is this that underlies Marxism's failures – both as a predictive 'science' and as a guide to future happiness.

Workers, according to the classical Marxists, would not be able to improve their living standards significantly through collective action, because the 'iron law of wages' would always keep them at or near subsistence level. The state, as a 'tool of the bourgeoisie', could not possibly pass and enforce legislation of primary benefit to the proletariat. Nor could the state, a mere reflection of economic forces, intervene to mitigate the 'anarchy' of the capitalist market through regulation of demand or investment. On all these points the Marxists were wrong. The future society was similarly cursed by Marxism's reductionist tendencies. For example, human rights, owing to their origin in capitalist society, had to be dismissed as mere guarantors of bourgeois selfishness. And since politics was nothing but disguised economics, collective ownership meant collective harmony; and such harmony (objectively present, despite 'superficial' evidence to the contrary) obviated the need for either safeguards against the abuse of political power or market mechanisms to accommodate the inherent diversity of material tastes and interests.

Modern Marxists, recognizing the follies of economic determinism, have – as shown earlier – placed greater stress on so-called superstructural phenomena. But these attempts to rescue Marxism by divesting it of its most distinctive feature only served to create confusion and highlight the increasing irrelevance of the doctrine. What is 'alive' in Marxism has already been absorbed into the general intellectual climate. To this extent, the Marxist project was a success. But it is ironic that a world-view which claimed to be vindicated by history should now be buried by history.

NOTES

1. 'Preface' to the first edition of *Capital* (1867), in L. Feuer (ed.), *Marx and Engels: Basic Writings on Politics and Philosophy*, Doubleday, New York, 1959, pp.135–7.
2. 'The German Ideology' (1846), in L.D. Easton and K.H. Guddat (eds), *Writings of the Young Marx on Philosophy and Society*, Doubleday, New York, 1967, p.414.
3. 'The Poverty of Philosophy' (1847), in Easton and Guddat, op. cit., p.480.
4. 'Preface' to *A Contribution to the Critique of Political Economy* (1859), in Feuer, op. cit., p.43.
5. Ibid., p.44.
6. 'Preface' to the first edition of *Capital* (1867), in Feuer, op. cit., pp.135–6.
7. 'Preface' to the second edition of *Capital* (1873), in Feuer, op. cit., p.144.
8. Ibid., p.146.
9. G. Plekhanov, *The Development of the Monist View of History*, Progress, Moscow, 1956, pp. 105, 107, 156. First published in 1895.
10. K. Kautsky, *The Class Struggle (Erfurt Program)*, Norton, New York, 1971, p.117.

11. *History and Class Consciousness*, Merlin, London, 1971, p.xiv.
12. *Which Socialism?*, Polity Press, Oxford, p.115.
13. *The Communist Manifesto* (1848), in Feuer, op. cit., p.20.
14. See, e.g. S. Carrillo, *Eurocommunism and the State*, Lawrence Hill, Westport, 1978.
15. See for instance, H.-G. Betz and G.A. Welsh, 'The PDS in the New German Party System', *German Politics*, no. 3, 1995.
16. H. Marcuse, *One Dimensional Man*, Routledge and Kegan Paul, London, 1964. p.200.
17. See in particular his *Political Power and Social Classes*, New Left Books, London, 1973.
18. 'Theses on Feuerbach', in Feuer, op. cit., p.243.

GUIDE TO FURTHER READING

Marx

Anthologies

Easton, L.D. and Guddat, K.H. (eds), *Writings of the Young Marx on Philosophy and Society*, Doubleday, New York, 1967. Includes only the early writings (up to 1847).

Feuer, L. (ed.), *Marx and Engels: Basic Writings on Politics and Philosophy*, Doubleday, New York, 1959. Second edition published in 1969 by Fontana of London. Both editions exclude the early (pre-1846) writings.

McLellan, D. (ed.), *Karl Marx: Selected Writings*, Oxford University Press, Oxford, 1977.

Pierson, C. (ed.), *The Marx Reader*, Polity Press, Oxford, 1996. The most useful collection of Marx's writings published since the fall of communism in Eastern Europe. The editor's introduction considers the importance of Marx after the events of 1989 and after the intellectual impact of post-modernism.

Commentaries

Berlin, I., *Karl Marx*, 4th edn, Oxford University Press, Oxford, 1978. First published in 1939, it remains the most elegant and entertaining study of Marx available in English.

Cohen, G.A., *Karl Marx's Theory of History: A Defence*, Oxford University Press, Oxford, 1978. A rigorous philosophical analysis of historical materialism, which insists on Marx's 'productive force determinism'. This apparently obvious thesis was, and still is, denied by many commentators.

Elster, J., *Making Sense of Marx*, Cambridge University Press, Cambridge, 1985. Meticulous and very long. Unlike most commentaries, it devotes considerable space to Marx's methodology.

McLellan, D., *The Thought of Karl Marx*, 2nd edn, Macmillan, London, 1980. Helpfully combines commentary with selected texts.

Singer, P., *Marx*, Oxford University Press, Oxford, 1980. An excellent introduction – brief and lucid.

Sowell, T., *Marxism*, Macmillan, London, 1985. Surprisingly sympathetic and sensitive introduction to Marx's thought by a right-wing economist. It offers a clear exposition of Marx's economic theories.

Torrance, J., *Karl Marx's Theory of Ideas*, Cambridge University Press, Cambridge, 1995. A systematic study of Marx's concept of ideology and its implications for the sociology of ideas.

General

Childs, D., *Marx and the Marxists*, Croom Helm, London, 1973. Combines theoretical analysis and historical narrative. Selective in its coverage (e.g. nothing on Lukács or Gramsci) but contains a useful chapter on 'Mao's Marxism'.

Femia, J.V., *Marxism and Democracy*, Oxford University Press, Oxford, 1993. Discusses the different Marxist conceptions of democracy, as well as the links between Marxism and totalitarianism.

Jessop, B., *The Capitalist State*, Martin Robertson, Oxford, 1982. Examines the various Marxist and neo-Marxist theories of the state. Notable for its detailed analysis of recent (since the 1960s) 'discourse' on the subject.

Kolakowski, L., *Main Currents of Marxism*, 3 vols, Oxford University Press, Oxford, 1978. Probably the best history of Marxism in any language – massive, comprehensive, subtle and eloquent. Contains sections on every important Marxist thinker, as well as a book-length discussion of Marx himself.

Lichtheim, C., *Marxism*, Routledge and Kegan Paul, London, 1961. A classic work of intellectual history, though the narrative ends in 1948.

Lukes, S., *Marxism and Morality*, Oxford University Press, Oxford, 1985. Not as narrowly focused as the title suggests. A stimulating and scholarly analysis of Marxist philosophy.

McLellan, D., *Marxism after Marx*, Macmillan, London, 1980. A good basic textbook, though its attempt to be comprehensive in just 333 pages makes for a certain superficiality.

Townshend, J., *The Politics of Marxism: The Critical Debates*, Leicester University Press, 1996. A clear and incisive exploration of the controversies that have divided Marxists for the past hundred years.

Main Marxist thinkers (excluding Marx and Engels)

Primary sources

Althusser, L., *For Marx*, Penguin, Harmondsworth, 1969.

Althusser, L. and Balibar, E., *Reading Capital*, New Left, London, 1970.

Hoare, Q. and Nowell Smith, G. (eds), *Selections from the Prison Notebooks of Antonio Gramsci*, Lawrence and Wishart, London, 1971.

Kautsky, K., *The Class Struggle*, Norton, New York, 1971.

Kautsky, K., *The Dictatorship of the Proletariat*, University of Michigan, Ann Arbor, 1964.

Lenin, V.I., *What Is To Be Done?* Penguin, Harmondsworth, 1988.

Lenin, V.I., *Imperialism, The Highest Stage of Capitalism*, in *Collected Works*, vol. 22, Progress, Moscow, 1960–70.

Lukács, G., *History and Class Consciousness*, Merlin, London, 1971.

Marcuse, H., *One Dimensional Man*, Routledge and Kegan Paul, London, 1964.

Plekhanov, G., *The Development of the Monist View of History*, Progress, Moscow, 1956.

Plekhanov, G., *Fundamental Problems of Marxism*, International, New York, 1969.

Sartre, J.P., *Critique of Dialectical Reason*, New Left, London, 1976. A massive and difficult work.

Sartre, J.P., *The Problem of Method*, Methuen, London, 1964. Prefatory essay to *Critique de la raison dialectique*, though not included in the English translation of that work. *The Problem of Method* offers an accessible exposition of Sartre's Marxism.

Waters, M.A. (ed.), *Rosa Luxemburg Speaks*, Pathfinder, New York, 1970. Includes her most important works.

Commentaries

Bellamy, R. and Schecter, D., *Gramsci and the Italian State*, Manchester University Press, Manchester, 1993.

Deutscher, I., *Stalin*, Penguin, Harmondsworth, 1966.

Femia, J.V., *Gramsci's Political Thought*, Oxford University Press, Oxford, 1981. Paperback edition in 1987.

Gay, P., *The Dilemma of Democratic Socialism: Bernstein's Challenge to Marx*, Schoeken, New York, 1962.

Geary, D., *Karl Kautsky*, Manchester University Press, Manchester, 1987.

Geras, N., *The Legacy of Rosa Luxemburg*, New Left/Verso, London, 1976.

Harding, N., *Lenin's Political Thought*, 2 vols, Macmillan, London, 1977.

Joll, J., *Gramsci*, Fontana/Collins, London, 1977. A brief and reliable introduction.

Knei-Paz, B., *The Social and Political Thought of Leon Trotsky*, Oxford University Press, Oxford, 1978.

Lane, D., *Leninism: A Sociological Interpretation*, Cambridge University Press, Cambridge, 1981.

MacIntyre, A., *Marcuse*, Fontana/Collins, London, 1970. Polemical but persuasive introduction. Very brief.

New Left Review (ed.), *Western Marxism: A Critical Reader*, New Left/Verso, London, 1977. A collection of essays on various Marxist thinkers. The essays on Althusser – one by N. Geras and the other by A. Glucksmann – are especially worth reading.

Parkinson, C.H.R., *Georg Lukács*, Routledge and Kegan Paul, London, 1977.

Rigby, S.H., *Engels and the Formation of Marxism*, Manchester University Press, Manchester, 1992.

Salvadori, M., *Kautsky and the Socialist Revolution*, New Left, London, 1979.

Schram. S., *Mao Tse-tung*, Penguin, Harmondsworth, 1966.

Warnock, M., *The Philosophy of Sartre*, Hutchinson, London, 1965.

6
ANARCHISM
Jeremy Jennings

——

ANARCHISM: THE PROBLEM OF DEFINITION

I must tell you first of all [proclaimed the American anarchist Alexander Berkman (1870–1936) in 1929] what anarchism is *not*. It is *not*
bombs, disorder, or chaos. It is *not* robbery and murder. It is *not* a war
of each against all. It is not a return to barbarism or to the wild state of
man. *Anarchism is the very opposite of all that.*[1]

What then is anarchism if its popular image is a misconception? Is it merely
an impractical Utopian ideal, doomed to failure and inappropriate to the
highly industrialized societies that have emerged since the nineteenth century? Is it an ideology in its own right or simply a version of socialism or of
liberal thought pursued to its radical conclusions? Is it a coherent doctrine
that should be taken seriously? Or rather a primitive form of revolt deriving
inspiration from conflicting and contradictory sources? Is it merely a pos-
ture, a form of role rejection displayed by a stubborn minority intent on
scorning the conformities and conventions of their age? Can we even speak
of 'anarcho-capitalism' and of right-wing anarchism? In short, anarchism
has been seen and characterized as all of these things.

Anarchism as a doctrine reached its fullest development in the early
decades of the twentieth century, but its origins lie deep in European history
and are to be found in a peculiar combination of what James Joll in *The
Anarchists* has described as 'heresy and reason'. To the tradition of religious
dissent associated with the millenarian Christianity of the Middle Ages was
wedded the secular and rationalist tradition born out of the Renaissance,
thus producing a doctrine that in its earliest formulation – for example, in
William Godwin's (1756–1836) *Enquiry Concerning Political Justice*[2] pub-

1798 – was part dissenting religious faith and part rationalist philosophy. No one, Godwin believed, was obligated to do anything that sacrificed his own independence of judgement. Yet anarchism as it developed was to draw sustenance from a wide variety of philosophical and psychological ideas, organizational principles and economic classes, as well as the experience of different countries. In 1843 the lonely and eccentric Max Stirner (1806–56) was to publish *The Ego and his Own*,[3] a work steeped in Hegelian philosophy and whose guiding principle was 'Nothing is more to me than myself'. In America in particular there came into existence a form of individualistic anarchism, hostile to all external authority and proud of its attachment to private property and the spirit of the frontiersman. Elsewhere, and especially in Russia, it was to be the peasant's communal and agrarian life that provided anarchists with both their vision of the future and the foundations of their critique of capitalism.

Tolstoy (1828–1910), and later Gandhi (1869–1948), turned their distrust of government and their calls for a moral purity into a defence of civil disobedience and pacifist resistance.[4] In France the 'man of paradox', Pierre-Joseph Proudhon (1809–65), the first person self-consciously to embrace the epithet of anarchist, first condemned the French Revolution of 1789 because it had been 'bewitched by politics' – 'No authority, no government, not even popular: that is the Revolution', Proudhon wrote – and then became involved in a bitter and acrimonious conflict with Karl Marx, a conflict which was to split the international labour movement and which Bakunin (1814–76), Kropotkin (1842–1921) and many later anarchists were to continue in their struggle to destroy the dead weight of Marxist orthodoxy.[5]

Where then, if anywhere, is to be found the common core of anarchist doctrine? What is it that makes an anarchist an anarchist? By common consent there is agreement that the lowest common denominator serving to unite anarchism and anarchists is a rejection and criticism of all state authority and of the power and coercion that combine to make up the machinery of government. 'The anarchist teachings', wrote the anarchist Paul Eltzbacher (1868–1928) in 1900, 'have only this in common, that they negate the State for our future'. Why do anarchists condemn the state and, beyond this negative stance, do they have any positive options to recommend?

ANARCHISM: THE THEORY

Central to the anarchist vision is the primacy of the individual and the virtue of moral autonomy, and it is within this perspective that the anarchist concludes that it is only the truly free individual who will create a worthwhile morality and who will be worthy of respect. To be coerced or constrained in any way is to be debased and demeaned. Of all the things which interfere with the free activity of the individual, which reduce liberty and compel us to act in ways different from those we would choose, the most powerful and pervasive is the state. Proudhon argued in his classic text *The General Idea of the Revolution in the Nineteenth Century*:

> To be governed is to be kept in sight, inspected, spied upon, directed, law-driven, numbered, enrolled, indoctrinated, preached at, controlled, estimated, valued, censured, commanded, by creatures who have neither the right, nor the wisdom, nor the virtue to do so ... to be governed is to be at every operation, at every transaction, noted, registered, enrolled, taxed, stamped, measured, numbered, assessed, licensed, authorized, admonished, forbidden, corrected, punished ... That is government.[6]

Legal government, in other words, was a hindrance to the self-development of the individual. Yet this is not all. The conventional defence of the state is that as an organization it preserves law and order and thus allows the individual to prosper in tranquillity and peace. According to the anarchist the reality of the state was the very opposite. Government filled the world with violence, with fraud and deceit, with oppression and misery. It corrupted and crushed everything it touched. As an act of self-justification it needed precisely to preserve disorder and thus was in its very essence counter-productive and dysfunctional. The people were blinded by the regalia that served to sanctify authority and in return were robbed and abused.

It is not surprising therefore that the prevailing anarchist image or metaphor of the state is that of the policeman. The state is fundamentally an instrument of coercion. Nor is it surprising that much anarchist literature concentrates upon attacking the specific instruments of state power. If the state in general is a threat to our liberty then its system of law and of law enforcement is made and operated in the interests of the ruling class and of the property owner. Its methods of punishment, and especially its prison systems (always a popular theme in anarchist writings), are seen as being barbaric, punitive, regressive and futile, designed, as Emma Goldman (1869–1940) remarked, 'that society might be "protected" from the phantoms of its own making'. The armed forces, far from protecting the peoples are institutions of brute force designed for war, sustained by the artificially induced emotion of patriotism and characterized by the degrading violence and perversion of military and barrack life. The state itself was costly to run and wasteful in operation, its bureaucracy inefficient, its taxes arbitrary and unfair.

How then did this instrument of oppression and exploitation preserve itself from overthrow and the wrath of its subjects? Most obviously through the police agent, the soldier and the gaoler but also, as Enrico Malatesta

(1853–1932) observed, by reliance upon 'the trader in lies, be he priest or schoolmaster'. The trick, in other words, had been to convince the people that the state was actually necessary, that without it we would rob and murder each other, and in this religion and education, protected and financed by government, had played a vital role in enslaving minds and encouraging us docilely to accept our yoke. All anarchists, therefore, were agreed that state education was nothing else but propaganda and indoctrination and that the church as an institution was a vital appendage to state power, the purveyor of subservience and submission. 'There is', wrote Tolstoy, 'no idea which has produced more evil, none more inimical to Christ's teaching, than the idea of a Church'. Other anarchists were prepared to categorize all forms of religion as an evil.

What should be obvious is that this hostile reaction to the state, government and organized authority was rooted in an earlier experience of monarchical and authoritarian despotism so typical of the nineteenth century, with Tsarist Russia cast as its very embodiment. But anarchists in the twentieth century have rejected *all* states, even the most advanced and democratic. The arguments here have been more complex. In part they derived from the view that voting and universal suffrage could never be a means of emancipation. To vote, to choose a representative, was to abdicate one's capacity for self-direction. Given the economic slavery and ignorance of the workers, they were incapable of using their vote to good effect. Voting produced the election of mediocrities and nonentities. More than this, participation in the electoral process was corrupting. A good democrat, the anarchists quickly learnt, would, with the exercise of power, inevitably become an autocrat. However, the charge was that such modern constitutional rights as the vote, the existence of political parties, and freedom of the press, were instruments in the hands of the dominant classes, primarily designed to divert and canalize protest and which were respected only so long as the people chose not to use them against their oppressors. Moreover, what did a change of personnel at the top signify? All government was oligarchy, the government of a few and therefore the government of a class. Democratic government was nothing but a mirage.

But what of so-called revolutionary government and the famous dictatorship of the proletariat? Here from Proudhon onwards the view of the anarchists has not varied and has, if anything, been strengthened in the twentieth century as it sadly received confirmation with the Russian Revolution of 1917. The Marxist analysis, drawing sustenance first from the experience of the Paris Commune of 1871 and then re-endorsed by Lenin, was that in the period of transition between capitalism and communism the state could be used by the proletariat against its enemies. Only when this function was unnecessary would the state disappear and wither away. The anarchist response was that it was in the process of revolution itself that the state had to be destroyed and this because, were it not, it would become a self-perpetuating institution directed not by capitalists but by party bureaucrats, with the citizen existing only under a new yoke. 'We know', wrote Kropotkin, 'that revolution and government are incompatible. One must destroy the other no matter what name is given to government, whether dictatorship, royalty or parliament.'[7] The revolution, in short, was not to be a simple change of governors but rather the spontaneous dissolution of all authority and all laws. And it was here that the Bolshevik Revolution, as the anarchists were among the first to recognize, had taken a wrong turn. To cite Kropotkin again: 'this effort to build a communist republic on the basis of a strongly centralized state communism under the iron law of party dictatorship is bound to end in failure'.[8] It did.

But was the authority and power of the state the only form of coercion that anarchists objected to? Did not coercion take other social and economic forms? And were they not linked either directly or indirectly to the state itself? Here too there are grounds for believing that anarchists were in substantial, if less categorical, agreement. Writing at the end of the eighteenth century William Godwin could recognize that each article of property ought to belong to the individual whose possession of it would yield the greatest good of the greatest number and this by extension led him to conclude that property should be distributed according to the claims of need. There should, in short, be a rough equality of wealth. With time the views of anarchists hardened. Proudhon, despite his famous slogan that 'property is theft', defended private property but in his advocacy of an economic system which he described as mutualism he sought to protect the individual producer both from exploitation and the robbery inflicted by the tax collector, the usurer and the middleman. By the beginning of the twentieth century the anarchist position was clear-cut. Emma Goldman proclaimed: 'The only demand that property recognizes is its own gluttonous appetite for greater wealth, because wealth means power; the power to subdue, to crush, to exploit, the power to enslave, to outrage, to degrade.'[9]

Anarchism meant communism. No state meant no capitalism. Not only, the argument went, was the institution of private property the principal cause of crime in society and therefore of the continued existence of the state, but it also served to divide humanity into two different classes: the exploiters and the exploited. Moreover, the particular form of production associated with capitalism was especially loathsome. It diminished both the quality of the goods produced and the quality of workers, reducing them to exhausted, unskilled automatons. A good society was one where people were free to choose their mode and conditions of work and where work could be an expression of individual personality. Real wealth consisted in producing things of utility and of beauty. Fortunately for the anarchist there were signs that a higher form of economic organization was coming into existence, a form of organization that would not reduce the individual to the rule of a slave to either the capitalist or the state. Kropotkin, for example, drew inspiration from the numerous models of voluntary association that he saw all around him – his particular favourite was the Lifeboat Association which he regarded as 'one of the noblest achievements of our century' – and which had nothing to do with the state: the International Postal Union, international railway links, learned societies, museums, public libraries, and so on.

The point to stress is that all anarchists, and not only those wedded to the predominant twentieth-century strain of anarchist communism, have been critical of private property to the extent that it was a source of hierarchy and privilege. Even such American anarchists as Benjamin Tucker (1854–1939) and Lysander Spooner (1808–87), the forebears of modern 'anarcho-capitalism', agreed with the proposition that property was legitimate only in so far as it embraced no more than the total product of individual labour. Equally, all anarchists have abhorred the dehumanizing tendencies of routinized labour – what George Woodcock (1912–   ) described as 'the tyranny of the clock' – and machine technology.

As a matter of fact, of course, property – especially under capitalism – was a source of abuse. Moreover, its possession was intimately linked to other forms of social oppression and its existence served to perpetuate the *status quo*. It was against such oppression, rooted in the norms and mores of the established order, that anarchists also rebelled. At its most basic level anarchism has represented a rejection of customary pieties and orthodoxies and as such at times its espousal indicated little more than the desire to shock. But the serious side of dilettantism was a scorn for the conventions of the age and it was this no doubt which explains the attraction of anarchism to such literary and artistic figures as Oscar Wilde, Herbert Read, William Morris, the painter Camille Pisarro and the controversial French writer Céline. The habit of obedience to traditional taste, dogma and ideas – especially when they had been defiled by a mercantile culture – was, on this view, not one to be admired. By the same token anarchists have been deeply critical of many of the institutions that structured our social life, most notably marriage and the bourgeois family. The first recognizable anarchist, William Godwin, berated marriage as a form of fraud and monopoly and for this was probably condemned more than for anything else. In the twentieth century subsequent anarchists such as Emma Goldman have continued this theme, condemning the enslavement of women as well as all forms of sexual hypocrisy and repression and in the process championing such causes as the right to abortion and birth control. Recently anarchists have been advocates of gay and lesbian rights.

It has to be said, however, that not all have shared this enthusiasm for the abolition of marriage and for freedom of sexual expression. Proudhon was an ardent admirer of the family, believing that the choice facing women was between housewife and prostitute, whilst Tolstoy – admittedly in old age – resolved upon a course of complete sexual abstinence. Where anarchists are united is in their conviction, as Emma Goldman proclaimed (in a phrase borrowed from Friedrich Nietzsche), that the new society, in whatever shape it might come, must be based upon a transvaluation of all human values.

THE GOAL OF ANARCHISM

The anarchist, by general agreement, is a passionate believer in individual freedom. 'Freedom', wrote Rudolf Rocker (1873–1958) in 1938, 'is the very essence of life'. And it was moreover a concrete possibility for every human being. Not unnaturally therefore it has frequently been assumed that the anarchists' aim is to create a society of untrammelled individual liberty. But is it as simple as that? Anarchism, Kropotkin argued, 'seeks the complete development of individuality combined with the highest development of voluntary association in all its aspects, in all possible degrees for all imaginable ends'.[10]

On this view, as Alan Ritter has argued in his *Anarchism: A Theoretical Analysis*, it is not freedom but individuality and community that are the anarchist's chief goals and the concern with liberty cannot be divorced from the desire to foster a real community.[11] It is in this context that the anarchist's preoccupation – voiced from Godwin onwards – with public censure and rebuke as a means of constraint have to be understood. If punishment in the conventional sense was to be avoided then, as Kropotkin put it, the evil-doer would be subject to the 'practical corrective' of 'fraternal treatment and moral support'. He would, in short, be encouraged and educated to change his or her ways.

But what was it that led the anarchist to believe that a society based upon individuality and community was a possibility? Underpinning all anarchist thought was the assumption that harmony was implicit to the world. Man was naturally social and it was only when this natural propensity was subverted that conflict arose. The law governing humanity, Enrico Malatesta argued, was solidarity and it was this alone that made progress and advance possible. The best known twentieth-century expression of this opinion is undoubtedly that presented in Kropotkin's classic text *Mutual Aid*. It was Kropotkin's belief that science proved – contrary to the views of vulgar neo-Darwinists – that evolution was governed not by the survival of the fittest but rather by solidarity within species:

> In short, neither the crushing powers of the centralized State nor the teachings of mutual hatred and pitiless struggle. which came, adorned with the attributes of science, from obliging philosophers and sociologists, could weed out the feeling of human solidarity, deeply lodged in men's understanding and heart, because it has been nurtured by all our preceding evolution.[12]

For Kropotkin, our future lay in the mutual support that had sustained humanity throughout the ages and which alone could guarantee our material and ethical progress.

Moreover, it should be clear from this that anarchists did not believe that their goal was a beautiful but impractical ideal, a Utopian dream. Anarchy was written into human history and was proved by science. Kropotkin, for example, denied that anarchism derived from abstract theory and rather concluded that its roots lay in the tendencies towards integrating labour and the fullest freedom of the individual that were intrinsic to the development of society. The goal of the anarchist, therefore, was a summing up of what was considered to be the next phase of society's evolution. By contrast, it was the presently existing order – with its crime and misery – that was doomed to fail and to disappear. Equally, the anarchist was convinced that anarchy had a sound basis in ethics. Man's moral sense was a natural faculty and only when his judgement had been perverted would he fail to recognize that what was good was what was of benefit and of use to humanity. Anarchist morality, therefore, boiled down to one simple maxim: 'Do to others what you would have them do to you in the same circumstances.' Furthermore, the anarchist recognized that society existed for humanity and not vice versa.

What then would the anarchist society of the future look like? Here, perhaps surprisingly, the anarchists tended toward caution. 'We are', wrote Malatesta, 'no more prophets than anyone else.' The important point, however, was that a society should be brought into existence that would make the exploitation and dominance of man by man into an impossibility. How was this to be achieved? Godwin again laid down the general principles from which later anarchists did not significantly diverge. Government, Godwin argued, had been allowed to flourish because of the existence of a complicated, large-scale social and economic system. This system needed to be broken down and in its place people should form small, completely voluntary federations – 'parishes' – around which they could organize co-operative projects. These parishes would occasionally select representatives to discuss matters with other parishes but no one would be bound by their decisions. They would not pass any laws. The guiding thread, therefore, was to be the idea of political and social simplicity. Accordingly, in the nineteenth century anarchists such as Proudhon were opponents of moves towards national reunification in Italy and Germany and this was extended in the twentieth century into a generalized preference for decentralization, local autonomy and mass participation in the decision-making process. As Berkman put it in his *ABC of Anarchism* published in 1929: 'Politically decentralisation means freedom: industrially, material independence: socially, it implies security and well-being for the small communities: individually it results in manhood and liberty.'[13] If what this meant in political terms was reasonably clear – there was to be no attempt to replace the state with another form of centralized decision-making machinery – what it implied for such difficult issues as the organization of the economy is less evident.

The aim of the revolution was to make possible the immediate improvement of the conditions of working people and this implied that the workers were to take hold of the factories and fields in which they worked. Anarchists came up with various schemes to support this argument – Proudhon's mutualism, Bakunin's collectivism – but by the early twentieth century anarchism as a movement had resolved upon a system of free consumption and exchange. Given that private ownership of the means of production and distribution would be abolished there would be no buying or selling. Personal possessions would remain only in the things of personal use. Money would be useless and disappear. Goods would be supplied on the basis of need. Wrote Kropotkin:

> We consider that an equitable organization of society can only arise when every wage-system is abandoned, and when everybody, contributing for the common well-being to the full extent of his capacities, shall enjoy also from the common stock of society to the fullest possible extent of his needs.[14]

Thus production itself was to be organized on the basis of voluntary productive and distributive associations, thereby simplifying what had formerly been a wasteful and irrational process. The satisfaction of essential needs – food, clothing and shelter – would come first and only later would luxuries be made available. Small-scale production was to be the norm but this did not mean that industrial machinery and the scientific cultivation of the land would be ignored. The individual worker, freed from tutelage and external direction, was to become a more conscious and determining factor in production. Brainwork and manual work were to be combined and wherever possible people were to enjoy the 'moral and physical advantages' that derived from dividing their labour between the field and the workshop. But how were we to be induced to labour? 'With us', Kropotkin replied, 'work is a habit and idleness an artificial growth.' People, in short, would not need to be forced to carry out agreements freely entered into. Everyone would have the opportunity of following whatever occupation appealed to their natural inclinations and aptitudes. Merit would be assessed on the willingness to be socially useful. Local committees would decide upon such matters as housing provision, food distribution and the organization of health and sanitary services. Education would be voluntary, not compulsory, free to all who desired it and would be purged of rigid dogma. The aim was to foster mental growth and independent thought.

Overall, anarchy was taken to mean the free and equal participation of all in the general work and welfare of society and in this way, it was assumed, the harmonious blending of individual and social instincts would be achieved.

FROM PROPAGANDA BY THE DEED TO CLASS WAR

When at his trial in 1883 Kropotkin declared that 'the social revolution is at hand. It will break out in the next ten years', there were many anarchists who believed that this was too cautious a prediction. Every street demonstration, every strike seemed to indicate that the revolution had already begun. But how would the great change come about? Here again among anarchists there was agreement on one basic principle: emancipation had to be self-emancipation. This in turn, however, provided anarchists with one basic and perennial problem: how could this enthusiasm for spontaneous, individual and direct action be reconciled, if at all, with the supposed need to structure and organize patterns of revolt?

The first anarchist, William Godwin, set himself against what he described as 'tumult and violence', preferring rather to trust to positive sincerity and the reasonableness of man as the means necessary to bring about the advance of knowledge without which all change was absurd and injurious. The best that Max Stirner could do was to recommend insurrection, not revolution, and the formation of a temporary 'Union of Egoists'. It was, however, in their clash first with Karl Marx and then with later generations of Marxists that anarchists came more precisely to define the means that they believed should be used to attain their ends. At one level this was seen by anarchists as a conflict between the Latin spirit and the German spirit – the Germans, especially after the victory of the Franco-Prussian war, being obsessed by the discipline of the barrack room and Bismarckian centralization – but, more seriously, the charge was that Marx and his supporters always wanted to create a centralized, bureaucratic organization of well-educated professional revolutionaries which would direct the masses in the revolution like an army general staff. With respect to the First International, for example, the anarchists never wanted to see it as anything more than a bureau for co-ordinating and circulating information. Indeed, the favourite image of an organization for an anarchist was always that of a post-box.

Furthermore, anarchists to this day do not share the Marxist enthusiasm for exclusively class-based organizations. For them the ideal has been the so-called 'affinity group', a group of like-minded individuals freely joined together who might well be drawn from different classes and which the twentieth-century anarchist Murray Bookchin (1921–   ) has described as 'a new type of extended family'. Accordingly, anarchists are prepared to turn their gaze beyond the proletariat, denying the Marxist postulate that all other classes were reactionary. Anarchists – especially those from Spain, Russia and Italy who had precious little knowledge and experience of the urbanized industrial worker – looked above all to the peasantry, to the disillusioned intellectual as well as to the vagabond and the city drop-out, Marx's loathed *Lumpenproletariat*. These people, the anarchists believed, were instinctively revolutionary, outsiders who were untainted by the corruption of bourgeois society and had no need to be controlled or directed by middle-class socialists.

There was, however, something of an irony here. Marxists, in their enthusiasm for political parties as the vanguard of the proletariat, were accused of turning the leadership of the revolution over to the charge of a small group of full-time, professional activists. Yet anarchists themselves constantly emphasized the importance of the committed and non-compromising minority in the revolutionary struggle. 'Every effort', Emma Goldman wrote, 'for progress, for enlightenment, for science, for religious, political and economic liberty, emanates from the minority and not from the mass.'[15] The vast majority of people, oppressed by poverty and stupefied by superstition and public opinion, were at best sheep and cowards. Of necessity, therefore, the spirit of revolt and of revolution in the masses would be awakened by the heroic acts of a dedicated minority.

It is only when anarchists came to realize that their hopes of gaining the ascendency in the international labour movement were ill-founded, and that the revolution might not be so near at hand as they had previously imagined, that they began to change their views on tactics. In the 1860s Bakunin – the very embodiment of an anarchist with his copious beard and Bohemian dress – created a whole series of secret, conspiratorial associations committed to the violent overthrow of society; but by the end of the century this had given way to other strategies that were themselves reflections of weakness and failure. One – for which Tolstoy became the most famous advocate – was passive resistance or civil disobedience. The state's demands were to be met by simple non-compliance. The refusal to obey – be it to pay taxes or to serve in the army – was the great weapon. The power of example (and Tolstoy's was immense) would do the rest. Another, less reputable alternative, articulated by Elisée Reclus (1830–1905), was individual expropriation or, put simply, theft and robbery.[16] Given that the people should not be constrained by the dictates of bourgeois morality and that all property was illegitimate it was perfectly proper that they should reclaim what had been unjustly taken from them and by any means. Many anarchists, including Kropotkin, were not impressed.

It was, however, so-called propaganda by the deed – individual attacks on both property and persons – that aroused the most controversy and which forever transformed the image of the anarchist into that of a bomb-thrower in a black cloak. To understand why this tactic appeared so useful we need to recognize that the anarchist movement throughout the world had been deeply influenced by the campaign of the Russian 'nihilists' who in 1881 had assassinated Tsar Alexander II. In France, for example, between 1892 and 1894 there was a veritable terrorist epidemic with innumerable bomb explosions, often on indiscriminate targets. The French Parliament was bombed and in 1894 the President of the French Republic, Sadi Carnot, was murdered. In America Alexander Berkman tried to kill the chairman of the Carnegie Steel Corporation, Henry Clay Frick, for his part in the repression of a strike by steelworkers in Homestead, Pennsylvania, an attempt he was later vividly to describe and justify in his *Prison Memoirs of an Anarchist*, published in 1912. The logic itself, as Emile Henry revealed in his trial, was a ruthless one. All members of the exploiting class, including women and children, were by definition guilty and therefore merited punishment by the self-appointed representatives of the people. 'That is why', Henry announced, 'I struck at random and did not choose my victims.'

Certainly the perpetrators of these acts of violence did not imagine that they would spark off the revolution itself but they did believe that these dramatic gestures would draw their true enemies to the attention of the exploited. In this they were to be disappointed. Far from eliciting support from among the people it brought only the reverse and provided governments with the pretext for systematic repression of anarchists everywhere. As Kropotkin observed: 'An edifice based upon centuries of history will not be destroyed by a few kilos of explosives.'

Anarchists were again therefore obliged to reconsider their methods. Two particular favourites, both of which succeeded in retaining their popularity throughout the twentieth century, were the establishment of schools and, wherever possible, communities based upon anarchist principles. Herbert Read (1893–1968) with his *Education through Art* and Paul Goodman (1911–72) with his *Compulsory Miseducation* were among the many anarchists to have set out the principles of a libertarian education. Another strategy was tireless, and selfless, propaganda through the publication of newspapers, brochures and pamphlets, the voice of the anarchist often lost in the wilderness. In Britain this activity has largely been carried out by the Freedom group through its newspaper founded in 1886 and still in existence today. Anarchists in France even published a multi-volumed *Encyclopédie Anarchiste* during the 1930s.

More importantly, prior to the First World War anarchists started to turn their attention towards syndicalism or revolutionary trade unionism. Anarcho-syndicalism as it came to be called represented too much of a compromise for those anarchists wedded to the purist ideal of individual action alone but for many – including Fernand Pelloutier (1867–1901), Goldman, Berkman and Rudolf Rocker (1873–1958) – it represented a serious attempt to fuse anarchist principles of spontaneous and decentralized agitation to the demands of a modern industrialized economy. The important point was that labour unions were to be built upon the principle of equal liberty for all members and were to avoid bureaucratic hierarchical patterns of organization. The union or *syndicat* was to be an instrument of resistance, a vehicle of revolution as well as the nucleus of the new society, the body around which consumption, production, education and social life were to be structured. Its tactics were, of course, to be non-political, the emphasis falling upon what was known as direct action in the form of sabotage and strikes. The revolution itself was to take the form of a general strike, although there was no agreement about either its duration, the number of workers who would be involved or the level of violence that it would entail. The goal, however, was clear: the removal of both the state and capitalism. Such ideas received extensive support in France, Italy, Spain, the USA (in the shape of the International Workers of the World) and even in Great Britain, where union leader Tom Mann launched not only the Industrial Syndicalist Education League in 1910 but also the periodical *The Industrial Syndicalist* a year later.[17] These ideas were later to be bitterly opposed and crushed by the international communist movement.

But these have not been the only compromises that anarchists have found themselves making in the twentieth century and, moreover, for the most part the others were singularly less successful. To what extent, for example, should anarchists intervene to save bourgeois democracy if the alternative was a military regime? In France this dilemma was faced at the very turn of the century with the Dreyfus affair, the anarchists being divided in their response to the demand that they should unite with the other parties of the left to save the Third Republic. But it was in Spain with the outbreak of civil war that the issue came to a head. There, as the republicans strove to defeat Franco's military insurrection, anarchists were to become ministers in the government, thus seemingly rejecting their own ultimate goal.[18] By the same token could anarchists accept the military discipline required to fight an armed campaign? First Nestor Makhno with his Ukranian Revolutionary Insurrectionary Army in the Russian Civil War and then the Spanish anarchists, by the side of their Communist rivals, found themselves obliged to imitate hierarchical patterns of command, although with only limited success. And what of a response to war itself? In 1914 anarchists such as Kropotkin and James Guillaume supported the Allied war effort on the grounds that it would destroy German militarism and imperialism. Most, however, maintained a steadfast neutrality, as they were also to do in the face of later wars.

It was, however, 1917 and the Russian Revolution that proved to be the real test. The situation initially seemed favourable to anarchism. There was a virtual breakdown of state authority, workers and peasants had seized control of the means of production and had formed soviets, and the Bolsheviks, including Lenin, seemed to be pursuing libertarian goals. 'They have opened the prison gates, declared the ancient government non-existent and, what is best, have one after another disarmed and expelled the police, high and low', Kropotkin proclaimed. Berkman described himself as being 'wild with joy'. Some anarchists, for example Victor Serge (1890–1947), joined the communists, others like Berkman and Goldman returned to Russia and many were prepared to work with the Bolsheviks, both at home and abroad. Not all, however, were taken in by the revolution's libertarian credentials and anarchists soon came to realize that for the Bolsheviks, as Lenin explained to Berkman, liberty was a luxury that could be dispensed with. Anarchists were prevented from speaking, were persecuted and arrested, treated like common criminals. The pacifist Tolstoyans were shot for refusing to serve in the Red Army. But it was the Bolshevik repression of the Kronstadt rebellion in 1921, led by the soldiers and sailors who had been instrumental in overthrowing the Tsarist regime, that finally blew sky-high the myth of the libertarian proletarian state. After this the anarchists recognized that the revolution in Russia was dead, drowned in a sea of despotism and terror. Even for such 1960s anarchist-inspired radicals of the New Left as Daniel Cohn-Bendit what occurred at Kronstadt remained of decisive symbolic importance.[19]

Disillusioned, those anarchists that survived the experience took up their travels again, involved themselves in new struggles and were to be among the first in articulating a critique of state socialism and the Bolshevik model. Their problem was that communism or, more accurately, Marxism-Leninism came to dominate the labour movement, strangling its political parties and trade unions in dogma and Stalinist orthodoxy, and within this context anarchists, always a minority group, were further marginalized. It was not, therefore, until the 1960s, when the personality cult of Stalin was dead and when many communist parties, particularly in the West, had been discredited by their inertia and conservatism, that anarchism made something of a comeback. Student radicals throughout the world found themselves drawn to a new type of non-authoritarian, spontaneous and libertarian protest, and if at times the inspiration came from Mao's China or Castro's Cuba then so too it derived sustenance from older anarchist ideals. In 1968 the black flag of anarchy flew over street barricades of Paris and the university campus at Berkeley, California. Anarchism found itself merged into a counterculture of youth, drugs, sexual permissiveness and rock and roll. Liberation, to cite the title of Richard Neville's provocative book, was to be through *Play Power*.[20] But this too proved to be a false dawn. Student protest quickly faded and the long-haired revolutionary soon found his way into the accountant's office and the world of conventional politics.

Has anarchism therefore died as a movement of revolt and rebellion? As a mass movement the answer is clearly yes; but it lives on. In Britain, for example, *Class War*, an anarchist organization that owes more to punk than it does to Kropotkin, frequently caught the headlines with its 'Bash the Rich' campaigns, violent demonstrations and often tasteless but effective propaganda. Disorder, it proclaims, is our power. More recently still, 'the eco-direct action community' has drawn inspiration from anarchist ideals and practices. A 'network' such as *Earth First!* proudly announces: 'It does not work to an agenda. Its response is emotional – to protect the environment, mainly through direct action'. What, then, is its aims? 'To replace capitalism and large-scale industry.' How is this to be done? As with all those inspired by anarchist principles, there is no definitive, programmatic answer: 'through involvement in situations of struggle to protect the earth, alternative strategies are being discovered.' And these take a variety of forms but all loosely fall into the category of 'non-violent' direct action 'without any one group being in charge': peace camps, raves against the machine, reclaiming the streets, street-party blockades, and, most famously, the tree-climbing and tunnelling that in protest after protest has brought immense publicity and even celebrity. So, too, anarchism continues to exhibit its affection for the dramatic gesture. Hitting the headlines, the pop group Chumbawamba, calling themselves 'anarchists', threw a very public bucket of water over British Deputy Prime Minister John Prescott in 1998. The spirit of anarchy at least survives.

PHILOSOPHICAL ANARCHISM

If we were asked to assess the constructive achievements of anarchism in the twentieth century we would have to acknowledge that they have been slight. George Orwell's graphic account of anarchist Barcelona in *Homage to Catalonia* and Borkenau's description of life in an Andalusian village[21] show that anarchist principles can be put into practice and that for those individuals involved it was an invigorating and liberating experience. But such examples have been both few in number and short in duration. It has, therefore, been more as a philosophical idea that anarchism, if at all, has had an impact and this has been especially true in the past twenty or so years. And with surprising consequences.

A key text has been Murray Bookchin's *Post-Scarcity Anarchism*. Written in the tradition of communist anarchism Bookchin sought to ally anarchism with contemporary ecological concerns, arguing not just that the goal of revolution was the liberation of daily life but that its precondition was the practice of ecological principles (see Chapter 10). The goal was to humanize society, to move out of the realm of necessity into the realm of freedom and this, he believed, was to be attained through the promise of decentralized, communitarian lifestyles or what he referred to as 'ecological forms of human association'. Gone was to be the emphasis on production for production's sake and the stress on quantity and standardization. Technology was to be employed on a human scale and in the interests of quality and artistry, the elimination of human toil and material insecurity. Human dependence upon the natural world would once again become a central and living part of our culture. More recently Bookchin, in criticizing what its advocates describe as deep ecology, has sought to articulate what he terms a social ecology that draws inspiration from 'such outstanding decentralist thinkers as Peter Kropotkin, William Morris and Paul Goodman among many others who have advanced a serious challenge to the present society with its vast hierarchical, sexist, class-ruled, statist apparatus and militaristic history'. His self-proclaimed aim is to attack the vested corporate and political interests of capitalism and this, he believes, can be done in alliance with the leftist tendencies of the German greens, extra-parliamentary street movements and radical eco-feminists.

From an altogether different perspective, in 1970 Robert Paul Wolff published *In Defense of Anarchism*. The work of a self-proclaimed 'philosophical anarchist', the starting point of Wolff's argument was that the fundamental assumption of all moral philosophy was that man was responsible for his actions. Men were 'metaphysically free' and as such were obliged to achieve autonomy wherever and whenever possible. Accordingly, in Wolff's view, anarchism was the only political doctrine consistent with the virtue of autonomy. What, however, did this actually mean in practice? If, as Wolff argued, the anarchist could occasionally grant the necessity of complying with the law under certain circumstances then this in no way implied that he was obliged to accept that the authority of the state was legitimate. The conflict between authority and autonomy was without possible resolution. Moreover, Wolff extends his critique to include states deriving supposed legitimacy from representative democracy, majority rule and even (his most difficult case) unanimous direct democracy. All are incompatible with the preservation of man's autonomy. What then was Wolff's own vision of a world without states? By his own admission he gives us something which falls 'far short of a coherent projection of an anarchist society' but the general guidelines are clear. Wolff wishes to show us that societies can be held together by something other than the state, that people when in full knowledge of their situation, can put aside private interest and pursue the common good. Voluntary compliance would be sufficient to generate an adequate level of social co-ordination, thus making possible national defence, the collective pursuit of internal goals as well as the maintenance of an industrial economy. Economic decentralization would be a necessity even if 'at the present time' it would produce economic chaos.

If the philosophical basis of Wolff's argument was derived from the eighteenth-century German philosopher Kant then Robert Nozick (1938–), in his highly influential *Anarchy, State and Utopia* published in 1974, returned to the seventeenth century and the ideas of John Locke, (see Chapters 2 and 3). For Nozick, anarchy – in effect, Locke's hypothetical state of nature – figures as a conceptual device designed ultimately to justify his assertion that only the minimal state limited to narrowly defined functions such as law enforcement is permissible. The important point, however, is that Nozick recognizes the legitimacy of the individualist anarchist's moral objections to the state. States, by claiming a monopoly of the use of force within their territory and the corresponding right to exact punishment, violate the rights of individuals. The detailed argument of how Nozick sets out to overcome this objection to the state need not detain us, but some knowledge of its content is vital if we are to understand its important implications.

In effect, Nozick argues that it is not necessarily the case that a state would arise out of a state of nature. It is just as likely that private protective agencies would emerge, paid for by individual citizens and designed exclusively to protect their clients and secure individual redress. Ultimately, Nozick argues, there will emerge a dominant protective agency and this, to all intents and purposes, will be a form of state, because everyone will recognize that it is in their interest to join. But crucially no one's rights are adjudged to have been violated and such a state would in no way be entitled, for example, to begin the task of wealth distribution or the provision of social services. 'Patterned principles of distributive justice', Nozick writes, 'involve appropriating the actions of other persons.'

The conclusion then is that the state's functions, where legitimate, should be severely limited and it was in this way that Nozick was to contribute to the emergence of the radical or 'New' Right in the 1970s, a trend which ultimately saw the election of Ronald Reagan and Margaret Thatcher. The real radicals, for example Murray Rothbard in works such as *For a New Liberty*, continued to see themselves as the defenders of 'anarcho-capitalism' and it was through them that demands for the privatization of prisons and the police force, as well as the privatization of much else, were heard. Every individual had an absolute right to private property and therefore taxation was a form of robbery, a system of coercive violence designed to sustain a class of exploitative rulers. The state – by nature an aggressive institution – was not even necessary to make or enforce law. Everything could be left to the market. Moreover, on this view, the advance of modern technology made anarchistic arrangements increasingly feasible.

However, it is hard not to conclude that these ideas – with roots deep in classical liberalism – are described as anarchist only on the basis of a misunderstanding of what anarchism is. And this is especially so when we are invited to consider the American conservative Ayn Rand, author of *Capitalism: The Unknown Ideal* and *The Virtue of Selfishness*, as one of their sources of inspiration. Anarchism, according to Rothbard, is defined by its articulation of 'the dissolution of the state into social and market arrangements' and thus it is compatible with an unrestrained capitalism and the pursuit of self-interest. Correctly perceived, anarchism does not stand for the untrammelled freedom of the individual (as the 'anarcho-capitalists' appear to believe) but, as we have already seen, for the extension of individuality and community. 'If anything', Peter Marshall writes in *Demanding the Impossible: A History of Anarchism*, 'anarcho-capitalism is merely a free-for-all in which only the rich and the cunning would benefit.'

More intriguing are recent attempts to elucidate the outlines of a 'post-structural anarchism'.[22] Drawing upon the analyses of the nature of power to be found in such writers as Foucault and Lyotard, the aim has been to describe a kind of politics that is 'more local and diffuse than the large-scale politics that is better suited to grant narratives'. As the sites of power and oppression are decentralized, so must resistance be, thus producing a 'micro-politics' of 'diffusion and multiplicity' focused upon 'multiple struggles' that stretch beyond 'the economic and state levels' to bring in the realms of the psychological, sexual, ethical, religious, etc.

ANARCHISM AT THE TURN OF THE TWENTY-FIRST CENTURY

If of late there has been much discussion of individualist anarchism and its affinities with the 'New' Right then it should also be clear from what has been said that to a large extent anarchism in the twentieth century and before has been on the side of the defeated and, not surprisingly therefore, it has frequently been characterized as either a reactionary or an outmoded doctrine. At best anarchists are seen as an absurd, romantic breed who cannot come to terms with the realities of a highly industrialized, bureaucratic and urbanized world. But can anarchism be so easily dismissed, especially in an age which has become increasingly sceptical about both the efficiency and the benefits of the state's actions, and where there is a need for radical solutions to our urban, ecological and industrial problems? For all its weaknesses, failures and naïvety anarchism might still have something to offer.

Writing in his 1973 text *Anarchy in Action*, Colin Ward argued that 'the anarchist alternative is that of fragmentation, fission rather than fusion, diversity rather than unity, a mass of societies rather than a mass society'. In line with this, contemporary anarchists continue to call for forms of human activity that are local and immediate and that call upon the involvement, ability and ingenuity of the people themselves. They argue for 'thinner cities', 'topless federations', urban renewal through citizen control and participation, open families, an education that is both child-centred and varied, workers' control in industry, the 'deinstitutionalization' of social welfare and health care and its replacement by a system based on self-help and mutual support, a decentralized Europe of the regions rather than a centralized European superstate. More generally, as a distinct intellectual current of social thought, anarchism continues to remind us that the individual is to be prized, that there is more to life than the routine-bound and soul-destroying pursuit of wealth, and that we can aspire to a more communal, less competitive, form of existence. More than this – and anarchists from Proudhon to Bookchin have not tired of repeating this lesson – anarchism tells us that goals cannot be divorced from means, that the attempt to construct a society of freedom through the tactics of slavery and oppression is doomed to ultimate failure. Anarchism also makes us aware that states – all states, whatever their shape, size, or ideological justification – have a tendency and the capacity to perpetuate themselves as institutions, to extend the range of their functions, and, if necessary, to turn themselves into instruments of oppression and censorship. Even today the vast majority of states – for example in Latin America or in Asia – fall into this latter category and even our much prized Western democracies are not above committing the occasional abuse. This in turn makes us reflect upon the ultimate justification of the state's authority – who exactly is it there to serve? – and on the importance of even the individual protest against its misused power. As Robert Paul Wolff eloquently puts it:

The belief in state authority comes naturally to men, it would appear. A band of robbers ride into town with guns drawn and demand all the gold in the bank. They are called criminals. They return the next year on the same day and repeat their demand. Again they are called criminals. They put on uniforms and return each year on the same day. Eventually they are called tax collectors. Finally, the smallest and least offensive of the bandits rides into town unarmed and the townspeople given him their gold without a struggle. The State has arrived.[23]

ACKNOWLEDGEMENT

The author wishes especially to thank Professor Neil Harding and the editors for their comments on the first draft of this chapter and Tom Bunyard, Françoise Blum and Colette Chambelland for providing invaluable primary material.

NOTES

1. A. Berkman, *ABC of Anarchism*, Freedom Press, London, 1977, p.2.
2. W. Godwin, *Enquiry Concerning Political Justice*, Penguin, Harmondsworth, 1976.
3. M. Stirner, *The Ego and his Own*, Fifield, New York, 1915.
4. See L. Tolstoy, *On Civil Disobedience and Non-violence*, Mentor, New York, 1968 and *The Kingdom of God is Within You*, University of Nebraska Press, Lincoln, NB, 1984. Also G. Ostergaard and C. Melville, *The Gentle Anarchists: A Study of the Sarvodaya Movement for Non-Violent Revolution in India*, Clarendon Press, Oxford, 1971.
5. See P. Thomas, *Karl Marx and the Anarchists*, RKP, London, 1980.
6. P.J. Proudhon, *The General Idea of the Revolution in the Nineteenth Century*, Pluto, London, 1989, p.294.
7. P. Kropotkin, 'Revolutionary Government', in his *Kropotkin's Revolutionary Pamphlets*, Vanguard, New York, 1927, p.243.
8. Kropotkin, 'The Russian Revolution and Soviet Government', in ibid., p.254.
9. E. Goldman, 'Anarchism: What It Really Stands For', in F. Goldman, *Anarchism and Other Essays*, Mother Earth, New York, 1917, p.60.
10. Kropotkin, 'Anarchism: Its Philosophy and Ideal', in his *Kropotkin's Revolutionary Pamphlets*, p.123.
11. A. Ritter, *Anarchism: A Theoretical Analysis*, Cambridge University Press, Cambridge, 1980.
12. P. Kropotkin, *Mutual Aid: A Factor in Evolution*, Beacon, Boston, 1914, p.292.
13. Berkman, op. cit., p.78.
14. P. Kropotkin, 'Anarchist Communism: Its Basis and Principles', in his *Kropotkin's Revolutionary Pamphlets*, p.59.
15. E. Goldman, 'Minorities versus Majorities', in *Anarchism and Other Essays*, p.80.

16. See M. Fleming, *The Anarchist Way to Socialism*, Croom Helm, London, 1979.
17. See P.F. Brissenden, *The Launching of the Industrial Workers of the World*, Columbia University Press, New York, 1920; F.F. Ridley, *Revolutionary Syndicalism in France: The Direct Action of its Time*, Cambridge University Press, Cambridge, 1970; and D.L. Roberts, *The Syndicalist Tradition in Italian Fascism*, University of North Carolina Press, Chapel Hill, 1979.
18. See H. Thomas, *The Spanish Civil War*, Hamish Hamilton, London, 1977 and G. Brenan, *The Spanish Labyrinth*, Cambridge University Press, Cambridge, 1969.
19. D. and G. Cohn-Bendit, *Obsolete Communism: The Left-Wing Alternative*, Penguin, Harmondsworth, 1968.
20. D. Caute, *Sixty-Eight: The Year of the Barricades*, Paladin, London, 1988.
21. F. Borkenau, *The Spanish Cockpit*, Faber and Faber, London, 1937.
22. See, for example T. May, *The Political Philosophy of Poststructural Anarchism*, Pennsylvania State University Press, Pennsylvania, 1994.
23. R.P. Wolff, *In Defense of Anarchism*, Harper, New York, 1976, p.113.

GUIDE TO FURTHER READING

The standard text on the history of anarchism is G. Woodcock, *Anarchism* (Penguin, Harmondsworth, 1983). To this can now be added P. Marshall, *Demanding the Impossible: A History of Anarchism* (HarperCollins, London, 1991). J. Joll, *The Anarchists* (Methuen, London, 1979) and D. Miller, *Anarchism* (Dent, London, 1984) provide excellent introductions to a wide range of anarchist ideas and movements. A very sophisticated examination of the cogency of anarchist ideas can be found in A. Ritter, *Anarchism: A Theoretical Analysis* (Cambridge University Press, Cambridge, 1980). See also D. Goodway (ed.), *For Anarchism: History, Theory and Practice* (Routledge, London, 1989). See also T. May, *The Political Philosophy of Poststructural Anarchism* (Pennsylvania State University Press, Pennsylvania, 1994).

A selection of anarchist texts appear in G. Woodcock, *The Anarchist Reader* (Fontana, London, 1980), I.L. Horowitz, *The Anarchists* (Dell, New York, 1964) and L.I. Krimmerman and L. Perry, *Patterns of Anarchy* (Anchor, New York, 1966). Less interesting and slightly dated are D.E. Apter and J. Joll, *Anarchism Today* (Macmillan, London, 1971), D. Guérin, *Anarchism* (Monthly Review Press, New York, 1970) and A. Carter, *The Political Theory of Anarchism* (Routledge and Kegan Paul, London, 1971). J.R. Pennock and J.W. Chapman, *Nomos XIX: Anarchism* (New York University Press, New York, 1978) provides an interesting collection of essays reflecting the upsurge of interest in anarchism in America after the publication of Robert Nozick's *Anarchy, State and Utopia* (Blackwell, Oxford, 1974).

On the great anarchists of the nineteenth century see C. Crowder, *Classical Anarchism The Political Thought of Godwin, Proudhon, Bakunin and Kropotkin* (Oxford University Press, Oxford, 1991) and C. Cahm, *Kropotkin and the Rise of Revolutionary Anarchism* (Cambridge University Press, Cambridge, 1989). Several articles can usefully be consulted: D. Novak, 'The Place of Anarchism in the History of Political Thought', *Review of Politics*, 20, 1958, pp.307–29; R.B. Fowler, 'The Anarchist Tradition of Political Thought', *Western Political Quarterly*, 25, 1972, pp.738–52; and D. Miller, 'Kropotkin', *Government and Opposition*, 18, 1983, pp.319–38.

Anarchism in Britain is explored in J. Quail, *The Slow Burning Fuse: The Lost History of the British Anarchists* (Paladin, London, 1978) and in H. Oliver, *The International Anarchist Movement in Late Victorian England* (Croom Helm, London, 1983); in Russia in P. Avrich, *The Russian Anarchists* (Princeton University Press, Princeton, 1967); in Spain in M. Bookchin, *The Spanish Anarchists: The Heroic Years* (Harper, New York, 1977); whilst the evolution of French anarcho-syndicalism can be seen in J. Jennings *Syndicalism in France: A History of Ideas* (Macmillan, London, 1990). On recent trends in Britain see also *Class War: A Decade of Disorder* (Verso, London, 1991), the anarchist quarterly *The Raven* and the fortnightly *Freedom* (published by Freedom Press, 84b Whitechapel High Street, London).

On the distinctive 'right-wing anarchism' associated with the USA readers can try to obtain J.J. Martin, *Men against the State: The Expositors of Individualist Anarchism* (Ralph Miles, Colorado Springs, 1970). A detailed biography of Emma Goldman is to be found in A. Wexler, *Emma Goldman: An Intimate Life* (Virago, London, 1984) and *Emma Goldman in Exile* (Beacon Press, Boston, 1989). To this can also be added R. Drinnon, *Rebel in Paradise: A Biography of Emma Goldman* (Chicago University Press, Chicago, 1961).

Excellent primary material illustrating the key themes in what has been the dominant strand of twentieth-century anarchism comes in the form of P. Kropotkin, *Kropotkin's Revolutionary Pamphlets* (Vanguard, New York, 1927), P. Kropotkin, *Mutual Aid* (Porter Sargent, Boston, MA, no date), E. Goldman, *Red Emma Speaks* (Vintage Books, New York, 1972), E. Goldman, *Anarchism and Other Essays* (Dover, New York, 1969), E. Malatesta, *Anarchy* (Freedom Press, London, 1974), A. Berkman, *ABC of Anarchism* (Freedom Press, London, 1977) and E. Pataud and E. Pouget, *How We Will Make the Revolution* (Pluto, London, 1990).

7
NATIONALISM
Roger Griffin

—

NATIONALISM AS A MODERN POLITICAL IDEOLOGY

Unlike most other ideologies treated in this volume, all closely associated
with modern 'Western' values, nationalism has an aura of antiquity about it,
even of the pre-historical. After all, the existence of distinct cultures can be
traced back into the mists of time, as the archaeological remains from Aztec,
Hittite and countless other archaic civilizations which adorn 'our' museums
still testify. Then there are the many ancient texts which refer to nations in
conflict, such as Herodotus's writings on the wars between Greeks and
Persians, Caesar's description of his military campaign in Gaul, or a passage
in the Gospel of St Matthew prophesying that in the Last Days 'nation shall
rise up against nation'. It would be tempting to conclude that nations and
nationalism are primordial human phenomena and as such are as old as
human civilization itself. Yet Ernest Gellner speaks for most scholars who
have reflected on this issue when he asserts:

> Nationalism tends to treat itself as a manifest and self-evident princi-
> ple, accessible as such to all men, and violated only through some
> perverse blindness, when in fact it owes its plausibility and compelling
> nature only to a very special set of circumstances, which do indeed
> obtain now, but which were alien to most of humanity and history.[1]

It will be a central theme of what follows that nationalism in its various
permutations and the nation-states based on them are indeed essentially
modern, even in the many instances when they are associated with ethnic
distinctiveness or with political states which may be as old as recorded
history.[2] In other words, while nationalists are wont to invoke a heroic past

stretching into the mists of time so as to legitimate claims they make on behalf of 'their' people, 'nationalism' as an ideology which defines the relationship of individuals to the state and which legitimates what that state undertakes on behalf of its citizens was literally inconceivable before the 'modern age'. Indeed, to the surprise of most of the Western intelligentsia, it has established itself in the last 100 years as one of the most pervasive and potent determinants of modernity itself.

The recentness of nationalism is borne out by its etymology. Nation is derived via the French from the Latin *natio*, whose root occurs in *nasci* to be born, and which in Classical usage tended to be a pejorative term for a race, tribe or 'breed' of people considered uncouth by Roman standards. In the various Romance languages which inherited the word 'nation' as part of the legacy of occupation, or the non-Latin languages which eventually adopted it under the influence of the Renaissance, 'nation' was to go through a number of semantic shifts before it was used expressly to denote the alleged cultural unity and political sovereignty vested in an entire people. Significantly, among the earliest documents of this usage are a pamphlet by the abbé Sieyès and the Declaration of the Rights of Man and Citizen, both composed in the heat of the French Revolution in 1789. It was only after this that the term 'nationalism' first started gaining currency in European languages to refer to the animating energy of the new 'people power' which events in France had revealed to be capable of overthrowing not just a monarch (as in the English Civil War), but monarchy itself, and not just in a seceding colony (as in the American Revolution), but in one of Europe's oldest established absolutist states.

Philology also highlights the fact that, far from being a universal datum of human experience, the concept of 'nationalism' with its revolutionary populist implications has a highly nuanced history as we move from society to society. Even in languages which have borrowed it, such as German or Polish, it acquires specific connotations, while those cultures which have in the last 200 years generated home-grown equivalents from native linguistic roots, such as Arabic or Chinese, have done so largely under the impact of contacts with the West and of modernization: indeed the appearance of the concept is a reliable litmus test for such an impact. In the process of coining the concept they have inevitably imbued it with untranslatable, culture-specific shades of meaning. Fascinating case studies in this are the Arabic term *watan*,[3] or the Japanese *kokumin*,[4] both of which only partially overlap semantically with the English term 'nation'.

It is not just the fact that nationalism is bound up with the complex force of modernity and has adapted itself to myriad unique histories, languages and cultures which frustrates those in search of simple definitions or snap judgements for it. What further complicates all discussions of nationalism is the ambivalent role which it has played in modern history. On the one hand it is indispensable to the cohesion of democratic institutions and values and hence takes the benign form of 'liberal' or 'civic nationalism', while on the other it acts as a malignant force which can pervert liberalism, and even lead to its wholesale destruction. In this case it is referred to by a number of terms, such as 'chauvinism', 'integral nationalism', 'hyper-' or 'ultra-nationalism', though for the sake of clarity we will adhere to the distinction 'liberal/ illiberal', well aware that, rather like national boundaries, the demarcation line between the two is rarely as straightforward as it might seem. The corruption of liberal nationalism by illiberal elements continues to be one of the most disturbing determinants of the maelstrom of events and processes we call 'the modern world'. Thus the study of any particular instance of nationalism should take account of whether it is primarily cultural or political, located in a thinker, a movement or a regime, and works to cement liberal values or destroy them.

AN EXPANDED DEFINITION OF NATIONALISM

After these preliminary reflections stressing nationalism's elusive, para- doxical nature, it is as well if we offer a working definition of the term, or what social scientists know (after Max Weber) as an 'ideal type'.[5]

> **Nationalism:** an ideology whose affective driving force is the sense of belonging to and serving a perceived national community. The carriers of this ideology attribute to their nation a distinctive cultural identity which sets it apart from other nations and gives it a special place in the historical process. This community is (usually subliminally) identified with a unique set of characteristics allegedly deriving from constitu- tional, historical, geographical, religious, linguistic, ethnic and/or genetic realities. The sentiments aroused by the sense of being a member of this community may be confined to a keen sense of pride in national culture and traditions without being associated with political demands ('cultural nationalism'). On the other hand, when such senti- ments play a major role in the dynamics of a *political* movement, the thrust of nationalism is generally for the national community to be assumed to form 'naturally' a state (whether autonomous or part of a federation or confederation of states) in which the sovereignty held to reside in the people is exercized by its elected or self-appointed repre- sentatives within territorial boundaries recognized by the international political community.
>
> As long as the resulting 'nation-state' upholds the principle of civil society on the basis of which all permanent residents fully enjoy the human rights conferred by citizenship, irrespective of ethnic criteria, then nationalism is indissociable from political liberalism and gives rise to 'liberal nationalism' (sometimes called 'civic nationalism'). Indeed a subjective 'secondary' national identity in the sense of 'love of one's

country' or patriotism), which may well not be coterminous with a primary sense of ethnic identity, is arguably vital to the social cohesion and political stability of all liberal democracies.

However, in post-traditional societies the universal human need for identity and belonging has often been fulfilled by a particularly intense form of affective attachment to one's 'own' homeland ('chauvinism') or people ('ethnocentrism'), one often maintained through the demonization of other nations or outgroups, ethnic or otherwise, within the nation. The emotions to which such an attachment gives rise has proved highly susceptible to being exploited for their own political purposes either by state oligarchies (in the form of 'official nationalism') or by demagogues of a revolutionary movement. In such cases nationalism may act as the legitimation of hatred directed at 'foreigners' (xenophobia) and of discrimination on grounds of ethnicity (racism), both of which axiomatically deny the universality of human rights and thus generate 'illiberal nationalism'. This then serves to underpin domestic or foreign policies which can lead to the subjugation, persecution or even the attempted extermination of national or ethnic communities perceived as alien, primitive or degenerate. In this form nationalism is one of the most potent enemies of a harmonious international community and the creation of a sustainable political and economic global society.

This definition, while complex, still artificially simplifies the phenomenon of nationalism by teasing out into distinct components elements which may 'on the ground' be closely bound up together. A classic example of this is provided by the career of one of the principal ideologues of the Jacobin phase of the French Revolution, Maximilien de Robespierre (1758–94). Though he started out as a highly committed and articulate activist within the movement of liberal nationalism which overthrew the *ancien régime*, his patriotism gradually degenerated into a fanatical chauvinism by which he justified dictatorship and terror, a perversion epitomized in the Revolutionary Tribunal's decision to redefine the crime of treason as *lèse-nation* instead of *lèse-majésté*.[6]

The capacity of nationalism to operate either as an emancipatory populist movement or a tendentially authoritarian state orthodoxy, a force upholding radical liberal values or destroying them, has caused some commentators to refer to its essential ambivalence in terms of its 'Janus-headed' quality.[7] An even stronger metaphor for nationalism's schizoid nature opens Minogue's book: 'Nationalism, as the story is generally told, begins as Sleeping Beauty and ends as Frankenstein's monster.'[8] However, as Jacobinism illustrates, it should not be assumed that European nationalism mysteriously degenerated as the nineteenth century wore on. As long as it has been an active force in history it has always contained the potential for promoting both genuine liberal democracy and its grotesque travesty, one which upholds the rights of one segment of humankind at the expense of others. After all, the American Declaration of Independence of 1776 went hand in hand with the destruction of Native American cultures, just as the British retained the institution of slavery in the West Indies long after the 'Glorious Revolution' of 1688 had on paper transferred sovereignty to the British people (though in reality to the ruling male élite). Throughout the twentieth century nationalism has continued to demonstrate its capacity for double-think, and at times to act both as an enlightened Dr Jekyll and a socio-pathological Mr Hyde.

LIBERAL THEORIES OF NATIONALISM

In their respective developments as political theories, too, nationalism's contradictory manifestations as both a liberal and an illiberal force is a history of parallel lives or cohabitation rather than degeneration or succession. It could be argued that as a doctrine liberal nationalism is as old as liberalism itself. Drawing sustenance from its deep roots in the Enlightenment's universal principles of rationalism and progress, it asserts the existence of basic rights on the grounds of a common humanity. However, these rights can only be enjoyed in the first instance within a particular civil society based on laws enforceable within clearly defined territorial limits. In other words liberalism presupposes the existence or formation of a constitutional nation-state, even if its ultimate vision is a global society made up of such states in which all human beings can coexist in peace and freedom. Within this scheme nationality comes to be identified primarily with statehood, citizenship and universal freedoms, and not with ethnic identity, racial homogeneity or a particular history. Since the late eighteenth century a number of important political theorists have contributed to the theoretical elaboration of the dream of a world order based on the peaceful coexistence of liberal nation, some of the most well known being Jean-Jacques Rousseau (1712–78), Immanuel Kant (1724–1804), Jeremy Bentham (1748–1832), Richard Cobden (1804–65), John Bright (1811–89) and Francisque Bouvet (1799–1871).[9]

Yet, as on so many other basic issues relating to liberalism, it is arguably still J.S. Mill (1806–73) who offers the contemporary student of political thought the most lucid exposition of liberal thinking on nationalism. In an essay written in 1840, for example, he attacked 'nationality in the vulgar sense of the term', which he associated with a 'senseless antipathy to foreigners; and indifference to the general welfare of the human race, or an unjust preference of the supposed interests of our own country'. But he saw nationality as the 'essential condition of stability in political society' when it consists in the 'feeling of common interest among those who live under the same government, and are contained within the same natural or historical boundaries'. Nationality in this sense he regarded as crucial to enable societies 'to pass through turbulent times without any permanent weakening of the securities for peaceable existence'.[10]

Nine years later he felt prompted to vindicate the Paris Revolution of February 1848 which put an end to the 'bourgeois monarchy' of Louis Philippe. In doing so he took issue with the judgement of Lord Brougham who had condemned what he saw as the true cause of the king's abdication, namely 'the principle, that new speculation in the rights of independent states, the security of neighbouring governments, and indeed the happiness of all nations, which is termed *Nationality*, adopted as a kind of rule for the distribution of dominion' – a comment which underlines just how recent the concept of popular sovereignty still was in 1848. However, while upholding nationalism as the mainstay of liberalism, Mill felt only revulsion for the evidence provided by the recent revolutions in Germany and eastern Europe that at times 'the sentiment of nationality so far outweighs the love of liberty, that the people are willing to abet their rulers in crushing the liberty and independence of any people not of their own race and language'.[11] Mill returned to the topic of nationalism in a chapter of his seminal work of liberal theory, *Considerations on Constitutional Government* (1861), entitled 'Of Nationality, as Connected with Representative Government', which contains one of the classic formulations of a people's right to self-determination:

> Where the sentiment of nationality exists in any force, there is a *prima facie* case for uniting all the members of that nationality under the same government, and a government to themselves apart. This is merely saying that the question of government ought to be decided by the governed. One hardly knows what any division of the human race should be free to do, if not determine, with which of the various collective bodies of human beings they choose to associate themselves.[12]

The term *prima facie* is an important qualification, however, for Mill has no intention of writing a blank cheque which would allow any self-appointed nationalist movement to constitute itself as a state. A few paragraphs later he adds the vital proviso that if 'different nationalities are so locally intermingled that it is not practicable for them to be under separate governments ... there is no course open to them but to make a virtue of necessity, and reconcile themselves to living together under equal rights and laws'. He also gives short shrift to separatist movements of smaller peoples, considering that it is to their advantage 'to be brought into the current of ideas and feelings of a highly civilized and cultivated people', a judgement which he applies to the Bretons, Basques, Welsh, Scots and, after some deliberation, the Irish. In the same essay, Mill deplored cases where an advanced people is taken over by a less civilized but more numerous one, commenting, in a passage which some would regard as prophetic, that if Russia were to absorb 'any of the principal countries of Europe' it would be 'one of the greatest misfortunes of the world'.[13]

A contemporary statesman who would endorse most of Mill's reflections on nationalism, not least the last of these, is Vàclav Havel (1936–   ), former President of Czechoslovakia and now president of the Czech Republic. His use of poetry and drama to appeal for basic freedoms had already made him the country's most famous dissident under Soviet rule, and after the Velvet Revolution of 1989 he set about becoming the ambassador of national self-determination in a spirit of universal humanism close to the heart of Enlightenment idealists such as Kant. He formulated the axioms of his vision when in 1991 he received an honourary degree at Lehigh University in Bethlehem, Pennsylvania. In his address he dwelt on the concept of 'home', stressing how vital it is to a sense of personal identity and purpose. Among the vital components of home which he identified were ethnic and national consciousness, which in his case he could distinguish into 'Czechness' and 'Czechoslovakness'. Yet the central theme of his talk was to reject the type of nationalism which Mill saw as liable to crush the liberty and independence of other peoples. For Havel home is to be pictured as a series of concentric circles extending from the local (family, friends, church, profession) to the supranational, namely Europe, modern civilization and the planet as a whole. The sole foundation for this multilevel sense of identity is a human sovereignty which 'finds its political expression in civic sovereignty'.

> I certainly do not want, therefore, to suppress the national dimension of a person's identity, or to deny it, or to refuse to acknowledge its legitimacy and its right to full self-realization. I merely reject the kind of political notions that attempt, in the name of nationality, to suppress other aspects of the human home, other aspects of humanity and human rights.[14]

Fortunately, the need for championing in theory and in practice a nationalism stripped of ethnocentrism and compatible with universal human rights has not just been the concern of humanistic philosophers or dissident artists. It lies at the very heart of one of the world's most important global institutions, the United Nations. The declarations and policies which emanate in a steady stream from its various component organizations are all informed by the vision which was born out of a tide of revulsion against the racist nationalism which had generated the horrors of the Second World War. At the heart of this vision is the conviction that all the world's peoples can eventually live in peaceful coexistence and collaborate in the alleviation of human-made misery. In other words they reflect a commitment (at least in principle, even if it has been so often compromised by the sectional interests of member nations in practice) to a radical egalitarianism on issues of nationality. Typical is the Declaration on Race and Racial Prejudice of 27 November 1978 issued by the United Nations Educational, Scientific and

Cultural Organization (UNESCO): 'The differences between the achievements of the different peoples are entirely attributable to geographical, historical, political, economic, social and cultural factors. Such differences can in no case serve as a pretext for any rank-ordered classification of nations and peoples.'[15]

THE CONTAMINATION OF LIBERAL NATIONALISM

In the context of twentieth-century political theory, then, the hallmark of a truly liberal nationalism is that the nation-state is considered to be a political unit indispensable to the modern age. Moreover, it acknowledges that a communal sense of ethnic or national identity helps guarantee the stability of an existing nation-state once formed and is a major criterion in deciding whether claims to autonomous statehood should be recognized by the international community. However, a self-consistent liberalism denies that the state's sovereignty resides in the nation on the basis of a common ethnic identity, locating it instead in a properly constituted civil society. Civil rights are a function of what Havel calls 'civic sovereignty', that is, of citizenship and statehood not ethnicity or race, and demands for secession which invoke an alleged cultural or racial homogeneity as their primary rationale are to be treated by the international community with the utmost scepticism.[16] Each human being's rights are perfectly compatible with the rights of all other ethnic groups or nationalities residing legally within the state, as well as with those of the citizens of all other nation-states which defend the cause of a common humanity.

Yet even in the artificially tidy world of theory the boundary between liberal and illiberal nationalism can often be fuzzy. J.S. Mill himself betrayed a Eurocentric bias in his portrayal of Britain's colonization of India and England's hegemony over the rest of the 'British' Isles as a benevolent civilizing force. Before him Gottfried von Herder (1744–1803) had upheld a typically eighteenth-century belief in the capacity of each nation to live in harmony with all others as different but equally valid facets of God's creation, humanity. Yet at the core of his world-view lay the belief that the nation was defined by a unique spirit (*Volksgeist*), thus pioneering a form of cultural nationalism which attached great significance to language, folk-myth and poetry, a position which proved later to be all too easily corruptible into deeply illiberal fantasies of Germany's alleged racial purity and superiority.

One of the nationalist theorists who took up Herder's ideas was Giuseppe Mazzini (1805–72), who inspired nationalist liberation or unification movements (e.g. Young Italy, Young Poland) in various parts of nineteenth-century Europe. His vision of the coming age of international harmony was ecstatic:

When in the presence of the Young Europe now arising, all the altars of the old world shall be overthrown, two new altars will be raised upon the soil made fruitful by the divine Word. And the hand of the initiator-people shall inscribe upon one the *Fatherland*, upon the other *Humanity*. As children of the same mother, as brethren gathered together, the peoples shall assemble around those altars, and make sacrifice in peace and love.[17]

Yet Mazzini's ideas also reinforced the tendentially illiberal belief that every state should be based on a unique, historically defined nationality with its own heroic mission to perform, first and foremost Italy, the 'initiator-people'. It is little wonder that he was adopted as a prophet of Fascist Italy two generations after his death.

Another way liberal nationalism can slip imperceptibly into illiberalism is when conservatives in the tradition of Edmund Burke (1729–97) place so much weight on the need for a sense of tradition, organic nationhood and cultural or ethnic homogeneity that they become oblivious of how easily this can prevail over any deep-seated commitment to the equal rights of all citizens, irrespective of their ethnicity. A more contemporary example is provided by the British political commentator, Paul Helm. Even before Ceauçescu's downfall and the dissolution of the Russian Empire, the flaring up of ethnic tensions between Hungarians and Rumanians in 1986 prompted him to observe that

The ties of brotherhood, of common history and culture and of blood are by any test firmer and longer lasting than the supposedly transcend-ent ties of economic destiny and class solidarity which, in Marxist theory, unite all socialist countries, and which are supposed to be destined to bind us all together.[18]

Yet for all his prescience, Helm failed to acknowledge the dangers to humane coexistence which an obsessive preoccupation with such ties bring with it, dangers which in the 1990s have been so chillingly illustrated in the campaigns of ethnic cleansing carried out in the Balkans and in Rwanda.

When we take into account the source of some of the most eloquent expressions of liberal nationalism in the twentieth century, namely the pronouncements of political leaders, the fuzziness intensifies even further. With the exception of Gandhi (1869–1948), few of even the most liberal-minded heads of state of the twentieth century have had the clear-sightedness of Havel in his absolute rejection of what Mill called 'vulgar' nationalism, whether we think of Woodrow Wilson (1856–1919), Winston Churchill (1874–1965), or Margaret Thatcher (1925–   ). Take Charles de Gaulle (1890–1970), for example, hero of France's liberation from Nazi occupation and the ultra-nationalist Vichy regime. In the opening pages of his memoirs he makes no bones about the irrational[19] affective core of his nationalism, crystallized in his image of France as 'the princess of fairy tales or the Madonna of church frescoes, destined for an outstanding, exceptional fate'.[20] Consistent with this is his idea of France as a supra-individual entity with a life of its own:

> France comes from the mists of time. It lives ... It has a constant character which means that in each period all the French depend on their ancestors and they in turn have a task to perform for their descendants. Unless it should ever break down, this human whole, living on this territory, at the heart of this universe, is thus made up of an indivisible past, present and future.[21]

Given this metaphysical vision of France it is hardly surprising that all de Gaulle's policies were geared to enhancing the country's pre-eminence on the world's political and cultural stage, and that it was his pragmatism, not his heart, that convinced him (only after eight years of the most bitter conflict) that France should renounce her colonial claims in Algeria, which duly became an independent state in 1962.

The Eurocentrism and illiberalism implicit in the nationalist assumptions of Western statesmen such as de Gaulle are thrown into particularly stark relief when they are contrasted with those of one of the most important revolutionary theorists of Southern (Third World) nationalism, Frantz Fanon (1925–61). Fanon acquired firsthand experiences of the racism endemic to colonialism during his childhood in Martinique, and especially as a doctor working in Algeria during the war of independence. Given the collusion he had witnessed between colonial repression and capitalism under the guise of liberalism, it is hardly surprising if Fanon was drawn towards a theory of revolutionary struggle profoundly indebted to Marxist theories of emancipation. However, the highly individual philosophy of liberation which underpins his critique of all oligarchical power, whether in the hands of white or black élites, means that he can be seen as a radical revisionist of liberal nationalism rather than its opponent. Certainly he was no apologist for the communist terror state as perfected under Stalin (1879–1953) or Mao Zedong (1893–1976).

Fanon was also keenly aware of the ambivalence of the ethnic consciousness which fuelled anti-colonial struggles and could easily turn benign liberal nationalism into 'ultra-nationalism, chauvinism and, finally, to racism'.[22] He warned all would-be freedom fighters that 'If nationalism ... is not enriched and deepened by very rapid transformation into a consciousness of social and political needs, in other words of humanism, it leads up a blind alley'. In other words he realized that in the artificial 'state-nations' which Africans had inherited from colonial rule, the development of a genuine sense of collective destiny could all too easily be destroyed by tribalism, either in the form of civil war between rival ethnic groups, or of dictatorship imposed by an indigenous bourgeoisie intent only on promoting the interests of its own ethnic faction. What then results is a home-grown racism or tyranny which makes a mockery of the slogans of pan-African solidarity. The result is 'anarchy, repression and the resurgence of tribal parties',[23] an insight relevant to all newly liberated democracies, whether in the Third World or the former communist Second World.

If it is to remain a truly liberal and hence benign force, nationalism must act as a force dedicated to the emancipation of peoples and individuals from all forms of tyranny, not just the 'home' nation's freedom from foreign invasion, occupation or colonization by other states or self-imposed despotism, but also the liberation of other nations from the same evils. It must balance a keen sense of national identity (which is not to be equated with ethnic homogeneity, let alone 'purity') with a profound respect for the rights of all fellow citizens whatever their ethnicity, and of all human beings whatever their homeland. On these points there is considerable common ground between thinkers as far apart in national background and historical experience as J.S. Mill, Havel and Fanon. Unfortunately, it is one of the hallmarks of twentieth-century history that such voices have been generally ignored in favour of the dulcet tones of a selective liberalism which puts the interests of the home nation (and then only sections of its population) before that of all others. Worse still, they have been all too often drowned out by strident forms of nationalism which regard liberalism as a source of decadence rather than of health.

ILLIBERAL THEORIES OF POLITICAL NATIONALISM

No major social theorist anticipated the possibility that illiberal nationalism would steal a march on all other modern political ideologies to become the dominant force of the twentieth century. Partially blinded by their Enlightenment heritage to the forces of irrationalism, liberal thinkers have in the past generally failed to anticipate the susceptibility of nation-states, no matter how sound their constitutional and judicial apparatus, to lapsing into new forms of autocracy rationalized by appeals to the interests of the people and the needs of the nation. Their revolutionary socialist counterparts have also tended to underestimate the strength of chauvinism both among the 'proletariat' and among the heads of state who claim to be carrying out a revolution on their behalf. Thus it was that when theorists began to project on to the nation longings usually associated with God, nature or Romantic love, they were generally given scant attention by the custodians of Western humanism.[24]

A symptom of this ominous shift towards ultra-nationalism at the level of theory is to be found in the writings of the German idealist thinker J.G. Fichte

(1762–1814). His convoluted philosophical defence of individualism, humanism and the French Revolution was dramatically abandoned after Napoleon's victory over Prussia at the battle of Jena in 1806. His response was to become the prophet of the Germans' Messianic destiny as the only people which possessed a healthy national character and soul, a claim legitimated in Herderian terms by pointing to the way they had retained their *Ursprache* or primordial language in such stark contrast to the French who, he claimed, spoke a degenerate form of a foreign language, Latin. Thus the Germans alone were in a position to inaugurate a new era of humanity which would rescue it from the universal decay of its spiritual life. The programme for fulfilling this mission was laid out in his *Addresses to the German Nation* of 1808, a work which was to have a major impact on later generations of German ultra-nationalists. The first stage was to be the imposition by the (Prussian) state of an all-encompassing system of education to raise a youthful generation devoted body and mind to the service of their nation. In this way a new Germany would rise from the ruins. He closed his last address with the warning to his youthful proselytes: 'If you go under, all humanity goes under with you, without hope of any future restoration'.[25]

Equally significant expressions of the 'new' nationalism inspired by the Napoleonic wars poured forth in the poems and pamphlets of another German, Ernst Arndt (1769–1860). His influential 'Catechism of a Patriot' (1814) imbues the German landscape with all the force of divine revelation, while his 'Song of the Fatherland' of the same period soon became a favourite of chauvinistic student fraternities (*Burschenschaften*), called upon men to fight to the death for their 'holy fatherland' in verses which fused religion, history, race, war and patriotism into a single fanatical emotion. By 1848 Arndt was specifically singling out Jews as a source of national *Zersetzung* (dissolution, decay), using language and ideas which adumbrate Nazi racism.[26]

Already fully elaborated in the writings of both Fichte and Arndt is a recurrent feature of illiberal nationalism, one which we have already encountered in de Gaulle's writings: the image of the nation as a living organism. In this conception all human existences are held to be shaped decisively by their relationship to this unique historical life-form which has slowly grown up in the seed-bed of history. The nation precedes and will survive the 'mere' individual (the focal point of liberal values), so that to live life in such a way as to nourish it is the highest, indeed the only, source of value. To be uprooted and cut off from the lifeblood of national culture is to fall into a black hole of anarchy and meaninglessness. Documentary proof of citizenship is not enough.

Here is another metaphor expressing the axiom that the nation is more than the sum of its parts. It comes from the pen of one Maurice Barrès (1862–1923), one of France's foremost protagonists of a new form of republicanism whose basic thrust was ultra-nationalist and hence profoundly illiberal. What gives it a sinister subtext is that it was written against the background to one of modern history's pivotal episodes of collective anti-Semitism, the Dreyfus affair.

> I would happily compare a nation to those compounds of small stones and mortar which occur naturally in running water ... If a single stone breaks off from the whole, it rolls quickly, gets worn down and becomes dust; even if it attaches itself to another mass, it is still half worn, diminished in value. Thus it seems to me that the individual is bound to all his dead ancestors by the efforts and sacrifices of individuals in the past, just as the stone is bound to the mass by the mortar formed by the successive layers.[27]

The vision of the nation as the patrimony of what Barrès called the 'soil and the dead' makes its protagonists the arch-enemies of any ideology which celebrates pluralism, multiculturality and rational individualism (i.e. liberalism), cosmopolitanism (e.g. global consumerism), or internationalism (e.g. Marxism or One-worldism) at the expense of that utterly *mythical* entity, the natural, homogeneous, organic national community. A direct corollary of this view is that ultra-nationalism also feeds on and feeds various types of racism and xenophobia (e.g. anti-Semitism, hatred of gypsies, foreigners, ethnic minorities, etc.), and fosters conspiracy theories about how certain groups (e.g. communists, liberals, feminists) are 'undermining' society. The policies which such ideas inspire are geared to realizing the fantasy of the 'healthy' or 'reborn' nation which has either fully 'assimilated' 'alien elements' (e.g. Jews) or, yet more sinisterly, 'cleansed itself' of the 'parasitic' elements to which it has become host, though the paranoia latent in the ultra-nationalist mindset is veiled by a confused pseudo-spirituality, so that Romantic or quasi-religious rationales are produced for the fighting machines and terror apparatus necessary to implement its slogans.

As long as the *ancien régime* and liberalism disputed ideological hegemony in the West, ultra-nationalism could do little more than carp from the wings or form impotent political movements. However, the exacerbated nationalist passions whipped up by the First World War and the vast socio-political upheavals which were its legacy, not least the Russian Revolution, created a climate in which authoritarian nationalism, in the form of military juntas, autocratic monarchy or personal dictatorship, could take root in all countries where absolutist regimes had collapsed and liberalism was not deeply entrenched. A case study in this pattern is provided by the changing fortunes of Charles Maurras (1868–1952) as a political activist. Though his blend of chauvinism, Catholicism, monarchism, anti-Semitism and Germanophobia was powerful enough to launch the *Action Française* and win a considerable following among Catholic nationalists abroad, Maurrassian ultra-nationalism was safely marginalized from mainstream politics till the end of the First World War. It was only after 1918 that it came to have a direct impact on ultra-right political movements in Belgium and Spain, and was incorporated into the dictatorships of Salazar (1889–1970) in Portugal, Pétain (1856–1951) in Vichy France, and Vargas (1883–1954) in Brazil. After 1945 Maurras and his ideas found himself once more relegated to the fringe of political life.

The most spectacular product of this new tide of political irrationalism and the most virulent modern permutation of ultra-nationalism was a new genus of political ideology which centred on the myth of the nation's rebirth within a *revolutionary* new order. It became known as 'fascism' after the Italian form of it became the first to wrest state power from the weak grip of liberalism. The structural weaknesses of Fascist Italy's industrial-military complex under Mussolini (1883–1945) meant that the potential for inhumanity latent in its ultra-nationalism was initially vented on Ethiopia (Abyssinia), a practically defenceless traditional society, an episode which distinguished itself from countless other acts of colonization by European nations only in the fact that it happened after the Scramble for Africa (1871–1914) by 'liberal' European powers such as Britain and France was over. A truly international crisis only materialized when two of the world's most powerful industrial powers, Germany and Japan, fell under the sway of regimes dedicated to the fulfilment of vast schemes of territorial expansion in their respective geo-political areas. In both cases these schemes were legitimated by the vision of the reborn nation, in Japan embodied by the 'divine' emperor Hirohito (1901–1989) and in Germany by the charismatic dictator, Adolf Hitler (1889–1945). All three regimes resorted to every possible form of social engineering to weld the population into a homogeneous national community (in German, *Volksgemeinschaft*), the dedicated SS officer and the *kamikaze* pilot were the supreme personification of this 'totalitarian'[28] nationalism. Indeed, as true fascist movements, Fascism and Nazism went beyond the dynamic conservatism of Japan in wanting to create a new social order based on a new type of human being, the *homo fascistus*, or New Man, who entirely existed for the nation.[29]

It is this profoundly illiberal concept of nationalism which underlies Hitler's *Mein Kampf* and surfaces in such statements as

> For us the State is nothing but a form. Its substance, or content, is the essential thing. And that is the nation, the *Volk*. It is clear therefore that every other interest must be subordinated to the supreme interests of the nation.[30]

In practice this meant that any alleged source of the decay of the German race was to be eliminated, at first through the denial of civil rights, and eventually through the systematic extermination of those deemed in bureaucratic terminology to be 'inferior' (*minderwertig*) or to have 'a life not worth living' (*lebensunwertes Leben*). This came to apply to Jews, Gypsies, communists, homosexuals, Russian soldiers, the mentally retarded and all other putative enemies of German rebirth.

Our allusions to Fichte, Barrès, Maurras, Mussolini and Hitler should not be taken to imply that any of them produced texts which directly influenced ultra-nationalism elsewhere. They are merely a minute selection of the countless ideologues who, to overcome a sense of national failure, mediocrity, humiliation, external danger or oppression, and the inferiority complex which this sense engenders, have evoked the mystic essence of the people or rhapsodized about the unique destiny of the race, and so provided legitimation for inhuman acts committed by movements or regimes against other segments of humankind. In capitalist or communist states, or just selectively liberal ones which have run colonies or apartheid systems, torrents of words have poured out in speeches, official reports, legislation, journalism, manifestos and textbooks in which the 'nation' is treated as a living entity to be created, completed, defended, expanded, purged or rejuvenated, whatever 'sacrifices' have to be made to achieve it. Nor has there been any shortage of movements dedicated to fighting the state to realize their rival, but equally illiberal, concept of the nation. In this sense Pol Pot's (1925–1998) Khmer Rouge in Kampuchea and Saddam Hussein's (1937–   ) Ba'ath party in Iraq, the most radical factions of Zionism and the Palestine Liberation Organization (PLO) in the Middle East, those Loyalists and Republicans in Northern Ireland still committed to the use of violence to achieve their ends, and the fascist groupuscules which are still active all over the developed world can be said to speak essentially the same ideological language. Here is a sample of its characteristic register or 'discourse':

The foreigner is not he who does not hold a certificate of nationality; rather, in our doctrine, the foreigner is he who does not feel as we do . . . even though he carries ninety such certificates and our cemeteries were sinking with the bones of his ancestors from a thousand years.[31]

Here is another specimen, from closer to home:

The modern world does not provide us with an identity, and for all their wealth and freedom from tyranny the peoples of the western world are joyless. If I am nothing more than myself, then what is the purpose of living? With no enemy I have no friends, with no hatred I am unloved and unloving. Only when a people unites for a common task, will the crisis of identity (the cause of the chaos of the modern world) be overcome. Nationalism reintegrates the human individual. Only by means of a national revolution can a people re-discover itself, and thereby its joy in living.[32]

THE MYTHIC DIMENSION OF NATIONALISM

So far we have concentrated on nationalism as a political theory. However the majority of social scientists have been less interested in it as a formal doctrine than as a socio-political myth. In other words they have approached it as a set of ideas and sentiments whose importance resides not so much in their rational cogency or conceptual coherence, but in the normative or mobilizing power of the irrational ideas and the Utopian images in which they are expressed. Typical is the sociologist Anthony Giddens, who sees the nation-state as the universal unit of government in the age of modernity for reasons of political and economic expediency, but regards nationalism itself as primarily a psychological rather than an ideological phenomenon, whose focus may or may not be the officially constituted nation-state. Its rise to become one of the most diffused and potent forces of the twentieth century is to be understood in terms of its ability to satisfy a chronic need for a sense of identity. This need has grown apace with modernity since two of its major components, 'globalization' and the 'disembedding' of experience of a specific time and space have eroded the instinctive sense of belonging provided by traditional societies. Paradoxically, then, modernity undermines traditional society but can intensify ethnic consciousness, especially where it serves to rationalize a sense of socio-economic distress or political impotence.[33]

The mythic dimension of nationalism has also been highlighted by Benedict Anderson who has studied the complex process by which the modern nation comes into being as an 'imagined community', inconceivable before the secularization of society, the rise of vernacular languages and the spread of modern communications. Despite its recentness its existence is projected back into the past through a creative editing, or even invention, of history till it becomes real enough in the minds of some to be something to die for, whether the imagining is promoted by the custodians of an existing nation-state or the activists of a movement dedicated to forming one.[34]

No social scientist has dedicated more intellectual energy to unravelling the mysteries of nationalism than Anthony Smith. A special focus of his attention has been the subtle relationship of pre-modern nationalities, which he terms *ethnies*,[35] to modern nations. He sees these as the product of a triple revolution: the transition from feudalism to capitalism, the centralization of administrative and military power by the state, and the standardization of cultural consciousness through modern education and communications. In order to work as a 'solidary, mobilizing force the nation must take over some of the attributes of pre-existing *ethnie* and assimilate many of their myths, memories and symbols or invent ones of its own'.[36] Smith thus argues a middle position between those who imply that nations have always been (primordialists) and those who stress their recent origins (modernists), maintaining that a major factor in the viability and stability of any modern state is the degree to which it can build on a pre-existing *ethnie* or successfully weld a plurality of them within a new national consciousness which respects their distinctiveness.

The briefest reflection on how a random sample of existing nation-states have been formed bears out Smith's thesis that there is no single or simple pattern in the relationship between them and their constituent *ethnies*. India contains several distinct religious and hundreds of linguistic communities, while the USA has over the last 400 years absorbed migrants from countless ethnic groups. Many modern states in the developing world were created from colonies whose territorial limits in no way reflected the ethnic realities of the peoples administered within them. Not even 'old' nations such as Spain and Japan, let alone England or France, are not as ethnically pure as conservative and ultra-right orthodoxy would have its inhabitants believe. Meanwhile, the existence of pan-nationalisms which can never correspond to a single national territory, such as pan-Africanism, pan-Arabism,[37] Pan-Islamicism or Pan-Aryanism, highlight the fact that there is no necessary connection between ethnic consciousness and the creation of a state, even though these 'cultural nationalisms' will often assume the form of a radically political movement within particular national contexts.

Smith emphasizes that it is ethnic consciousness which tends to be fostered by the prevailing stresses and *anomie* of modern society, rather than the more recent and artificial state-sponsored 'official nationalism':

> In the confusion and rootlessness of the modern world, ethnic mythologies and symbolisms can restore the collective heritage and explain 'who we are' to ourselves and to others, by clearly demarcating what is 'ours' from what is alien, in much the same way that traditional religions distinguished the sacred from the profane.[38]

He predicts we are entering an era characterized by growing tensions between what he terms the civil (i.e. liberal or civic) nationalism which is the only possible basis of a harmonious world order, and the insistent demands of egoistic nationalisms, both official and ethnic, fed by mounting demographic and resource crises.

There are other features of nationalism which point to its irrational dynamics. One is the pathological behaviour it inspires once it becomes the motor of national conflict, racial persecution or ecological terrorism. To heirs of the humanist tradition of whatever complexion the destruction (or what nationalists like to call 'sacrifice') in the last hundred years of countless millions of lives in the name of 'God and Country', 'the leader' or 'the rebirth of the race' is eloquent proof in itself of just how perverted the human need for self-transcendence can become when a heightened sense of solidarity with one segment of human beings depersonalizes others into 'the enemy'. The corpse-strewn killing fields of Flanders, the hi-tech extermination ovens of Nazi-occupied Poland, the charred city-scape of Nagasaki, and the burning oil wells of Kuwait are emblems of how technology, far from eradicating human unreason, has only increased its destructive potential when harnessed by nationalist passions.

It might be objected that irrational, mythic forces underpin adherence to any ideology when it operates as a mobilizing force, and that liberalism, anarchism, socialism can all inspire violent acts. Even ecologism has produced a faction calling itself 'Earth First!' whose members commit terrorist acts of 'ecotage' against selected targets. However, nationalism is special to the extent that it is a pervasive component of modern consciousness. All citizens of the modern world are carriers of some form of national consciousness, benign or otherwise, which cannot be said of any of the other ideologies considered in this volume. This universality also relates to nationalism's promiscuity as an ideological force. It can be incorporated equally well into liberalism and Marxism, First World and Third World consciousness, state orthodoxy and revolutionary movements. In that sense it can be treated as a component or constituent of ideologies rather than an ideology in its own right, one which helps impart affective impetus and mobilizing energy to a wide range of political value systems.

Another feature of nationalism which underlies its irrationality is the absence of any single criterion which forms the basis for the forging (in both senses of the word) of a national identity. One defining property may be 'natural' geographical frontiers, such as a mountain range, plains conveniently bordered by major rivers, a continuous coastline. Language, too, can play a vital role in its capacity to act as a signifier distinguishing the 'home' national community from 'outsiders', especially if it tends to act as an impenetrable barrier to them (e.g. Japanese, Hungarian, Basque or Finnish). Religion also lends itself to serving this discriminatory or signifying role once it has been corrupted into a fundamentalist variant with overt political implications. Modern science has provided another prolific source of nationalist rationalizations in feeding scientistic (i.e. pseudo-scientific) fantasies of ethnic homogeneity, whether conceived in terms of strictly biological, genetic or physical anthropological distinctiveness (biological racism), or in vaguer notions of cultural, social anthropological uniqueness (cultural racism). Often nationalist myth will be an amalgam of several of these components, welded together by a web of historical truths and half-truths which suggest a glorious heritage from the past and a special destiny to fulfil on the world stage.

The reason why the various 'nations' constructed by such mental operations are to be regarded as essentially 'mythic', no matter how real they seem to their more zealous protagonists, is that no academic discipline sanctions the claim that nations possess discrete sets of defining properties which allow them to be distinguished like separate species of flower or rocks. Once operated professionally as a natural or human science, history, geography, philology, linguistics, social and physical anthropology, ethnography and genetics, all serve to demystify nationalism and refute the claim that any ethnic group can legitimately regard itself as somehow 'pure' or 'primordial'.

For instance, modern science has completely discredited the thesis that humanity consists of distinct races derived from different evolutionary ancestry (polygeny). On the contrary, it has been proved beyond doubt that in strictly genetic terms all human beings really do form 'One World' and that ethnic differences are never rooted in biology alone. Nor can any 'higher' religion in its original orthodox form be called on to vindicate the use of revelation to justify nationalist claims of popular sovereignty or the state's right to territorial expansion. The fundamentalist permutations, sceptics would say perversions, of the Christian, Jewish, Islamic and, more recently, Sikh and Hindu faiths which currently feed a number of the world's nationalist conflicts are historically speaking recent reactions to the rise of aggressive nationalism in more secularized societies since the late eighteenth century and to the threat which modernization poses to a traditional way of life.[39]

The mythical basis of the nation is particularly thrown into relief when there is more than one imagined national community available to woo a nationalist's attachment. Consider the dilemma of someone temperamentally predisposed to nationalism and living in Egypt. Is he (and nationalism has tended, like so many potentially destructive ideologies in history, to be a predominantly male preserve) to identify with Egyptian history which can be traced from the 'glorious' age of the Pharaohs right up to the achievements of Nasser (1918–70), or with Arabian history, which enters its own 'magnificent' phase of cultural expansion and foreign conquest with the rise of Islam in the sixth century AD (by Christian reckoning, that is). If he is drawn to neither an Egyptian or a pan-Arab nationalism, he may still fall prey to the spell of Islamic fundamentalism.[40] This virulent form of political religion has had a profound impact on a swathe of states stretching from Morocco to Afghanistan, in each of which it has spawned, if not regimes, then its own highly active political parties and factions with marked ultra-nationalist tendencies. Our imagined Egyptian nationalist may, of course, be a Christian, a Jew, or a Marxist, in which case the sense of belonging would be complicated still further. Though we have taken an extreme case of hypothetical 'multiple choice' in matters of nationhood, each attempt to probe into any form of it beyond a certain point, be it Britishness, Italianness, Jewishness, Mexicanness or any other, will ultimately reveal it to be a tissue of intangible qualities which defy rational analysis, no matter how powerful and palpable they are at the level of visceral emotions.

NATIONALISM AT THE TURN OF THE TWENTY-FIRST CENTURY

'Two prisoners looked out from the bars. One saw mud the other stars.' Peering out from behind the bars of their cage of reason with the aid of the 'electronic media', liberal humanists concerned with nationalism's impact on history had good grounds to see both mud and stars as the 1990s sped towards their rendezvous with the third millennium.[41] In an optimistic frame of mind they could point to the end of the cold war and the emergence of a host of nation-states liberated from the yoke of Russian imperialism or communist dictatorship and officially committed to liberal democracy. This applied not only to the newly united Germany and a string of countries from Latvia to Albania, but the creation of a Commonwealth of Independent States out of the former USSR. Less well publicized, but in its own way equally impressive, had been the shift from autocracy towards greater democracy in a number of profoundly multi-ethnic and multicultural Latin American, African and Asian countries, including Argentina, Chile, Ethiopia, South Africa, Iran and Cambodia. In Northern Ireland too, 1998 finally saw a consensus emerge amongst all but a small minority that the conflict between the Republican and Loyalist imaginings of Irish history, identity and nationhood can only be resolved, or at least accommodated, through democratic processes and institutions.

On the other hand, pessimists could underline the rapid rise in the early 1990s of both paramilitary and electoral forms of anti-Semitism, xenophobia and neo-fascism in the new Germany (where the state persisted in defining citizenship legally as a function of ethnicity) and in a number of former East bloc countries, notably in Russia itself, where the bizarre blend of liberal economics with ultra-nationalist Utopianism peddled by Zhirinovsky for a time won a sizeable electoral following. Even in stable democracies, such as Italy, Sweden, Belgium and Austria, there were parties actively promoting a highly restrictive liberalism and fomenting anti-immigrant feeling along lines pioneered by the French National Front, which under Jean-Marie Le Pen had developed into a nation-wide movement. Meanwhile, in Yugoslavia ethnic tensions, suppressed but unresolved after four decades of state communism, had erupted into a fierce civil war and the collapse of the federation amidst terror campaigns carried out against civilian populations in the name of 'ethnic cleansing'. The savage conflict in Rwanda between the Hutu and the Tutsi, like the mass slaughter of over a million Armenians by Turks between 1895 and 1915, also underlined the fact that the fomenting of racial hatreds to genocidal levels of intensity by illiberal government and military machines is not an exclusively European phenomenon. These were also the years in which Saddam Hussein's Iraq reminded the world, as if it needed reminding, that autocratic nation-states (if sufficiently supported by First World finance and arms) could ruthlessly exploit the military and propaganda power of official nationalism (Ba'athism) to persecute an ethnic group living within its territory (the Kurds), and to commit aggressive acts against a neighbouring state (Kuwait).

Three manifestations of the vitality of populist nationalism at the end of the twentieth century are particularly disturbing. The first is the continuing vigour of movements struggling for greater political autonomy, which continue to enlist support for devolutionist, secessionist or irredentist causes in both the North and the South, some using liberal tactics, others having recourse to naked acts of terrorism, and some (as in the case of the Irish republican movement which for so long embraced both Sinn Fein and the IRA) maintaining an uneasy mixture of both. The progress of the peace processes under way in Northern Ireland and Israel at the end of the 1990s will provide valuable litmus tests to indicating how far the demands of nationality can be accommodated without recourse to bloodshed.

The second is the growing power of religious fundamentalism, especially in Muslim countries, notably in Iran, Egypt and Afghanistan. This understandable bid to stem the incursion of modernity and hence the breakdown of tradition, can all too easily tip into aggressively anti-Western domestic and foreign policies. In Algeria an unprecedented situation came about in 1992 when a military *coup* was staged in order to preserve democratic institutions by forestalling the possibility of a democratically elected Muslim party, the National Salvation Party, from taking power. Six years later in India its Hindu counterpart, the fanatically anti-Muslim Bharatiya Janata Party, finally became head of a seventeen-party coalition. Though it had by then moderated its programme, it soon displayed its commitment to restoring national pride and warding off threats from neighbouring (Muslim) countries to India's sovereignty by detonating five nuclear weapons. This symbolic gesture not only unleashed a wave of patriotic fervour at home, but provoked Pakistan into carrying out atomic tests of its own, while also reawakening further afield spectres of nuclear confrontation which many had thought laid to rest with the ending of the cold war. In the USA as well the Christian Identity movement, though highly marginalized within the arena of national politics, has seized the opportunities offered by cyberspace to disseminate its hatred of racial mixing and its paranoid fantasies that it is the Federal Government (also known by the ultra-right as ZOG, Zionist Occupation Government) which is the real enemy of true Americans.[42]

The third manifestation of the unabated force of contemporary populist nationalism is that all over the world, in both the North and the South, minorities are asserting their ethnicity, whether they are Puerto Ricans in inner cities or Aborigines in the Australian outback. The positive side of this is that a profound sense of impotence and isolation can be resolved as long as this self-assertion remains at the level of reclaiming cultural identity and civil rights eroded through colonization or racism. However, the quest for identity can, as in the case of the brutal conflict between Azeris and Armenians over Nagorny Karabakh, and between Serbs and Croats or Albanians over 'their' 'homeland', lead to routinized racial hatred and calculated atrocities in which the only definitive outcome is that the lives of innocent men, women and children are destroyed on both sides and hundreds of thousands more become refugees. The demand that civic rights and nationhood are to be based exclusively on membership of an allegedly organic or homogeneous *ethnie* leads to 'ethnocracy', a perversion of the legacy of the French

Revolution (which made no such mythic claims about the 'people').

In the late 1990s ethnocracy shows every sign of becoming the post-war equivalent of fascism in terms of the power it has to undermine liberal humanist principles and the civic nationalism they underpin.[43] Ethnocratic assumptions about the need to protect the 'home nation' from the catastrophic effects of mass immigration and multiculturalism form the common ground between such highly contrasting political formations as the British National Party in England, the Republicans and the German People's Union in Germany, the National Front in France, the Northern League and National Alliance in Italy, the Austrian Freedom Party, the Progress and New Democracy parties in Scandinavia, the Flemish Block in Belgium, the Liberal Democratic Party of Russia, and the One Nation party in Australia, not to mention the White Aryan Resistance movement in the USA and their neo-Nazi equivalents all over the world to whom the Internet now offers possibilities of communication and collaboration undreamt of by the propaganda ministry of the Third Reich.[44]

What is to be made of a situation where signs of nationalism's capacity for benign evolution are repeatedly contradicted by manifestations of its power to wreak havoc on human societies? One expert who at the beginning of the 1990s incarnated widespread faith in the ultimate triumph of liberal nationalism over its many enemies was Francis Fukuyama, author of a famous article published in 1989 called the 'End of History'.[45] Two years later he could be found reassuring his readers that the globalization of liberal democracy he had predicted was in the long term unlikely to be jeopardized by ultra-nationalism. Instead he saw the 'young nationalisms' causing problems at present in various parts of the world, especially in the former Russian empire, gradually entering 'a period of maturity as national identities become better recognized and more secure'. The 'sense of national unity' which would then prevail would then fulfil its role as the 'only truly necessary precondition for the emergence of stable democracy'.[46]

There are many analyses of the world situation which are less sanguine than Fukuyama's. One is proposed by the French (and now pan-European) New Right, which see in the globalization of technology and culture a force which will inexorably erode cultural identities to create a humanity homogenized on American lines. Their praise of cultural difference, extolled in an apparent spirit of xenophilia ('love of foreigners') rather than xenophobia, has encouraged many of the more sophisticated ideologues of the extreme right to attack multiculturalism and 'mondialization' or 'one-worldism' in terms of defending the integrity and homogeneity of all *ethnies*, and of an alleged sense of solidarity with the societies of the North at the mercy of the cultural imperialism of the North (a stance known as 'Third Positionism'). However, differentialism, despite its libertarian and philanthropic claims, is at bottom a form of racism.[47] Translated into concrete measures, its mission to purge (European) societies of the effects of multiculturalism would involve the enforced repatriation (to countries doubtless reluctant to reabsorb the descendants of their former émigrés or diasporic populations). This in turn would transform any state attempting to carry out such a programme *de facto* into an authoritarian state based on racial principles on a par with apartheid South Africa or contemporary Croatia.

An alternative prognosis at loggerheads with Fukuyama's is the one offered by the British 'liberal' sociologist Anthony Giddens, who identifies a profound ambiguity which lies at the heart of the modernization process. As it destroys traditional societies, the nation-state becomes a standard unit for the organization of economic, cultural and political life. Yet, given the mounting pressures exerted by demographic and subsistence crises in the South and resource and ecological crises in the North, there are four 'high-consequence risks' involved in the inexorable globalization of modernity: the growth of totalitarian power, large-scale warfare, the collapse of economic mechanisms and ecological decay or disaster. If a deteriorating planetary political and economic situation generated even a partial mix of these phenomena, nationalisms, both populist and official, would tend to be increasingly egoistic and centripetal, rather than universalist and centrifugal. If, however, the global political order could be co-ordinated and economic mechanisms socialized, then Giddens foresees the possibility of major war being averted and a sustainable society being developed, so that humanity would at last enter a 'post-scarcity system' beyond the radical consequences of modernity through which we are now living.

If Giddens is right the implications for nationalism are clear. Modernity's progressive destruction of traditional society will continue to call forth sporadic rearguard actions in the form of aggressive ethnic nationalism, Balkanization[48] and tribalism. Meanwhile, if nothing changes at the level of global policy-making, rich nations, even when operating as part of supranational alliances, will continue to exploit poor ones, while escalating environmental decay and catastrophic demographic explosions in the developing world will feed interethnic and interstate conflict.[49] However, there is still time (just) for major planetary dysfunctions (i.e. disasters) to be avoided if those who are both powerful yet committed to humanistic goals are prepared to work towards the creation of an international community which will neutralize or minimize their impact and ensure the triumph of civic nationalism world-wide.

One indicator of which road human history is taking will be how the European Union will have evolved by the year 2010. Will it have become an inward-looking, egotistic superstate, a 'Fortress Europe', or a major protagonist of international initiatives to address the (largely North-made) social and political dilemmas of the South and the (largely North-made) ecological crises.[50] Whatever happens, ethnic identities, nationalities, nationalisms, and multicultural societies are here to stay, and will continue to evolve and interact in ways which no political scientist can predict with certainty. A major issue is whether globalization can become a prevalently creative rather than a destructive force, one which underpins the resolution of local conflicts, sustainable development, and international harmony. This will largely determine the degree to which liberalism will remain contaminated by 'interests', and nationalism will slide into ultra-nationalism, provoking a chain of *evitable* human and 'natural' catastrophes.

NOTES

1. E. Gellner, *Nations and Nationalism*, Blackwell, Oxford, 1983, p.125.
2. On the substantial role played by pre-modern ethnic nationalism as the foundation for modern nationalisms and successful state-building see A. Smith, *The Ethnic Origin of Nations*, Basil Blackwell, Oxford, 1983.
3. See R. Scruton, 'In Defence of the Nation', in *Ideas and Politics in Modern Britain*, Macmillan, London, 1990, pp.58–9; B. Lewis, *'Watan', Journal of Contemporary History*, 26, 1991.
4. See C. Gluck, *Japan's Modern Myths*, Princeton University Press, Princeton, 1985.
5. One advantage of this phrase is the way it emphasizes that there is no such thing as an absolute definition of any key term in academic research. Each of the many essays or books on nationalism can be seen as the application of different ideal types by academics with idiosyncratic angles on its theory and practice.
6. See for example J.M. Eagan, *Maximilien Robespierre: Nationalist Dictator*, Octagon Books, New York, 1978.
7. See for example A. Giddens, *A Contemporary Critique of Historical Materialism*, Macmillan, 1981, p.192; T. Nairn, *The Modern Janus – Nationalism in the Modern World*, Hutchinson, London, 1990.
8. K.R. Minogue, *Nationalism*, Batsford, London, 1967.
9. See E.K. Bramsted and K.J. Melhuish, *Western Liberalism*, Longman, London, 1978, pp. 278–88, 352–83.
10. J.S. Mill, *Essays on Politics and Society*, Routledge and Kegan Paul, vol. 10, 1977, pp.134–5. Mill's stress on nationalism's consolidating role in the creation and maintenance of civic society echoes the conservative strand within liberalism which ever since Edmund Burke has stressed the role of traditional loyalties, whether social, ethnic or national, to the cohesion of the state. For a contemporary example see R. Scruton, 'In Defence of the Nation', p. 68: 'Until sustained by a national idea, the liberal state is a solvent of unity and therefore contains the seed of its own destruction'.
11. Mills, *Essays*, vol. 20, p.347.
12. Ibid., vol. 19, p.547.
13. Ibid., p.550.
14. Vàclav Havel, 'On Home', *New York Review of Books*, 5 December 1991, p.49.
15. Quoted in J. Crawford, *The Rights of Peoples*, Oxford University Press, Oxford, 1988, p.191.
16. See A. Buchanan, *Secession*, Westview, Boulder, CO, 1992.
17. G. Mazzini, *Life and Writings of Joseph Mazzini*, vol. 3, *Autobiographical and Political*, Smith, Elder and Co., London, 1890, p.133.
18. P. Helm, *The Salisbury Review*, January 1987, p.33.
19. Or rather 'non-rational', since all nationalisms are susceptible to rationalization and blend subjective perceptions with objective 'facts'.

20. C. de Gaulle, *Mémoires de Guerre, l'Appel. 1940–1942*, Plon, Paris, 1954, pp.1–2.

21. C. de Gaulle, *Mémoires d'Espoir. 1958–62*, Plon, Paris, 1970, p.1.

22. F. Fanon, *The Wretched of the Earth*, Penguin, Harmondsworth, 1967, p.125.

23. Ibid., p.165.

24. See I. Berlin, 'Nationalism. Past Neglect and Present Strength', in *Against the Current*, ed. Henry Hardy, The Hogarth Press, London, 1979, p.350.

25. J.G. Fichte, *Addresses to the German Nation*, ed. G.A. Kelley, Harper Torchbooks, New York, 1968, p.228.

26. See L. Yahil, 'National Pride and Defeat: A Comparison between Danish and German Nationalism', *Journal of Contemporary History*, 26, 1991.

27. Quoted in J.S. McClelland (ed.), *The French Right*, Jonathan Cape, London, 1970, p.163.

28. *Totalitario* was a positive term in the Fascist doctrine of the state.

29. R.D. Griffin, *The Nature of Fascism*, Pinter, London, 1991.

30. A. Hitler, *Mein Kampf*, (trans. James Murphy), Hurst and Blackett, London, 1939, p.470.

31. The words are from a major ideologue of pan-Arabism and forerunner of Iraqi Ba'athism, Shawakat. See S. Al-Khalil, *Republic of Fear*, Hutchinson Radius, London, 1989, p.178.

32. The author is Michael Walker, foremost intellectual of British neo-fascism and editor of *The Scorpion*, from which this quotation is taken (1983, no. 4, p.4).

33. See particularly A. Giddens, *A Contemporary Critique of Historical Materialism*, Polity Press, London, 1985; *The Consequences of Modernity*, Polity Press, Cambridge, 1990.

34. B. Anderson, *Imagined Communities*, Verso, London, 1991.

35. A French term which he uses only in the singular even when the context demands, as here, a plural.

36. A. Smith, *The Ethnic Origin of Nations*, Basil Blackwell, Oxford, 1986, p.152.

37. See B. Rubin, 'Pan-Arab Nationalism: The Ideological Dream as a Compelling Force', *Journal of Contemporary History*, 26, 1991.

38. Smith, *Ethnic Origin of Nations*, p.202.

39. On this aspect of Islamic fundamentalism see Y.M. Choueiri, *Islamic Fundamentalism*, Pinter Press, London, 1990. For an extended discussion of nationalist mythopoeia at work see B. Shafer, *Faces of Nationalism*, Harcourt, Brace, Jovanovich, New York, 1972, chs 11 and 12.

40. See B. Lewis, '*Watan*'.

41. That is if we accept the system of time-reckoning adopted first by Christianity and now by globalization. This passage was written in the spring of 1992. Clearly by the time it is read yet more manifestations of the power of contemporary nationalism will have taken place to indicate which of the two perspectives is more 'realistic'.

42. See Jeffrey Kaplan, *Radical Religion in America*, Syracuse University Press, New York, 1997.

43. See Roger Griffin, 'Last Rights?': Afterword to S. Ramet (ed.), *The Radical Right in Central and Eastern Europe*, 1999, Penn State Press, Pennsylvania.

44. On the emergence of a new type of neo-fascist International through the increasing co-operation between USA and European racists see Jeffrey Kaplan and Leonard Weinberg, *The Emergence of a Euro-American Radical Right*, Rutgers University Press, New Brunswick, 1998.

45. F. Fukuyama, 'The End of History', *The National Interest*, Summer 1989.

46. F. Fukuyama, 'Liberal Democracy as a Global Phenomenon', *PS. Political Science and Politics*, 24, December 1991. For a more extensive treatment of his views see F. Fukuyama, *The End of History and the Last Man*, Hamish Hamilton, London, 1992.

47. See Pierre-André Taguieff, 'From Race to Culture: The New Right's View of European Identity', *Telos*, nos 98–9, 1993–94, pp.109–22.

48. Balkanization refers to the collapse of an entire geopolitical area into the anarchy of ethnic nationalist rivalries and separatist or irredentist claims, after the political chaos engendered by this process in the Balkans which helped precipitate the First World War.

49. N. Brown, *The Strategic Revolution*, Brassey's, London, 1992.

50. See D.H. Meadows, D.L. Meadows and J. Randers, *Beyond the Limits*, Earthscan, London, 1992.

GUIDE TO FURTHER READING

The proliferation of new nation-states, of virulent nationalist and extreme right-wing movements and parties, and of violent ethnic conflicts, notably in the former Yugoslavia, which followed in the wake of the collapse of the Soviet empire in the late 1980s triggered a boom in nationalism as a subject for books, learned articles and conferences. A profusion of new literature came into being on how nations are 'built', ethnic identities are 'constructed', and national communities are 'imagined'. Studies in the extreme right also underwent an unexpected revival, particular attention being devoted to the fascist legacy or novelty of populist parties such as the Front National which uphold the 'ethnocratic' principle that citizenship is a function of (an allegedly pure or homogeneous) 'ethnic identity' (*ius sanguinis*) rather than of civic rights (*ius soli*). A book which captures brilliantly the heady, and often disturbing, 'reawakening' of national consciousnesses which occurred in the early 1990s in Europe is Michael Ignatieff's *Blood and Belonging. Journeys into the New Nationalism* (Penguin, Harmondsworth, 1994). A text constantly alluded to (if not always read) has been B. Anderson, *Imagined Communities. Reflections on the Origin and Spread of Nationalism* (revised edition Verso, London, 1991), the closest thing yet to a modern classic on the dynamics of nationalism. Though unlikely to achieve the same mythic resonance as Anderson's book, David Miller's *On Nationality* (Oxford University Press, Oxford, 1995) offers a defence of nationalities as a rationally defensible reality of identity (whatever the non-rational processes involved in their formation), and analysis of consequences to be drawn from its existence as the basis of a community founded on civic nationalism. Craig Calhoun, *Nationalism* (Open University Press, Buckingham, 1997) is a brief-text example of the plethora of new works.

This new spate of fresh scholarly literature has partly compensated for the notable paucity of outstanding works on nationalism up to the 1980s. Given the diversity and complexity of nationalism, it is perhaps inevitable that traditional scholarship produced no 'standard work' on the subject, though certain texts acquired the status of classics, such as H. Kohn, *The Idea of Nationalism: A Study of Its Origins and Background* (Macmillan, New York, 1944), E. Kedourie, *Nationalism* (Hutchinson, London, 1966), K.R. Minogue, *Nationalism* (Basic Books, New York, 1967), and E. Gellner, *Nations and Nationalism* (Blackwell, Oxford, 1983). In this context one should mention Isaiah Berlin's seminal essay 'Nationalism' in *Against the Current* (ed. Henry Hardy, The Hogarth Press, London, 1979) and reprinted in *The Crooked Timber of Humanity* (London, John Murray, 1990). One of the most stimulating and wide-ranging treatments of the subject was B. Shafer, *Faces of Nationalism* (Harcourt, Brace, Jovanovich, New York, 1972).

The academic who has perhaps carried out the most sustained, wide-ranging, and authoritative investigation of the subject is Anthony Smith in his *Theories of Nationalism* (Duckworth, London, 1971), *Nationalism in the Twentieth Century* (Martin Robertson, Oxford, 1979), *The Ethnic Origin of Nations* (Basil Blackwell, Oxford, 1986), *National Identity* (Penguin, Harmondsworth, 1991) and *Nations and Nationalisms in a Global Era* (Polity Press, Oxford, 1995). Together with John Hutchinson he also produced the two excellent anthologies of source material in the Oxford Readers series, *Nationalism* (Oxford University Press, Oxford, 1994) and *Ethnicity* (Oxford University Press, Oxford, 1996). He is also associated with the most important periodical to cover nationalism in its many aspects, both theoretical and empirical, *Nations and Nationalism* (Cambridge University Press), which since 1996 has been published three times a year by the Association for the Study of Ethnicity and Nationalism (ASEN) based at the London School of Economics and Political Science.

A very readable introduction to the subject is provided by P. Alter, *Nationalism* (Arnold, London, 1989), which also provides a very useful 'select bibliography', while a highly sophisticated Marxian analysis of the subject is to be found in E.J. Hobsbawm, *Nations and Nationalism since 1780* (Cambridge University Press, Cambridge, 1990). One of the most comprehensive accounts of the different permutations of nationalism at work in modern history is John Breuilly's *Nationalism and the State* (Manchester University Press, Manchester, 1982), which also contains valuable insights into the 'initial conditions' which foster a particular type at the expense of another. For an insight into the fascinating diversity of nationalism as a topic of specialist study see *Journal of Contemporary History*, 1991, 26, nos 3-4 and volume 15 of *History of European Ideas* (September 1992) which publishes over 50 papers presented at a conference on European nationalism held in 1990. On British nationalism a valuable recent contribution is B. Crick (ed.) *National Identities* (Blackwell, Oxford, 1991), while as an equivalent for continental nationalism one could recommend R.M. Mitchison (ed.), *The Roots of Nationalism: Studies in Northern Europe* (Donald, Edinburgh, 1979).

A teaching cassette which serves as a valuable introduction to those new to the subject is M. Savigeor, *European Nationalism 1789-1848* (London, Audio Learning, 1977). Case studies in the emergence of two contrasting European national identities can be gained by reading L.L. Snyder, *The Roots of German Nationalism* (Indiana University Press, Bloomington, 1978) and J. Hutchinson, *The Dynamics of Cultural Nationalism: The Gaelic Revival and the Creation of the Irish State* (Allen and Unwin, London, 1987). On the tangled legal and political questions raised by the concept of a global community of nations an important, though somewhat technical, book is J. Crawford (ed.), *The Rights of Peoples* (Oxford University Press, Oxford, 1988), while J. Tomlinson, *Cultural Imperialism* (Pinter Press, London, 1991) offers stimulating insights into the problem of retaining political and cultural identity under the globalizing impact of modernity. Two works which cast important light on the dynamics of nationalism in a non-European context are Frank Füredi, *Colonial Wars and the Politics of Third World Nationalism* (I.B. Tauris, London, 1994), and Peter van der Veer, *Religious Nationalism. Hindus and Muslims in India* (Berkeley, London, University of California Press, 1994). Contrasting appraisals of the sudden resurgence of nationalism in the early 1990s can be found in F. Halliday, 'The Siren of Nationalism', in C. Hartman and P. Vilanova (eds), *Paradigms Lost* (Pluto Press, London, 1991), T. Nairn, *The Modern Janus – Nationalism in the Modern World* (Hutchinson, London, 1990). The whole issue is placed in the context of an overarching theory of where modern history is leading by F. Fukuyama in his controversial *The End of History and the Last Man* (Hamish Hamilton, London, 1992).

On the mythic and psychological dynamics of modern nationalism I would recommend L. Hunt, *Politics, Culture and Class in the French Revolution* (Methuen, London, 1986), J.L. Talmon, *The Myth of the Nation and the Vision of Revolution. The Origins of Ideological Polarization in the Twentieth Century* (Secker and Warburg, London, 1981), G.M. Platt, 'Thoughts on a Theory of Collective Action: Language, Affect and Ideology in Revolution', in M. Albin (ed.), *New Directions in Psychohistory* (Lessington, MA, 1980) and R.D. Griffin, *The Nature of Fascism* (Routledge, London, 1993) chapter 7. Finally I would like to recommend Salmon Rushdie's 'Is Nothing Sacred?' printed in his *Imaginary Homelands* (Penguin, Harmondsworth, 1992), and Stuart Hall's 'Cultural Identity', in S. Hall (ed.) *Modernity and Its Futures* (Polity Press, Cambridge, 1992). They are timely reminders that any quest for an 'identity' in the late twentieth century must start out not by mourning but by celebrating the loss of cultural and ethnic purity (which is anyway a strictly mythical entity).

8
FASCISM
Roger Eatwell

——

AN ELUSIVE IDEOLOGY

'Never before was the relation of masters and slaves so consciously aestheti-
cized ... The color is black, the material is leather ... the fantasy is death.'[1]
Today, the term 'fascism' often denotes little more than a style: authoritarian, violent, morbid, perversely hyper-sexual. Even many historians and
social scientists consider fascism to be an incoherent, or nihilistic form of
nationalist dictatorship. A brief overview of the main historical examples of
fascist regimes will help explain why fascism is such a problematic 'ism'. (See
the end of Chapter 1 too, as methodological debates are especially important
to defining fascism.)

Listing these examples is easier said than done. For some, only Italian
Fascism should be included in the fascist pantheon, though most would add
Nazism ('Fascism' is henceforth used to refer specifically to the Italian
variant, and 'Nazism' to the German one; 'fascism' in the lower case is a
generic term). More controversially, others would include regimes such as:
inter-war Japan; General Franco's Spanish dictatorship (1939–75); Colonel
Perón's first period of government in Argentina (1943–55); General Pinochet's Chile (1973–88); and the contemporary Saddam Hussein regime in
Iraq.

Even if analysis is restricted to the two 'classic' regimes, serious defini-
tional problems still emerge. The term 'fascism' was coined in 1919 at the
time of the founding of the Italian Fascist movement.[2] The first Fascist
programme was adopted in the same year, but by the time of the consolidation of the Fascist dictatorship after 1925 policy had been modified
considerably in a more moderate vein. Also formed in 1919 was the Nazi, or
German National Socialist Workers' Party (initially under a different name),

which went through similar mutations. Even after coming to power in 1933, Nazism pursued a complex mix of pragmatism and fanatical ideology. Put more analytically, in the 'movement' phase before coming to power, both German and Italian fascism tended to be hostile to vested interests (though both movements had notably different factions within them). During the 'regime' phase both were more accommodating, although fascism regained a more radical rhetoric in the programme of the Italian Salò Republic (1943–45), which was set up after Mussolini had been rescued from his Italian captors by the Germans. In spite of this notable example of fascist fraternalism, there were significant differences between Italian and German fascism. In particular: Fascism, unlike Nazism, was not premised upon biological racism; and Fascism, although highly statist, exerted much less 'totalitarian' and brutal social control than Nazism. Italy's leading historian of Fascism, Renzo De Felice, has even argued that Fascism grew out of the left, whereas the more atavistic Nazism had its roots on the right![3]

The problem of where to place fascism on the left–right spectrum can be seen more clearly by considering briefly some of the major commentators who have taken fascist ideology seriously. Ernst Nolte has seen fascism as a form of 'resistance to transcendence', an attempt to hold back the forces of modernism, embodied especially in Marxism. George Mosse has similarly traced the right-wing roots of Nazism, though he sees fascism as revolutionary rather than reactionary. Zeev Sternhell sees fascism as owing more to the left, a product of the synthesis between radical socialism and nationalism, in order to achieve 'renewal and the birth of a new world'. The idea of 'rebirth' also appears in the very different writings of A.J. Gregor, who has argued that Italian Fascism was a form of left-inspired 'developmental' dictatorship (a conclusion he expands to claim that fascism has been common in the Third World, even in nominally communist countries like Cuba). Totalitarian theorists like Brzezinski and Friedrich have similarly confused regime style and power structures with ideological goals – holding that Nazi Germany and Stalinist Russia were essentially similar. Finally, picking up as his key term a word first used in this context by the leading Italian historian Emilio Gentile (whose works deserve to be translated more widely into English), Roger Griffin sees fascism as 'a *palingenetic*' (reborn) form of 'populist ultra-nationalism'.[4]

There is much of importance here, though all miss the point that fascist ideology emerged from an attempted *set* of syntheses. This, together with the national mutations of fascism, means that doctrinal content has varied notably. Moreover, fascism has often focused on activist and propagandist appeals rather than developing doctrine: 'rebirth' plays an important propagandistic role here, for the concept helps hide whether what fascism sought was essentially a return of the old or something new. This, together with its post-1945 pariah status, means that there has been no substantial body of fascist intellectuals to develop the ideology. Indeed, the argument which follows is that in some ways fascism is form more than content – though this is not to argue that fascism is little more than an alienated 'style'.

THE BIRTH OF FASCIST IDEOLOGY

Occasionally the witch-hunt for the origins of fascism leads back to the writings of Plato (c.428–348 BC), who advocated ideas such as the need for rule by an élite, which would manipulate popular opinion. More frequently, the two 'Most Wanted' men are Rousseau (1712–78), whose concept of a 'general will' is seen as prefiguring a holistic one-party state, and Hegel (1770–1831), who is portrayed as elevating the community above the individual.[5] Such approaches are a useful corrective to the belief that fascism was totally alien to the Western tradition. However, the argument requires a very one-sided reading of the philosophies of those demonized in this rogue's gallery. Moreover, the approach offers no insights into why fascism exploded on to the scene as a concrete movement when it did.

In terms of a history of ideas approach, it is more helpful to focus on the impact of the two broad developments in the late nineteenth century, and at the turn of the twentieth. These were: the rise of a more holistic form of nationalism and racist thought; and the attack on the optimistic assumptions about progress, which were central to the Enlightenment.

Nationalist doctrine began to emerge clearly in the eighteenth century (see Chapter 7). Much of it was associated with the attack on dynastic, autocratic monarchies, and linked to the rallying cry of 'sovereignty of the people'. If the 'people' were now the masters, it became necessary to define who they were. As such, nationalism was clearly linked to democracy and liberalism. But there was always a strand which had linked the nation more to an emotive sense of 'culture' or 'blood'. In the nineteenth century, this became central to the German *völkisch* movement. After the Prussian victory in 1870 such ideas began to gather support in France too. Similar ideas gathered force in Italy in the early twentieth century, often linked to the quest for colonial expansion and the belief that Italy was an emerging nation in search of a greater place in the sun. The rise of racist thought, epitomized by Arthur de Gobineau (1816–82), furthered these trends. New racial thinking, often bolstered by Social Darwinism, saw national and racial conflict as endemic in history.

Crucial to the rise of what Sternhell has termed anti-'positivism', were developments in three areas. Key developments in psychology, involving individuals such as Sigmund Freud (1856–1939) and Gustave Le Bon (1841–1931), stressed the individual subconscious, and the power of the amorphous crowd. Where did this leave the rationalist ideologies, like liberalism or Marxism, which held that people could be converted and 'perfected'? In philosophy, a powerful challenge to Enlightenment rationality came from Friedrich Nietzsche (1844–1900), who proclaimed the importance of the will and leadership. The belief in the power of 'vitalism', was also proclaimed by Henri Bergson (1859–1941). In sociology, élite theorists such as Roberto Michels (1876–1936) and Vilfredo Pareto (1848–1923) argued that democracy was an illusion, that a governing class always emerged: the key issue concerned how dynamic this group was.

The impact of this attack on positivism can be seen clearly in the writings of Georges Sorel (1847–1922), a man to whom both Lenin and Mussolini (1883–1945) were to acknowledge a debt. Sorel developed the idea that the working class needed to be swayed by great myths (understood as sweeping, empowering ideas) rather than rational discussion: he believed that preaching the cause of a general strike to overthrow capitalism could provide such a myth. However, it is important not to identify these intellectual precursors with fascism itself. Michels was to become a leading defender of Fascism, and Pareto defended Mussolini's appointment as Prime Minister (see Chapter 2). But in general fascist 'precursors' differed notably. Nietzsche, for instance, was not anti-semitic and he mocked emotional German nationalism. And Sorel remained a revolutionary socialist, albeit one disillusioned with past forms of left-wing thought.

In terms of explaining the actual formation and rise of the first fascist movements, it is more fruitful to see them as emerging from a crisis of the left and right during the period culminating in the post-1918 era. This is not to agree with those, like the British fascist leader Sir Oswald Mosley (1896–1980), who have claimed that fascism was a form of authoritarian centrism. There seems something bizarre in calling what is essentially a radical and extreme ideology 'centrist'. Nor is it to claim that fascism drew equally from the left and right: the right-wing influences seem clearer in general, and certainly fascism found it easier to make alliances with the right than with the left. Indeed, Hitler (1889–1945) and Mussolini would almost certainly not have come to power but for the connivance of right-wing élites – although it is important to stress that they did have genuine mass popular support, especially Hitler (a fact often glossed over, especially by Marxist accounts). The point is more that at the core of fascism was a set of syntheses which adapted positions both from the left and right.

By 1918, the left and especially the right were undergoing important developments. On the right, there was a fear of the rise of socialism and an organized working class. The Bolshevik Revolution, and outbreak of violence in other European countries after 1917, petrified many in the Establishment, especially when faced with major economic problems. There was also an ambivalence, even hostility, towards modernity – especially given the clear signs of declining religious faith, which led many on the right to fear the effects of social anomie. Some reactionaries sought to turn the clock back, but the most perceptive right-wing politicians and theorists realized that the task was more how to attract the newly enfranchised working class (in some countries, the vote was restricted only to males). This led to a growing interest in propaganda and organization, often in the belief that these were crucial factors in the rise of the left, though the use of state propaganda during the First World War also had a crucial impact here. There were fears on the left too. Some pondered what had happened to the revolutionary working class, predicted by Karl Marx. Others wondered why the middle class and/or intellectuals always seemed to dominate socialist movements. This led to interest in forms of organization which fostered working-class leadership. In themselves, these developments were not necessarily fascist, and could simply produce new forms of left and right-wing movement. For example, on the one hand, they produced Christian democratic movements based on Catholicism, appealing above class; on the other, they helped spawn syndicalism, based on trade unions and a belief in the use of the mythical general strike.

Nevertheless, there were crucial points of contact. The industrial basis of social organization envisaged by syndicalism had affinities with the development of corporatist thought on the right. In some forms, the latter was little more than back-to-the-Middle-Ages reactionary or romantic thought, as can be seen in the *völkisch* movement. However, corporatism had a more radical side too. Social Catholics in particular sought to ensure social unity (and the maintenance of Faith) in the face of industrialization and the rise of divisive parties and pressure groups by bringing together employer, worker and state in a way that would help ensure justice to the working class. More generally, there was growing interest in the power of the state as a vehicle for securing both social unity, and economic transformation. This was especially true after the First World War had demonstrated the state's powers – and the willingness of people to accept a loss of liberty for the cause of nationalism (which some syndicalists, like many on the right, now saw as the crucial myth).

The pioneer French fascist Georges Valois (1878–1945), who before 1914 had sought to link the radical Catholic right with syndicalists like Sorel, held that nationalism + socialism = fascism. This formulation helps illustrate the vital mutations at the heart of fascism, but it is important not to see fascism as a form of heretical radical socialism. There are several Marxist analyses of nationalism, but no true Marxist holds that the nation is the basis of social organization. Those from the left who turned to fascism were apostates, not heretics. Even the more left-inclined fascists, for example Gregor and Otto Strasser (1892–1934 and 1897–1974 respectively), tended to be anticapitalist rather than socialist. They certainly did not proclaim international fraternity, hostility to private enterprise, a belief in radical income and wealth redistribution, yet alone engage in class analysis. Although still misleading, it would be more accurate to say that nationalism + conservatism = fascism. Nevertheless, the hostility of fascist doctrine to old, dominant élites, and its commitment to radical social reorganization, mean it cannot be seen as unequivocally right wing, at least in the sense that this term was understood up until the inter-war period.

This point can be seen more clearly by considering the case of the man who first popularized the term 'national socialist', the French author Maurice Barrès (1862–1923), a man who has often been seen as a key ideological link between the pre-fascist and fascist eras.[6] Barrès was very influenced by General Boulanger (1837–91) and other important French forerunners of fascism. During the late nineteenth century these movements demonstrated the power of nationalism to rally mass support. They also revealed the resonance of attacks on parliamentary democracy, for Boulanger and others bitterly attacked the corruption and social divisiveness of the Third Republic, traits which were often associated with Jews. Like many at the turn of the twentieth century, Barrès came to see nationalism and racism as crucial to integrating the working class into the national community. However, although his views changed through time and exhibited some contradictions, he ultimately sought to conserve an idealized France, in the same way that Charles Maurras's (1868–1952) *Action Française* sought restoration more than synthesis:

> I see in our history, in our literature in which the themes of *order*, and the sense of *honour* dominate, my true being. Any modification in these forces is detrimental to my happiness and negates part of myself. I ask that France, or rather the ideal of the French, Ronsard, Racine, Chateaubriand, Corneille, Napoleon continues to blossom. I do not need it to be altered.[7]

Fascism was something more radical, and fundamental than this. The Italian writer-adventurer Gabriele D'Annunzio (1863–1938), provides a better example of the ideological developments which led to fascism in the early twentieth century. Before 1914 he had flirted with the left, though in general his ideas had more in common with the right, albeit not the conventional Italian parliamentary right, which he associated with decadence and factional politics. He became a First World War hero (helped by his ego-centric self-publicism), and during 1919–20 led a brief occupation of Fiume, which he sought to claim for Italy rather than the newly created polyglot state of Yugoslavia. In Fiume he established an authoritarian regime complete with elaborate ceremony and uniforms. The sense both of action and of style clearly influenced Fascism. However, the crucial linkage was his growing emphasis on synthesizing progress with tradition, and the desire to create a 'new man'. He saw Italians as literary and creative, but by 1918 he wanted to forge a new Italian who was aggressive, independent, inventive as well as creative.

THE THEMES OF CLASSIC FASCIST IDEOLOGY

At worst, this syncretic style of argument produced bombastic paradoxes, with little if any meaning, other than perhaps in the context of propaganda. Mussolini, for example, could seek to rally Italians of different political persuasions by talking of Fascists being both 'aristocratic and democratic', 'conservatives and progressives', 'law-abiding and law-breaking'. Such language is often seen as confirming fascism's often proclaimed activist, anti-ideological and anti-intellectual nature. Certainly anyone who reads Hitler's book *Mein Kampf* (1925) would find it hard to believe that fascism should be taken as an ideology with serious roots. Hitler offered a rambling concoction of (half) reasoned arguments, combined with a celebration of the power of emotion over reason.

However, these points should not detract from the fact that there was a more serious side to fascist thought. This can be glimpsed in Mussolini's claim that fascism was:

> a synthesis and a unit inclusive of all values ... From beneath the ruins of liberal, socialist, and democratic doctrines, Fascism extracts those elements which are still vital ... supercede[s] socialism and supercede[s] liberalism ... create[s] a new synthesis ... Man is integral, he is political, he is economic, he is religious, he is saint, he is warrior.[8]

Mussolini, like most fascist leaders, was not capable of a high level of theoretical debate, but this quote clearly illustrates both the syncretic form and the way in which fascists saw their ideas in relation to earlier ideologies.

In order to help unravel this ideology, it is useful to set out the themes which tended to recur throughout classic fascist thought. These can usefully be grouped under three headings: natural history, geopolitics and political economy. It is important to note that these themes are not offered as a list-type definition of fascism (e.g. nationalism, leader principle, authoritarianism, militarism, corporatism, etc.). List-definitions fail to bring out the subtleties and complexities in terms ('militarism', for instance could involve violent aggression or the communal 'blood socialism' of the First World War trenches). They also fail to state what is at the core and what is peripheral to the definition. The argument here is that fascism is best understood in more discursive terms. However, in order to help provide an introductory outline of the nature of fascist ideology, a one sentence definition is provided, with its ideological core italicized:

> **Fascism** is an ideology that strives to forge social rebirth based on a *holistic-national radical Third Way*, though in practice fascism has tended to stress style, especially action and the charismatic leader, more

than detailed programme, and to engage in a Manichaean demon-isation of its enemies.[9]

Natural history

Fascism's view of man (the term seems appropriate in view of its focus on male dominance) derived both from scientific developments and through a particular reading of history. Often the two were synthesized. The major philosopher Martin Heidegger (1889–1976), for example, in his Rectoral address to the University of Freiburg shortly after the Nazis came to power in 1933, spoke of the need to 'will that science be informed by the historical spiritual mission of the German people'. In terms of science, the key influ-ences were Social Darwinism, and the irrationalist and vitalist aspects of the new discipline of psychology. In terms of history, there was a similar major bifurcation of influence. Nietzsche's emphasis on the role of 'Supermen' and 'will' in history clearly underpinned many of the scientific lessons. So too did the ideas of the élite theorists.

These approaches only combined to help produce a specifically fascist form of thought when linked to an analysis of the contemporary condition of man, and other factors. Running through fascist thought was a sense of alienation, or decadence. 'Progress', in the form of the onset of individualist materialist values, allegedly left man lacking a true community, and sense of purpose. Existing élites were powerless to prevent these changes. Indeed, they were often seen as actually fostering such decadence. Sometimes, this argument took a more specifically racist form. In particular, powerful Jewish élites were seen as the source of both materialism and international Marxism (the apparent contradiction of Jews being both capitalist and communist was usually explained away by their alleged, rootless, desire to destroy Western civilization). Clearly such arguments gathered force against a background of the Bolshevik victory in 1917, and the chaotic economic and political conditions of countries such as Germany and Italy in the period after 1918.

However, the resulting ideology was not the pessimistic, or cyclical, doctrine of the type which typified much turn of the twentieth-century right-wing thought. Fascism synthesized natural and vitalist arguments to hold that *new* élites with the vision and will to succeed could shape history. As the important philosopher of Fascism, Giovanni Gentile (1875–1944), argued in the 1920s:

> What were the creative forces of the *Risorgimento*? The 'Italian peo-ple', to which some historians are now tending to attribute an important if not decisive role in our struggle for national unity and independence, was hardly on the scene at all. The active agency was

always an idea become a person – it was one or several determined wills which were fixed on determined goals.[10]

This emphasis on new élites and will can be found too in the thought of other leading fascists, for example, the Romanian Iron Guard's leader, Corneliu Codreanu (1899–1939), who wrote that 'This country is dying because of a lack of men not programmes ... We do not need to create new programmes, but new men.'[11]

The Iron Guard is sometimes regarded as not being fascist, usually on account of its mystical Christian element. This misses the point that Christianity has been adaptable enough to accommodate itself to all the main Western ideologies. Fascism too could accommodate itself to the church in order to consolidate its power, a trait which can be seen most clearly in Italian Fascism, which in 1929 settled a long-standing state problem by formalizing relations with the Vatican. However, fascism in general tried to syncretize religion with its own system of values, or used religious imagery largely for propaganda purposes. Thus the image of rebirth, which can often be found in fascism, was part of a broader use of Christian themes (faith, disciples, sacrifice). Fascism saw man as in need of 'religion', of faith, but the main focus was on creating a new secular religion.

What was this new credo to be? An interesting insight into the development of 'new man' thought can be seen by considering Enrico Corradini (1865–1931), a leading figure in the Italian Nationalist Association (ANI), another example of the new blend of conservatism and nationalism which emerged at the turn of the twentieth century. Corradini, influenced by Japan's victory over Russia in 1905, advocated instituting what he saw as the Japanese religion of nature and heroes. Japan's sudden emergence as a world power had a significant impact in some European circles. (Interestingly, the influence of Japan on fascism is universally ignored in favour of the reverse influence, though fascism, defined precisely, was only a marginal influence in Japan.)[12] However, most later fascists who looked to Japan did not believe that its emperor-dominated traditional culture could be imported to Europe. The point was more to draw specific lessons, like the emphasis on the martial values which had helped make Imperial Rome great, before decadence had led to its fall.

Geopolitics

The nation is seen as the 'natural' unit of state organization by fascists, and is central to fascist ideology. However, there was a sense in which fascism stressed the defence of shared European values rather than the nation against alien threats. In some cases this was an attempt to hide the planned reality of German domination, but there could be a deeper feeling of shared identity too. At the intellectual level, Heidegger serves as an example of someone who believed that the struggle was to preserve an endangered European culture. At the activist level, several thousand West Europeans, including the Belgian fascist leader Léon Degrelle (1906–96) fought with the Germans against the dreaded new version of the Eastern hordes: Bolshevism.

Nevertheless, it is important not to overstate this Europeanism, which was mainly a trait of some fascist intellectuals. More central to fascist thought was the issue of what constituted the basis of the nation. In some cases, for example Italian Fascism, the nation was defined mainly by culture. In the case of Nazism, the basis was biological. Thus for most Nazis, a Jew could not be German, as Jews were held to be a separate racial type, whereas in Italy many Jews joined or supported the Fascist party. However, there was an element of synthesis even in Nazi racial thought. Alfred Rosenberg (1893–1946) is often seen as one of the high priests of 'blood' Nazism on account of his lengthy *The Myth of the Twentieth Century* (1930), but in this pretentious and rambling book Rosenberg wrote of race as resulting from 'the formation of a mystical synthesis'.[13] (The book was second only to *Mein Kampf* in the Nazi 'bestseller' list.)

In fact, there were significant differences even among the Nazis over racism. Most Nazi leaders, notably Hitler and Heinrich Himmler (1900–45), held a deep-rooted belief in the existence of a Jewish conspiracy to dominate the world, a belief which helps explain Nazism's genocidal impulse. This view held that it was the Jews who believed *they* were the 'chosen people'. Others were less concerned with conspiracy than with alleged Jewish materialism and lack of national loyalty. For example, the Nazi economist Gottfried Feder (1883–1941) distinguished between productive and finance capital, with the Jews allegedly dominating the parasitic latter form. Yet other leading Nazis, notably Hitler's 'court' architect and later Minister of Armaments Albert Speer (1905–81), saw anti-semitism more in terms of its propaganda appeal, or ability to court favour with Hitler. These differences help explain why the Nazis did not begin systematically killing Jews until after the Second World War had begun, though the major factor in the development of Jewish policy was a complex mix of pragmatism and fanaticism. Initial Nazi policy towards the Jews after 1933 was influenced by the need to retain in Germany certain types of (skilled) Jews, and fear of international opinion. The later genocide, which tied up considerable logistical resources, must largely be explained in terms of Hitler's fanatical anti-semitism.[14]

Whilst there were differences over the basis of nationalism and racism, Fascists and Nazis shared a belief in the necessity of an expansionary foreign policy. However, it is important to note that the militaristic aspect of fascist thought has sometimes been misunderstood, especially in list-definitions. As well as the obvious connotations of foreign conquest and violence, militarism could encompass ideas of 'blood socialism', a community of the trenches, finding a purpose in the service of the nation. Moreover, outside Germany and Italy, expansionism was not a necessary aspect of fascist thought. British fascism sought more to preserve an empire, which was already showing signs of disintegration in the face of the twin threats of indigenous liberation movements, and the rise of new world powers. Fascist movements in most smaller European countries did not harbour dreams of major empire, though they sometimes sought specific border revision. In the case of the Eastern European countries there was a strong fear of invasion by the Soviet Union, which raised the twin spectres of both the communist and the Jewish menace. The belief that Jews dominated Soviet communism was particularly appealing in these countries, which had strong anti-Russian and anti-semitic traditions. Indeed, they proved fertile recruiting grounds for the German forces during the Second World War, and would have yielded even more help to the Nazi cause had not many Nazis' racist views encompassed Slavic inferiority.

What linked these different views was a set of beliefs drawn from geopolitical thought. This involved the belief that conflict was ultimately inevitable as nations and alliances rose and fell, and that society needed to be prepared for this. This link between the creation of a new political culture at home and foreign policy was stated by Hitler in *Mein Kampf*:

> Yes, from the past we can only learn that, in setting an objective for our political activity, we must proceed in two directions: *Land and soil as the goal of our foreign policy, and a new philosophically established, uniform foundation as the aim of political activity at home.*[15]

Hitler became committed to the importance of expansion partly as a result of coming into contact with academic geopolitical ideas. The geopolitical method was particularly attractive to fascism because it involved a synthesis of history, economics, politics and the physical sciences. However, as with many of the influences on Hitler, the original ideas were plundered rather than faithfully reproduced. For example, the key German geopolitical academic, Karl Haushofer (1869–1946) believed in environmental rather than racial cultural determination, and believed that Britain, although in decline, needed to be appeased by Germany. (It could be argued that Hitler accepted the latter view, at least until he realized during 1940–1 that Britain would not concur with German expansion in the east.)

Most Nazis saw Eastern Europe as a natural sphere for their expansion. This was not simply a question of destroying communism. It was also to provide land for Germany's growing population, and to forge links with the large German communities in some parts of Eastern Europe. Within this new sphere, an autarchic unit of economic activity would make the German economy immune to external influence.

Similar geopolitical influences also encouraged the Italian quest for a new empire around the Mediterranean, beginning with the invasion of Abyssinia (now Ethiopia) in 1935. However, there was an important difference in

legitimation. Nazi expansion was closely linked to theories of racial supremacy. Although Italian Fascism was inherently racist in the sense that it
accorded inferior status to the conquered peoples, and suppressed them with
great cruelty, this was not accompanied by a panoply of racial theory. The
new empire was legitimized more in terms of work and economic opportunities for the Italians.

Political economy

It has generally been held that fascists had few views on economics, other
than a vague commitment to expansion and recovery through rearmament
and aggrandizement. Economic policy in fascist regimes, therefore, tends to
be seen as something which owed much to circumstance, and especially to
the influence of non-fascist élites. In fact, by the 1930s the Nazis had
relatively clear economic policies. This is not to deny that there were some
tensions within the Nazi movement, in particular between those who
stressed the need for economic modernization and those who advocated a
form of proto-ecological ruralism. There were also some tensions caused by
the 'socialist' Nazis, like the Strassers, who advocated more radical policies.
However, by the mid-1930s this group had largely been removed from
influence (Gregor Strasser was killed in the 1934 'Night of the Long Knives',
when Hitler ordered the killing of some of his leading radical rivals). By this
time, most leading Nazis were agreed on the need for an economic policy
which sought in the short run to come out of the slump by increasing public
expenditure. In the longer, the aim was to make the private market responsive to national needs, and to seek stability rather than the maximization of
production.[16] Moreover, most recent studies of policy have shown that
politically inspired motives, rather than business and other interests, were
the main determinant of policy.[17]

When Hitler wrote in *Mein Kampf* that economics was of only second- or
third-rate importance, he was stating a central fascist belief that economics
had to be seen as part of a wider set of goals. This was not simply a question
of the fact that expansion required a relatively high level of technology and
national wealth. The point was to synthesize economics with more fundamental values. As Mosley, one of the fascist leaders with the clearest views on
economics, wrote: 'We have in unison in our cause the economic facts and
the spiritual tendencies of our age.' Or in the words of Juan Perón
(1895–1975) during the fascist phase of Peronism: 'Virtuous nations are
such as unite material economies with spiritual values.'[18]

Fascists saw the nature of work and society under liberal democratic
capitalism as essentially alienating. Individualistic materialism could not
provide the cement necessary to bond society. The liberal democratic emphasis on the existence of different parties and pressure groups similarly led to
division: worker was set against employer, for example. Fascists saw the

freedoms of democracy as essentially an illusion: the worker had no real freedom, as power resided in the hands of élites. In the mocking parody of the leader of the Spanish Falange, José Antonio Primo de Rivera (1903–36):

> 'You are free to work as you like ... but remember, being rich, we offer you whatever conditions we please; as free citizens, you are by no means obliged to agree to them; being poor citizens, though, if you will not agree to the conditions we impose, you will die of hunger in the midst of the utmost liberal dignity' ... That is why socialism was bound to emerge, and rightly so.[19]

The sympathetic reference to socialism did not mean that fascists accepted the abolition of private property. This was seen as a law of nature. The point was more to mould in a suitable way the value system and institutional structure which accompanied private property – though state ownership was not ruled out if it was in the national interest. The goal was to create what was sometimes referred to as a 'third way' (neither socialism nor capitalism), a term first popularized by German 'conservative revolutionaries' after 1918. In particular, the emphasis was on making man less money-centred, more co-operative (see Chapter 3).

In Italian and many other forms of fascism, a key institutional idea to help achieve both economic development and social unity was corporatism. However, there were some notable differences in theory about what this involved. In practice, the Italian Corporate State which was set up during the late 1920s was largely a façade. Society was divided into different sectors, and representatives of government, employers and workers held meetings, but this should not divert attention from the fact that corporatism was premised upon the brutal destruction of independent workers' organization. Real power on a day-to-day basis was firmly in the hands of the employers, though, as in Germany, on most major issues politics determined economics rather than vice versa. In Germany the Nazis made no real attempt to create even a façade of corporatism, though unions again were suppressed. Arguably the most original Nazi contribution to industrial organization was its commitment to help end worker alienation through the programme to beautify factories. The original Volkswagen ('people's car') was made in such a factory (the vision of extensive car ownership helps underline the point that mainstream Nazism was not anti-modernist in an economic sense).

Part of this difference over corporatism can be explained by the fact that Fascism was more clearly statist than Nazism (although there were ambiguities and divisions within both). To some extent, this was simply an extension of the Italian tradition of looking to the state as a way of securing unity. However, Alfredo Rocco (1875–1935), an academic legal expert, a key figure in pre-1914 Italian radical nationalism, and a Fascist Minister of Justice, offered a more specifically Fascist rationale by distinguishing between two types of state. First, there was the mechanical/atomical; secondly, there was the organic. The first varied widely, from Athenian direct democracy to modern liberal democracy. The latter was seen as deriving more from the thought of Plato, through Machiavelli (1469–1527) and others. Rocco saw Fascism as a successor to the latter tradition, with its emphasis on 'efficient' élites, authority, its suspicion of the gullible masses, and ultimate goal of unifying the Italian nation. Indeed, Italian Fascists sometimes talked of a 'totalitarian' state, not in the hostile sense to be used by later Western social scientists and others, but as a positive reference to a system in which social divisions had been eliminated, in which people felt truly part of the system. (One reason why early Italian Fascism was not anti-semitic was the tendency to see the nation as an extension of the state rather than vice versa: thus the state could make a Jew a citizen).

Discussion of the fascist state raises again the important distinction between theory and practice. Not all fascist theory was highly statist. Indeed, Hitler's *Führerprinzip* was opposed to a mechanistic state, supporting a natural or spiritual leadership: he even claimed that Nazism sought to destroy not strengthen the state. However, the ultimate reality of fascist regimes was varying degrees of arbitrary and brutal dictatorship. This is not to deny that there was an element of independent power centres in the main fascist regimes (the armed forces, church and business in particular retained some influence). Nor is it to say that Hitler and Mussolini made all the key decisions (historians debate the powers of these 'dictators'). The point is more to remember that in practice the fascist state was powerful, though often confused in terms of principles. The Nazi system of 'justice' helps illustrate this. The Nazis sometimes talked of replacing Roman Law with German Law, but in practice the legal system was a witches' brew of the system which had been used during the Weimar Republic (1919–33), onto which were grafted vague principles, such as the need for the law to respect 'healthy popular feeling', or the 'Führer's will'. The rule of law had little meaning, particularly for those the regime deemed politically and socially undesirable – groups which included gypsies and homosexuals, as well as communists and Jews. The rule of the SS, and other party para-state organizations, was the day-to-day reality.

THE CLASSIC FASCIST 'STYLE'

Many commentators, most notably Stanley Payne, have argued that classic fascism should be defined by its negations, and especially its 'style' as much as, if not more than, its ideological content.[20]

Certainly an important aspect of fascism's rhetoric was a series of attacks on other ideologies. In particular, it was anti-communist, anti-liberal and anti-conservative. However, these negations, especially the first two, derived from the more fundamental themes set out above. Moreover, fascism was a 'latecomer' to the political scene, and it was therefore forced to define itself, and seek support, by attacking the established ideologies.

It is true that the classic fascist movements were usually characterized by a particular style. This included the creation of an organized mass party, led by a charismatic leader, and using extensive propaganda. Thus by 1932 the Nazis claimed over a million members, and Hitler's plane trips in the presidential election (the first major campaigning use of flight by a European politician) allowed him to address a large number of rapturous rallies. There were also the attendant para-military formations, used to protect these rallies, and willing to use violence for domestic ends. Fascism's iconography was male dominated, young and virile. Its rhetoric often included an anti-intellectual and violent streak: the death-head banners (which pre-dated Nazism), or the slogan (taken from Italian First World War shock troops) 'I don't care a damn'.

However, the exact relationship of such style-features to fascism needs probing carefully, both in practice and theory. Firstly, it is possible to question how important were features such as the party, especially in Italy. Moreover, organization was an area where many fascists believed that they were learning from the rise of the left. They also were influenced by the development of left-wing myths, such as the revolutionary general strike, or the commitment to Utopian social equality, which many fascists saw as central to the appeal of the left. Some myths were even modified to suit fascist purposes. Thus the 'myth of the two hundred families' in France began as a left-wing critique of the alleged domination of France by a small number of people; anti-semites found it easy to convert the myth to the claim that these were Jewish families. Indeed, anti-semitism is sometimes referred to as 'idiots' socialism'.

Secondly, fascist views on questions such as organization and propaganda must be seen in the light of other, more fundamental, principles. An important approach to fascism comes from Noël O'Sullivan, who sees it as an 'activist' challenge to the, in some ways personally unfulfilling, dominant Western style of 'limited' politics.[21] His arguments point to how the (Kantian) idea of freedom, involving internal liberation from dominant norms, could lead to self-actualization through violence. Or how the (Rousseau-esque) view of evil as being essentially secular and social, could lead to fanatical attacks on the existing order. As such, this approach discerns interesting counter-traditions to, even tensions within, liberal democracy. It points to the fact that fascism was opposed to a certain sort of intellectual, rather than to all serious thought: namely, it despised the rationalistic, positivistic heirs of the Enlightenment, who believed that man could be perfected or society remade from scratch (a criticism first seriously developed by Joseph de Maistre (1753–1821)).[22] Fascism is thus better seen as an ideology which stresses anti-rationalism, rather than the 'irrationalism' discerned by most commentators. The concept of rationalism is a complex one, but fascist intellectuals believed their views were founded on a valid basis, derived from scientific, historical and other sources. They thought that this was more than could be said for the 'rationalistic', *a priori*, views of liberalism and Marxism. Fascism's rationalism was also more than just an intellectual affair, for a handful such as Gentile or Heidegger. The mass appeal of fascism cannot be simply understood in terms of the usual arguments of sociologists and psychologists. It was more than just pathology, or rootless anomie. The arguments presented above combined to provide a vision of a world in which people, and especially the community, were threatened by destruction – both physical and emotional. This sense of imminent destruction is vital to help explain why people joined extremist groups, and subsequently engaged in extremist acts.

Nevertheless, the exact nature of fascist 'activism' needs probing carefully. This could be illustrated by looking at concrete events. For example, how active were most of the large numbers of members of the Nazi party; did those who were active in work-organizations such as the Italian *Dopolavoro* see them largely in terms of outings and holidays? In the context of this book, it seems more helpful to return to the basic fascist themes, and in particular how they differed from populism.

It is important to ask whether the activism that fascism sought was essentially manipulative, or based more on the idea that activism = political enlightenment and fulfilment. There is a problem here in the sense that fascists held somewhat different views about human nature. Some believed that decadence was a feature of the corrupt existing social order, and (rather like Leninism) that after a transitional period of fascist rule, extensive state control would not be necessary. Others took a more pessimistic, hierarchical view of man, seeing him as always in need of leadership and direction. The latter produced an essentially manipulative view of mobilization, whereas the former could encompass a more genuine mass activism. The French literary fascist, Pierre Drieu La Rochelle (1893–1945), for example, rejected the proletariat as capable of independent action: their decadence went too deep. He also had little interest in party and organisation, seeing fascism as essentially involving an élite freeing itself from decadence. This distinction can also be seen in the debates among fascists about whether they should seize power through a coup (Nazism in its early days was '*Putschist*'), or whether it was possible to acquire power through mass support, adopting more populist themes. In the former camp was the Italian fascist theorist Julius Evola (1898–1974), who held that Fascism was too democratic in the sense that it sought popular support. (Note: Evola was never a member of the Fascist Party, and before 1945 was in some ways closer to Nazism.) The people were a 'mass'; only an élite could be a true 'race', an élite which would require a 'new man' fusion of military and priestly élite values. There was nothing here that was populist in any sense of the word (be it 'popular'; the celebration of the people for their simple, traditional ways; or the advocacy of a direct relationship between leaders and led).[23]

Fascists, therefore, held very different views about key aspects of activism, which in turn affected their views on 'style'. Yet the absence of style factors, such as a mass mobilizing party, is frequently seen by commentators as a ground for viewing particular regimes, such as inter-war Japanese ones, as *not* being fascist. This argument not only misses the historical point that it is highly debatable how important style-features were to core fascist ideology. It also glosses over the fact that classic fascism emerged at a particular stage in the rise of party politics: namely the entry of the 'masses' to universal franchise. Much of what has become embedded in basic definitions of fascism is in fact contingent to an era. The main reason why inter-war Japan was *not* fascist should be seen as stemming more from the fact that key elements were missing from the ideology and programme of dominant groups, for example the desire ultimately to overthrow the existing order and create a new political culture. (There were of course individual fascists in Japan, mainly converts from the left, like Kita Ikki [1881–1937].)

Francisco Franco (1892–1975), whose revolt against the Spanish Republic in 1936 received military aid from Germany and Italy, established a regime which had notable similarities to the Italian Fascist state, especially in its earlier phases (later, there were clear international reasons to play down the more fascist side). Key points of linkage included the emphasis on organic national identity and unity in a quest for greatness, corporatism, and (until the very closing years) the ruthless suppression of opposition. However, Franco was a reactionary more than a radical. In particular, he was a devout Catholic, and defender of a past order – though by the 1960s his regime was increasingly stressing rapid economic development. On the other hand, the early Spanish Falange was certainly fascist, though it played no significant part in Franco's victory, which was achieved by force of arms. And subsequently it became part of the manipulative Francoist-state apparatus rather than a vehicle for radical ideology.

Early Peronism, too, is often omitted from the fascist pantheon on account of style factors, or on the grounds that it was populist more than fascist.[24] It is also usually noted that there was a degree of pluralism in Peronism, particularly in relation to labour unions. However, as has been argued, fascism should not necessarily be associated with rigid statist dictatorship. Moreover, Perón, who believed Mussolini to be the greatest man of the century, was a great exponent of the syncretic form of argument. To those who might counter that male-dominated fascism could never have used the Evita-myth, it is worth pointing out the deferential opening words to the Preface of Eva Perón's (1919–52) autobiography: 'All that I am, all that I have, all that I think and all that I feel, belongs to Peron.'[25] Although later Peronism sought to distance itself from fascism, during the 1940s there were clear links.

NEO-FASCISM

In the decades immediately after 1945, full employment and the growth of welfare systems in Western countries alleviated the social tensions which had helped spawn fascism. Moreover, fascism had become a political pariah. It thus mainly attracted an activist and alienated fringe. Indeed, virtually no one has termed themselves 'fascist' during this period (the prefix 'neo-' will be added to post-1945 fascism in order to stress this break). Major regimes which have sometimes been seen as fascist, for example Pinochet's Chile, have usually been military dictatorships, lacking any serious ideological resemblance to fascism – though a case could be made that Hussein's Iraq has close similarities.[26] Indeed, Pinochet's Chile during its early years espoused 'monetarist' and other individualist economic policies which would have been anathema to classic fascism.

Fascism's pariah status has led some neo-fascists to try to rewrite history. This can be seen most clearly in relation to arguments about Hitler, and especially the claim that the Holocaust is the 'hoax of the century'. (Note: Holocaust denial work can come from non-fascist sources, for example pro-Palestinian groups, seeking to de-legitimize Israel.) Whilst some of this revision may reflect a genuine questioning of the past, it is clear that much is deceitful.[27] Indeed, the Holocaust denial serves as a useful reminder of the need to distinguish between ideology and propaganda: it is even more important in the post-war era not to assume that public ('exoteric') statements are a reflection of inner ('esoteric') beliefs. Such historical revisionism is common among most neo-fascists, but it is important to realise that there are different types of neo-fascist, including some who even celebrate Hitler's anti-semitism.

One type of neo-fascist might be termed *recidivist*, namely those who have sought to stay faithful to mainstream pre-1945 fascism. In the immediate post-war era, this group included the leading members of the German Socialist Reich party (SRP), which claimed Germany was under American and Soviet occupation, and effectively defended the Nazi legacy (it ended up being banned in 1952 as the Basic Law prohibits non-democratic parties). Since the 1960s there have been similar, though weaker, continuities in the National Democratic party (NPD), and German People's Union (DVU). The now-defunct Italian Social Movement (MSI), too, had links with the Mussolini era, including a leader, Giorgio Almirante (1914–89), who was a Fascist official. He coined the revealing slogan 'Back to the Future' (*Nostalgia dell'avvenire*). This, like much of the MSI's propaganda, combined a fascist kernel with allusion and ambiguity. As such, it appeals to a select few, whilst mocking the masses. During the 1990s, German neo-Nazi youth groups attracted considerable media attention on account of their riots and killings. However, the actions of such neo-fascists are best understood in terms of social tensions, and as the expression of an alienated style, rather than political theory, though some of those who sport Nazi insignia and chant fascist slogans may be inducted into a more serious ideological milieu.

More interesting in terms of ideas, have been the relatively small number of ideologically *radical* neo-fascists, like the French writer Maurice Bardèche (1907–1998). They have sought to delineate a 'true' fascism which is somehow part of, yet different from classic fascism. (Almirante was in many ways radical, but his leadership period of the MSI forced him towards a more conservative position.) Thus Bardèche wrote in a book which begins with the remarkable (post-war) claim 'I am a fascist writer':

> Nothing is more stirring in the history of Italian Fascism than the return to sources achieved under the iron fist of defeat. The programme of the Salò Republic in 1944, this is what Mussolini ought to have fought for twenty years earlier. This is where the real fascism lies.[28]

Bardèche thus saw the Salò Republic as an attempt to retrieve Fascism's early radicalism, for example its hostility to the bourgeoisie. (He glossed over the regime's brutal aspect, and Mussolini's continuing tendency towards erratic judgement and posturing.) Predictably, Bardèche, was unwilling to accept contemporary Latin American dictatorships, or even Franco's Spain, as fascist, seeing them as too conservative, too deferential to the existing order to be considered fascist (though he saw classic Peronism as fascist on account of pro-worker policies).

There have been several other varieties of radical neo-fascism. One seeks to argue that fascism is 'socialist', and could appeal to the masses (though the need for élite leadership is usually stressed). Unlike Bardèche, most in this category do not seek inspiration in the Salò Republic, which was a short-lived failure, and survived under German tutelage. A more common source of this form of neo-fascism is the Strasser brothers. 'Strasserism', for example, frequently emerged as an issue within German neo-Nazi groups during the 1970s–90s, having been carefully nurtured in fascist coteries by Otto Strasser, who had survived Nazism by going into exile.

Another variety of radicals looked to German 'conservative revolutionaries' of the 1920s, such as Ernst Jünger (1895–1998), for inspiration. This group had been closely allied to 'third way' thinking, but some of its leading members, like Jünger, had gone on to criticize the Nazi search for a mass base and the compromise with traditional forces. A particularly notable group influenced by this source was the French *Nouvelle Droite* (New Right), which emerged in the late 1970s, centring around the writings of the polymath Alain de Benoist (1943–   ), who claimed that although many of the key ideas came 'from the right, they are not necessarily of the right'[29] (see Chapter 3). Indeed, a key element of de Benoist's thought came from the Marxist Antonio Gramsci (see Chapter 5). Influencing cultural norms, for example through the media, was seen as a crucial way forward. Conservative revolutionary thought was also influential in Italy, though here Evola was more central to the revision of fascism. Although owing far more to the right than the left, Evola too became associated with 'third way' policies, and the idea of withdrawal from formal politics in favour of cultural struggle as a preparation for the revolution.

However, some of Evola's followers turned to a further major revision of fascism. They interpreted Evola's hostility to conventional politics as involving military organization. Codreanu and José Antonio, both fascist martyrs, were often invoked, too, as models of the 'Political Soldier', the dedicated, ascetic, individual, willing to die for his beliefs. In some cases, this military discipline was seen largely in spiritual terms, a form of self-control and discovery. However, there was a clear terrorist side as well, though the exact rationale of how small fascist groups could gain power through terrorism was far from clear. (Neo-fascist terrorism, especially in Italy, raises complex factual issues concerning manipulation by the 'forces of law and order', which could hope to benefit from destabilization.)[30] Indeed, neo-fascist terrorism has produced some remarkably muddy thinking, such as the claim to being 'Nazi-Maoist' – though this does point to the continuing clear left-wing influence on fascist thought, and attempts to forge links with the terrorist left.

Two final versions of radicalism are worth noting. Some neo-fascists have advocated Europeanism, albeit very much not of the European Union variety. For instance, Degrelle wrote prolifically about the international brotherhood of the Waffen SS who fought to save Europe from communism. Another form of neo-fascist revisionism concerns ecology, which has often drawn its inspiration from Nazi 'blood and soil' and proto-ecological thinking. However, ecology offers the further possibility of being a surrogate theme, useful for parties which seek broad support in a world where fascism is still a pariah. Thus when the French Front National (FN) – which has been consistently the most electorally successful of the new radical nationalist parties since the early 1980s, averaging over 15 per cent in the late 1990s – speaks of defending the patrimony, the enemy is clearly immigration and ethnic minorities as well as industrial despoliation.

Jean-Marie Le Pen's (1928–   ) FN points to a further form of neo-fascism, the *hybrid*. There is much controversy as to whether Le Pen and his party should be seen as ideologically fascist. Those who hold that the FN is fascist point to facts such as Le Pen's charismatic leadership and large, stylized rallies, or his dismissing the Holocaust in 1987 as a 'detail' of history – which many equated with endorsing Holocaust-denial arguments (a claim repeated on subsequent occasions, for example in 1997).

However, many would see Le Pen and the FN as an extreme form of conservatism, or a form of populist protest, rather than fascism ('national populism' is arguably the most common term among French commentators).[31] The Front National claims to have accepted the free-market economy, and liberal democratic state. It also tends to employ what some have termed 'new racism', which is not always easy to disentangle from mainstream views. This does not talk in terms of racial hierarchies so much as 'naturalness' and 'democracy' – North Africans, so the argument runs, are not inferior, it is just that they belong in their own culture back 'home' (the FN was clearly influenced in this area by the writings of the *Nouvelle Droite*). Le Pen's likely successor as leader, Bruno Mégret, has certainly sought to keep down the cruder type of racist appeal which sometimes surfaces in the FN and has made strong appeals to mainstream parties.

Part of the problem is that political parties tend to be ideological coalitions: this was true of classic fascism, and it is certainly true of the FN. Nevertheless, Le Pen and the Front National seem best understood as a hybrid form of fascism. At the core of Le Pen's thought is a series of classic fascist syntheses, on to which have been grafted aspects of liberal, conservative, populist, even socialist imagery and rhetoric. Thus man is seen as constrained by nature, but capable of change through leadership. France is seen as threatened by an enemy both within and without (with Islam increasingly replacing communism as this enemy), but France is seen as capable of salvation by dynamic leadership. Le Pen talks of learning from the inspiration of socialism before it became perverted by Marxism, of reconciling the security of workers with economic dynamism. He may at times celebrate the free market, but he termed the Maastricht Treaty in the 1992 referendum: 'strictly materialist and mercantile'.[32] Le Pen has promised privatization, but this seems mainly to allow shares to be given to heads of households, and move towards a societal rather than state form of corporatism. Le Pen's rhetoric overall is no simple eulogy to the past, but more an attempt to synthesize progress and tradition. Revealingly, in the late 1990s the language of the 'third way' has increasingly emerged in FN rhetoric. Even the apparent coming to terms with liberal democracy is accompanied by bitter attacks on current élites, and ominous, if vague, promises to institute a more presidential state. Moreover, it is vital to note the dynamics of Le Pen's position in terms of democracy. There is a paradox of toleration here. Freedom will be possible precisely because France will be culturally and ideologically harmonious (if Le Pen has his way).

FASCISM AT THE TURN OF THE TWENTY-FIRST CENTURY

The FN is one of several new nationalist parties which recently have shown an ability to make electoral breakthroughs. Electorally the most successful in the late 1990s has been the Austrian Freedom Party (FPÖ), led by the charismatic Jörg Haider, which has averaged approaching 30 per cent of the vote. Also of note is the successor to the MSI, the Alleanza Nazionale: another party with a media-genic leader, Gianfranco Fini, this has averaged more like 15 per cent of the poll recently. It is important to stress that, whilst Haider has at times seemed to support aspects of Nazism, he rejects the fascist label. Fini claims that his party is 'post-fascist', and certainly there are notable differences with the past – including a rejection of totalitarianism and racism (Italy adopted Nazi-type Nuremberg laws in 1938). Some critics argue that there are hidden agendas, but overt distancing of these parties from classic fascism has undoubtedly been important to their appeal. Indeed, in general across Western Europe insurgent right-wing parties have tended to be most successful where they can clearly distance themselves from classic fascism: for instance, the Italian regionalist and free market Lega Nord, or the Scandinavian parties – though there have been ominous exceptions, for instance the 13 per cent of the vote won by the DVU in 1998 in a Länder of the old East Germany where economic conditions had some parallels with the dark days of the inter-war era.

Fascism in the form it took during the inter-war years is dead as a major force, at least in Western Europe. Here it lives on primarily as a style movement among the alienated young. Nevertheless, Le Pen and the FN show the potential for new forms of fascism to gather support – and to influence the mainstream agenda, for their impact has been notable on the programme of others. Even more ominously, there are interesting parallels with turn of the twentieth-century politics. Socially, there are renewed signs of anomie and political alienation, accompanied by growing criticism of mainstream politicians. Ideologically, there are signs of a new crisis of both left and right. The moderate left may have won many recent elections, but it has failed to delineate a new philosophy and faces major socio-economic problems. The fashion for the New Right has waned against a background of an ailing Western economy, and the sense of a loss of community and national identity particularly in Europe. Geopolitically, there seems a new threat from the East, not least in the shape of militant Islam. Last, but by no means least, fears of massive population transfers, including illegal immigration, threaten to undermine integrationist and anti-racist policies. It is therefore a serious mistake to write off the salience of fascism, especially when adapted by shrewd leaders to fit the context of the turn of the twenty-first century.

NOTES

1. S. Sontag, 'Fascinating Fascism', in *Under the Sign of Saturn*, Writers and Readers, London, 1983, p.105.
2. *'Fascio'* means 'group' in Italian; it also means 'bundle', and can refer to the axe, bound with rods, which was a Roman symbol of authority – a symbol adopted by the Fascists.
3. R. De Felice, *Interpretations of Fascism*, Harvard University Press, Cambridge, Massachusetts, 1977, p.ix *et passim*.
4. C.J. Friedrich and Z. Brzezinski, *Totalitarianism, Dictatorship and Democracy*, Praeger, New York, 1961; A.J. Gregor *The Fascist Persuasion in Radical Politics*, Princeton University Press, Princeton, 1974; R. Griffin, *The Nature of*

Fascism, Pinter, London, 1991; E. Nolte, *Three Faces of Fascism*, Holt Rinehart and Winston, New York, 1969; C.L. Mosse, *The Crisis of German Ideology*, Grosset and Dunlap, New York, 1964; Z. Sternhell, *Neither Right nor Left*, University of California Press, Berkeley, 1986.

5. For a somewhat longer introduction to the birth of fascist ideology see R. Eatwell, *Fascism: a History*, Chatto and Windus, 1995. For the classic attempt to trace the roots of fascism and communism deep in Western thought see K. Popper, *The Open Society and its Enemies*, 2 vols, Routledge and Kegan Paul, London, 1945.

6. For an interesting work which views Barrès as a forerunner of fascism, see R. Soucy, *Fascism in France: The Case of Maurice Barrès*, University of California Press, Berkeley, 1972.

7. *Mes Cahiers*, vol. 4, 1904–06, Plon, Paris, 1931, pp.69–70. Emphasis in original.

8. B. Mussolini, *Fascism: Doctrine and Institutions*, Ardita, Rome, 1935, pp.11, 25–6, 58, 59.

9. R. Eatwell, 'On Defining the "Fascist Minimum"': The Centrality of Ideology', *Journal of Political Ideologies*, 1, 1996.

10. G. Gentile, 'The Philosophic Basis of Fascism', *Foreign Affairs*, 1927–28, p.291.

11. C. Codreanu, *La Garde de Fer*, Editions Prometheus, Paris, 1938, p.282.

12. For example, W.M. Fletcher, *The Search for a New Order: Intellectuals and Fascism in Pre-War Japan*, University of North Carolina Press, Chapel Hill, 1983.

13. Cf the historians and sociologists who do not accord Hitler and ideology a significant role in the Holocaust, e.g. Z. Bauman, *Modernity and the Holocaust*, Polity Press, Oxford, 1989.

14. Noontide Press, Torrance, CA, 1982, p.63.

15. Heinemann, London, 1969, p.593. Emphasis in original.

16. See A. Barkai, *Nazi Economics*, Berg, Oxford, 1990.

17. For example, P. Hayes, *Industry and Ideology*, Cambridge University Press, Cambridge, 1987.

18. Sir Oswald Mosley, *The Greater Britain*, BUF Publications, London, 1932, p.154; Juan Perón, *The Theory and Complete Doctrine of General Perón*, Ministry of Foreign Affairs and Worship, Buenos Aires, 1946, p.6.

19. H. Thomas (ed.), *The Selected Writings of José Antonio Primo de Rivera*, Jonathan Cape, London, 1972, p.51.

20. S Payne, *Fascism: Comparison and Definition*, University of Wisconsin Press, Madison, 1980; cf. his *A History of Fascism*, University College Press, London, 1996, where he clearly takes ideology more seriously.

21. N. O'Sullivan, *Fascism*, Dent, London, 1983.

22. For an example of those who have sought to trace fascism's origins back to major thinkers like de Maistre, see I. Berlin, 'Joseph de Maistre and the Origins of Fascism', in *The Crooked Timber of Humanity*, John Murray, London, 1990.

23. On populism see M. Canovan, *Populism*, Junction Books, London, 1981.

24. For example, G. Germani, *Authoritarian Populism, Fascism and National Populism*, Transaction Books, Brunswick, New Jersey, 1978.

25. Eva Perón, *My Mission in Life*, Vantage Press, New York, 1951, p.1.

26. R. Eatwell, 'Universal Fascism: Approaches and Definitions', in S. Larsen (ed.), *Fascism outside Europe*, Social Science Monographs, Boulder, 1999.

27. See R. Eatwell, 'How to Revise History (and Influence People?), Neo-Fascist

Style', in L. Cheles *et al.* (eds), *The Far Right in Western and Eastern Europe*, Longman, Harlow, 1995.

28. M. Bardèche, *Que'est-ce qu le fascisme?* Les Sept Couleurs, Paris, 1961, p.20.
29. For example, *Vu de Droite*, Paris, Copernic, 1979, p.15.
30. See F. Ferraresi, *Threats to Democracy. The Radical Right in Italy after the War*, Princeton University Press, Princeton, 1996.
31. For the best introductory work in English see H.G. Simmons, *The Front National*, Westview, Boulder, 1996.
32. *Pour la France*, Editions Albatros, Paris, 1985, esp. pp.14, 31; *National Hebdo*, 10–16 September 1992.

GUIDE TO FURTHER READING

Antecedents

Arendt, Hanna, *The Origins of Totalitarianism*, André Deutsch, London, 1986. Classic work covering communism as well as fascism.

De Grand, A.J., *The Italian Nationalist Association and the Rise of Fascism*, University of Nebraska Press, Lincoln, 1978. Detailed monograph.

Gregor, A.J., *The Young Mussolini and the Intellectual Origins of Fascism*, University of California Press, Berkeley, 1979. Sees Mussolini as a serious thinker.

Mosse, George L., *The Crisis of German Ideology*, Grosset and Dunlap, New York, 1964. Major writer on the cultural background to fascism.

Mosse, George L., *Towards the Final Solution*, Howard Fertig, New York, 1978. History of ideas approach to racism.

Stemhell, Zeev, Sznajder, Mario and Asheri, Maia, *The Foundations of Fascist Ideology*, Princeton University Press, Princeton, 1993. Sees fascism as a serious ideology, though Sternhell controversially holds that Nazism was *not* fascist on account of its racism.

Inter-war fascism

Bendersky, J.W., *Carl Schmitt. Theorist for the Reich*, Princeton University Press, Princeton, 1983. Mongraph.

Blinkhorn, Martin (ed.), *Fascists and Conservatives*, Unwin Hyman, London, 1990. Historial surveys from high quality contributors.

R.J.B. Bosworth, *The Fascist Dictatorship*, Edward Arnold, London, 1998. Opinionated history textbook.

Brooker, Paul, *The Faces of Fraternalism*, Clarendon Press, Oxford, 1991. A functionalist account which includes Japan as fascist.

Burleigh, M. and Wippermann, W. *The Racial State: Germany, 1933–1945*, Cambridge University Press, Cambridge, 1991. Excellent on Nazi racist policy.

Costa Pinto, António, *Salazar's Dictatorship and European Fascism*, Social Science Monographs, Boulder, 1995. Excellent discussion of Portugal.

De Felice, Renzo, *Interpretations of Fascism*, Harvard University Press, Cambridge, MA, 1977. Survey by leading Italian scholar of fascism who has stressed the 'movement' vs 'regime' phases of fascism, its alleged irrationalism and middle class basis.

Durham, Martin, *Women and Fascism*, Routledge, London, 1998. Clear survey including post-1945 coverage of Britain.

Eatwell, Roger, 'Towards a New Model of Generic Fascism', *Journal of Theoretical Politics*, 4, 1992. Long and often cited article.

Eatwell, Roger, *Fascism: a History*, Chatto and Windus, London, 1995. Brings the story up to the 1990s; narrative but takes ideology seriously.

Eatwell, Roger, 'On Defining the "Fascist Minimum": The Centrality of Ideology', *Journal of Political Ideologies*, 1, 1996. Critique of Sternhell, Payne and Griffin.

Gentile, Emilio, *The Sacralization of Politics in Fascist Italy*, Harvard University Press, Harvard, 1996. Fascism as a secular religion.

Gregor, A.J., *Interpretations of Fascism*, Transaction Books, New York, 1997. Reissue with new introduction of classic work on why fascism emerged.

Griffin, Roger, *The Nature of Fascism*, Pinter, London, 1991. Broad, sophisticated, survey.

Griffin, Roger (ed.), *Fascism*, Oxford University Press, Oxford, 1995. Short-text reader.

Griffin, Roger (ed.), *International Fascism: Theories, Causes and the New Consensus*, Edward Arnold, London, 1998. Useful set of key secondary works.

Hitler, Adolf, *Mein Kampf*, Heinemann, London, 1969. Banned in most countries.

Kershaw, Ian, *The Nazi Dictatorship*, Edward Arnold, London, 1993. Excellent short, analytical textbook.

Kershaw, Ian, *Hitler: 1889–1936 Hubris*, Allen Lane, London, 1998. Best biography.

Lane, Barbara Miller and Rupp, Leila (eds), *Nazi Ideology before 1933*, Manchester University Press, Manchester, 1978. Selected texts.

Laqueur, Walter (ed.), *Fascism: a Reader's Guide*, Penguin, Harmondsworth, 1979. Includes some notable contributions, particularly by Sternhell, and Juan Linz.

Larsen, Stein, Hatgvet, Bemt and Myklebust, J. (eds), *Who Were the Fascists?* Universitetsforlaget, Oslo, 1980. Includes some notable contributions.

Linz, Juan, 'Totalitarian and Authoritarian Regimes', in F. Greenstein and N. Polsby (eds), *Handbook of Political Science*, Addison-Wesley, Reading, MA., 1975. Excellent typological essay.

Lyttelton, Adrian (ed.), *Italian Fascisms: from Gentile to Pareto*, Jonathan Cape, London, 1973. Set of texts.

Mosse, George L. (ed.), *International Fascism*, Sage, London, 1979. Articles from the important *Journal of Contemporary History*.

Mussolini, Benito, *Fascism: Doctrine and Institutions*, Rome, Ardita, 1935.

Neocleous, Mark, *Fascism*, Open University Press, Buckingham, 1997. Neo-Marxist textbook which takes ideology fairly seriously.

Noakes, Jeremy and Pridham, Geoffrey (eds) *Documents on Nazism*, Jonathan Cape, London, 1974. Very good selection.

Nolte, Ernst, *Three Faces of Fascism*, Holt Rinehart and Winston, New York, 1965. Classic view of fascism as a European inter-war force.

O'Sullivan, Nöel, *Fascism*, J.M. Dent, London, 1983. Excellent political philosophy overview.

Payne, Stanley G., *Fascism: Comparison and Definition*, University of Wisconsin Press, Madison, 1980. Influential typology.

Payne, Stanley, *A History of Fascism, 1914–1945*, University College London Press, London, 1996. Excellent general history, including minor fascisms like the Romanian Iron Guard.

Poulantzas, Nicos, *Fascism and Dictatorship*, Verso, London, 1979. Sophisticated Marxist analysis.

Preston, Paul, *The Politics of Revenge: Fascism and the Military in Twentieth Century Spain*, Routledge, London, 1995. Excellent history.

Rockmore, T., *On Heidegger's Nazism and Philosophy*, Harvester, London, 1992. One of several works branding the major philosopher as Nazi.

Soucy, R., *Fascism in France: the Second Wave, 1933–1939*, Yale University Press, New Haven, 1995. Sees fascism more as a form of conservatism; note there is a preceding volume covering 1924–33.

Stemhell, Zeev, *Neither Left Nor Right*, University of California Press, Berkeley, 1986. Major work which sees France as a key source of fascist ideas, which owed much to the left.

Thomas, Hugh (ed.), *The Selected Writings of José Antonio Primo de Rivera*, Jonathan Cape, London, 1972. Leading Spanish fascist.

Thurlow, R., *Fascism in Britain*, I.B. Tauris, London, 1998, revd edition. Good history coming up to the 1990s.

E. Weber, *Varieties of Fascism*, Van Nostrand, New York, 1964. Dated, but still useful, especially on the 'minor' fascisms.

Woolf, S.J. (ed.), *European Fascism*, Methuen, London, 1981. Good, if dated, wide-ranging set of essays.

Neo-fascism

Betz, H.-G. and Immerfall, S. (eds), *The New Politics of the Right*, St. Martin's, New York, 1998. Broad national coverage.

Cheles, Luciano *et al.* (eds), *The Far Right in Western and Eastern Europe*, Longman, Harlow, 1995. Good wide-ranging set of essays, mainly nationally based.

Eatwell, Roger, 'The Dynamics of Right-Wing Electoral Breakthrough', *Patterns of Prejudice*, 32, 1998. Critique of existing approaches and new theory, which highlights the importance of ideology.

Hainsworth, Paul (ed.) *The Politics of the Extreme Right*, Pinter, London, 1999. Good, broad, mainly national coverage.

Larsen, Stein (ed), *Modern Europe after Fascism, 1943–1980s*, 2 vols, Social Science Monographs, Boulder, 1998. Encyclopaedic; mainly national studies.

Merkl, Peter H. and Weinberg, Leonard (eds), *The Revival of Right-Wing Extremism in the Nineties*, Frank Cass, London, 1997. Includes the often-neglected states in Central and Eastern Europe and the USA.

9
FEMINISM
Valerie Bryson

——

INTRODUCTION

> Women constitute half the world's population, perform nearly two
> thirds of its work hours, receive one tenth of the world's income, and
> own less than one hundredth of the world's property.
>
> United Nations Report, 1980.

A common starting-point for all feminist ideas is the belief that women are
disadvantaged in comparison with men, and that this disadvantage is not a
natural and inevitable result of biological difference but something that can
and should be challenged and changed. Unlike traditional political theories
and ideologies, feminism provides a way of looking at the world that sees
women's situation and the inequalities between men and women as central
political issues; as such, it provides a fundamental challenge to dominant
assumptions about the scope and nature of politics. Beyond this, there is
enormous disagreement as to the nature, causes and cure for women's
inequality, subordination or oppression, for feminism is certainly not a
unified ideology but contains many competing strands. These have frequently been identified as 'liberal', 'Marxist', 'radical' and 'socialist'
feminisms; 'black feminism' and, increasingly, 'post-modern feminism' also
represent distinct and important approaches. This classification provides a
useful way of approaching feminist ideas which I will use throughout this
chapter; it is, however, essential to remember that reality is much more
complex than such labels can suggest, and that in practice few writers or
theories fit exactly into any one slot.

Bearing this reservation in mind, liberal feminism can be understood as
'equal rights' feminism. It asserts that women are rational beings like men,

and that they should therefore have the same legal and political rights, and the opportunity to compete equally with men in politics and paid employment. Marxist feminists argue against this, that women's oppression is essentially a by-product of class society, and that full equality will only be achieved when capitalism is replaced by genuine socialism. Both these approaches use existing male theories and apply them to the situation of women; radical feminists, however, claim to provide a new perspective based on women's own experiences, and they argue that the patriarchal domination of women by men is both the most basic form of power in society and one that has its source in such apparently private areas of life as the family and sexual relationships. This analysis involves a redefinition of power and politics, and an attack on the allegedly artificial distinction between public and private life. Modern socialist feminism seeks to combine this radical perspective with Marxist class analysis by exploring the interrelationship between capitalism and patriarchy. Feminism has frequently been seen as the preserve of white middle-class women; some feminists now argue that the experiences of black women must not only be included in feminist analysis, but taken as its starting-point. Finally, a number of feminists have recently endorsed post-modernist critiques of western philosophy, and are attempting to use these as a basis for exploring new woman-centred forms of knowledge and understanding.

All of these ideas will be explored in later sections. Here it is important simply to point out the diversity of approaches that are contained in the one word 'feminism', and to stress that feminism is very much more than a catalogue of the wrongs that have been done to women. Far from being a static ideology, it involves a complex and dynamic set of ideas that has evolved over the last 300 years and that is still constantly developing and challenging its own assumptions, as well as contributing and reacting to what many feminists now refer to as 'malestream' ideologies.

FEMINISM BEFORE THE FIRST WORLD WAR

Early liberal feminism

Although the term 'feminist' first came into use in English during the 1890s, the origins of modern feminism can be traced back at least to the late seventeenth century, when early capitalist development involved a marked change for the worse in the legal and economic situation of many women, and liberal challenges to established political authority were extended by some writers to question the arbitrary power of men.[1] It is, however, Mary Wollstonecraft's *Vindication of the Rights of Woman*, written in 1792 during the early years of the French Revolution, that provides the first full expression of early liberal feminism. At this time women not only lacked the vote, but were deemed unfit for education, were debarred from many occupations and had no more legal standing than children; a married woman had no legal property of her own, anything she might earn was legally the possession of her husband, and even if he abused her she had no real right to a divorce. Forcefully rejecting contemporary belief in female inferiority, Wollestonecraft (1759–97) argued that women are, like men, rational individuals and that, as such, they should have equal rights; and she established the principles underlying later campaigns for women's right to education, employment, property and the vote. Half a century later, these principles found concrete expression at the first ever Women's Rights Convention held at Seneca Falls in America in 1848, and the latter part of the nineteenth century saw the growth of equal rights feminism throughout the industrializing world.[2] In England, the eminent philosopher John Stuart Mill (1806–73) introduced the question of women's suffrage to the House of Commons in 1867, and his *The Subjection of Women*, first published in 1869, provided a full-scale analysis of women's situation and the advantages to society of giving them full legal and political equality with men; although many rights have now been won, his arguments still have a striking relevance today.

Some early feminist demands met with considerable success. By the end of the nineteenth century, women in Britain and America had won a considerable degree of legal independence and increased access to education and employment, and they were no longer completely excluded from public life and political debate. They were, however, still denied the franchise, and the frustrated demand for 'Votes for Women' was to produce an unprecedented wave of feminist activity by the turn of the century.

Early socialist and Marxist feminism

Although many of the early liberal feminists were highly critical of class inequalities, they did in general think that their demands could be met within the existing socio-economic system. For the 'Utopian socialists' of the early nineteenth century, however, existing relationships between men and women could only be understood as part of the competitive capitalist society which, they argued, not only produced women's subordination but was also upheld by it. This led some to attack not only legal and economic inequalities between men and women, but also marriage, the family and the gender division of labour, and to develop an analysis that linked sexuality to economic and political issues. From this perspective, the goals of feminism and socialism were inextricably interlinked; these early socialists also believed that a better society would be brought about through reform, persuasion and example, and not through violent revolution.[3]

Feminism was not similarly central to the revolutionary socialist ideas developed by Karl Marx (1818–83) later in the century. Nevertheless, his theory did claim to provide a comprehensive analysis of human history and society, and later writers have applied it to feminist issues. It implied that the family and sexual relationships are, like other forms of social organization, the product of a particular stage of economic development; as such, they cannot be altered at will, but only as a result of socio-economic change expressed through class conflict and revolution. This understanding was developed by Frederick Engels in *The Origin of the Family, Private Property and the State*, first published in 1884. In this Engels (1820–95) argued that women's oppression has not always existed, but that it began with the first private property and class society, for it was only then that men's desire to pass property to known heirs motivated them to control women. This motive would, Engels argued, disappear with the overthrow of capitalism, when women would no longer be economically dependent upon men, and the socialization of housework and childcare would liberate them from domestic chores. Similar ideas were produced in Germany by August Bebel (1840–1913), and developed and defended within the Social Democratic Party by Clara Zetkin (1857–1933); they also provided the starting-point for the analysis of women's oppression by Marxists in Russia.

By the end of the nineteenth century, there was in many European countries a sharp split between 'bourgeois' liberal feminists with their demands for equal rights, and Marxists socialists with their talk of class war and revolution. In America and Britain there was much more of a continuum: in America Charlotte Perkins Gilman (1860–1935) developed a highly popular woman-centred theory of history, and argued that society was evolving towards what she saw as the 'womanly values' of socialism;[4] in Britain the dominant form of socialism owed little to Marxist ideology and seemed readily compatible with a feminism based on ideas of social justice and a better life for all. Issues of gender and class seemed however to some to conflict when it came to the campaign for women's suffrage.

The campaign for the vote

The campaign for women's suffrage developed during the second half of the nineteenth century, and reached a dramatic climax in Britain in the brief but famous period of suffragette militancy before the First World War. However, although many different groups seemed to be demanding the same thing, the campaign did not represent a united feminist movement; rather, it provided a rallying-point for an extraordinarily diverse range of political ideologies and interests.[5]

At one level, it was simply the logical extension of liberal feminist ideas of equal rights. Others, however, demanded the vote on the basis of women's *difference* from men rather than their equal worth: women, they argued, possessed sex-specific virtues such as pacifism and temperance which should be allowed to improve political life, and the demand for political rights involved no challenge to their traditional role as wives and mothers.

Others anticipated the modern radical feminist concern with sexual oppression, and argued that political rights were needed because they gave women the power to resist men's sexual demands (with the attendant dangers of venereal disease or pregnancy) – a view encapsulated in Christabel Pankhurst's famous slogan 'Votes for Women: Chastity for Men'. From this perspective, the vote would never be won through reason or persuasion, but only by a demonstration of women's strength, and the suffragettes (the term given to those in the militant wing of the suffrage campaign) therefore declared war on a system that denied them their rights. Most suffrage campaigners in fact rejected illegal methods, but the campaigns of arson, window-smashing and general political disruption certainly drew public attention to their cause; the often brutal reaction of the authorities and the bravery of women in prison who faced the dangers of hunger-strikes and forced-feeding (experienced by over 1000 women) also gained them support.

This approach further implied that sex oppression was more basic than class, and at times it become intertwined with a strongly conservative and anti-democratic strand in the movement, which demanded votes for women as a necessary counter to the power of working-class men in Britain, former slaves in America and new immigrants in Australasia. In this context, it is unsurprising that socialist attitudes to women's suffrage were ambivalent. Although alliances with 'bourgeois feminists' were rejected, however, the official Marxist line came to see it as an important weapon in the class struggle, and in many European countries the campaign was spearheaded by the new mass socialist parties. In Britain, there was a strong working-class suffragist movement in the north of England,[6] some prominent members of the Labour Party gave their full support (most notably George Lansbury and Keir Hardy),[7] and the suffragette leaders Emmeline, Sylvia and Christabel Pankhurst (1858–1928, 1882–1960 and 1880–1958 respectively) began their political lives as socialists. Many socialists were, however, antagonized by what they saw as the middle-class nature of the campaign; the Labour leadership fudged the issue and refused to prioritize female suffrage; some suffrage supporters (including Lansbury) responded by leaving the party, and others followed Emmeline and Christabel Pankhurst in an increasingly right-wing direction (although Sylvia Pankhurst retained her socialist commitments). In general, as the issue became entangled with party politics, political expediency rather than principle often seemed to dominate the debate.

By the time of the First World War, feminism represented both a complex set of ideological positions and a powerful mass movement held precariously together by a common goal. Once the vote was won, there could be no basis for united action, and feminism dissolved more clearly into its constituent parts.

FEMINISM BETWEEN THE WARS

Britain and America

The first country in the world to enfranchise women was New Zealand in 1894, and most 'modern' nations did so shortly after the First World War. In Britain, most women over 30 were given the vote in 1918 (this was extended to all women on the same terms as men in 1928), and in America the 1920 Constitutional Amendment enfranchised all adult women. The reasons for this were complex, but included the hope by some politicians that women would provide a conservative and stabilizing force, the fear that the militant and illegal campaigning methods that had characterized some sections of the suffrage movement in the pre-war years would be renewed, and the belief that women's contribution to the war effort had demonstrated their entitlement to full citizenship.

Although the following period has often been seen as the 'silent years' of feminism, it was in fact characterized by new forms of activity and by significant debates.[8] The liberal demand that women should be treated as individuals on the basis of complete equality with men and that state intervention should always be avoided, clashed head-on with the belief that women have sex-specific needs and attributes, that their prime role is that of wife and mother and that state intervention is needed to promote women's welfare. Translated into the politics of the day, this became 'equal rights' versus 'welfare' feminism. A key issue at the time was the question of protective legislation, aimed at protecting women from the worst effects of dangerous and unhealthy occupations and long working hours: for liberal feminists this represented an undesirable form of discrimination, but for welfare feminists it was a practical and necessary response to the immediate problem of exploitation.

In general, equal rights feminism was abandoned during this period by all but a small minority of middle-class women. However, in America the small Women's Party managed to secure the introduction of an Equal Rights Amendment before Congress every year from 1923; issues of equal pay and opportunity were now on the political agenda, and were to surface dramatically in the 1960s. Welfare feminism was particularly influential in Britain, where it was bound up with the growth of the Labour Party and the early years of the welfare state.[9] Here an important issue was the demand for family allowances associated with Eleanor Rathbone (1872–1946), which was met in a modified form after the Second World War. In America, women's campaigns on welfare issues met with little success until the 1930s, but meant that women's needs could not be entirely ignored in the New Deal, although women did not receive state aid to anything like the same extent as men.

Winning the vote did not have the immediate and dramatic effect that many had hoped or feared. There was no great influx of women into public life, no moral transformation of politics, and women's issues were not at the forefront of the political agenda. Nevertheless, during the inter-war years some concrete gains were made on both equal rights and welfare issues, and although they may have been dormant, the ideas of active feminism were far from dead.

Marxist feminism in Russia

> The new morality is created by a new economy, but we will not build a new communist economy without the support of a new morality.
>   Alexandra Kollontai.[10]

By the time of the 1917 Russian revolutions, there was a well established Marxist feminist position that argued both that the oppression of women was a product of class society that would be ended under communism, and that the achievement of communism itself required the active participation of women. The tumultuous years that followed saw fierce debates over the role of women and experiments with new forms of family and sexual relationships. Lenin himself appeared to take women's issues seriously and supported the establishment of a special Women's Department in 1919, and for a few years there was a genuine attempt to put Marxist feminist ideas into practice.[11]

Here the leading figure was Alexandra Kollontai (1873–1952) who, until she was effectively removed from power in 1923, fought to prioritize women's issues and who confronted issues of personal morality avoided by many other Marxists. As the first woman in the world to hold cabinet office, she did not simply give women full legal, economic and political rights (including the right to abortion), but committed the Communist Party to the principle of the collective provision of housework and good quality child care. She aimed at involving women in the processes that she believed would liberate them, and she insisted that questions of sexuality and family organization would not automatically be resolved through economic change, but must be tackled directly. Here she claimed that possessiveness in relation to both children and sexual partners was a reflection of bourgeois individualism that would become unnecessary in a more caring and cooperative society; she also believed that collective child care and the avoidance of extreme sexual intensity would themselves foster the communist virtues of caring, co-operation and comradeship.

In practice, the resources to implement Kollontai's ideas were never available, and the kind of 'revolution from below' with which she was associated did not survive for long. Under Stalin, her ideas were declared erroneous, most of her policies were reversed, the 'Woman Question' was officially declared solved and a woman could become a 'Mother Heroine' of the Soviet Union by having ten children.[12] Nevertheless, her ideas represent an important attempt to extend Marxist analysis into new areas, and she anticipated a major stand of modern feminist debate.

SIMONE DE BEAUVOIR AND THE ORIGINS OF MODERN FEMINISM

One is not born, but rather becomes, a woman. No biological, psychological, or economic fate determines the figure that the human female presents in society; it is civilization as a whole that produces this creature, intermediate between male and eunuch, which is described as feminine.

Simone de Beauvoir.[13]

The years immediately after the Second World War represent the low point of feminism during the twentieth century, as earlier ideas seemed old-fashioned or irrelevant at a time when most political and legal rights had been won, and when the most general desire was for a return to 'normality'. Many women who had entered male occupations during the war returned to the home, and although labour shortages meant that more continued to enter paid employment, this was seen as contrary to their own interests, as the dominant cult of domesticity taught that true fulfilment for women lay with the family.

In this context, the ideas expressed in Simone de Beauvoir's *The Second Sex* (first published in 1949) seemed both shocking and inspiring. De Beauvoir's own life (1908–86) represented a decisive rejection of the traditional female role: refusing domestic responsibilities or the restrictions of female 'respectability', she lived very much like a man in the male world of the French intelligentsia; the central relationship of her life was with the existentialist philosopher Jean-Paul Sartre, but this was not based on sexual exclusiveness and they never married, had children or shared a home. In *The Second Sex*, she assembled a wealth of philosophical, psychological, anthropological, historical, literary and anecdotal evidence to argue that femininity and domesticity are not natural attributes of womanhood, but artificial creations which limit women's freedom and deny them the expression of their full humanity. In the past, she argued, women's biology made their secondary situation inevitable, but modern technology and contraception now make biology irrelevant. The task is therefore to expose the processes by which femininity is manufactured and to show women the possibility of living differently; in doing this, de Beauvoir looked at hitherto unarticulated areas of female experience such as menstruation and sexuality, which she discussed with a frankness unprecedented in a serious academic work.

Although de Beauvoir's ideas were very much bound up with existentialist philosophy, they struck a chord with many women who neither understood nor accepted her philosophical premises, but who agreed that women had been denied an independent existence or sense of self, and who were excited by the idea that women could be free to take responsibility for their own lives. Today many of her ideas may seem commonplace or false, and critics have accused her of accepting male assumptions, denying the value of women's experiences and ignoring men's interests in maintaining their 'first sex' status. At the time, however, by breaking the silence that surrounded women's experiences, she enabled some women to see the world in a different way. She therefore provided inspiration for a new generation of feminists, who from the 1960s were to attempt to translate feminist analysis into political practice.[14]

MODERN LIBERAL FEMINISM

Betty Friedan and the National Organization of Women

> We aim ... To take action to bring women into full participation in the mainstream of American society *now*, exercising all the privileges and responsibilities thereof in truly equal partnership with men.
> National Organization for Women. Founding Statement, 1966.[15]

The central premise of modern liberal feminism is that women are individuals possessed of reason, that as such they are entitled to full human rights, and that they should therefore be free to choose their role in life, and to compete equally with men in politics and paid employment. Despite formal gains, such freedoms had nowhere been realised in the 1960s, and 'Second Wave' feminism began in America as an essentially liberal protest against the failure of that society to deliver to women the promises of independence, self-expression and fulfilment that seemed part of the American dream. It demanded that women should be liberated from domesticity, and that the existing 'rules of the game' be applied to women in the same way as to men. It did not seek to overturn the economic, social or political system, and unlike de Beauvoir and later radical feminists, it did not attack traditional morality and family values.[16]

The most famous statement of this position was Betty Friedan's best-selling *The Feminine Mystique*, first published in 1963. In this Friedan claimed, rather like de Beauvoir, that women had been socialized and manipulated into believing that their only fulfilment lay in the home, and that the purpose of their life should be to catch and keep a husband, and to service the needs of him and his children. So pervasive and successful was this 'feminine mystique', she argued, that the frustration and despair experienced by millions of American housewives could not be expressed, for each unhappy woman believed that she and not her situation must be at fault. In identifying this 'problem that has no name', Friedan was sounding a clarion call to women, for she believed that the gains won by earlier feminists meant that the door to freedom had been opened, and that women could now walk through it and join men in pursuing careers in the public sphere.

Friedan accepted, however, that some discrimination against women remained, and that this must be actively fought. To this end, she and others in 1966 founded the National Organization for Women (NOW), which was intended to act as a national pressure group that would use the law and existing political processes to challenge both discrimination and the assumptions of traditional gender ideology; for many years a focal point of the organization was the campaign to secure an Equal Rights Amendment to the constitution (the ERA). More recently, Friedan has called for greater child care provision by the state, for greater involvement by men in domestic work and child-rearing, and for a basic restructuring of employment patterns to allow both men and women to combine domestic responsibilities with a career. Other campaigners have also supported the active promotion of gender equality in schools, and have argued for more positive measures including 'reverse discrimination' in employment and political appointments, in order to compensate women for their disadvantages. In 1993, Naomi Wolf's *Fire with Fire* restated the liberal approach for a new generation; she argued that women must refuse to see themselves as victims; rather, they must embrace what she calls 'power feminism', which demands that women realize their right to determine their own lives and teaches them to overcome their fear of success.

Radcliffe Richards, Okin and liberal political theory

Liberal feminism has tended to represent the 'common sense' application of existing values to women's situation rather than theoretical innovation. As such, it has had a significant impact on the political agenda in many nations, and its assumptions lay behind legislation such as the Sex Discrimination Act (1975) and the establishment of the Equal Opportunities Commission in Britain.

More recently, Janet Radcliffe Richards and Susan Moller Okin have attempted to develop more sophisticated ideas using the language of philosophy and political theory. In *The Sceptical Feminist* (1982), Richards uses the ideas of the modern liberal theorist John Rawls to develop a theory of justice that would allow women as well as men to develop their full potential. She accepts that such justice might require temporary 'reverse discrimination', and both she and Okin (in *Gender, Justice and the Family*, 1990) agree with American activists on the need for state support for child care, more flexible patterns of employment and a sharing of domestic work with men. Both also believe that gender equality is not only in accordance with reason and justice, but that it is in the interest of men and society as a whole; from this perspective, there is no reason why their proposals should be opposed, and neither explores the possibility that women's progress might be blocked by powerful conflicting interests.

Criticisms of liberal feminism

In practice, liberal feminism has been attacked not only by anti-feminists defending the sexual *status quo*, but also by other feminists who claim that it does not understand women's true interests and cannot provide a strategy for their liberation.[17] Such criticism focuses on five main areas. First, it is claimed that, even within its own terms, liberal feminism has failed. Despite the well-publicized gains of a few women, there is still no real equality in the worlds of work or politics: positions of power and authority continue to be dominated by men, women's earning power remains dramatically less than men's and the defeat of the ERA in America meant that even the goal of full legal equality has not been met. Second, its goals themselves are rejected by many who argue that they can have meaning only for middle-class career women, and that they ignore the realities of a competitive, hierarchical society in which most must be losers and in which many men as well as women are oppressed by class and race. They are also rejected by those who claim that they are based on male norms which deny the value of activities and attributes traditionally associated with women. If the goal is to become like men, the ability to give birth can only be seen as a handicap, and the caring and domestic work of women is an inferior form of activity. Critics however claim that 'womanly values' must be asserted rather than abandoned, and that we must recognize the interdependence that is the essential basis of human society – so that male ideas of autonomy, competition and rationality must be supplemented or replaced by nurturing, co-operation and empathy.

Third, liberal feminists are said to be thoroughly confused as to the nature of state power and gender interests. Their belief that a just society is in the interest of all implies that men as well as women can be feminists; this assumption is attacked by those who argue that men have a vested interest in maintaining their power, and that this is built into all the institutions of state and society. Liberal feminists are therefore criticized for naïvely thinking that the state is a neutral institution that can be used to promote gender equality. Some critics further claim that the state is not only dominated by men, but that it also reflects the needs of the capitalist economic system; when the needs of women come into conflict with those of men or the pursuit of profit, they will therefore be opposed. This confusion over the nature of the state is increased by liberal feminist demands for state action (such as the provision of child care and the monitoring of employment practices) – for this is contrary to liberal principles of limited government and non-intervention.

Fourth, critics claim that the liberal perspective on power and politics is based on an uncritical acceptance of male definitions which serve to conceal the real roots of women's oppression. In particular, it accepts an artificial distinction between the public world of politics and the private world of personal relationships. It is therefore unable to see that such apparently 'private' areas of life as the family may be the site of sexual politics, and that domestic violence and rape are not simply unfortunate personal experiences but are related to the power structures of society. It is also unable to conceptualize the value and importance of women's work within the home. As many an exhausted 'superwoman' will testify, domestic and caring work does not disappear when women enter paid employment, nor is it shared equally with men; until this problem is confronted, the liberal promise of emancipation may represent an increase in women's burdens, and women will be unable to compete equally with men in paid work or politics.

Finally, it is hard to reconcile the individualistic assumptions of liberalism with a feminist politics based on shared gender interests: the liberal belief that it is up to each person to make the best of his or her own life clashes with feminist awareness of group disadvantage and the need for collective action.

All this means that although liberal feminism represents an important ideology, there are tensions within it. For some critics, there is a fundamental incompatibility between the assumptions of liberalism and the demands of feminist politics. Others, however, argue that liberal ideas of freedom, justice and equality embody important principles that can be extended to women, and that in the process they can be re-examined and improved.

MODERN RADICAL FEMINISM

The theory of patriarchy and its critics

> Women are an oppressed class. Our oppression is total, affecting every facet of our lives ... We identify the agents of our oppression as men. Male supremacy is the oldest, most basic form of domination ... All men receive economic, sexual and psychological benefits from male supremacy. *All men* have oppressed women.
> New York Redstockings Manifesto, 1969[18]

Modern radical feminism arose from women's experience in the Civil Rights, anti-war, New Left and student movements in the 1960s. In these, young women often found that they were treated as sex-objects, secretaries or housewives rather than equal political partners, and that any attempt to challenge this was met with silence, ridicule or contempt. Resistance to such treatment led to a new and revolutionary ideological position that offered a direct and fundamental challenge to all existing perspectives, as women discovered that problems which they had assumed to be theirs alone were in fact widely shared. This led to the approach known as 'consciousness-raising', through which, in women-only groups, women expressed and shared personal experiences so as to bring out their political implications and to develop a strategy for change. Radical feminism has since developed and fragmented, and the label has been applied to a confusingly diverse range of ideas. Nevertheless four key elements can be identified that distinguish it from other approaches.

In the first place, it is essentially a theory of, by and for women. As such, it is based firmly in women's own experiences and perceptions, and it sees no need to compromise with existing political perspectives or agendas. Secondly, it sees the oppression of women as the most universal and fundamental form of domination, and its aim is to understand and end this; here 'patriarchy' is the key term. From this it follows, thirdly, that women as a group have interests opposed to those of men. These interests unite them in a common sisterhood that transcends the divisions of class or race, and means that women should struggle together to achieve their own liberation. Finally, radical feminism involves a redefinition of the very nature of politics. It insists that male power is not confined to the public sphere, but that it extends into such 'personal' areas of life as the family and sexual relationships, both of which are seen as central instruments of patriarchal domination. It argues that the identification of male power is itself a political act; from this perspective, the invisibility of gender issues in dominant political ideologies is no unfortunate accident, but a part of the process by which male power is maintained. The role of feminist theory, therefore, is to show the political nature of areas of life that have hitherto been deemed personal, and to challenge male power by naming it.

For many women, such ideas seemed to express truths which conventional analysis denied, and from the late 1960s, consciousness-raising groups sprang up throughout America and Europe. The new ideas were popularized in such books as Germaine Greer's *The Female Eunuch* (first published in 1970), but it is Kate Millett's *Sexual Politics* (also 1970) that provides the first systematic account of the theory of patriarchy.

Millett argued that in all known societies, the relationship between the sexes has been based on power, and that it is therefore political. This power takes the form of male domination over women in all areas of life, and it is so universal, so ubiquitous and so complete that it appears 'natural'. The patriarchal power of men over women is maintained by a process of socialization which begins in the family and is reinforced by education, literature and religion; it also rests upon economic exploitation and, ultimately, force (particularly sexual violence and rape).

The radical feminist theory of patriarchy has had an enormous impact on feminist thought, and represents a fundamental challenge to conventional political theory. It has also been heavily criticized by other feminists, for some see it as based on a false idea of 'man as the enemy', that leads logically only to lesbian separatism, and that can have little appeal or relevance for the majority of women. Others argue that the theory is a-historical and based on a 'false universalism' that reflects only the experiences of white middle-class women. It is also said to be descriptive rather than analytical, unable to explain the origins of male power and therefore unable to provide an adequate strategy for ending it. Finally, in describing the wrongs done by men over the centuries, it is said to see women simply as passive victims, rather than as makers of history.

Such criticisms are true of some radical feminist theories. The concept of patriarchy has however also been developed to produce a more sophisticated analysis. In particular, many writers now distinguish between the structures of male domination on the one hand, and individual men on the other. This means that the enemy remains male power in all its manifestations, but that this power is seen to be socially constructed rather than embodied in all biological males. Others also attempt to analyse how patriarchy has changed over time, and the ways in which it interacts with other forms of oppression; from this perspective, patriarachy is not a monolithic, universal or bio-logically determined system, but the changing product of particular circumstances which may be modified by collective feminist action.[19]

The bases of patriarchal power

Unlike most political ideologies, radical feminism does not see state power as the central political issue. Instead, it treats the state as but one manifestation of men's political power, reflecting other deeper structures of oppression; women's well-documented exclusion from its formal institutions is therefore a symptom rather than the cause of gender inequality. It also rejects the classic Marxist claim that women's oppression is a product of class society that will be ended with the overthrow of capitalism; it argues that male power cannot be reduced to economics, but is embedded in the family, in reproduction, in sexuality or in the very language that we use.

Many radical feminists see *the family* as the key to men's patriarchal power.[20] Far from being a 'natural' arrangement based on mutual love and respect, it is, they argue, a social institution in which women's labour is exploited, oppressive gender identities and modes of behaviour are learned, and men's sexual power is often violently expressed. As such, it both sustains male power in the 'public' world, and is itself a source of oppression. Others have focused upon *reproduction*. Some see pregnancy and childbirth as barbarous relics of a lower stage of human development from which women will be 'liberated' by reproductive technology.[21] Others argue that, on the contrary, these can be fulfilling and creative experiences, and that mothering is the source of superior 'womanly values' to do with nurturing, co-operation and peace.[22] Such arguments have led to the development of 'eco-feminist' theory; here feminists are further divided over whether women's planet-friendly attributes are biologically preordained, or whether they can in principle be learned by men (see Chapter 10). Such disagreements are profound. Nevertheless, these radical feminists are united in their perception that reproduction is politically significant, and that men's attempts to control it are an important limitation on women's freedom: all can therefore unite behind the slogan of 'A woman's right to choose'.

For other radical feminists, it is *sexuality* that is the prime source of male power.[23] It is argued that this involves a 'forced heterosexuality' that is inherently unfulfilling for women, and that is a means of dividing and controlling them. Heterosexual intercourse, it is claimed, is irretrievably entangled with men's social power and should be rejected: this is not simply a matter of personal choice, but a politically empowering act that liberates women from the need to please men. For some, the central issue is not heterosexuality as such, but its association with violence. Here it is argued that sexual violence is not a rare occurrence, but that it is built into our society and culture, and maintained by a vast pornographic industry. This means that it effectively restricts women's lives and leads to them being seen as sex-objects rather than full human beings. It is further argued that *all men* benefit from pornography and rape, whether or not they personally condemn them, for such violence forces women to seek protection from some men against others, rather than competing equally with them. Such arguments have led some women to the most 'extreme' feminist position: that of lesbian separatism. Most feminists reject this on a number of grounds, and refuse to accept that gender issues can be reduced to sexuality. Nevertheless, the radical feminist analysis has had a significant impact on public opinion, as the implications of pornography are more widely discussed, the extent of sexual abuse is gradually revealed, and it becomes harder to dismiss sexual harassment as 'harmless fun'.

Yet another strand of radical feminism argues that the basis of women's oppression does not lie in social organization or physical domination, but in male control of *culture, language and knowledge*.[24] This, it is claimed, limits the ways in which we can think, and causes patriarchal assumptions to be internalized by women as well as by men (for example, a mother at home with young children will say she is not working; there is no available word to describe what she does do). Feminists must therefore attempt to create a counter-culture and to expose male bias and assert female knowledge at all levels, ranging from the rediscovery of women's history to the development of gender-neutral language.

Each of the areas outlined above has generated a vast literature; despite the claims of some writers, none on its own can provide a full analysis of women's situation. It is essential to note that radical feminism does *not* represent a unified ideological position, and that it need not necessarily imply a politics based on man-hating and separatism. Its central insight is that 'the personal is political'; this must be combined with the understanding that complex issues cannot be reduced to a simple cause, and that patriarchy cannot be isolated from other forms of inequality and oppression.

MODERN MARXIST AND SOCIALIST FEMINISM

Theoretical developments

Many radical feminists have described Marxism as yet another patriarchal ideology. In so-called communist societies, they argue, patriarchal structures remained intact, while Western Marxists have treated questions of gender equality as trivial, diversionary and almost indefinitely postponable. Now that Marxism itself is in disarray, the status of Marxist feminism is particularly vulnerable; it does however represent an influential strand of modern feminist thought, and it is important to examine its contribution.

Central to all Marxist feminism is the belief that women's subordination is not a permanent, natural or inevitable feature of human relationships, but the historically specific product of class society. As such, it cannot be ended at will or in accordance with abstract notions of justice, but only as part of more general socio-economic change. In its most 'orthodox' form, this is an argument of economic determinism, which rejects any idea that gender relations might have a dynamic of their own, or that women may have common group interests cutting across class divisions. However, many modern writers have developed a more flexible form of Marxism, and others have added radical feminist perspectives to explore the interrelationships between capitalism and patriarchy, and to develop what is often described as a 'socialist feminist' position.

During the 1970s, the attempted application of Marxist economic concepts to women gave rise to the so-called 'domestic labour debate'. This involved disagreements over the precise meaning of such terms as 'value', and might at first sight appear of interest only to academic or sectarian Marxists. It did however represent an important attempt to make visible the work done by women in the home, to explore its relationship to the capitalist economy and to assess the implications of this for achieving socialist or feminist change. A minority developed the analysis to demand 'wages for housework' as part of a wider socialist strategy; rather more agreed that the housework done by women does not simply represent a personal service to individual men, but that it serves the interests of the capitalist economy by reproducing and maintaining the workforce in a particularly cheap and efficient way. Others have further argued that capitalism has benefited from being able to treat women as a 'reserve army of labour', which can be employed or dispensed with as the economy goes through its inevitable cycles of expansion and recession.

The idea that women's subordination serves capitalist interests has led

some writers to argue that we have a system of *capitalist patriarchy*. Others
however claim that although capitalism and patriarchy are often mutually
reinforcing, they may also come into conflict (as when the capitalist need for
women's labour is opposed by the patriarchal demand for personal services
within the home). They therefore argue that there are two dynamic forces at
work in history, which must be understood in terms of both class and gender
struggle; this has come to be known as the *dual systems* approach.[25]

The above arguments are based on economic analysis; others have tried to
use Marxist ideas to explore spheres of life traditionally considered 'private'
or non-political. Here important pioneering work was done by Juliet Mitchell, who has argued that women's situation is determined by four structures:
production, reproduction, sexuality and the socialization of children.
Although she accepts the classic Marxist position that production is the most
basic of these, she also argues for the relative autonomy of the other
structures; she further claims that the ideas of Freudian psychoanalysis
should be used by feminists to analyse the situation of women. Such ideas
reflect more general changes in Marxist theory, and have been explored by
later writers, some of whom have also used the Marxist concept of *alienation*
to discuss women's lack of control over reproduction and their own sexuality.

All this means that, although important disagreements remain, there is
now a wide body of thought that believes that gender issues can neither be
isolated from their socio-economic context nor reduced to it. Such an
approach does not think that gender is more basic than class, that all women
are united in a timeless sisterhood, or that all men are the enemy; rather, it
argues that both women and men will gain from the socialist transformation
of society which will make possible the elimination of all forms of oppression. It does accept the importance of the 'personal' oppression identified by
radical feminists, but it insists that this is bound up with the economic system
in ways which must be understood if it is to be challenged and changed.

Socialist feminist strategies

Since the early 1970s, left-wing talk of incipient revolution in advanced
industrial societies has largely faded, to be replaced by a more pragmatic
approach which prefers piecemeal reform to class struggle. For many socialist feminists, the immediate political tasks are to challenge sexism within
trade unions and left-wing political parties, and to organize around particular class, gender, race, community or environmental demands in the belief
that these are interconnected, and that they can have a cumulative effect
upon society.

Socialist feminism is now in many ways on the defensive. Not only are
many of its assumptions increasingly out of line with the general political
environment, but it has been accused by other feminists of élitism and racism.

Nevertheless, the perception that economic relationships can limit or determine what it is possible to achieve remains important, and helps explain the failure of apparently 'reasonable' feminist demands. In its more sophisticated forms it may therefore help in the formulation of an effective feminist politics based on an understanding of the interrelationships between economic, political and personal life.

BLACK FEMINISM

> black women felt they were asked to choose between a black movement that primarily served the interests of black male patriarchs, and a women's movement which primarily served the interests of racist white women.
>
> bell hooks[26]

The feminist ideas discussed in this chapter reflect the experiences, interests and priorities of white western women. Such women have frequently claimed to speak on behalf of the whole of their sex; the perspectives of 'other women' have either been ignored or treated as an optional extra. In thus treating one particular group as the norm, feminism has marginalized other groups in much the same way that male ideologies have marginalized women, and has too often fallen into the trap of thinking that ideas only really exist if they can be found neatly bound on library shelves.

Black women in many countries are now both rediscovering their own history and developing their own ideological positions. Writers and activists such as Angela Davis, Andre Lorde, bell hooks and Patricia Collins have moved beyond a critique of the racism of some white feminists to assert the primacy and validity of black women's own experiences.[27] They argue that, precisely because they are the most disadvantaged group in society, with no institutionalized inferiors, black women have a special vantage point and a particularly clear understanding of the world from which we can all learn. A focus on the experience of women of colour also enables us to see the interconnecting and interactive nature of different forms of oppression; this in turn opens up feminist analysis to other previously marginalized or excluded groups, such as disabled women or lesbians.

Increasingly, white Western feminists are beginning to acknowledge their own limitations, and there has been much beating of breasts over past insensitivities. The problem remains, however, of whether it is in principle possible to build a feminist ideology and develop a feminist politics that can encompass the needs and perspectives of all women. Here it must also be noted that 'black women' or 'third world women' are no more a united group than are 'white women'; it is important too to understand that racism is not simply a matter of individual prejudice or injustice, but also the product of particular historical situations which has become embedded in the structures of society; on a global scale, this means that differences amongst women cannot be understood outside of the context of colonialism, imperialism and nationalistic struggles for independence.

Some writers have recently suggested that an understanding of women's differences means that the radical feminist idea of *sisterhood*, which implies an oppression shared by all women, should give way to that of *solidarity*, which is based on the belief that the struggles of all women are inter-connected, but that they are not the same. Such an approach would allow women to unite on some demands, but would also give them scope to ally themselves with men of their own race or class on other issues.

POST-MODERN FEMINISM

Attacks on the 'false universality' of feminist ideas have coincided with developments in linguistic and psychoanalytic theory which some think offer radically new ways of understanding that can be of use to feminism. These new theories are highly complex, and involve a plethora of overlapping schools of thought which have been variously labelled as post-structuralist, discourse, 'French' or post-modernist. They reject Western philosophy's search for truth and certainty, arguing that this is now meaningless in societies that are increasingly characterised by fragmentation, diversity and transience. From this perspective, it is individual subjectivity that is impor-tant, and such labels as 'woman' or 'working class' can only conceal the multiplicity of particular experiences.

Such an approach can usefully alert us to the dangers of overgeneraliza-tion. It also involves an exploration of the ways in which power is dispersed, and how it is constructed through language, knowledge and sexuality, which has affinities with some radical feminist approaches, and which many find very exciting. However, it also has many dangers. In particular, critics argue that it easily collapses into a woolly relativism and an individualistic reduc-tionism that negates all possibility of collective action and paralyses political will. It is also said to be deliberately obscure and inaccessible. This means that although it may provide a fashionable retreat for erstwhile Marxists, and although post-modern feminism is an increasingly influential school of thought, post-modernism is an essentially conservative ideology, and its inability to understand that women have collective as well as individual experiences rules it out as the basis for a coherent feminist practice.

FEMINISM AT THE TURN OF THE TWENTY-FIRST CENTURY

Women have made important gains during the twentieth century, and many of the principles for which they have fought are now seen as obvious entitlements rather than feminist demands. Few in Western democracies would now challenge the right of women to education, employment or the vote, or advocate a return to the gross legal inequalities of the nineteenth century; for young women today, feminism can therefore seem at best outdated and at worst a threat to loving relationships between men and women or an anti-male obstacle to genuine gender equality.

Nevertheless, even in the most 'advanced' countries, women remain disadvantaged in comparison with men. Positions of public power remain largely in male hands, women as a group continue to work much longer hours than men (particularly within the home) and to receive far less financial reward, while fear of sexual violence restricts their lives and they are denied full control over their own reproduction.

In this context, media talk of a 'post-feminist era' is nonsense. Feminism may seem less fashionable than a few years ago, but its assumptions have entered the consciousness of too many people to be easily cast aside. It has, however, lost the easy certainties that sometimes characterized it in the past, and feminist ideology has not produced a united feminist movement – it seems there can be little common ground between those who seek success in the boardroom, those who insist that feminism is inseparable from socialism, those who argue that 'womanly values' must be learned by men, and those who would like to replace men by sperm banks or parthenogenesis. Nevertheless, there are signs that different perspectives are coming closer together, as they move away from their origins in male theory and become increasingly based on the realities of women's lives and struggles. This trend is apparent in the more recent works in the bibliography at the end of this chapter. Although the fragmentation of feminist ideas and activities reflects important ideological disputes, it may therefore also indicate a new sense that complex problems cannot have a simple cause, and that different approaches give rise to complementary rather than alternative forms of feminist politics. It may also involve the recognition that gender division is not the only significant source of inequality, and that for many women, race or class are more important.

An important area of agreement is an increasingly general acceptance of the radical feminist claim that 'the personal is political', and that power relations are not confined to the 'public' worlds of law, the state and economics, but that they pervade all areas of life. This means that such issues as child care or domestic violence are redefined as political, and can be the focus of collective feminist action; it means too that politics is not simply something 'out there', but a part of everyday experience. At the same time, it is becoming clearer that gender issues cannot be isolated from their socio-economic context, and that apparently moderate feminist demands may come into conflict with dominant economic interests and assumptions.

Disagreements remain over the role of men in aiding or opposing feminist goals. Liberal feminism started from the premise that all will gain if society is based on principles of justice and equal competition, for men as well as women will be able to realise their full individuality, and society will benefit from the talents of all its members. Marxists and socialists too have argued that there is no fundamental conflict of interest between men and women, for the ending of sex oppression cannot be disentagled from wider social progress. In this sense, therefore, many liberal, Marxist and socialist writers would agree in principle that men as well as women can be feminists. At the same time, however, radical feminist theories and the experience of feminist politics have produced an increasingly widespread perception that men as a group are privileged by existing inequalities, at least in the short term, and that they therefore have an interest in maintaining them. This is not to say that all men consciously or actively oppress all women, or that they may not be in some ways disadvantaged by present arrangements, but simply to note that at a general level they are systematically favoured over women, and that the structures of society are likely to support their interests. Male support for feminist goals need not therefore be rejected out of hand; it should however be treated with caution, and it is unsurprising to find that, with some notable exceptions, few male writers or politicians have seen gender issues as central or made original contributions to feminist understanding.

Feminism's redefinition of politics means that it represents a profound challenge to other political ideologies which, it argues, are all too often based on the experiences, interests and perceptions of only half of the human race. The issues which it addresses are both basic and quite extraordinarily complex. As the other chapters to this volume have shown, men have always been deeply divided over political methods, goals and values; it is therefore not surprising that feminism too cannot be understood as one cohesive ideology.

NOTES

1. See Moira Ferguson (ed.), *First Feminists. British Women Writers 1578–1799*, Indiana University Press, Bloomington, 1985.
2. See Richard Evans, *The Feminists. Women's Emancipation Movements in Europe, America and Australasia 1840–1920*, Croom Helm, London, 1977, and Olive Banks, *Faces of Feminism*, Basil Blackwell, Oxford, 1986.
3. For a fascinating account, see Barbara Taylor, *Eve and the New Jerusalem. Socialism and Feminism in the Nineteenth Century*, Virago, London, 1983.
4. Discussed in Mary A. Hill, *Charlotte Perkins Gilman. The Making of a Radical Feminist*, Temple University Press, Philadelphia, 1980. On anarchist feminism in America during this period, see Margaret S. Marsh, *Anarchist Women*

1870–1920, Temple University Press, Philadelphia, 1981.

5. The classic account is Ray Strachey, *The Cause. A Short History of the Women's Movement in Great Britain*, Cedric Chivers Ltd, Bath, 1974. Good recent contributions include Philippa Levine, *Victorian Feminism 1850–1900*, Hutchinson, London, 1987, and Susan Kingsley Kent, *Sex and Suffrage in Britain*, Routledge, London, 1990. See also Jane Marcus (ed.), *Suffrage and the Pankhursts*, Routledge and Kegan Paul, London and New York, 1987, and notes 6 and 7 below.

6. See Jill Liddington and Jill Norris, *One Hand Tied Behind Us. The Rise of the Women's Suffrage Movement*, Virago, London, 1978.

7. See Jonathan Schneer, *George Lansbury*, Manchester University Press, Manchester and New York, 1990, ch. 2.

8. For a good general account of feminism at this time see Olive Banks, op. cit. On American feminism, see Nancy Cott, *The Grounding of Modern Feminism*, Yale University Press, New Haven and London, 1987.

9. See Jenny Dale and Peggy Foster, *Feminists and State Welfare*, Routledge and Kegan Paul, London, 1980.

10. *Selected Writings*, with an Introduction by Alix Holt, Allison and Busby, London, 1977, p.270.

11. See Vladimir Lenin, *On the Emancipation of Women*, Progress, Moscow, 1977, and Richard Stites, *The Women's Liberation Movement in Russia. Feminism, Nihilism and Bolslhevism 1860–1930*, Princeton University Press, Princeton, NJ, 1978.

12. See Mary Buckley, *Women and Ideology in the Soviet Union*, Harvester Wheatsheaf, New York and London, 1989.

13. *The Second Sex*, Penguin, Harmondsworth, 1972, p.295.

14. See Mary Evans, *Simone de Beauvoir. A Feminist Mandarin*, Tavistock, London and New York, 1985, and Judith Okely, *Simone de Beauvoir. A Re-Reading*, Virago, London, 1986.

15. Quoted in David Bouchier, *The Feminist Challenge*, Macmillan, London, 1983, p.45.

16. For accounts of this period see for example David Bouchier op. cit., and Jo Freeman, *The Politics of Women's Liberation*, Longman, New York and London, 1975.

17. For more detailed theoretical discussion, see Zilla Eisenstein, *The Radical Future of Liberal Feminism*, Longman, New York and London, 1981, Alison Jaggar, *Feminist Politics and Human Nature*, Harvester, Brighton, 1983, Valerie Bryson, *Feminist Political Theory: An Introduction*, Macmillan, Basingstoke, 1992, and Carole Pateman, *The Sexual Contract*, Polity Press, Cambridge, 1988.

18. In Robin Morgan (ed.), *Sisterhood is Powerful. An Anthology of Writings from the Women's Liberation Movement*, Vintage, New York, 1970, p.598.

19. See for example Sylvia Walby, *Theorizing Patriarchy*, Basil Blackwell, Oxford, 1990.

20. These include Christine Delphy, *Close to Home. A Materialist Analysis of Women's Oppression*, Hutchinson, London, 1984. A rather different approach is taken by such writers as Nancy Chodorow and Dorothy Dinnerstein who apply psychoanalytic theory to discuss the destructive and oppressive effects of present family arrangements: Nancy Chodorow, *The Reproduction of Mothering*, University of California Press, Berkeley, Los Angeles and London, 1978, and Dorothy Dinnerstein, *The Rocking of the Cradle and the Ruling of the World*, The Women's Press, London, 1987.

21. Most famously Shulamith Firestone, *The Dialectic of Sex*, The Women's Press, London, 1979.
22. See for example Adrienne Rich, *Of Woman Born: Motherhood as Experience and Institution*, Virago, London, 1977, and Sarah Ruddick, *Maternal Thinking. Towards a Politics of Peace*, The Women's Press, London, 1990. For criticism of this kind of approach, see Lynne Segal, *Is the Future Female? Troubled Thoughts on Contemporary Feminism*, Virago, London, 1987.
23. Key essays on this are: Anna Koedt 'The Myth of the Vaginal Orgasm', in Lesley Tanner (ed.), *Voices from Women's Liberation*, Mentor, New York, 1970, and Adrienne Rich, 'Compulsory Heterosexuality and Lesbian Existence', *Signs, 5,* no. 4, 1980.
24. See Dale Spender, *Man Made Language*, Routledge and Kegan Paul, London, 1985, and Mary Daly, *Gyn/Ecology. The Metaethics of Radical Feminism*, Beacon Press, Boston, 1978.
25. For the debate on this, see the essays collected in Lydia Sargent (ed.), *The Unhappy Marriage of Marxism and Feminism: A Debate on Class and Patriarchy*, Pluto Press, London, 1986.
26. *Ain't I A Woman? Black Women and Feminism*, South End Press, Boston, 1981, p.9.
27. In addition to the more recent books in the bibliography, see bell hooks op. cit., and *Feminist Theory: From Margin to Center*, South End Press, Boston, 1984; Angela Davis, *Women, Race and Class*, The Women's Press, London, 1982; Audre Lorde, *Sister Outsider. Essays and Speeches*, The Crossing Press, New York, 1984.

GUIDE TO FURTHER READING

The available literature has expanded enormously in recent years, as new ideas are developed and earlier writers are republished. The following provide general accounts of feminist ideas, with extensive bibliographies.

Bryson, Valerie, *Feminist Political Thought: An Introduction*, Macmillan, Basingstoke, 1992.
Coole, Diana, *Women in Political Theory*, Wheatsheaf, Sussex, 1988.
Pateman, Carol and Gross, Elizabeth (eds), *Feminist Challenges: Social and Political Theory*, Allen and Unwin, London, 1986.
Tong, Rosemary, *Feminist Thought: A Comprehensive Introduction*, Unwin Hyman, London, 1989.
Walby, Sylvia, *Theorizing Patriarchy*, Basil Blackwell, Oxford, 1990.
Whelehan, I., *Modern Feminist Thought. From Second Wave to 'Post-Feminism'*, Edinburgh University Press, Edinburgh, 1995.

Some key texts of feminism before the 1960s are, in order of first publication:

Wollstonecraft, Mary, *Vindication of the Rights of Woman*, Penguin, Harmondsworth, 1978.
Mill, John Stuart, *The Subjection of Women*, published in one volume with Harriet Taylor's, *The Enfranchisement of Women*, Virago, London, 1983.
Engels, Frederick, *The Origin of the Family, Private Property and the State*, in Marx and Engels, *Selected Works*, Lawrence and Wishart, London, 1968.

Kollontai, Alexandra, *Selected Writings*, translated and with an introduction by Alix Holt, Allison and Busby, London, 1977.
de Beauvoir, Simone, *The Second Sex*, Penguin, Harmondsworth, 1972.

As discussed above, different strands of feminist ideology frequently overlap. The following subject areas are therefore not intended to represent a rigid classification of modern writings, but simply an initial guide to key works.

Liberal feminism

Eisenstein, Zilla, *The Radical Future of Liberal Feminism*, Longman, New York and London, 1981.
Friedan, Betty, *The Feminine Mystique*, Penguin, Harmondsworth, 1963.
Okin, Susan Moller, *Justice, Gender and the Family*, Basic Books, New York, 1990.
Richards, Janet Radcliffe, *The Sceptical Feminist*, Penguin, Harmondsworth, 1982.
Wolf, Naomi, *Fire with Fire. The New Female Power and How It Will Change the 21st Century*, Chatto and Windus, London, 1993.

Radical feminism

Bell, Diane and Klein, Renate (eds) *Radically Speaking. Feminism Reclaimed*, Zed Books, London, 1996.
Dworkin, Andrea, *Pornography. Men Possessing Women*, The Women's Press, London, 1981.
Eisenstein, Hester, *Contemporary Feminist Thought*, Unwin Paperbacks, London and Sydney, 1984.
Firestone, Shulamith, *The Dialectic of Sex*, The Women's Press, London, 1979.
Greer, Germaine, *The Female Eunuch*, Paladin, London, 1971.
Millett, Kate, *Sexual Politics*, Virago, London, 1985.
Rich, Adrienne, *Of Woman Born: Motherhood as Experience and Institution*, Virago, London, 1977.
Spender, Dale, *Man Made Language*, Routledge and Kegan Paul, London, 1985.

Marxist and socialist feminism

Barrett, Michele, *Women's Oppression Today: The Marxist/Feminist Encounter*, Verso, London, 1988.
Mitchell, Juliet, *Women's Estate*, Penguin, Harmondsworth, 1971.
Rowbotham, Sheila, Segal, Lynne and Wainwright, Hilary, *Beyond the Fragments*, Merlin Press, London, 1979.
Sargent, Lydia (ed.), *The Unhappy Marriage of Marxism and Feminism: A Debate on Class and Patriarchy*, Pluto Press, London, 1986.
Vogel, Lise, *Marxism and the Oppression of Women*, Pluto Press, London, 1983.

Black feminism

Collins, Patricia Hill, *Black Feminist Thought*, Unwin Hyman, London, Sydney and Wellington, 1990.
Davis, Angela, *Women, Culture and Politics*, The Women's Press, London, 1990.
hooks, bell, *Yearning. Race, Gender and Cultural Politics*, Turnaround, London, 1991.
Mirza, Heidi (ed.), *Black British Feminism. A Reader*, Routledge, London, 1997.

Post-modern feminism

Assiter, Alison, *Enlightened Women. Modernist Feminism in a Postmodern Age*, Routledge, London, 1996.
Nicholson, Linda (ed.), *Feminism/Postmodernism*, Routledge, New York and London, 1990.
Weedon, Chris, *Feminist Practice and Poststructuralist Theory*, Basil Blackwell, Oxford, 1987.

10
ECOLOGISM
Andrew Dobson

——

ORIGINS AND TRADITIONS

The history of political ecology – or ecologism as I shall call it – is in dispute, and there are three views in contention.

The first is that the roots of ecologism are to be found wherever and whenever people either thought or acted in ways similar to those advocated by the modern green movement. On this reading, the bands of hunter-gatherers (for example) that roamed the earth up until about 10,000 years ago coexisted in a non-exploitative way with their environment and only took from it what was necessary to satisfy their vital needs. They may also have been animated by the view that nature has value in itself rather than only having value in as much as it is useful for human beings. On both these scores, Paleolithic humans are close to modern green sentiments and are therefore sometimes cast as early political ecologists.[1]

Much more recently, eighteenth- and nineteenth-century romantics throughout Europe reacted to what they saw as the blight of rapid industrialization by demanding the re-establishment of links between society and the natural world. Romantic poets wrote of the natural world as a source of moral and aesthetic value, and stressed the supposed unity between humanity and nature which industrialization had broken down. Such 'back to nature' views are clearly a part of contemporary green ideology.[2] Similarly, craft-orientated thinkers such as William Morris (1834–96) with an aesthetic regard for the non-human natural world advocated closeness to nature as an antidote to what he regarded as the philistinism and ugliness of industrial life, and pressed the value of the countryside against urban life. Again these views are reflected in some aspects of contemporary ecologism.[3]

In the USA one important present-day debate was prefigured in the

nineteenth century when John Muir (1838–1914) and others argued strenu-
ously for the preservation of wilderness for its own sake, while Gifford
Pinchot (1865–1946) took a more practical line in arguing for the conservation of natural resources because of their utility value.[4] This battle between
camps that came to be known as the 'preservationists' (like Muir) and
'conservationists' (like Pinchot) has been handed down to us today, and I
shall say more about it in a subsequent section.

In various ways, then, the history of ecologism can be shown to have deep
roots, and analyses of this sort serve usefully to remind us that while
ecologism is a modern political ideology it has old resonances.

The second view of ecologism's history begins with those scientists in the
nineteenth century who began to build on Thomas Malthus's (1766–1834)
famous argument that population would increase geometrically and food
production only arithmetically, thus causing widespread famine. Studies in
the biological and earth sciences in France, Britain, the USA, Russia and
Germany led to an awareness of the possibility of resource and energy
scarcity, some geographers began to view the earth as an organism,[5] and the
Oxford English Dictionary credits the German zoologist Ernst Haeckel with
the first use of the word 'oecology' in 1873. Contemporary scientists' views
(on scarcity in particular) have played a big part in today's green movement
and so it makes good sense to see their nineteenth-century counterparts as
contributing to the history of ecologism.

In some quarters, people believed that these scientific views had normative
implications for the behaviour of human beings in the sense that natural
ways of living were cast as the best ways of living. Throughout the first three
or four decades of this century this argument was advanced by people with
whom today's predominantly leftist political ecologists would rather not be
associated, such as romantic nationalists and conservative back-to-the-
landers, whom Anna Bramwell describes as the 'soft, alternative Right'.[6]
More notoriously, German fascism hooked on to traditional German pre-
occupations with nature as a source of both pleasure and moral guidance,
and many Nazi policies on, for example, ruralization, would not look far out
of place in today's Green Party manifestos. Similarly, Hitler was a vegetarian
and organic gardening experiments were carried out at Dachau concentration camp. Indeed, the Nazis' use of biological and organic metaphors, their
stress on the mystical aspects of the human condition, and their desire to
have the individual submit to the wider interests of the community, all have
an echo in political-ecological writings (see Chapter 8).

The merits of this second view of ecologism's history, then, are that it
stresses the vital importance of science to ecologism, and it points to the
diversity and complexity of ideas relating to nature and so alerts us to the
possibility of political contradictions in the modern movement.

Some argue, though, that the problem with both these views of ecologism's
history is that they ignore the conditions that made possible the modern
movement in its full-blown form. Those who locate ecologism's origins in

distant history underplay the very modern nature of ecologism as a response to events set in train by the Industrial Revolution and the forces it unleashed. Those who favour the nineteenth-century interpretation both neglect the importance for the green case of the global nature of many contemporary environmental problems, and overstress science at the expense of politics. It is no accident that public concern in developed countries over the environment peaked during the late 1980s when two things became clear: that the ozone layer was disappearing, and that 'global warming' was a reality. The green movement has grown in size and importance at a time when it has become possible to argue that the scale of human activity relative to the biosphere has reached the point where the latter's capacity to withstand the former is in doubt. This argument is important to ecologism and it could not have been made at all persuasively until very recently.

The third view as to the origins of ecologism takes this on board and points up the historical specificity of ecologism: environmental calamities have been with us since the dawn of time, but the ones brought about by human beings have only recently amounted to a threat to the integrity and complexity of global life-support systems. Without this possibility, it is argued, ecologism, with its tapestry of descriptions and prescriptions for economic and political change, could not exist. At this contemporary point, the ecology movement became a global movement, driven by an ideology with global implications.

At the same time, disillusionment with the achievements of socialist parties, the demise of communism, decreased levels of loyalty to all parties and a corresponding increase in the volatility of voters, many of whom (from all parts of the political spectrum) were prepared to transfer their allegiance to the greens, the events of May 1968, the peace movement of the early 1980s and its association with environmental politics – particularly in the former West Germany – all combined to create the circumstances in which the greens could make headway.

Similarly, it has been argued that in Europe and America a generation without direct experience of war, living in societies wealthy enough to fund a welfare state and therefore provide occupations in the 'caring services' such as health and education, has been produced. This, it is suggested, is a generation with its basic needs satisfied, and therefore in a position to pursue 'higher order' values beyond the satisfaction of material wants.[7] It would be wrong to say that this generation 'caused' the rise of modern ecologism, but it is appropriate that what is, at heart, a post-material ideology should encounter a post-material generation to articulate it.

This third view on the history of ecologism places its origins in the 1960s or 1970s when an influential number of writers and reports began to reassess the relationship between society and the 'natural' world. One of the most striking contributions was Rachel Carson's *Silent Spring* (1962), which emphasized the fragility of ecological relationships, and argued for the embedding of human beings in those relationships rather than beyond them, and called traditional notions of scientific progress into question. All these themes have remained central to the modern ecology movement and Carson's book is often used to date its beginnings.

Then *The Limits to Growth* report (1972) showed, to the satisfaction of its supporters at least, that there were limits to growth in a number of fundamental features of existence such as population growth, industrial growth, food per capita, resources and pollution. The report's basic conclusion, and one which has informed most green policy ever since, is that infinite growth in a finite system is an unfulfillable fantasy. Ted Trainer puts the issue this way:

> Our way of life assumes an endless increase in affluence. If American per capita use of resources continued to increase by at least 2 per cent per annum, as it did in the period 1950–70, then by 2050 each American would be using four times as much each year as in the mid-1970s. If we are willing to endorse an already affluent society in which there is continued growth on this scale, then we are assuming that after 2050 something like *forty times* as many resources can be provided each year as were provided in the 1970s, and that is in order for people in a few rich countries to live in this super-affluent way while the other 9.5 billion people in the world do not. Some savage implications follow this analysis. Unless extremely implausible assumptions are made there is no chance of all people ever rising to the levels of material affluence enjoyed by Americans in the late 1970s, let alone to the levels Americans will reach if growth in material living standards continues.[10]

Then, again in 1972, *The Ecologist* magazine's *A Blueprint for Survival* proposed a strategy for change and outlined the decentralized social structures most appropriate to a sustainable society. It would be wrong to imagine that *Silent Spring*, *The Limits to Growth* and *A Blueprint for Survival* either 'caused' the ecology movement or are exhaustive examples of the literature that led to its modern form; nevertheless they each represent durable features of the movement and so are central to its archaeology. All this gave rise to a growing number of writers and activists calling the desirability of what has come to be called 'industrialism' into question.[8] In the words of Jonathon Porritt (1950–):

> The politics of the Industrial Age, left, right and centre, is like a three-lane motorway, with different vehicles in different lanes, but *all* heading in the same direction … Both [capitalism and communism] are dedicated to industrial growth, to the expansion of the means of production, to a materialist ethic as the best means of meeting people's needs, and to unimpeded technological development. Both rely on increasing centralization and large-scale bureaucratic control and co-ordination. From a viewpoint of narrow scientific rationalism, both

insist that the planet is there to be conquered, that big is self-evidently beautiful, and that what cannot be measured is of no importance.[9]

MAXIMALISM AND MINIMALISM

The debate as to the historical origins of ecologism, represented by the three views outlined above, is matched by disagreement as to how best to approach the ideology itself. There are essentially two positions on this, which I shall call maximalist and minimalist. Maximalist commentators on political ecology define ecologism tightly: people and ideas will have to pass stringent tests before they can be properly called political-ecological. Minimalists cast their net wider so that the definition of ecologism is subject to fewer and/or less stringent conditions. The distinction is evident in the debate over ecologism's historical origins – minimalists will be more happy than maximalists to locate its roots before the twentieth century.

The strength of the minimalist view is that it stresses the very real diversity of the environmental movement, and allows room for discussion of (for example) its radical and reformist wings. Maximalism can give too exaggerated a picture of unity by stressing the inner coherence of political-ecological ideas rather than the diversity of actual political positions within the environmental movement. Maximalism's advantage, though, which is important in the context of this book, is that it brings out the radicalism of the green project and therefore allows for clear distinctions to be drawn between ecologism and the other ideologies.

I should stress that while this is a distinction drawn by those who write about political ecology, it is matched (but not in perfect reflection) by a distinction among those who actually profess environmental beliefs: that between ecologism and environmentalism. Environmentalists and political ecologists are united by their concern for the environment but they differ in two important ways. First, environmentalists usually act on the symptoms of environmental damage while political ecologists have a quite specific view of its political and economic causes; and second, the former believe that such damage can be corrected by tinkering with 'industrialism' while the latter think it needs to be dismantled and replaced.

In public debate it is not very common to distinguish between environmentalism and ecologism, and most people will make green politics wholly synonymous with the former. This is largely because the public face of the green movement is its high-profile international pressure groups such as Greenpeace and Friends of the Earth, whose explicit task has been to raise awareness of the visible symptoms of environmental degradation. They are less inclined to produce the generalized critique of present practices (and prescriptions for different ones) associated with any transformative ideology – in this case, ecologism.

Another way of grasping this important distinction is to consider the 'greening' of major political parties, both in Britain and elsewhere. Almost all major political parties have policies for the environment, and it is notable that these policies have been seamlessly grafted on to already existing manifestos without affecting their fundamentals in any way.[11]

What this indicates is the major parties' belief that environmental degradation can be successfully confronted within existing practices – political, economic and social. In other words, it is possible to be a socialist, conservative or liberal *and* an environmentalist. It is less easy, though, to be a socialist, conservative or liberal *and* a political ecologist, because ecologism calls into question too many of the assumptions on which socialism, conservatism and liberalism are based.[12] It is true, of course, that ecologism contains elements of these three ideologies (as will become clear in what follows), but it remains distinct from them.[13]

THE GREEN CRITIQUE OF MODERN INDUSTRIAL SOCIETY

Limits to growth

Ecologism is unique as a political ideology in its concern for the relationship between human beings and their environment, as well as among human beings themselves. Its critique of modern industrial society can be summarized by saying with Fritz Schumacher, author of *Small is Beautiful*, that 'the modern industrial system, with all its intellectual sophistication, consumes the very basis on which it has been erected'.[14] We are used to thinking of 'capital' as something we create and then spend or invest. But from a green point of view the planet and its non-renewable resources amount to a capital that is not created and certainly cannot be increased. A business that was profligately eating away at its capital would hardly be considered to be on a sound footing, suggests Schumacher, yet that is exactly what industrial societies are doing. We believe, mistakenly he says, that 'the problem of production' has been solved. Industrial societies, on this reading, are digging their own collective grave.

Worse still, political ecologists argue that so-called developed societies are dragging the rest of the world with them into the abyss, and this for two reasons. First, this is because rates of production and consumption in such societies are much higher than in developing countries, and so per capita rates of resource use and pollution creation are disproportionately high. According to Ted Trainer, for example, each American uses 617 times as much energy per year as the average for Ethiopians.[15]

Second, such high rates of production and consumption are the aspiration of all developing countries; the seductive power of the developed world's style of life has been demonstrated by events in Eastern Europe since 1989. Political ecologists argue that such an aspiration cannot be fulfilled across the planet with our incurring untold and possibly irreversible damage to the ecosystem. The Chinese, for example, comprise almost a quarter of the world's population, and most of them ride bicycles. Life in Chinese cities is already chaotic at rush hour, but political ecologists believe that the environmental damage that will be done if every Chinese who now rides a bicycle eventually drives a car, or even rides a motorcycle, is unimaginable. Besides, they say, there must come a point where the resources required to build and run a car economy on such a scale will simply not be available.

Schumacher's point about the 'problem of production' is, of course, a restatement of the limits to growth thesis, and there are two other implications of this thesis that deserve mention here. The first is that it is not enough to deal in isolation with this or that symptom of the environmental problematic. This is because their causes and effects are interrelated, and dealing successfully with one may not mean dealing successfully with all the others, and may even make them worse.

This thesis of interdependence accords with the lessons of the science of ecology itself. Ecologism is the only political ideology that takes its name from a science, and the principles of ecology form part of the green critique of industrial society. They also inform the green view of the ideal sustainable society, as I shall show. Denis Owen has written that, 'Ecology is concerned with the relationships between plants and animals and the environment within which they live'.[16] The important word here is 'relationship'. Just as Schumacher, above, warned that we forget our dependence on the non-human natural world at our peril, so political ecologists argue that the problems we face as a result of environmental degradation are interdependent. Because they are interdependent they need to be dealt with simultaneously. This amounts to the suggestion that successful change will be wholesale change, and in this sense ecologism is a radical political ideology.

The second lesson to be drawn from *The Limits to Growth* report, say political ecologists, is that technological answers to environmental problems might be temporarily successful but they cannot provide lasting solutions. As the report itself concluded once its computer simulations had been run: 'The application of technological solutions alone has prolonged the period of population and industrial growth, but it has not removed the ultimate limits to that growth.'[17] It is at this point that ecologism properly becomes a politics, for it is suggested that technical ingenuity cannot overcome problems that are, at root, economic and social.

Ecologism's critique of modern industrial society can be summed up in the claim that industrialism's tendency to expand production and consumption is incompatible with the finite nature of the planet. Sooner or later, it is argued, the limits to expansion will be reached, either as resources run out or the planet's capacity to absorb toxic waste is exhausted, or both. Along the way, the environment is despoiled and our quality of life (if not our standard of living) worsens. As Jonathan Porritt has put it: 'Sustainability and industrialism are mutually exclusive.'[18]

It should be clear by now that in making absolute scarcity a fundamental determinant of political and economic life, ecologism makes a clean break with most other modern ideologies, and therefore with their recommendations for the 'Good Life'. With the possible exception of some strands in the anarchist and socialist traditions, no other major political ideology calls into question the productivist aims and assumptions of industrial society. Nor is it just a question of whether it is *possible* to fulfil such aims; greens also wonder whether it is *desirable* to try to fulfil them, in terms of the kind of human life their fulfilment seems to entail. Ecologism's alternative to this state of affairs will be outlined in the section on the sustainable society, but the green critique of modern industrial society has a second informing strand beyond that of the limits to growth thesis, yet connected to it.

Human beings and the natural world

Ecologism is unique as an ideology in its placing the relationship between human beings and the natural world at the centre of its concerns. We are familiar with liberalism's advancing the cause of the rights of human beings (or the rights of 'man'), and much of ecologism's momentum is controversially engaged in widening the community of rights holders to animals, trees, plants, and even inanimate nature.[19] In other words:

> All ethics so far evolved rest upon a single premise: that the individual is a member of a community of interdependent parts. His instincts prompt him to compete for his place in that community, but his ethics prompt him also to co-operate (perhaps in order that there may be a place to compete for). The land ethic simply enlarges the boundaries of the community to include soils, waters, plants, and animals, or collectively: the land ... In short, a land ethic changes the role of *Homo Sapiens* from conqueror of the land-community to plain member and citizen of it.[20]

Another way of expressing this is to say that ecologism berates other ideologies for their anthropocentrism. This means that they base their prescriptions for political life on the assumption that the world has been made for human beings, and that human beings are not only the source but the measure of all value. It is not that other ideologies state this assumption and defend it, but rather that it is such a long-standing part of the political furniture that it goes unobserved and unnoticed. It is a large part of ecologism's project to expose this assumption, bring it to our attention, and replace anthropocentrism with *biocentrism*, according to which all life (and not just human life) has value. On the minimalist interpretation of ecologism, of course, biocentrism is not a defining feature of the ideology, for from this point of view ecologism is simply a matter of being more mindful of the environmental impact of our actions than has hitherto been the case.

For maximalist ecologism, though, the reasons we give for caring for the environment are as important as care for the environment itself, and an example will serve to illustrate this. There are many defenders of the rain forest nowadays, and most of them give respectable reasons for why deforestation should be halted, or at least slowed down. They will argue that valuable genetic material for new medicines is being lost; that trees absorb carbon dioxide and thus help reduce global warming; that indigenous tribes are being wiped out; that soil erosion silts up rivers and causes floods; and even that contemplation of such wondrous beauty and complexity can bring about the spiritual renewal of senses dulled by urban industrialism.

What is common to these arguments against deforestation is that they are all informed by human interest. The forest is seen as *instrumentally* useful to human beings, and this is the source of its value. Political ecologists will want to add that the forest is valuable in itself: that it is intrinsically valuable. In other words, the non-human natural world is not to be regarded simply as a stockpile, and our attitude towards it should not simply be the utilitarian one of the efficient management of resources, but rather of the defence of the natural world's intrinsic right to life. Sometimes we encounter the terms 'deep ecology' and 'shallow ecology' in the context of this debate, after a distinction created by the Norwegian philosopher Arne Naess in 1972.[21] The distinction has become complex of late, but we will not be far wrong if we think of the former as encompassing intrinsic value defences of the natural world, with the latter reserved for instrumental defences.

Political ecologists argue for intrinsic value mainly because they believe that anthropocentrism underpins our troubled relationship with the environment. Instrumental-value defences of the natural world are an extension of anthropocentric principles rather than an attack on them, they claim. What is needed is a system that refuses human beings as the measure of value, and intrinsic value defences of the non-human natural world do just that.

So ecologism's critique of modern industrial societies can be summed up under two headings. First, such societies are not sustainable because they aspire to continued and unending growth in a finite system – finite both in terms of non-renewable resources and its capacity to absorb the waste (including pollutants) we produce. Not only do greens claim such an aspiration to be impossible to fulfil, but also undesirable in itself because the pressures it creates contribute to human unhappiness. In global terms it is also argued that our affluence is bought at the cost of the Third World's deprivation by siphoning off their resources, encouraging inappropriate development, and operating a global economic system that consistently works in the developed world's favour.

Second, our unsustainable political and economic systems are both symptom and cause of an anthropocentric perspective that places human beings at the apex of existence, makes us the measure of value, and encourages us to see the natural world as simply a means to the end of human satisfaction. The strong claim being made here is that a sustainable society cannot be built on human self-interest alone, or at the very least that the foundations of such a society would be fragile. The obvious objection is simply that a sustainable society can be constructed on such a basis (some forms of minimalist ecologism would go along with this), and I shall consider such a view further towards the end of the chapter. Now I turn to a consideration of ecologism's prescriptions for society.

THE GREEN SOCIETY

Economics

Not surprisingly, green economics is organized around alternatives to the traditional economics of growth. More accurately – for it is wrong to characterize green economics as no-growth economics – political ecologists are opposed to growth that involves the exponentially increasing consumption of raw materials, and the accompanying increase in pollution that threatens global life-support systems. Necessarily this introduces a new dimension into economic decision-making: the needs of future generations. Greens hold that no economic theory or practice is sound unless it promises to leave a sustained and sustainable environment to future generations. Progress must not be bought, they say, at the expense of the ability of future generations to satisfy their vital needs.

The simplest way to conceive the green view of economics is to consider the production and consumption process, ask why greens object to present practices within it, and then examine their proposed alternatives. The American economist Herman Daly describes the production and consumption process as *throughput*, which looks like this:

$$\text{depletion} \to \text{production} \to \text{consumption} \to \text{waste}[22]$$

Political ecologists suggest that the success of an economy in standard (and unsustainable) terms is measured by its ability to maximize the first three terms in the throughput process. More particularly, the health of contemporary economies is usually measured by either the gross domestic product (GDP) or the gross national product (GNP): an increase in either or both from year to year is taken to indicate a growing, and therefore healthy, economy.

Greens object to GDP and GNP yardsticks for a variety of reasons, not the least of which is that they make no distinction between environmentally damaging and environmentally benign economic activity and they don't measure unpaid work as a contribution to the economy. Thus any contribution to GDP is considered good even if it compromises the long-term future of economic activity itself. Political ecologists (and not a few others) have recently been developing alternative economic indicators (sometimes called the adjusted national product, or ANP), which would have the social and environmental costs of growth subtracted from GDP rather than included in it.

Most fundamentally, though, political ecologists object to such indicators because of their tendency to legitimate undifferentiated growth, or the maximization of throughput. Sooner or later, they claim, the growth economy will come up against the physical limits imposed by the biosphere because it refuses to live within the planet's budgetary constraints. A green economy would be concerned to *minimize* the four factors of throughput rather than maximize them, as at present, and for this reason greens talk of maintaining *stock* and minimizing *flow*. An example will serve to make this clear.

Before the Industrial Revolution human beings made almost exclusive use of energy derived ultimately from the sun – whether wind to drive windmills, or wood to make fire. The switch to fossil-fuel energy (coal, oil), however, involved a switch to stored energy on earth. As Daly points out: 'This shift is extremely significant because these two ultimate sources of life differ in their patterns of scarcity.'[23] This is to say that energy from the sun is virtually unlimited as stock, but its flow rate (the amount we can use at any one moment) is limited. Conversely, the stock of energy stored in fossil fuels is limited, while its flow rate is largely up to us.

Fundamentally, then, the kind of energy we use at the moment is limited as stock, and so any sustainable economics will need to concentrate on its conservation. This will mean minimizing flow rates, and it will also be clear that it makes sense, from a green point of view, to develop renewable sources of energy because they are virtually unlimited as stock. The stress on the minimization of throughput, which characterizes the 'steady-state economy' is a characteristic of maximalist ecologism. The much vaunted trend of 'green consumerism', for example, will be criticized by political ecologists because while it affects *patterns* of consumption it allows *aggregate* consumption to be maintained and even increased. Minimalist ecologists seek simply to get the environment taken into account when economic decisions are made, and in this respect the main issues at stake concern the instruments used to do so. The argument here has revolved around the respective merits of market-based incentives (essentially, pricing goods so as to reflect their environmental cost),[24] and government regulation. An example of the former (sometimes referred to as an aspect of 'eco-capitalism' or 'green capitalism' by virtue of its proponents' belief that capitalism can be made sustainable) would be taxing leaded petrol at a higher rate than unleaded petrol, while establishing quotas for the sale of leaded and unleaded petrol would be a case of government regulation.

This is part of a wider debate concerning the best way to bring about environmental protection. Those who have come to be known as green capitalists advocate free-market solutions on the grounds that private owner-ship, backed up by courts willing and able to prosecute when environmental damage is caused to another's property, encourages good stewardship. Green capitalists argue that rather than trying to make government control more efficient, the best strategy is to improve the definition and enforcement of property rights where they exist, and bring them into being where they do not. This, they believe, is the best way to ensure responsible and accountable political behaviour.

The point of green economics, in the end, is to reduce rates of depletion and pollution to the point where the first is as close to the capacity of regeneration as possible, and the second does not exceed the capacity of the environment to assimilate it safely. It will be clear that non-renewable resources cannot 'regenerate', and so their careful conservation must be accompanied by a corresponding increase in both recycling and the use of renewable resources.

Society

Amid the welter of recent excitement over green consumerism (or 'buying a better planet'), it is often forgotten that green recommendations involve organizing society so as to make the minimum impact on the environment consistent with providing a full and satisfying life for all. Political ecologists believe that this will involve changing our habits in much more profound a way than simply buying a different type of detergent.

Most fundamentally, and focusing for a moment on the developed world, this will mean accepting and enjoying lower levels of consumption than is currently the case. While this might be seen as a lowering of our standard of living, measured in terms of the possession and replacement rates of con-sumer durables, greens argue that it would be accompanied by an increase in the quality of life, measured in terms of intangibles such as better relation-ships, closer communities, more time for leisure, better leisure, and so on. The need for profligate consumers of the planet's wealth to rein in their material appetites and desires can be derived from the comments made in the previous section on green economics. For from a green point of view it is clear that to continue to deplete and consume at current rates is to follow the path of unsustainability. Resource substitution, recycling and more efficient use of energy can all contribute to doing more with less, as industries have shown over the last several years. But greens argue that resource substitution often involves the development of materials that are hard to dispose of (indeed there is no such thing as 'disposal' in a closed system like the planet), and the use of resources that in turn are finite. They will also argue that some things simply cannot be substituted for in any meaningful sense – a favourite 400 year-old oak tree, for example.

Recycling also uses resources and causes pollution and is therefore not in itself an answer to sustainability, from a maximalist green point of view; and in the medium to long term even the efficient use of finite sources of energy will not prevent them from running out. As renewable sources of energy are unlikely to satisfy the energy needs of contemporary developed societies, let alone those of the developing world as it aspires to higher living standards, all these factors point to the need for a decrease in throughput, and therefore to a decrease in consumption levels in developed countries.

The green interpretation of the limits to growth thesis, then, gives political ecologists what they see as a series of hard-headed practical reasons for reduced consumption in contemporary developed societies. At the same time they press less material reasons for 'living lightly on the earth'. First, they believe that the endless round of consumption and accumulation impoverishes the human spirit and comprises an obstacle to the achievement of intangible goals such as the development of relationships and the cultivation of wisdom. Second, they refer to the obligation (already mentioned) that we have to future generations to leave the environment capable of sustaining a satisfying life.

Third, most political ecologists will agree that the affluent world's consumption patterns are woven at the cost of the developing world's deprivation. This is because the developed world's political and economic leverage has encouraged the Third World to produce for export markets rather than for its own populations' needs. Talent, land, factory space and resources are all geared to First World satisfaction instead of to Third World needs. The argument runs that if we cut our consumption significantly, resources would be released for use where they were most needed – not a sufficient condition for relieving Third World poverty (because corruption and poor infrastructures would still play a role), but a necessary one.

Ecologism's view of the 'Good Life', then, is radically at odds with the styles of life of many people in countries like Britain and the USA. The practical imperatives of sustainability and the less tangible benefits of a lower-consumption society lead to a rejection of such profligate lifestyles. At the root of all this is the perceived need to reduce the level of human impact on the biosphere, and in what follows it will be seen that this is the driving force, too, behind the political arrangements in a green society.

Politics

Despite the newness of ecologism as a political ideology, many of the things it has to say about the proper political relationships between people in society can be found in other traditions. This should not surprise us, for it would be strange if political ecologists had suddenly found ways of talking about such relationships other than in familiar terms such as liberty, equality, the individual and community. What ecologism does, though, is to advance new arguments for – if you like – old positions.

At the bottom of all green prescriptions for the sustainable society is decentralization – complicated by an undetermined role for the state outlined below.[25] The reasons given for decentralization revolve, once again, around the need to reduce our impact on the biosphere. How would decentralization do this? First, greens argue, it would encourage communities to meet their needs as far as possible from local resources. This would eliminate the necessity for dependence on large and centralized networks of transport and trade, which are both wasteful of energy and conducive to the import of luxuries from far away whose cost to the environment is simply not reflected in prices. The idea is that ecologically responsible living at the local level will necessarily result in the same at the global level. Another way of putting this is to say that bringing the points of production and consumption closer together reduces waste and encourages self-reliance. At the same time this local living, it is claimed, will not be as petty and self-referential as many fear because it would be based on global awareness rather than local rivalries.

Second, it has always been argued by decentralists that political decentralization will improve the quality of decision-making because the people most likely to make the best decisions are those closest to their effects. Greens give a twist to this by claiming that communities are more likely to care for their own environment than anyone else's, and, given the devolution of political power that decentralization entails, they would be able to implement the necessary measures. To the obvious objection that much environmental damage is brought on the winds from far away (acid rain, radiation poisoning), radical greens will reply that most of this damage is caused by just those present-day large and centralized production techniques that will have no place in a decentralized society, while others recognize a role for traditional state and international politics in these cases.

The extent of decentralization is a matter of dispute among green theorists. At one extreme are the *bioregionalists*, such as the American Kirkpatrick Sale, who argue that the size, shape and character of communities should be based on the population that any given area of land can support:

> A bioregion is a part of the earth's surface whose rough boundaries are determined by natural rather than human dictates, distinguishable from other areas by attributes of flora, fauna, water, climate, soils and landforms, and the human settlements and cultures those attributes have given rise to. The borders between such areas are usually not rigid – nature works with more flexibility and fluidity than that – but the general contours of the regions themselves are not hard to identify, and indeed will probably be felt, understood or sensed, in some way known

to many of the inhabitants, and particularly those still rooted in the land, farmers and ranchers, hunters and fishers, foresters and botanists, and most especially, across the face of America, tribal Indians, those still in touch with a culture that for centuries knew the earth as sacred and its well-being as imperative.[26]

Bioregionalism has obvious affinities with the anarchist tradition in its bypassing of the state, although its opposition is not to the state as such, as a source of political unfreedom, but to any political formations that induce forgetfulness of our ties to the earth.

At the other extreme lie those theorists who believe that, while decentralization should remain the guiding star, states and governments have a role to play in promoting it. They can do this by devolving power while retaining some planning and legislative prerogatives. Similarly, they can take measures to encourage local self-reliance without it necessarily being desirable to move to fully fledged community politics. The tensions in some green thinking between the competing claims of central and local politics can often amount to a contradiction, but whatever the disagreements between political ecologists as to the extent of decentralization, all of them will be convinced of its desirability in principle. The general idea is that no decision should be taken at a higher level if it can be taken at a lower one. This creates the presumption in favour of 'low-level' decision-making that political ecologists support for the reasons outlined above.

There is one further reason they advance. Greens argue not only for the need to care for nature, but to learn from it as well – particularly in respect of how human relationships should be conducted. It is extremely unusual for modern left-leaning political ideologies to take nature as a guide for human activity because such a move has traditionally been associated with right-wing ideologies such as fascism.[27] In a radical form, this has involved combining Social Darwinism with the idea that human beings are really just a special sort of animal, to produce justifications for raw competition on the basis that the fittest will – and should – survive. This is further underpinned by the idea that this is natural, and what is natural is good.

Greens do indeed want us to behave more 'naturally', and they would also urge us to see ourselves as just another member of the biotic community rather than the ruler of it. This allows them to link human nature and the nature of nature much more closely than if human beings were conceived as 'separate' from nature. This can lead to deeply divisive views on the relationship between human beings and the natural world, as I shall show in the penultimate section, but as far as relationships among human beings themselves are concerned, greens deploy a completely different view of nature to that of the Social Darwinists. It is this that allows them – at least to their own satisfaction – to use nature as a teacher without falling into a right-wing trap. Their view of nature, not surprisingly, is an ecological one.

Greens will explain that ecological relationships as they interpret them are neither centralized nor hierarchical, and that, therefore, neither should human ones be. This is where a further argument for decentralization is located, and also a predisposition towards relations of equality. Further 'evidence' for equality is drawn from the notion of interdependence, already mentioned as a standard category in the science of ecology. Political ecologists hold that webs of interdependence create obligations of equal respect both among human beings themselves and between human beings and their environment. In standard terms, it is these arguments for equality – shaky though they may be – that ease ecologism leftwards on the political spectrum, although as I shall point out, its development has not been free of right-wing accusations.

We should also note the problems associated with moving from a description of how things 'are' to a prescription of how we 'should' behave. Many would argue that the former (however accurate it may be) does not entail any necessary conclusions about the latter. In other words, even if ecological relationships are not hierarchical (description), that cannot necessarily entail that relationships between human beings should not be either (prescription). There are disagreements among political ecologists about how valid a move this is, but at the level of ecologism as a functioning ideology, the consensus seems to be that ecological description implies political prescription.

This is the place to mention that concern for nature has given rise to a strand in feminism that has come to be called 'ecofeminism', with implications for ecologism as a whole (see Chapter 9).[28] Ecofeminists believe that women and nature have a common cause, in that the historical association of one with the other has contributed to the exploitation of both. Most feminist strategies in the face of this association involve disengaging women from it, in order to claim a place for women in the more valued realms of culture. Some ecofeminists believe this to be wrong, for two reasons. First, because women 'free' themselves at the cost of leaving nature undervalued and defenceless and, second, because denying women their association with non-human nature amounts to denying them their own 'true' nature. The point, then, is to re-evaluate nature positively, and to celebrate women's association with it. This, it is held, will both help nature and liberate women in the sense of allowing them to be 'themselves'.

There are implications here, too, for the wider movement. Political ecologists are likely to believe that the denigration of women and nature is accompanied by the invalidation of characteristics traditionally associated with them (and particularly with women), such as caring, nurturing, co-operation, empathy, emotion and intuition. Greens do not argue that these characteristics should completely replace those usually associated with men (such as rationality and competitiveness), but that we should aim for a better balance. In this sense the sustainable society would be more informed than our present one by what have come to be known (controversially) as 'feminine values' – not exclusive to women, but more usually associated with them. In sum, the green sustainable society is designed to reduce the impact of human activity on the biosphere, in the belief that such activity has reached a level at which both medium- to long-term human survival and the integrity and complexity of the biosphere itself are in danger.

> [T]he alternative to the maximum-feasible society would involve a sharp break with the principles of the modern era, for the simpler frugal sustainable society would be characterized by a relatively low-throughput, income-energy economy designed to elicit an optimal amount of material goods from nature – in other words, a modicum or a sufficiency of material well-being rather than a maximum. Although many different varieties of frugal sustainable society are conceivable, it seems likely that they would all share more or less completely certain basic features (relative to the maximum-feasible society) – decentraliza-tion and local autonomy; a simpler, smaller-scale, face-to-face life closer to nature; labour-intensive modes of production; a de-emphasis on material things; individual self-sufficiency (versus dependence on complex systems for the fulfilment of basic needs); and cultural diver-sity.[29]

Economic theory and practice should be organized around the principle of the conservation of non-renewable energy and mineral stock, together with increased deployment of renewable stock. Social habits should be marked – in parts of the developed world at least – by a willingness to live more frugally, and political decentralization should be accompanied by moves towards greater political and social equality. All of this, say political ecolo-gists, needs to be underpinned by the removal of human beings from the apex of creation to a more humble place alongside other members of the biotic community. As I remarked earlier, sociological studies suggest that this is a picture that appeals most to young highly educated, professional middle-class people, usually employed in the public sector, who have been dubbed (and seem happy to dub themselves) 'post-materialists'.

PROBLEMS WITH ECOLOGISM

What follows is not intended to be an exhaustive account of the difficulties associated with ecologism, but rather a pointer to further thinking – to be done in conjunction with the reading recommended at the end of the chapter. Similarly it will be clear that some of these problems are more serious for maximalist than minimalist ecologism.

Limits to growth

In the first place, I have suggested that the limits to growth thesis is fundamental to ecologism. Political ecologists believe that current rates of growth are impossible to sustain in a finite system, and they base their recommendations for political and economic change on such a belief. What, though, if the limits to growth thesis were wrong – would this invalidate ecologism as a political ideology?

It has often been suggested that limits to growth is no more than scare-mongering – a millenarian thesis born of end-of-century angst. Its opponents point to technological solutions to scarcity – either developing more resources or making better use of those we have. They refer to severe underestimations of resources, and claim that every 'limit' announced by political ecologists is soon passed with no discernible difficulty.[30]

Others say – completely heretically, from a green point of view – that growth is essential for protection of the environment, because environmental preservation is a costly business, and the only way to make the money to pay for it is to operate a growing economy. On this view – which is also a feature of green capitalism – growth, far from being the enemy of the environment, is its best friend. Still others, less forthright in their opinions (or perhaps less honest), say that growth and environmental protection are not necessarily incompatible, but that we have been insensitive until now to the damage that can be done. On this view – compatible with a minimalist interpretation of ecologism – consumers must make more environmentally responsible choices, and industrialists must clean up their dirty act. Both these things can be done, it is claimed, without hindering growth – indeed (as The Body Shop has found out) they may be the catalyst for further growth.[31]

Biocentrism

Beyond the issue of limits to growth there are difficulties with the notion of biocentrism, and this for at least two reasons. First, I have suggested that greens (at least on the maximalist interpretation of ecologism) believe a move away from anthropocentrism to be essential for sustainability. Depending on what we mean by sustainability, this may be doubtful. Sustainability, after all, is usually seen in human terms, and is understood to mean a state of affairs under which human populations of more or less their present size satisfy their vital needs without prejudicing the possibility of future genera-tions doing the same. Put differently, from a planetary perspective life of some sort (but maybe not human life) will exist for a very long time to come. In other words our present practices are perfectly sustainable (even if lethal to humans) from a biocentric point of view.

A second difficulty with biocentrism that deserves close attention is the worry that it dethrones human beings to the point where they are no more worthy of consideration than, say, bacteria. The most notorious example of this came with the announcement by some members of the radical American *Earth First!* organization (always with the '!') that the AIDS virus was a good thing because it would reduce human populations, and therefore help towards the recovery of the biosphere. While the *Earth First!* comment was soon retracted it was seized upon by opponents of biocentrism as evidence of the dangerous anti-humanist lengths to which it could be taken. The most vociferous attacks came from the American theorist Murray Bookchin whose notion of 'social ecology' has it that the exploitation of the environment by human beings stems from the exploitation of human being by human being, and that eradication of the latter is a necessary condition for dealing with the former. Bookchin's view is that to blame 'humanity' (all of it) for environmental destruction is both to legitimize viewing human beings as a blight on the planet, and to ignore the way in which some human beings and their activities (what Bookchin likes to call 'corporate interests') are more destructive than others (see also Chapter 6).[32]

The issue of population reduction has always left ecologism open to criticism. Some have objected to Draconian proposals such as *Earth First!*'s, while others have pointed to the spectre of Nazi eugenics lurking behind the selection of populations for decrease. Some early population theorists of the 1960s and 1970s certainly came close to racist solutions to the population problem. Greens have also been on the receiving end of criticism from the left over the immigration implications of the attempt to stabilize populations within any given community.

So the ethical implications of biocentrism certainly need clearly spelling out, but in the meantime it is safe – and important – to say that political ecologists seek only to establish a presumption in favour of leaving the non-human natural world alone, rather than in favour of interfering with it, as at present.

Authoritarianism and collectivism

It has been suggested that ecologism's commitment to principles such as liberty and democracy is compromised by apparently laying such a great emphasis on the *ends* rather than the *means* of political association. The argument goes that if the end is of overriding importance then the means for getting there do not matter too much – the ends 'trump' the means. Some have remarked in our context that the impression is given by greens that the threat posed by industrialism to sustainability is so great and so immediate that Draconian measures to avert it might be justified. Certainly in the early days of the modern environmental movement there were those who seemed ready to countenance authoritarian measures, on the grounds that time was short, and that if people were left to their own devices they would come round too late – if at all.[33] Similarly, some hold greens guilty by association by pointing out how some authoritarian right-wing parties (such as the Nazi Party) have advocated policies on, for example, non-industrialized farming practices similar to those of contemporary greens.

The worry about authoritarianism should not be confused (although it nearly always is) with a parallel concern about collectivism. Collectivist arrangements do not necessarily imply authoritarian rule, although collectivism and authoritarianism are by no means incompatible. Collectivism is perceived as a threat to the freedom of individuals to do what they want as long as they do not compromise similar freedoms of other individuals, while authoritarianism denies the individual the right to participate in political decision-making. What is at stake in both cases is the integrity of the individual conceived in liberal terms, and in these terms the green project can read like a series of prohibitions that will be forced upon unwilling individuals by a coercive and paternalistic state.[34]

While authoritarian solutions to the environmental crisis might be a permanent possibility within ecologism, it needs to be said for the sake of accuracy that the overwhelming bulk of the contemporary green movement is opposed to such solutions. Either through parliamentary participation or grass-roots activity greens seem committed to taking a majority of citizens towards sustainability of their own free will, or not at all. It is worth noting here that the principle of equality 'derived' from the science of ecology goes some way towards underpinning notions of political equality that are central to democratic theory. Likewise, while greens will agree that restraint is required, their belief is that self-imposed restraint is more effective and lasting than if it is coerced.

ECOLOGISM AT THE TURN OF THE TWENTY-FIRST CENTURY

Like any other radical political ideology, ecologism faces the problem of putting its ideas into practice. The gap between what we have now and where greens would like us to go is so wide that ecologism's practical credibility is in question. Green political parties and pressure groups have certainly made an impact, as have exhortations to change lifestyles either in the home or in sustainable communities, yet industrialism remains the practice across most of the planet, and the aspiration of the rest of it.

In deciding the future of ecologism we need, as at the outset, to distinguish it from environmentalism. The latter has a clear role to play in public policy-making from now on. Its profile will vary with the perceived state of the environment and it will certainly not always command centre stage, but governments at least pay it lip-service. To the extent that this has been brought about by the green movement's insistence on the environment as a political issue, ecologism has already won a significant battle.

But it would be wrong to think that ecologism's future is already behind it, because the more radical demands for the dismantling of industrialism, the examination of the assumptions of anthropocentrism, and the move towards a decentralized, low-impact society are as far as ever from being met. In this respect it will continue to attract and repel in equal measure according to the constituencies to which it speaks: the only solution to industrialism's failure for some, and a doom-laden irrelevance for others. Its actual future probably lies somewhere between these extremes, acting as a pure and good conscience for the paler green environmentalism which seems to have taken hold of governments around the world. Barring a sudden deterioration in the state of the environment, ecologism in the new millennium will play the role of all such movements: a source of inspiration to activists, and a position against which to 'check' less principled and radical forms of environmental politics.

NOTES

1. See Max Oelschlaeger, *The Idea of Wilderness: From Prehistoric to the Age of Ecology*, Yale University Press, New Haven and London, 1991, ch. 1.
2. See Anna Bramwell, *Ecology in the 20th Century*, Yale University Press, New Haven and London, 1989.
3. See Peter C. Gould, *Early Green Politics: Back to Nature, Back to the Land and Socialism in Britain 1880–1900*, Harvester and St Martin's Press, Brighton and New York, 1988.
4. See Douglas H. Strong, *Dreamers and Defenders: American Conservationists*, University of Nebraska Press, Lincoln and London, 1988, chs 3 and 4.
5. James Lovelock's *Gaia*, Oxford University Press, Oxford, 1979, argues similarly, and has had an important influence on contemporary ecologism.
6. Bramwell, op. cit., p.161.
7. See Ronald Inglehart, *The Silent Revolution: Changing Values and Political Styles among Western Publics*, Princeton University Press, Princeton, 1977, for his influential theory on 'post-materialism'.
8. See Andrew Dobson, *Green Political Thought*, Routledge, London, 1990, ch. 1 for more detail on this view.
9. Jonathon Porritt, *Seeing Green: The Politics of Ecology Explained*, Blackwell, Oxford, 1984, pp.43–4.
10. Ted Trainer, *Abandon Affluence!*, Zed Books, London, 1985, p.3.
11. For useful surveys of the environment and politics in Britain, see John McCormick, *British Politics and the Environment*, Earthscan, London, 1991, and Mike Robinson, *The Greening of British Party Politics*, Manchester University Press, Manchester, 1992.
12. There are, of course, green socialists and Martin Ryle's, *Ecology and Socialism*, Radius, London, 1988, comprises a very good discussion of the relationship between the two ideologies. But there are those who argue that 'ecosocialism' only works if the dominant traditions in socialism (welfare through growth, productivism, state as the agent of political will) are underplayed. See also Dobson, op. cit., ch. 5.
13. For a discussion of the relationship between ecologism and other political

252 **ANDREW DOBSON**

ideologies, see Peter R. Hay, 'Ecological Values and Western Political Traditions: From Anarchism to Fascism', *Politics*, 8, no. 2, 1988.

14. E.F. Schumacher, *Small is Beautiful*, Abacus, London, 1973, p.16.
15. Trainer, op. cit., 1985, p.2.
16. Denis Owen, *What is Ecology?*, Oxford University Press, Oxford, 1980, p.1.
17. Donella Meadows *et al. The Limits to Growth*, Pan, London, 1972, p.141.
18. Porritt, op. cit., p.49.
19. See Holmes Rolston III, 'Challenges in Environmental Ethics', in David E. Cooper and Joy A. Palmer, *The Environment in Question*, Routledge, London, 1992, for a succinct summary of the arguments.
20. Aldo Leopold, *A Sand County Almanac*, Oxford University Press, Oxford, 1968.
21. See Arne Naess, 'The Shallow and the Deep, Long-Range Ecology Movement: A Summary', *Inquiry*, 16, 1973, for the original article.
22. The most succinct expression of Daly's views is to be found in Herman Daly, 'The Steady-State Economy: What, Why and How?', in D. Pirages, *The Sustainable Society: Implications for Limited Growth*, Praeger, New York and London, 1977.
23. Herman Daly and John Cobb, *For the Common Good*, Green Print, London, 1990, p.11.
24. See David Pearce, Anil Markandya and Edward Barbier, *Blueprint for a Green Economy*, Earthscan, London, 1989, for an influential discussion of this.
25. This is discussed in Robyn Eckersley, *Environmentalism and Political Theory: Toward an Ecocentric Approach*, UCL Press, London, 1992, chs 6 and 7.
26. Kirkpatrick Sale, 'Mother of All', in Satish Kumar (ed.), *The Schumacher Lectures*, vol. 2, Abacus, London, 1974, pp.226–7.
27. Indeed some will say that the green use of nature as a guide for human behaviour marks it as right wing at the outset.
28. A useful comparison of ecofeminism with other types of feminism can be found in Karen J. Warren, 'Feminism and Ecology: Making Connections', *Environmental Ethics*, 9, 1987.
29. William Ophuls, 'The Politics of the Sustainable Society', in D. Pirages (ed.), *The Sustainable Society: Implications for Limited Growth*, Praeger, New York and London, 1977, p.164.
30. See Julian L. Simon and Herman Kahn (eds), *The Resourceful Earth: A Response to 'Global 2000'*, Blackwell, Oxford, 1984, for a statement of this view.
31. This point is argued by John Elkington and Tom Burke in *The Green Capitalists: Industry's Search for Environmental Excellence*, Gollancz, London, 1987.
32. The *Earth First!* position is put by Christopher Manes in *Green Rage*, Little Brown and Co., Boston, Toronto and London, 1990, while Murray Bookchin's most complete statement is to be found in *Remaking Society*, Black Rose Books, Montreal, 1989. For an assessment of Bookchin's thought from a green point of view, see Robyn Eckersley, 'Divining Evolution: The Ecological Ethics of Murray Bookchin', *Environmental Ethics*, 11, 1989. Bookchin replies in 'Recovering Evolution: A Reply to Eckerslev and Fox', *Environmental Ethics*, 12, 1990.
33. See Andrew McHallam, *The New Authoritarians: Reflections on the Greens*, Institute for European Defence and Strategic Studies, London, 1991, Occasional Paper no. 51.
34. For a useful discussion of the relationship between ecologism and liberal principles, see Mark Sagoff, *The Economy of the Earth*, Cambridge University Press, Cambridge, 1988.

GUIDE TO FURTHER READING

The best general guide to the politics of ecology by an 'insider' is still Jonathon Porritt's *Seeing Green* (Blackwell, Oxford, 1984). For an American view in the same vein, see Brian Tokar, *The Green Alternative* (R. and E. Miles, San Pedro, 1987). The Australian critic Ted Trainer's *Abandon Affluence!* (Zed Books, London, 1985) is an uncompromising attack on industrialism and its effect on the Third World. A radical German perspective can be found in Rudolf Bahro, *Building the Green Movement* (GMP, London, 1986).

There is a growing number of academic books on the general themes of ecologism. Andrew Dobson's *Green Political Thought* (2nd edn, Routledge, London, 1995), was one of the first, and his edited anthology, *The Green Reader* (Andre Deutsch, London, 1991) provides easy access to some of the most important texts of contemporary green thinking. Robyn Eckersley examines the socialist, Marxist and anarchist traditions from an 'ecocentric' point of view in her *Environmentalism and Political Theory: Towards an Ecocentric Approach* (UCL Press, London, 1992). Tim O'Riordan's *Environmentalism* (2nd edn, Pion, London, 1981) is a path-breaking book covering a wide range of issues from growth to public policy and environmental law, and it also has a useful, if now slightly outdated bibliography. David Pepper's *The Roots of Modern Environmentalism* (Croom Helm, Beckenham, 1984) covers the historical, philosophical and ideological background to environmentalism from a Marxist perspective. Tim Hayward's *Ecological Thought: An Introduction* (Polity Press, Cambridge, 1994) organizes discussion of environmental political theory around its relationship with modernity, and John Dryzek's *The Politics of the Earth* (Oxford University Press, Oxford, 1997) is an accessible introduction to the politics of ecology. Anna Bramwell presents a provocative and influential interpretation of the contemporary history of political ecology in *Ecology in the 20th Century: A History* (Yale University Press, New Haven and London, 1989), and the subtitle of Mary Mellor's *Breaking the Boundaries: Towards a Feminist Green Socialism* (Virago, London, 1992) says all you need to know about her ground-breaking book.

The new systems thinking, derived from advances in modern physics, which greens believe amounts to a new 'paradigm' to replace the Newtonian one, is inspiringly described in Fritjof Capra's *The Turning Point* (Flamingo, London, 1985), while Adrian Atkinson's *Principles of Political Ecology* (Belhaven Press, London, 1991) provides a more academic but still partisan historical survey' of the roots of environmental crisis in European attitudes and practices.

Rachel Carson blends scientific fact with campaigning passion in *Silent Spring* (Houghton-Mifflin, Boston, 1962), often cited as the book that got the modern environmental movement going. Paul Ehrlich's *The Population Bomb* (Pan, Ballantine, London, 1972) illustrates the concern about growing populations that was at the heart of early 'limits to growth' arguments. Donella Meadows *et al.*, *The Limits to Growth* (1972) (Pan, London, 1983) is central to green thinking, and should be read in conjunction with its sequel, *Beyond the Limits* (Earthscan, London, 1992), and alongside Edward Goldsmith *et al.*, *A Blueprint for Survival* (Penguin, Harmondsworth, 1972). Many of the themes that inform political ecology are to be found in E.F. Schumacher's elegant and popular *Small is Beautiful* (Abacus, London, 1973), again with a slant on the developing world. Ernest Callenbach's novel *Ecotopia* (Pluto, London, 1978) is worth reading as a fictionalized account of a green society.

Denis Owen introduces the science of ecology in *What is Ecology?* (Oxford

University Press, Oxford, 1980), and Herman Daly and John Cobb's *For The Common Good* (Green Print, London, 1990), together with Paul Ekins (ed.), *The Living Economy* (Routledge and Kegan Paul, London, 1987) give a clear and full expression of green economics. Most of the themes in environmental ethics are covered in R. Elliot and A. Gare, *Environmental Philosophy* (Open University Press, Milton Keynes, 1983), and this should be read alongside Michael Zimmerman *et al*'s excellent anthology, *Environmental Philosophy: from Animal Rights to Radical Ecology* (Prentice Hall, New Jersey, 1993), while Bill Devall, *Simple in Means, Rich in Ends* (Green Print, London, 1990) and Arne Naess, *Ecology, Community and Lifestyle* (Cambridge University' Press, Cambridge, 1989) develop the theory and practice of 'deep ecology'.

Murray Bookchin's *Toward an Ecological Society* (Black Rose Books, Montreal, 1980) is a good source for his notion of 'social ecology', brought up to date in *Re-Enchanting Humanity* (Cassell, London, 1995), and the ideas and tactics of his *Earth First!* opponents are to be found in Dave Foreman and Bill Haywood (eds), *Ecodefense: A Field Guide to Monkeywrenching* (Ned Ludd Books, Tuscon, 1989).

11
ISLAM AND FUNDAMENTALISM
Youssef Choueiri

—

What are the Arabs without Islam? What is the ideology that they gave, or they can give to humanity if they abandon Islam? What value can a nation have without an ideology which it may present to mankind? Every nation which assumed the leadership of humanity in any period of history advanced an ideology.[1]

Sayyid Qutb

ISLAMISM AND MODERNITY

Islamic fundamentalism is an ideology that seeks to re-establish the religion of Islam as a political system in the modern world. It does so either by reinterpreting key elements in Islam, or by inventing new categories that are deemed to be self-evident and unique in their configuration. In this sense, Islam becomes a total organic system that rivals in its comprehensiveness and scope other ideologies and state systems. By coining new terms and reinterpreting conventional concepts,[2] Islamic fundamentalism invents a novel paradigm composed of theoretical and empirical elements. It is the configuration of these elements, and the manner in which they seem to cohere into an architectonic system that lends Islamic fundamentalism its distinct character.[3]

There are, of course, varying shades of emphasis in the way a certain element is given prominence, or attached to another one in a slightly modified form. But this is to state the obvious: all ideological systems are held together in a state of tension whereby historical circumstances and cultural diversities dictate the rhythm of development or accentuate certain features at the expense of others. Hence, at the ideological level fundamentalists in both Pakistan and Egypt entertain similar notions as regards the West, the nature of political power and the role of faith in human affairs. However, at the political level, these same notions may undergo subtle modifications until they become, over a period of time, noticeably different policy and practice.[4]

As a political movement and system of thought, Islamic fundamentalism came into being in response to modern challenges, both internal and external. By and large, one could postulate modernity itself, particularly in its colonialist and post-colonialist manifestations, as the ultimate generator of this response. Modernity, represented by the industrial and French Revolutions, brought about a cluster of transformations which had a direct or indirect impact on the evolution of societies throughout the globe. Islamic societies were caught up in these social upheavals as they formed a chain of regions which were of strategic, economic and military importance to the new European states.[5] Islamic fundamentalism is understood in this context as the response of certain social groups and political élites in the community of Islam (Islamdom) to the institutions, concepts and ideals generated within the world of modernity.

VARIETIES OF ISLAM

However, the emergence of Islamic fundamentalism does not exhaust the multivalent presence of Islam in the modern world. Contemporary Islam makes its presence felt in the form of official dogma, popular beliefs, sufi practices and modernist interpretations.[6] In this sense, fundamentalism is one current competing with other trends for cultural hegemony or political legitimacy.

Official Islam is almost a daily invention devised by the state, its officials and religious establishment as an extension of policies and programmes of action. Although there may exist varying shades of emphasis between a civil servant and a religious cleric, their ultimate purpose remains the defence of state legitimacy, civil order and political stability. Hence, a conservative ethical dimension is injected into Islam as the official religion of a particular political regime. Muslims are thus exhorted to be obedient citizens, serving the interests of their homeland, and law-abiding subjects who shun violence and adhere to the peaceful characteristics of their religion.[7]

Moreover, this particular aspect of Islam has become more pronounced over the last two decades. Its rise was the outcome of a number of factors, such as the failure of nationalist and socialist ideologies as well as the reconfiguration of global forces with the collapse of the Soviet Union and the emergence of the USA as the sole superpower. Hence, Islamism in its official incarnation manifests itself in varying degrees of intensity across the Muslim world. Egypt, Pakistan, the Sudan, Saudi Arabia and Morocco, under their monarchical or republican regimes, represent this particular trend. The Islamic Republic of Iran can be said to have joined this trend, particularly after the death of Ayatollah Khumayni in 1989 (b. 1900?).

Popular Islam is the most widespread and spontaneous expression of a religious inclination that is a mixture of conventional wisdom, local culture and personal piety. It may thus assume various forms and contents, depending on cultural contexts, social affiliations and historical backgrounds. Islam in this respect is taken for granted and invoked as a cultural reference. Merchants and industrialists, who are normally urban dwellers and operate within a global system of financial transactions, may choose to express their Islamic credentials by subsidizing the building of new mosques, hospitals and schools. This public demonstration of pious and charitable acts goes hand in hand with the practical pursuit of profit-making, interest-earning and credit advances – practices which are considered contrary to Islamic strictures on usury. On the other hand, industrial workers are the least attracted by fundamentalist interpretations of Islam. Yet, their Islam may consist of adhering to a number of religious obligations: fasting, praying and performing the pilgrimage to Mecca. Islam in rural or tribal areas is yet again attuned to a different rhythm of pious acts which are interwoven with inherited traditions and levels of social development. It is in these areas that superstitions and specific cultural beliefs intermingle with the official image of Islam, mediated by a local religious preacher or the distant echoes of ideas that circulate in urban conglomerations.

Islamic fundamentalism enters this rich array of attitudes and beliefs as an austere abstract formulation, often bereft of the subtleties of unique conditions and individual differences. It is an abstract system that is meant to apply to all human circumstances irrespective of time, place or social background,[8] and a dogmatic endeavour aimed at redefining Islam by restating its premises and first principles.

THEORETICAL MODELS

A puritan and scripturalist world religion does not seem necessarily doomed to erosion by modern conditions. It may on the contrary be favoured by them.

Ernest Gellner.[9]

One cannot perform a feat of oversimplification by opposing all varieties and trends of Islamic culture to a Western-inspired concept called secularism. One has to widen the concept and practice of secularisation itself in order to discover its equally multifarious guises and embodiments. While fundamentalists, be they Muslim, Christian or Jewish, postulate an irreconcilable gulf between religion and secularism, the modern world has learnt to accommodate both within the same society.

Secularism may signify a number of meanings and functions in the context of the relationship between state and religion. Like liberalism or nationalism, secularism is a child of the modern world; it is an integral part of the project of modernity and its associated institutions. Its history is bound up with the rise of the European nation-states, as well as the American, the French and the industrial revolutions. These revolutions heralded the triumph of reason and the application of the scientific approach to political organization, economic development and cultural growth. To the universalism of religion, they affirmed the integrity of territorial boundaries, whereby the state imposes its sovereign rights as the ultimate authority. With territorial integrity and national sovereignty, legislation lost its divine and metaphysical origins. Hence, the idea of citizenship replaced divisions of religion, locality and social background, introducing thereby the mechanisms for ensuring equality before the law. Some states enshrined the separation of state and religion in their constitutions (USA and France), while others achieved a similar outcome by incorporating religion into state institutions (Britain and Turkey).

I use secularization in this context to signify the application of the principles of secularism in the conduct of state affairs, both domestically and internationally. Since the modern state assumes direct or indirect responsibility for a wide range of policies and institutions, it is to be expected that secularization or its counterpart would figure in the fields of education, law and order, banking, housing, trade and industry, culture, social welfare, development, and so forth.

A number of models have been developed by social scientists in order to account for contemporary trends towards desecularization in the Islamic world. One model, echoing the rhetoric of fundamentalism, conjures the image of an obdurate Islam, whose vitality and energy defy suppression or dissipation. It has, therefore, managed to survive almost intact into the modern world as a result of two factors: 1) Islamist resurgence is a mere index of the persistence of traditional social and political structures;[10] 2) the renewal of Islam is a manifestation of a deeper cyclical pattern that keeps repeating itself irrespective of time and place.[11]

The other model, imbued with Weberian overtones, situates Islamism in the context of global change and readjustment. It postulates Islamist resurgence as a belated, albeit earnest, response of particular societies to the impact of capitalism and the industrial societies. Islamism is thus the expression of a collective desire to retrace the birth of industrial cultures and norms. Seen in this perspective, fundamentalism reasserts a belief system or a set of values reminiscent of the early days of the Reformation and the advent of the Protestant ethic.[12]

Nevertheless, even in this sophisticated version, Islam remains immune to secularization. Unlike Christianity, confucianism and Hinduism, Islam is perceived to have managed to fend off the onslaught of the Enlightenment and the age of reason by clinging to its pure doctrine and elaborate laws. Thus, both its doctrine and divine laws precluded the possibility of separating religion and legislation. By the sheer fact of its finality and divinity, Islamic law ensured the ascendancy of the community of believers over the state, which acted as its executive arm. Moreover, the absence of a clerical order, in the Christian sense, made Islam an egalitarian religion deeply associated with the daily rhythm of its adherents. The dualism of Christianity, pitting church against state, was therefore pre-empted, rendering the community itself a living incarnation of a divine state.

According to Ernest Gellner and his disciples, Islam in the modern world has been transformed in the image of High as opposed to Low Islam. It is High Islam – urban, scholarly and sober – that launches periodic acts of purification by asserting the paramountcy of puritanism and scripturalism. The modern era has thus witnessed the slow erosion of Low Islam with its saint-cults, sufi orientations, tribal affiliations and rural origins. The centralized state, be it in the West or East, has finally inflicted a crushing defeat on its outlying regions. The birth of a national market, labour migration and urbanization have all impelled populations in the direction of High Islam.[13]

High Islam and nationalism are as a result interchangeable or a mirror image of each other: they provide the Muslims of a given country with a well-defined national identity. More importantly, this model sees High Islam or fundamentalism as the generator of congruence between a modern economy and its attendant cultural norms. High Islam's rationality and thrift, discipline and belief in a free market are, according to Gellner, strikingly similar to what Max Weber thought to constitute the basic elements of the Protestant ethic. It was this ethic that ensured the birth and irreversible growth of the spirit of capitalism.[14]

These two models, notwithstanding the differences in their essentialist and historical approaches, freeze Islam either in the past or the present by excluding the relevance of secularism to its pace of development. Absolute categories such as the social contract, civil liberty and the triumph of tolerance are used to uncover the entrenchment of Islam in an enclosed world that glimpses secularism either as an enemy, or at best an alien presence to be yet decoded at an indefinite stage. The interplay between state and society, modernity and indigenous endeavours of resistance or assimilation are obscured and lost sight of under the shadow of an overarching theory.

It is at this juncture that a discussion of Islam as a religion in its historical evolution becomes pertinent. By so doing a number of questions posed by our two models are either refuted or confirmed. One could ask the following questions, often posed by fundamentalists themselves: what is Islam? How valid are its first principles in a modern scientific world? How can Islam be restored to its former glory without modernity and its institutions?

If the realities of the Islamic heritage can be frankly faced – its historical actuality good and bad, the problems which it presents as well as the spiritual opportunities it offers – then Islam as a heritage might conceivably prove able to serve flexibly in the Modern crises.[15]

ISLAM: DOGMA AND EVOLUTION

Islam is a religion that first emerged in Arabia in the seventh century AD. Its founder was a Prophet named Muhammad (c. 570–632). In 610 he declared himself a messenger charged with conveying divine revelations entrusted to him by God. These revelations, received and delivered over a period of 23 years, were shortly after the Prophet's death collected in a single holy book known as the Qur'ān.

The Qur'ān is divided into 114 chapters and classified by its collectors in order of length. However, it is generally agreed that the long chapters, which are given precedence in this scheme, belong to the second or Medinese phase of the Prophet's mission, whereas the shorter ones, distinguished by rhyming utterances and verses, belong to the first, or Meccan phase. Moreover, the Medinese chapters deal in the main with legislative and worldly affairs, in contrast to the Meccan ones which are largely confined to matters of dogma, eschatological forewarnings and moral exhortations.

Mecca, the birthplace of Muhammad, was a commercial and religious centre. Before the rise of Islam, it acted as the principal symbol of tribal paganism and its deities, both male and female. Its paganism was symbolized by its shrine and sanctuary housing a number of idols presided over by a supreme deity, Allah. In the middle of the sanctuary featured the Ka'bah, a cube-like structure with the Black Stone built into it. This high god had no monopoly of worship, nor did he appropriate the title of the only deity. He, for example, had daughters called al-Lāt, al 'Uzzah and Manāt, each charged with a particular function. There were also sacred enclaves throughout the Arabian Peninsula. The guardians of Mecca's pagan shrine as well as its leading merchants belonged to the tribe of Quraysh, to which Muhammad was affiliated through his clan, Banū Hāshim.

Moreover, Mecca was the site of seasonal trade gatherings and the destination of an annual pilgrimage from all over the Peninsula. As a result of their engagement in long-distance and local trade, in addition to servicing its pilgrims, its Qurayshite merchants and notables amassed large fortunes and attained a corresponding social status. On the eve of Islam, they were the leading members of Meccan society in wealth, power and status.

Through trade, the Meccans became acquainted with the cultures, religions and politics of their neighbours: Iran, Byzantium, Abyssinia and India. Arabia was also the target of a number of military expeditions, in particular by the Romans and Abyssinians. And in the heart of Arabia lived compact communities of Jews and Christians. The Jews had a particularly strong presence in Yemen in the South, and in Medina, or Yathrib, to the north of Mecca. Christian communities were scattered across Arabia, with strong concentrations in territories adjacent to the two superpowers of the day: the Sasanian and the Byzantine empires.

In the struggle between the two empires Mecca maintained a studied neutrality – an early indication of a desire to forge a separate identity which Islam embodied and fostered. Moreover, the Arabians of the peninsula had also forged a common literary language which found its most eloquent expression in vivid poetry and rhymed prose.

Into this society Muhammad was born an orphan in c.570 AD. He grew up under the care of his uncle Abū Ṭālib, the father of the future fourth caliph (656–661), and the would-be first Imam of the Shi'ite sect of Islam, i.e. 'Ali. Since his twenties, Muhammad is said to have shown an inclination towards metaphysical questions and the ultimate meaning of life. He also, as a member of the clan of Banū Hāshim, a branch of the powerful Quraysh, became a competent trader who was employed by a wealthy widow, Khadī-jah, whom he subsequently married. At the age of 40, Muhammad is said to have received his first revelation. In it he was summoned to worship God to the exclusion of all other deities. This first recitation, transmitted from Allah by the medium of the angel Gabriel, commanded Muhammad thus:

Recite in the Name of thy Lord who created,
    created man of a blood-clot.
Recite! And thy Lord is the most
Generous
Who taught by the pen,
Taught man what he knew not
(Qur'ān 96: 1–5)

According to Muslim tradition and historical accounts, this first revelation left Muhammad bewildered and troubled. Relating this fearful experience to his wife, she reassured him of its positive connotations, interpreting his experience as a sign of prophethood bestowed on him by the Almighty. In other words, the birth of Islam and the correct interpretation of its implications was a joint intellectual and emotional endeavour witnessed and corroborated by a husband and his wife, a fact that contemporary fundamentalists are reluctant to admit or contemplate.

With the multiplication of revelations a novel concept of God began to emerge, threatening the pagan beliefs and material riches of Muhammad's fellow Meccans. These early revelations, spanning the years between 610 and 622, speak directly of images conjuring up the last day of judgement, hell and paradise, God's mercy, His uniqueness and oneness. It was a moral God who wanted justice and fairness for the poor, the orphans and the weak. A

God who figured as the creator and ruler of the universe, the regulator and sustainer of His creatures, and who was the sole owner and dispenser of wealth.

Allah, the Compassionate and the Merciful, called upon the individual to eliminate all mediators and interceders and worship Him alone in His omnipotence and beneficence. The idols of Mecca, the gods of Quraysh and the various deities worshipped by the tribes had no power or validity. Possessed of a fraudulent belief, it was a false world that had to be swept away.

Faced with the hostility of Meccan notables and merchants, and after several aborted attempts to seek help or temporary accommodation, Muhammad decided to leave this hostile Meccan environment and migrate with his circle of followers to the agricultural oasis, Yathrib (renamed Medina). Having been invited to act as arbitrator in settling a feud between rival factions of tribal groups, Muhammad soon emerged as the ultimate authority in the social and political life of Medina. And it was in the new Medinese context that the legislative verses of the Qur'ān became more explicit and frequent. They covered topics such as marriage and custody, drinking alcohol and gambling, custody, commercial matters and the duty of *jihad*. It was in Medina, and following Muhammad's success in building his polity under a new 'constitution', that the concept of holy struggle or *jihad* was first elaborated. It was also in the Medinese period that Muhammad was ordered to pray in the direction of Mecca rather than Jerusalem. Moreover, Islam was declared to be the final and most perfect divine message and Muhammad the Seal of the Prophets. In this sense, Islam inherits and supersedes both Judaism and Christianity, representing religion in its purified and final substance.[16]

In other words, Islam was pronounced to be a dynamic re-enactment of Abraham's career and his monotheistic creed. Nevertheless, Muhammad never claimed superhuman qualities, nor did he boast of wondrous powers or the ability to perform miraculous deeds. His was a mission that became firmly placed within the universal orbits of other Semitic prophets, with Abraham acting as the founding figure, Jesus reaffirming and deepening its unadulterated monotheism and Muhammad confirming and restating its undistorted tenets. It is this dual character of Islam – its practicality and inclusiveness – that ensured the enthusiastic support it received throughout the Middle East, North Africa, Central and South Asia.

LAW AND THEOLOGY

Qur'ānic rules and injunctions were in the ensuing centuries of expansion elaborated and interpreted to form together with customary laws the divine law of Islam, or the Shari'a. The function of interpreting the Shari'a was based on a number of sources and principles. These principles (*uṣūl*) were used in varying degrees of emphasis by the four schools of law in Sunnite Islam as well as the mainstream shi'ite school, The Twelvers. Dubbed the sources of jurisprudence (*uṣūl al-fiqh*), they include the following: 1) the Qur'ān; 2) the sayings and deeds of the prophet (*al-sunna*); 3) consensus of the Companions of the Prophet or the religious scholars (*ijmā'*); and 4) logical analogy (*qiyās*).

Underpinning this whole theoretical structure was the idea of *ijtihād*, or the right to individual interpretation according to strict limits imposed either by legal requirements or the interests of the community. Reasoning by analogy was in this respect the most effective instrument used to elaborate and explore new areas of commands and ordinances. The expected silence of Islamic law on novel issues made it possible to update the Shari'a without risking its explicit violation. It was this task which successive generations of fundamentalists would claim for themselves as a religious obligation.

In addition to law, theology emerged during the same time as the hallmark of a new religion capable of organizing all facets of life, including their metaphysical dimensions. Theology, which was an endeavour to construct a metaphysical belief system and an elaborate effort to enumerate the attributes of God, was soon combined with philosophical speculations ultimately inspired by Hellenistic notions of essence and accident, necessity and contingency.

These religious sciences – juridical, theological and philosophical – were perfected during the golden age of Islam and which extended from the eighth century to the end of the tenth. They also coincided with the astonishing flowering of a vibrant secular culture that spanned poetry, *belles-lettres*, music, medicine, astronomy, chemistry, historiography and geography, as well as commercial and industrial innovations. This secular culture is often ignored by fundamentalists or subsumed under derogatory labels, except for purely scientific subjects.

The attributes of God, such as life, knowledge, will and unity, were seized upon by sufi scholars and developed, after the tenth century, into an all-embracing system of beliefs, practices and rituals. Although sufism as a doctrine emerged in its early spiritual form in the ninth century, it did not become a powerful social and cultural force until the twelfth century. Islamic mysticism developed an ascetic and pious dimension which was suffused with a popular appeal lacking in both theology and philosophy.

Based on the concept of love and adoration of God, it fuses elements of earlier mystical systems, turning them in the process into a moralistic world in the mould of Islam. Hence, whereas the elucidation of Qur'ānic injunctions and the study of theology were the preserves of official and semi-official exponents, sufism crossed the social hierarchical divide, infiltrated the lower popular orders and emerged in the medieval period as a formidable movement in both urban and rural areas.

The most remarkable feature of sufism is the veneration of the master of a particular order and the absolute obedience he exacts from his disciples. It is this feature which is most noticeable in contemporary Islamist movements, which are invariably led by 'a master' who is dubbed either *amīr* (commander) or *murshid* (guide).[17]

THE VIABILITY OF POLITICAL ISLAM

Politically, Islam after the Prophet's death was endowed with the institution of the caliphate as the corner-stone of its state system. Nevertheless, by 1258 the caliphate after its destruction at the hands of the Mongols in Baghdad had ceased to provide a unifying symbol of an Islamic polity. Side by side with the caliphate, the institution of the Sultanate began to emerge in the course of the tenth century. Presided over by a military chieftain, it embodied the political and secular arm of a Muslim state, relegating the caliph to a spiritual and cultural entity. Although it lingered on as a nominal institution under the Mamluk Sultanate (1250–1517), it was not revived, albeit in a modified and less compelling form, until the nineteenth century. This was the claim put forward by the Ottoman Sultans who combined in their person the spiritual and political leadership of the community. Moreover, it was the Ottoman empire, as the last formidable Islamic power, which managed the entry of the central Muslim lands into the modern world. Its programme of reform and Westernization, coinciding with the industrial and French revolutions, and stretching into the twentieth century, had as its direct result the abolition of both the institution of the sultanate (1922) and that of the caliphate (1924). The restoration of the latter has nowadays become the central aim of Islamist organizations.

Militarily, and following the initial waves of conquests which embraced between 732 and 750 AD, Iraq, Syria, Egypt, Iran, North Africa, Spain and parts of Central Asia and India, the Arabs began to lose their predominant position in military affairs. This was particularly the case after the ninth century, whereby the Mamluk institution, dominated by Turkic elements, established itself as the standard military structure throughout Islamdom. This system persisted down to the nineteenth century, and did not come to an end until modern reforms forced local rulers to rely on native recruits. By so doing, they paved the way for the rise of well-defined administered territories which began to look upon themselves as nascent nation-states in the European sense of the term. The disappearance of the caliphate and the Mamluk institution announced the arrival of modernity in the Islamic world, turning it into an internal feature of state structures and polities. In other words, it heralded the advent of nationalism and secularism, the twin enemies of fundamentalism in its radicalist phase.

Socially, modernity destroyed the symbolic relationship between sufi orders and craft guilds and undermined their ability to organize public life in urban centres. This was the basis of a civil society that Islamists allude to and lament its annihilation under the relentless growth of the nation-state and its modern institutions. Economically, the dual system of land assignments (*iqṭā'*) and tax-farming (*iltizām*) dominated property ownership and agrarian management until it was swept away by the turn of the twentieth century. The advent of the notion of private ownership, accompanying European expansionism and internal reform movements, the existence of an Islamic economic system, lost its viability or attraction. Islamic fundamentalism has so far failed to offer its own economic system, except in the most vague and general terms. This is particularly the case in the realm of banking, insurance, investment and profit-making.

To all intents and purposes, Islam entered the twentieth century bereft of institutions and structures that had been refined and developed ever since its inception in the seventh century. It is in this context that the idea of creating Islam anew becomes a plausible hypothesis capable of mobilizing a new generation of believers. Whereas official Islam is in the main satisfied with ensuring the observance of the five pillars of religion, Islamic fundamentalism posits the necessity of establishing a totalitarian system equipped with the most advanced technological and industrial innovations.

By the time of the Prophet's death, the five pillars of Islam had been firmly established. These were: 1) the profession of faith proclaiming the absolute unity of God and the Prophethood of Muhammad; 2) the five daily intervals of prayer; 3) paying charitable alms or *zakāt* for the relief of the poor and the needy; 4) observing the annual fast of the month of Ramadan; and 5) performing the pilgrimage to Mecca at least once in a lifetime. It is these pillars, alongside family law in a modernized or reformed state, which have survived into the modern world.

THE THREE FACES OF FUNDAMENTALISM

Thus, in the modern period, and beginning with the eighteenth century, the initial response of Muslim leaders and scholars was to call for an internal movement of renewal. This movement, best exemplified by the Wahhabites of Arabia (so called after their spiritual founder, Muhammad b. 'Abd al-Wahhāb (1703–92) aspired to invigorate Islam by sweeping away centuries of corruption, distortion and sinful practices. Proclaimed in regions which had relapsed into pagan practices and superstitious beliefs, it identified sufi orders and official Islam as the main culprit. The West, either as an ideological challenge or a socio-political system, was still absent in this revivalist endeavour.

In order to cleanse Islam of superstitious accretions, revivalism aspired to simplify the chain of command by repositioning the individual in a direct relationship with Allah, the sole sovereign and creator. This measure entailed the removal of interceders and the prohibition of visiting saints' tombs or invoking the spiritual powers of inanimate objects such as trees and stones. In other words, revivalism constituted an attempt to purify Islam by restating its message in a simple and unencumbered form, and under the leadership of a learned renewer or a Mahdi-Messiah, the Master of the Age. Although this movement accompanied or coincided with the age of European expansionism in the commercial and military fields, its message was confined to regions which had weak systems of government or non-existent state institutions. With the onset of the Industrial Revolution and the transformation of the global economy under the impact of a new order of European expansionism, revivalism began to crumble and lose its relevance.

European overseas investments, the desire to capture new markets for industrial commodities and the drive to seize control of raw materials created a relationship of political and economic dependency in non-industrialized countries, including the Islamic world. Facing direct military occupation or demonstrably overwhelming naval and territorial power, Muslim political élites and religious scholars were forced to turn their erstwhile internal debate into a tentative dialogue with European culture and civilization. It was now recognized that Europe had surpassed all Muslim countries in the fields of technology, industry, military organization and political institutions. Reformism, straddling the purity of early Islam and the modern world, was the second wave in this endeavour to reverse the state of decline.

It was in this period (c. 1839–1924) that the spiritual, ritualistic and legal aspects of Islam began to assume a dominant position. By contrast, the political, military and economic institutions of Islam lost their conventional or normative value. In this sense, the idea of creating a secular society with its own civil space and institutions became a strong possibility for the first time in the history of Islam. Thus, in 1924 Atatürk (1881–1938) declared his Turkish republic a secular, nationalist, Western-type state. More importantly, the birth of official secularism in Islamdom took place in the heartland of the former seat of the caliphate and the sultanate. Both had represented the imperial institutions of Islam and its symbolic role as a world power.

It is in this context that the third wave of Islamic fundamentalism entered the intellectual and political scene. Its task consisted of re-establishing Islam in the face of secularism, nationalism and democratic notions of popular sovereignty.

By invoking the heritage of Islam, Islamic radicalism, as the embodiment of the third fundamentalist wave, highlights the indissoluble link between worldly and metaphysical affairs to the extent that politics subsume all other objectives. Moreover, by attempting to resurrect Islam in its political dynamism, a new religion is fashioned out of the ideological heritage of modernity itself.[18]

FUNDAMENTALISM AND MODERNITY

An Islamic state does not spring into being all of a sudden like a miracle; it is inevitable for its creation that in the beginning there should grow up a movement having for its basis the view of life, the ideal existence, the standard of morality, and the character and spirit which is in keeping with the fundamentals of Islam.

Abu al-'Ala Mawdudi.[19]

Modernity in its cultural, political and economic dimensions is assumed by contemporary Islamic fundamentalists to have caused the gradual decline of Islam, or its virtual disappearance as an active force in international and state affairs. The institutions and concepts of secularism and liberalism, nationalism, Marxism and democracy are blamed for eroding the religion of Muslims, leading them to forsake its way of life for other ideologies and Western models.

In this scheme of things, Islam itself is absolved of its responsibility for such an outcome. Rather, both the West and a tiny minority of local collaborators are accused of colluding in an overall conspiracy to sap Islam of its energetic qualities. To Islamic fundamentalists, the doctrine of Islam has remained sound and perfect, escaping the vicissitudes of history and innumerable conspiracies launched throughout the ages to distort its pristine essence. It thus transcends time, place and human interference. Lying outside history, it could not have emerged in response to economic needs, political conditions, or geographic determinants. It is both timeless and eternally valid.

Moreover, the rise of Islam was a sign of God's magnanimity. Its triumph, spanning the career of the Prophet Muhammad (610–632), indicated the steadfast and unadulterated faith of a new group of believers. If the precepts of Islam declined or went in abeyance in the modern age, this was a direct result of a faltering faith on the part of Muslims. Islam itself possesses an independent existence over and above the historical conditions of its human carriers. Its reactivation or restoration requires no more than a creative endeavour modelled on the two phases of the Prophet's career: the Meccan and the Medinese. In the first phase (610–22), the doctrinal principles of Islam were received, propagated and inculcated. In the second phase (622–32), these principles were translated into concrete institutions and practices. Consequently, the fundamental principles of Islam and the injunctions of its law are one single whole: the latter are simply a practical translation of the former. Knowledge of God, His law and acts, as revealed by the Qur'ān, is the only immutable and valid activity. Scientific knowledge, dealing with the outward structure of the universe and matter is changeable, offering mere relative certainties. In the realm of religious truths, revelation is the ultimate authority. Reason may play its part as a logical instrument serving to elucidate the function and relevance of particular divine ordinances.[20]

GOD'S LORDSHIP

In this sense, the doctrine of Islam in its underlying principles demonstrates the necessity of God's will to create all beings and fix their functions. Laws of nature and those governing human affairs are derived from a single source and enjoy the same validity and regularity. The regular movement of the cosmos is created anew every moment by God to express His willingness to continue every time the operation of its harmonious motions. Similarly, injunctions explicitly pronounced in the Qur'ān have to follow the same pattern and be applied with all the rigour of a physical law. Furthermore, the suspension of one law, be it natural or religious, is bound to cause chaos and upset the harmonious order of the cosmos and human society. In the words of Ayatollah Khumayni:

> The fundamental difference between Islamic government, on the one hand, and constitutional monarchies and republics, on the other, is this: whereas the representatives of the people or the monarch in such regimes engage in legislation, in Islam the legislative power and competence to establish laws belongs exclusively to God Almight.[21]

Such a contention is made more explicit by a leading Egyptian fundamentalist:

> Man is a part of the universe; the laws which govern human nature are no different from the laws governing the universe. God is Creator of the universe as well as of man . . . He who has created the universe and man and who made man obedient to the laws which also govern the universe, has also prescribed a shari'ah for his voluntary actions. If man follows this law, then his life is in harmony with his own nature. From this point of view, this shari'ah is also a part of that universal law which governs the entire universe, including the physical and biological aspects of man.[22]

Furthermore, man-made laws are invariably meant to dominate and exploit others. It is for this reason that the principle of God's oneness and lordship excludes the human agency in its pretensions to formulate laws. By restoring divine law into the human sphere as the ruling principle, God becomes the sole legislator represented by a government that is his mere executive arm. Whereas particular matters and certain details may warrant issuing non-divine decrees, in the realm of 'fundamental matters', there is no substitute to God's law and His injunctions. The idea that religion is confined to the individual's conscience and his private life is, therefore, dismissed out of hand and considered an outright conspiracy against Islam. Thus, divine law is more concerned with the public rather than the private domain of human affairs. It seeks to regulate people's lives in order to ensure their conformity to a high ideal. Without such a law, man would be 'like an animal', or worse.[23]

Man's impulsive traits of passion, anger and greed can only be tamed by a superior power whose authority is beyond the whims of the world of appearances. Only divine law, as a direct expression of a metaphysical source, commands the necessary sanction to be fully enforced. This metaphysical dimension is first and foremost the product of efforts exerted by a chain of prophets since the dawn of history. These efforts find their culmination in Islam as the perfect religion which succeeded in creating a harmonious unity between the material and spiritual realms:

> Islam has taken all the dimensions of man into consideration and provided for them. The law of Islam is restricted neither to the unseen realm nor to the manifest dimension, in the same way that man himself is not restricted to a single dimension. Islam came to fashion true and complete human beings, complete in all their dimensions. It did not cultivate exclusively either the spiritual dimension of man, which would have fostered in him an aversion to the natural realm, or the natural dimension, which would have made him satisfied with the natural realm. The natural dimension is the means, and the spiritual, the end.[24]

Creation itself would cease to exist if the divine will was to withdraw 'its rays' from the world. Hence, Islamic fundamentalism singled out God's sovereignty as being of overriding importance. This notion presupposes the assertion of God's will to realize His order in the world, irrespective of the wishes of His creatures. It is, moreover, designed to preempt the concept of free will and the principle of democratic rights whereby social and political laws are the result of popular consensus or majority rule. Despite the unfathomable nature of divinity, an axiom reiterated by fundamentalists and non-fundamentalists, God's sovereignty is deemed to exclude human intervention in devising the essential laws of human societies. God sustains, guards and regulates the universe according to a meticulous plan. His absolute will fashions every movement and event without being bound by them. Moreover, this direct creation of physical and human acts does not abrogate God's bestowal on the individual the responsibility of voluntary acquisition (*kasb*).

In other words, human beings have been given the choice between faith and atheism – to follow God's ordinances or their own whims. Human history consists of the conflict between two opposing forces: belief and unbelief, polytheism and monotheism, faith and atheism. Historical evidence is also irrefutable in contradicting evolutionary theories which see monotheism as being a progression from lower to higher forms. In other words, Islam as the belief in the oneness of God preceded polytheism and could not, therefore, have been the culmination of a long line of evolutionary development. The cosmos, human history and the religion of Islam testify to the prior existence of a well-co-ordinated plan and a divine design to shape animate and inanimate objects by fiat and *ex nihilo*. The Qur'ān itself is not concerned with formulating proofs for the existence of God. Rather, its main purpose is to assert God's will, revealing His intention in regulating the human and metaphysical dimensions of life.[25]

A NEW RELIGION

Unfortunately, true Islam lasted for only a brief period after its inception.

Imam Khomeini.[26]

Islamist movements operating in countries stretching from Indonesia to Turkey, postulate the necessity of re-establishing Islam in varying degrees of emphasis and intensity. Whereas some movements refrain from postulating the complete disappearance of Islam either at the popular and official levels, others have no compunction in bestowing on themselves the responsibility of creating the whole religion afresh. They do so by accusing Muslims of renouncing their religion in favour of what is dubbed 'secularism'.

Consequently, Islamic fundamentalism becomes an act of conversion to a new religion and an oath of loyalty to a system of ideas and practices that are devised and elaborated by a new generation of Muslim scholars. Religious scholarship and the ability to be conversant with the idioms of the heritage, so as to underline its relevance to the modern world in sophisticated deductive exercises, become in this respect essential prerequisites for an aspirant leader of a fundamentalist organization.

All leaders of Islamist movements are accordingly practitioners of this art of building bridges between the past and the present, while insisting on the purity of their traditions. The Egyptian Supreme Guide of the Muslim Brotherhood, Hasan al-Banna (d.1949), his leading radicalist disciple and founder of a new school of thought, Sayyid Qutb (d.1966), the founder of the Pakistani Jama'at-i Islami Party, Abu al-'Ala al-Mawdudi (d.1979) and Ayatollah Khumayni (d.1989), have all produced tracts, treatises and commentaries on the Qur'ān as part of their claim to be the pioneers of a new political vision. The same feature of producing interpretative works, dealing with both historical subjects and contemporary issues, figures in the careers of a number of prominent members of the Syrian Muslim Brotherhood, the

Algerian Islamic Salvation Front and the Tunisian Islamic Renaissance Movement.[27]

What all these leaders and ideologues have in common is a concept of history and politics that may vary in some of its details, but is essentially informed by the same underlying assumptions. In this scheme of things, history, politics and morality intermingle as interconnected categories, illuminating each other, exchanging places and entering the daily discourse of believers. In other words, the past, the present and the future are deliberately made to prefigure each other as abstract models. These models are then repeatedly recycled by the sheer force of an intellectual argument. Moreover, the destruction of Islam as a system of government is deemed to be a perpetual conspiracy hatched by Jews, Christians, Marxists and their secular collaborators in the Islamic world.

These allusions to conspiracies, collusions and concerted assaults are often used as tools of analysis in order to justify the call to renew a religion that has suffered temporary defeat in the face of overwhelming odds. Nevertheless, such a temporary defeat only succeeded in causing the decline of the bearers of the religion, while the dynamic essence of Islam has remained sound and perfect. The soundness and perfection of Islam make it possible to relaunch a new political movement in its name and rescue humanity from its heartless materialism.

By a process of elimination, all the modernistic connotations attached to Islam by secular or reformist leaders are ruled out. The basis of such a fundamentalist stance has, however, nothing to do with an historical approach that perceives events and concepts in terms of their unique socio-political context, or as a result of a heightened sense of the past and its cultural distance. Islamic fundamentalism simply declares its discovery of a unique system of belief and action. It does so by performing a creative reading of God's will whereby the interlocking presence of the physical and the metaphysical dimensions of life are enumerated by referring to Qur'ānic verses, on the one hand, and the latest scientific theories, on the other. Moreover, its perception of a harmonious organic totality between the visible and the invisible reduces human reasoning and conduct to predetermined responses. If the same source of energy and custodianship governs both human affairs and cosmic laws, and God's sovereignty ensures the preservation of the fundamentals of religion in their literal meaning or permanent relevance, politics itself is rendered redundant and utterly oppressive.

Nevertheless, Islamic fundamentalists go out of their way to stress 'the modern and revolutionary' dimensions of their dogma. Their movement, it is contended, has no intention of restoring the institutions and structures of a bygone age. On the contrary, their aim is simply to relive the spirit of early Islam, re-enact its method and apply both in a creative manner.[28] This reference to the spirit and method of an historical experience, entailing the abrogation of its institutional and political practices, highlights the hybrid character of fundamentalism. Its dilemma is born out of an uneven encounter with the tidal waves of modernity which engulfed the Islamic world, turning in the process into an internal factor of destruction and change. It is precisely this internal dynamism of modernity that allows fundamentalists to differentiate between its material and cultural dimensions. Thus, nationalism, secularism and democracy are denounced for their non-religious implications, while technological advances and economic prosperity are embraced and amalgamated into Islam's original blueprint.

The rejection of nationalism, secularism and democracy is justified by referring to their Western roots and inimical opposition to the universality and divinity of Islam. However, this vehement hostility is anchored in a negative reaction against local movements and political systems which openly adopted these ideologies and made them an essential element of official policies. Hence, the fundamentalist argument against these ideologies is largely an internal debate, rather than a mere instinctive condemnation of things Western. It is argued, for example, that nationalism was turned into a political philosophy that made the nation-state an idol and an object of worship. By doing so, the aim of the worshippers of the nation-state was an insatiable desire for domination and the oppression of other nations. War was the inevitable outcome of such a belief. No sooner had the Islamic world suffered military defeats at the hands of Western powers, than it fell under the impact of their culture:

> It is one of the tragic consequences of these very influences that Muslims accepted the concept of nationalism that was unknown to them until the 19th century ... The nation to whom the idea of territorial nationalism was simply foreign ... adopted the non-believers' cult of nationalism and tore to pieces the precious mantle of international brotherhood it had inherited.[29]

It is further argued by fundamentalists in the Arab world that Islam excluded nationalism from its message, despite the prevalent conditions in Arabia which favoured the emergence of a movement with a nationalist message. After all, parts of Arabia were under the direct or indirect control of the Byzantine and Sasanian empires. But the Prophet Muhammad, inspired by God's divine guidance, chose faith and the universal message of all the Prophets, his fellow predecessors.[30] Accordingly, Arab nationalism, the official creed of various Arab states, becomes a pagan reversion and a clear violation of Islam's pristine nature.

However, not all fundamentalists maintain such a clear-cut hostility towards their nation-states. This is particularly the case in Shi'ite fundamentalism which rejects nationalism as an ideological allegiance, but accepts at the same time a mild version of patriotism. Such an aspect of contemporary radical Shi'ism is noticeable in Iraq, Lebanon and Iran. Thus, the spiritual leader of the Iranian Islamic revolution declared in the course of a speech:

To love one's fatherland and its people and to protect its frontiers are both quite unobjectionable, but nationalism, involving hostility to other Muslim nations, is something quite different. It is contrary to the noble Qur'ān and the orders of the Most Noble Messenger.[31]

This line of argument is also used to rule out democracy as a process of government, whereby elected deputies enjoy the right to legislate and make laws irrespective of religious strictures. Since God's sovereignty is indivisible, only His law as revealed in the holy book should claim the ultimate authority in the life of an individual and his community. The task that Islamic fundamentalism assigns to its disciples is to retrace the journey of Muhammad's prophethood. This task is not confined to the elaboration of a theoretical refutation of existing ideologies. Rather, it is a dynamic system of belief and practice embodied in a group of new converts – a vanguard. The vanguard cannot succeed unless it separates itself from its social and political surroundings. The new élite then embarks on a well-co-ordinated plan of action which may assume different forms of political struggle, including the holy obligation of *jihad*, or fighting in the path of God.

A counter-society with its own rules and codes of behaviour is gradually built up and prepared for the final encounter between the Party of Satan and the Party of God. Martyrdom and triumph are two options which have their guaranteed reward either in paradise or in this world. Sooner or later, God's promise to his soldiers will be fulfilled, and Islam as a political power will resume its leadership of the world.

Whereas Sunnite fundamentalists do not stipulate the leadership of the clergy or religious scholars, their Shi'ite counterparts single out the legitimate designated Imams, beginning with the fourth caliph 'Ali (d.661), as those who have the right to rule. Pending the return of the twelfth Imam who entered into his greater occultation in 941 AD, the 'ulama (religious leaders) are to be charged with his worldly tasks. The religious leaders, Khumayni argued, have the obligation to proclaim an Islamic government in the name of the absent Mahdi. The 'ulama, as the heirs of the Prophets and the custodians of their message, have the duty to topple illegitimate governments, be they monarchical or democratic, and install the rulership of the jurist (*wilayat al-faqih*). In 1979, Khumayni became the first supreme jurist and was succeeded upon his death by the present leader, 'Ali Khame'ni.

FUNDAMENTALISM AT THE TURN OF THE TWENTY-FIRST CENTURY

Iran is the only country which has so far experienced a genuine Islamic revolution, whereas in other Muslim countries, such as the Sudan, fundamentalism was imposed from above in a haphazard manner. With the election of a new president in May 1997,[32] Iran itself began to undergo subtle changes characterized by the emergence of new groups of youth and women who posit the idea of reactivating civil society as an autonomous space capable of developing its own momentum and which does not necessarily correspond with the austere injunctions of the state and its official institutions – the judiciary, the revolutionary guards and Parliament.

Throughout the Islamic world, and despite the tragedies of Algeria and the obscurantist rule of Taliban in Afghanistan, fundamentalists are beginning to accept the necessity of political as opposed to armed struggle. This is not to say that *jihad* as a method of gaining political power has completely disappeared. However, most Islamist groups which persist in following this particular violent strategy have either been defeated and discredited (this the case of Syrian, Iraqi and Egyptian Islamists), or have been contained and marginalized, as in Libya, Morocco, Algeria and Saudi Arabia. Other fundamentalists have gradually become less strident in their demands and express their willingness to join the political process, if granted the opportunity, in order to achieve their aims. The Tunisian Renaissance Movement, led by Rashid al-Ghannushi who lives in exile, has undergone such a transformation.

Founded in 1981, the Renaissance party, initially called the Islamic Tendency Movement, adopted the terminology of the Islamic Revolution in Iran and the radical stance of the Egyptian fundamentalist ideologue, Sayyid Qutb. Following its repression by the Tunisian state and the imprisonment of its leading figures, it began to develop a strategy of non-confrontation with the government. In 1989 it formally adopted its present name, hoping to gain official recognition and participate in the legislative elections. Despite the government's insistence on maintaining its ban on religious parties, the Renaissance fielded 'independent' candidates and succeeded in capturing 15 per cent of the vote, scoring higher proportions in a number of urban centres. This promising result prefigured the participation of the Algerian Islamic Salvation Front in the local and national elections of 1990 and 1991. In both countries, the Algerian and Tunisian authorities remain adamant in their rejection of fundamentalist politics, while their mainstream Islamist parties renew their pledges to respect the rule of law and the democratic alternation of power.

In Turkey, the courts disbanded the Islamist Welfare Party in early 1998, despite the fact that its leader Necmettin Erbakan had occupied the office of Prime Minister in a coalition government with a secular party. Nevertheless, the Welfare Party has reemerged under a new name (Virtue) and continues to profess adherence to the principles of democracy and fair play. The Turkish Islamist party enjoys electoral support that is to a large extent an index of a number of Muslim countries. Such support, ranging from 15 to 25 per cent, underlines the emergence of opposition groups with an Islamist programme and a political discourse steeped in the terminology of the spiritual founders – al-Mawdudi, Sayyid Qutb and Khumayni.

In this respect, real politics has outstripped the religious rhetoric, rendering the message a mixture of social democracy, piety and a genuine desire to reform the moral fibre of society. The religious rhetoric still represents a distorted reflection of a blocked system that is unable to respond to the democratic aspirations of its citizenry. Under such circumstances, widespread riots and destruction may figure as the only available outlet. This was the case in Indonesia (May 1998), where a regime built on nepotism, corruption and erratic economic performance generated a genuine movement for democracy in the largest Muslim state. The Indonesian experiment is perhaps a harbinger of things to come, in the sense that fundamentalism ceases to be the only option available to an effective opposition in a Muslim country.

It is true that movements, such as Hamas in the Palestinian occupied territories and the various Islamic Jihad organizations in Egypt and elsewhere, will continue to uphold armed struggle as a religious duty. However, this strategy, where a case of national liberation or resistance does not obtain, is likely to diminish in intensity, with other more legitimate means becoming an established norm.

Finally, the paradox of Islamic fundamentalism consists of its alleged belief in the priority of political activity and decision-making, whereas the concrete application of its ideology confiscates the political process and its participants. The recent events in Iran (the election of Khatami) and Indonesia (the downfall of Suharto) testify to the diversity of political life in the Islamic world and its ability to invent modern mechanisms to resolve the dilemmas of the twenty-first century.

NOTES

1. *In the Shade of the Qur'an*, vol. 30, translated by M.A. Salahi and A.A. Shamis, MWH, London, 1979, p.306.
2. Terms coined include *hākimiyya* (ultimate authority) and *tali'a* (vanguard) in reference to an Islamist party. Conventional terms range from the idea of *jihad* to the institution of the caliphate.
3. According to a leading fundamentalist scholar, Islam 'is a complete way of life with acts of worship and rites as well as individual and collective obligiations that are mutually complementary', Qutb, *In the Shade of the Qur'an*, p.316.
4. On the divergence between doctrinal purity and practical politics in Pakistan, see Seyyed Vali Reza Nasr, *The Vanguard of the Islamic Revolution: The Jama'at-i Islami of Pakistan*, I.B. Tauris, London, 1994, part 3.
5. On the repercussions of the Industrial and French Revolutions, see E.J. Hobsbawm, *The Age of the Revolution*, Mentor, London and New York, 1962.
6. On the different aspects of Islam in the modern world, see Michael Gilsenan, *Recognizing Islam*, I.B.Tauris, London, 1986.
7. Salwa Ismail, 'Confronting the Other: Identity, Culture, Politics, and Conservative Islamism in Egypt', *International Journal of Middle East Studies*, 30, 1998, pp.199–225 is a case study of this type of Islamism.

8. François Burgat and William Dowell, *The Islamic Movement in North Africa*, University of Texas, Austin, 1997, pp.212–23, discuss the nature of this abstract articulation in its Tunisian context.

9. *Postmodernism, Reason and Religion*, Routledge, London, 1992, p.22. See my review of Gellner's book in *Journal of the Royal Asiatic Society*, Series 3, 4, 1, 1994, pp.83–5.

10. See, for example, Emmanuel Sivan, *Radical Islam: Medieval Theology and Modern Politics*, Yale University Press, New Haven and London, 1985. Sivan's argument is based on the premise of 'the survivals of the past' and the persistence of 'medieval modes of thought' as well as 'the resilience of Arab traditional mentalities', pp.ix–x and 182.

11. This model is impregnated with the discourse of orientalism as expounded by Edward Said in his work *Orientalism*, Penguin, Harmondsworth, 1985.

12. This version is associated with the sociological and philosophical theory of Ernest Gellner in his numerous works. See, in particular, his *Postmodernism, Reason and Religion*.

13. Gellner, *Postmodernism, Reason and Religion*, pp.9–10 and 15.

14. For more details, see Max Weber, *The Protestant Ethic and the Spirit of Capitalism*, Unwin University Book, London, 1974.

15. Marshall G.S. Hodgson, *The Venture of Islam*, vol. 3, University of Chicago Press, Chicago and London, 1974, p.440.

16. There are a number of biographies of the Prophet. The most recent include Maxime Rodinson, *Muhammad*, Penguin, Harmondsworth, 1976, and Martin Lings, *Muhammad*, Allen and Unwin, London, 1983.

17. Sufism has received extensive treatment in Western scholarship, particularly in its spiritual dimension and metaphysical connotations. My brief account is based on Annemarie Schimell's *Mystical Dimensions of Islam*, University of North Carolina Press, Chapel Hill, 1975 and J. Spencer Trimingham's *The Sufi Orders in Islam*, Clarendon Press, Oxford, 1971.

18. The above account of revivalism, reformism and radicalism is partly based on my book *Islamic Fundamentalism*, revd edn, Pinter, London and Washington, 1997.

19. *The Process of Islamic Revolution*, 8th edn, Islamic Publications, Lahore, 1980, p.17.

20. Sayyid Qutb, *In the Shade of the Qur'an*, pp.80–81, 138–9, 220–21, 301–2, 351–3; Imam Khomeini, *Islam and Revolution*, translated and annotated by Hamid Algar, Mizan Press, Berkeley, 1981, pp.38–9, 302–5, 341; Abul A'la Maududi, *Unity of the Muslim World*, Islamic Publications, Lahore, 1982, pp.17–19.

21. Khomeini, *Islam and Revolution*, p.55.

22. Sayyid Qutb, *Milestones*, I.I.F.S.O./Beirut and Damascus, 1978, pp.163–4.

23. Khomeini, *Islam and Revolution*, pp.329–31.

24. Ibid., p.332.

25. Sayyid Qutb, *Muqawwimat al-tasawwur al-islami* (fundamentals of Islamic ideology), Dar al-Shuruq, Beirut, 1986, pp.247–316.

26. *Islam and Revolution*, p.332.

27. Some of these leaders' works have been translated into English. See, for details, 'Guide to further reading', below.

28. Kamal al-Sa'id Habib, 'Wathiqat al-ihya' al-islami', (Charter of Islamic revival), in Rifaat Sayyid Ahmad, *al-Nabi al-musallah*, vol. 2, Riad El-Rayyes Books, London, 1991, pp.242–3, n.105. It is significant that Habib, a former leader of

the Egyptian Jihad organization, chooses to reveal the modernity of his theory in a long endnote, while the bulk of his monograph (pp.199–238), originally published in 1986, highlights the recurring nature of Islamic renewal.

29. Abul A'la Maududi, *Unity of the Muslim World*, Islamic Publications, Lahore, 1982, pp.1–2 and 17.

30. Qutb, *Milestones*, pp.41–4.

31. Khomeini, *Islam and Revolution*, p.302. Khumayni's criticism of nationalism is here directed against Arab nationalism, particularly in its Ba'thist Iraqi variation.

32. Muhammad Khatami swept to power with nearly 70 per cent of the vote. A liberal cleric and former minister of culture, Khatami defeated his hard line rival in a landslide election victory which heralded a new era of reform and gradual improvement of relations with the USA. Khatami's idea of 'a civil society based on the rule of law' resulted in relative freedom of expression and improvement of women's rights.

GUIDE TO FURTHER READING

Muhammad and Islam

The study of Islam may be initially tackled by making use of good and accessible introductory surveys. Three stand out: H.H. Gibb, *Islam* (Oxford University Press, Oxford, 1978); David Waines, *An Introduction to Islam* (Cambridge University Press, Cambridge, 1995); Malise Ruthven, *Islam in the World* (Oxford University Press, Oxford, 1984).

The career of the Prophet and its political and social implications have been studied by W. Montgomery Watt, *Muhammad: Prophet and Statesman* (Oxford University Press, Oxford, 1976); a controversial view is offered in M.A. Cook, *Muhammad* (Oxford University Press, Oxford, 1983). However, M. Rodinson, *Mohammed*, trans. A. Carter (Penguin, Harmondsworth, 1971), strikes the right note.

Two general magisterial surveys study Islam in its various aspects: M.G.S. Hodgson, *The Venture of Islam* (3 vols, University of Chicago Press, Chicago, 1974, and several reprints); and I.M. Lapidus, *A History of Islamic Societies* (Cambridge University Press, Cambridge, 1988).

Islamic fundamentalism

The controversial nature of fundamentalism in Islam has given rise to a number of conflicting interpretations. One school sees fundamentalism or Islamic resurgence as a perennial phenomenon and part of an ongoing tradition. Emmanuel Sivan's *Radical Islam. Medieval Theology and Modern Politics* (Yale University Press, 1985), is a good example of the above school. Another school of thought sees fundamentalism as an expression of local resistance to Western domination and a political attempt to grapple with the complicated world of modernity and its secular ideologies. The reader may consult the following studies: Nazih Ayubi, *Political Islam* (Routledge, London, 1991); Sami Zubaida, *Islam, the People and the State* (I.B. Tauris, London, 1993); and Youssef M. Choueiri, *Islamic Fundamentalism* (Pinter, London, 1997).

Two edited books with contributions by a number of eminent scholars introduce the study of Islam and fundamentalism in their various political and social contexts. *Shi'ism and Social Protest*, edited by Juan R.J. Cole and Nikki R. Keddie (Yale University Press, New Haven, CT, 1986); and *Islamic Fundamentalism*, edited by A.S. Sidahmed and A. Ehteshami (Westview Press, Boulder, CO, 1996).

A deeper understanding of fundamentalism is best achieved by reading the works of its original spiritual founders in the contemporary period. Almost all of the works of the Pakistani radicalist Abul al-A'la al-Mawdudi have been translated into English. Most works are in the form of booklets or short monographs. See, in particular: Abul A'la Maududi, *Jihad in Islam* (2nd edn, Islamic Publications Ltd, Lahore, 1978) and *idem, First Principles of the Islamic State* (Islamic Publications Ltd, Lahore, 1983). Khumayni's theoretical contributions and some of his public speeches have been translated and annotated by Hamid Algar in Imam Khomeini, *Islam and Revolution* (Mizan Press, Berkeley, 1981). Another leading ideologue and whose works in Arabic have been translated into several languages is the Egyptian Sayyid Qutb. Two books give a clear summary of his principal ideas: *Milestones* (The Holy Koran Publishing House, Beirut and Damascus, 1978) and *In the Shade of the Qur'an* (MWH, London, 1979). An important pamphlet written by 'Abd al-Salam Faraj, leader of the *Jihad* organization which plotted the assassination of the Egyptian President, Anwar Sadat, has been translated into English by Johannes J.G. Jansen in *The Neglected Duty* (Macmillan, New York, 1986).

Islam and modernity

The history of Islamic societies in the twentieth century and their encounter with colonialism and modernism is meticulously chronicled in Reinhard Schulze, *A Modern History of the Islamic World* (I.B. Tauris, London, 1998). In *Islam and Modernity*, edited by Ron Nettler, Muhammad Mahmoud and John Cooper (London, 1998), the contemporary modernist and liberal aspects of Islam are highlighted as part of the missing image of Islam nowadays. Akbar S. Ahmed's *Islam Today* (I.B. Tauris, London, 1998), offers a succinct and robust defence of Islam in its historical and contemporary contexts.

12
CONCLUSION: THE 'END OF IDEOLOGY'?
Roger Eatwell

—

THE END OF IDEOLOGY AND DÉJA VU

During two periods in the second half of the twentieth century, we have been told that the age of ideologies is coming to a close, that a form of pragmatic liberal-capitalism has won. At the turn of the 1960s, writers like the French and American sociologists Raymond Aron, Daniel Bell, and Seymour Martin Lipset wrote of the 'end of ideology'.[1] Thirty years later, an American State Department official named Francis Fukuyama (1952–   ) caught the mood of the post-communist hour when he predicted the 'end of history'.[2] Fukuyama stressed that the decline during the 1970s and 1980s of authoritarian government in Europe, South America and elsewhere (Greece, Spain, Argentina, Brazil, etc.) predated the more spectacular collapse of communism after 1989. He portrayed the movement towards democracy and capitalism as part of a pattern of a general historical evolution. The occasional state might slip back into dictatorship, but the politico-economic die for the twenty-first century world was firmly cast.

These two sets of 'endist' arguments, especially Fukuyama's more recent prognostications, offer a useful starting-point to a discussion of ideological trends in the twentieth century, because each involves overt and implicit assumptions about how ideologies rise and fall (see also Chapter 1 on the earlier set).

In his much discussed book, *The End of Ideology* (1960), Bell celebrated the triumph of a socially concerned, liberal pragmatism. This development was, allegedly, accompanied by the decline of extremist ideologies, namely ones based on features such as *a priori* truths and 'monist' reasoning (i.e. 'scientific', allegedly unchallengeable intellectually, non-pluralistic, bodies of thought – like the communist view of the inevitable collapse of capitalism and the need for a single political party). Critics argued that this end of ideology thesis was itself ideological. It certainly seemed to echo the development of the 'totalitarian' model in the 1950s, which was covertly encouraged by the US government through funding academic conferences and other means. This model sought to damn both the USSR and Nazi Germany as 'ideological' political systems, which had led to brutal dictatorships, and murderous world war.[3]

Nevertheless, the end of ideology thesis was not simply Western triumphalism. It was based on a methodological view about how ideologies arose, and fell. First, there was the belief that the spread of affluence had undermined the social conflicts on which radical ideologies were premised. In other words, ideologies were not something inherent in all societies as a means of social bonding or change, but rather something which emerged at times of strain or crisis. Secondly, there was the belief that ideologies such as communism and fascism had been a form of secular religion, requiring both faith and ultimately irrational styles of thought. These were seen as being undermined not only by the growth of popular education, but also by a growing intellectual awareness that such beliefs were 'irrational', or 'mythical'. In this context, a crucial intellectual figure was the Austrian *émigré* Karl Popper. His post-1945 writings attempted to associate the scientific method with falsificationism, namely, a belief was rational, or scientific, if it was clear what was required to falsify it. Ideologies were seen as ultimately unfalsifiable (for example, what would it be necessary to do to *prove* that capitalism would not eventually be succeeded by socialism?; or what evidence could *prove* that but for capitalist socialization, people would behave in an egalitarian and co-operative way?).

During the late 1960s and 1970s, the end of ideology thesis fell from favour. In much of the world communism seemed to be growing: witness America's humiliating withdrawal from South Vietnam in 1975 following defeat in the battle against North Vietnamese communist insurgence. More generally in the Third World there were signs of growing radicalism and anti-Western sentiment: the installation of an Islamic fundamentalist regime in Iran during 1979 was dramatic evidence of this pattern. Nor did Bell *et al.*'s crystal ball seem attuned to Western developments. The 1960s proved a time of growing dissent, especially from groups such as students and blacks in the USA. Intellectually, this era witnessed the rise of a New Left, which had a notable following among academics especially, and a New Right, which was to have a far more profound policy effect on governments. Such varied developments seemed to damn the end of ideology thesis to the intellectual dustbin.[4]

However, with the dramatic collapse of communism at the turn of the 1990s, 'endism' enjoyed a revival, most notably in the work of Fukuyama, who argued in a much translated article which he later turned into a world best-selling book:

> The twentieth century saw the developed world descend into a paroxysm of ideological violence, as liberalism contended first with the remnants of absolutism, then bolshevism and fascism, and finally an updated Marxism that threatened to lead to the ultimate apocalypse of nuclear war. But the century that began full of self-confidence in the ultimate triumph of Western liberal democracy seems at its close to be returning full circle to where it started ... to an unabashed victory of economic and political liberalism.[5]

Like the earlier 'end of ideology' debate, there was an element of Western triumphalism, but there was also a methodological core. Fukuyama held (following Hegel and Marx) that there is an underlying pattern in the evolution of history, that there is an end state in which society finally conforms to the underlying pattern of human nature, which involves a quest for 'recognition' and the freedom only to be found in a liberal democratic-capitalist society.

Human nature is one of the three key factors which Fukuyama sees as directing history, and leading to the triumph of liberal democracy. These three factors are 1) the struggle for what he calls 'recognition'; 2) the logic of science's mastery over nature; and 3) the absence of major contradictions in liberal democracy. It is worth expanding the last point first, as it helps reflect the idealist aspects of Fukuyama's analysis. Fukuyama sees this as a direct refutation of the Marxist position – where the base determines the superstructure (see Chapters 1 and 5). He also saw it as a refutation of what he called 'the Wall Street Journal school' of determinism – the belief that man is essentially a rational, profit-maximizing individual – rather than one swayed by great ideas such as freedom or democracy. He accepts an idea going back to Lipset in the 1950s that economic development helps establish and stabilize democracy, but he sees the triumph of liberalism more in terms of ideologies than economics.

Fukuyama sees contradictions as helping to undermine competing twentieth century ideologies. In the context of other ideologies, he is presumably here thinking of failings like Soviet communism's promise of democracy, but practice of dictatorial élitism; or, communism's promise of economic success, but practice of bureaucratic incompetence and shortages – its inability to foster innovation and new thought. The last aspect leads on to Fukuyama's point about science's mastery of nature. By this Fukuyama seems in particular to mean the efficient and technocratic organization of production which capitalism has brought about. This has not just produced great wealth, thus raising living standards. He holds that those countries with capitalist economies give such societies a decisive military edge. Communism simply bankrupted itself and caused social discontent in its attempt to match and overtake Western military technology, symbolized most dramatically by Ronald Reagan's commitment to science-fiction like 'Star Wars' technology in the early 1980s.

Although many have endorsed the broad sweep of this analysis, it is important to note that Fukuyama's 'endism' is open to a variety of objections.[6] He has a somewhat rose-tinted view of the social tensions and inequalities within contemporary liberal-capitalist societies, and plays down the ecological dangers of ever-greater capitalist growth. Moreover, he has a one-sided reading of developments in the Third World, and international relations. He neglects that fact that some of the Third World is becoming relatively poorer: international capitalism is not a game in which everyone is a winner. More ominously, he plays down nuclear proliferation in the non-Western world, such as India and Pakistan, both of which provocatively tested such weapons in 1998. More surprisingly still, he does not seriously consider the impact of the rise of Islam, the world's fastest growing religion, and its militant fundamentalist strand.

As such, he offers a very different analysis to the one put forward later in the 1990s by fellow American, Samuel Huntington (1927–   ). Huntington agrees that ideological and economic conflicts are in decline at the world level, but argues:

> It is my hypothesis that the fundamental source of conflict in this new world will not be primarily ideological or primarily economic. The great divisions among human kind and the dominating source of conflict will be cultural. Nation states will remain the most powerful actors in world affairs, but the principal conflicts of global politics will occur between nations and groups of different civilizations. The clash of civilizations will dominate global politics.[7]

Huntington sees American-led capitalist globalisation as a new form of imperialism, which is inevitably producing an anti-Western response in the form of Islamic fundamentalism, or new nationalist movements based on the politics of identity. Rather than a Coca-Cola one-world culture, Huntington predicts a 'clash of civilizations'.[8] However, like Fukuyama, Huntington's views are open to objection.[9] For instance, he fails to perceive the continued vitality of ideological traditions other than nationalism and fundamentalisms. Moreover, he glosses over the internal divisions even within these ideologies: Islam, for instance, has many strands, and some new forms of micro-nationalism threaten existing state stability within the West. Nevertheless, Huntington's analysis points to the dangers of sweeping prophecies of the world victory of liberalism and capitalism – and highlight especially the weakness of forms of economic determinism which still dominate much academic thinking about the future.

THE RISE AND FALL OF IDEOLOGIES IN THE TWENTIETH CENTURY

The arguments of Fukuyama and other 'endists' do more than just echo turn of the 1960s' thought. The late nineteenth century saw perhaps an even greater wave of liberal triumphalism, proclaiming the victory of democracy and capitalism. However, by 1900 liberalism was coming under a two pronged attack from the left and right, though there was also an element of symbiosis in this process.[10]

The rising forces of the left tended to see liberalism as both morally wrong, and damned by a series of problems and tensions. Liberal democracy, with its concomitant claims of equality before the law, or rights, was viewed as a sham, hiding the interests of the rich and growing middle class (the 'bourgeoisie'). The reality of capitalist freedom, according to socialists, was great income and wealth inequalities. Ultimate power in 'democracies' was seen as laying in the hands of the rich. The proclaimed dynamism of the market was marred by trade cycle depressions. Moreover, liberalism's individualism, and linked apolitical vision of human existence, were seen by most socialists as alienating. 'Man' was inherently a social and political animal (before 1900 few socialists focused on women's rights).

The conclusions drawn by socialists about this analysis of liberalism could vary notably. Most Marxists and some other socialists, for example Sorel, believed that violence would be necessary to overthrow the (capitalist) state. Others, in particular the forerunners of modern social democracy, like Bernstein, held that it was possible to achieve change through the legislative process. This meant that some liberal views, for example about the neutrality of the state, were accepted by this form of socialism. By 1900 most socialists were turning to the (socialist) state as the vehicle to liberate the people. Here again, there was sometimes an element of symbiosis with liberalism, for 'new' liberals, such as Hobhouse, were putting forward arguments about why the power of the state could be expanded. In particular, activities which could be seen as increasing individual autonomy and freedom, for example extensive education and welfare provisions, were accepted by these new liberals. Even the most moderate socialists tended to view the state in broader terms than this, but the growth of statism within liberalism was to be an important point of linkage between the two ideologies. However, other socialists – especially anarchists and to a lesser extent syndicalists – were hostile to any form of state, seeing it as promoting élitism and authority.

Authority was central to the right-wing critique of liberalism, but here the fear was more that liberalism was undermining the authority necessary for social stability. From the time of the French Revolution, right-wing critics, such as de Maistre, had argued that people had duties as well as rights, that the 'masses' were largely ignorant and easily swayed, and that social stability was ultimately founded upon consensual values which could not be created from scratch according to *a priori* principles ('man' was ultimately neither rational, nor perfectible). Even many liberals shared some of these suspicions of the masses, and the doctrine of popular sovereignty. This could lead to the 'tyranny of the majority' in John Stuart Mill's terms. In the nineteenth century there was no necessary equation between liberalism and democracy, as the masses could be seen as a threat to individual rights, and rational government.

By 1900, notably different forms of right-wing thought had emerged, in the way that there were different forms of socialism. A more reactionary strand, associated with thinkers like Maurras, stressed traditional authority, and was usually monarchist and/or religious. As it was often tied to these particular interests, this strand found it difficult to exert mass appeal in a Western world which was witnessing the onset of the universal franchise. A moderate strand of the right, typified by Burke, was more willing to encompass change, if it were really needed and could be achieved gradually. This moderate right was also willing to accept some aspects of liberalism, for example the rule of law, and more grudgingly the economic dynamism of liberalism. In the latter context, there remained a hostility to radical *laissez-faire* views, seeing its individualism as essentially a threat to social solidarity and its economic conception of life as alienating. By 1900 this more moderate right saw the ultimate bonds of society not so much in terms of economic interest, or in the religious and monarchical devotion of the reactionary right, as in nationalism, a force which at the turn of the nineteenth century had been associated more with the left through its critique of established authority and celebration of the 'sovereignty of the people' (a cry which inevitably raised the issue 'who are the people?') This nationalism was often linked, especially in Europe, to welfare policies in a form of 'social imperialism', an attempt to attract the masses both through self-interest and myth. There was an element of this in America too, though the American dream was more individualistic, and usually isolationist.

During the inter-war years, liberalism seemed in terminal decline, particularly in Europe. Political parties based on its principles found themselves squeezed, losing members and supporters to left and right. The great slump which began following the Wall Street crash in 1929 seemed to remove any final legitimacy for free market production. Even in the citadel of capitalism, the USA, great public works were needed in the 'New Deal' to alleviate poverty and restore confidence. The great slump contrasted with a new age of Soviet planning, which began in the late 1920s, ten years after the revolution. The 1930s was the age of 'guided tours', when selected Westerners visited the USSR and returned (in the main) to sing the praises of what they believed was a full-employment, happy and prosperous 'New Civilization' – to use the title of a book written by Beatrice and Sidney Webb, who had earlier done much to develop gradualist-technocratic Fabian socialist theory.

Fascism, too, posed problems for liberalism. Interventionist economic policies in Italy and Germany during the 1920s and 1930s, apparently curing unemployment, seemed another confirmation of the death knell of *laissez-*

faire. More ominously, the emergence of mass, popular nationalism in economically developed countries did not fit easily within liberalism's view of 'history' leading to ever greater 'rationality'. In particular, it seemed to confirm the Sorelian idea that the masses were swayed by collective myths, rather than guided by individual rationality – a conclusion reached by many after the nationalist fervour of the First World War. The violence of fascism during its rise, too, raised issues about toleration and freedom which troubled liberalism (as did communist violence). Was it possible to tolerate the intolerant, to permit political movements which were based on ideologies which sought the overthrow of the liberal democratic system? Would the world not have been a better place if the ban on Nazi activity, imposed after its violent attempted *coup* in Munich during 1923, had remained in force?

Fascism was defeated by war, but in the initial post-1945 era communism seemed to have been strengthened. Indeed, during the 1960s–70s a growing number of peoples lived under communist rule. It is true that there were differences between communist systems, including a significant split between China and the USSR over both domestic policy and foreign interests. Nevertheless, communism was viewed by most commentators as an enduring force in world politics. Sympathetic commentators, and there were many in the West, often glossed over the problems of these countries' economic systems, their brutality and lack of civil rights. Some even managed to portray the brutality and chaos of Mao Zedong's 'Cultural Revolution' in favourable terms (an error only partly explained by lack of knowledge about aspects of these events). Radical-chic students of the late 1960s waved Mao's 'Little Red Book', chanted revolutionary slogans, plotted sit-ins, and engaged in other forms of activity which would have led to their arrest in communist countries. More seriously, admiring comparisons were often made by commentators between capitalist and 'democratic' developing countries – such as contrasting China's apparent absence of gross poverty with India's starving, often begging, millions (and India was one of the more successful developing countries, though it could not compete in terms of economic growth with what until the late 1990s seemed to be the Asian 'tiger' economies, bent on ever upward wealth-creation).

In the West, particularly in Europe, the first two decades after 1945 were characterized by an era of statism. This was the great age of Keynesian macro- and micro-economic policy, designed to level out the trade cycle, and ensure a prosperous full-employment economy. These truly were years of economic growth, which helped fund new welfare programmes and provide standards of living (judged in economic terms) undreamed of by nineteenth-century socialists. Cars, televisions and a host of consumer goods became the playthings of the masses. Pockets of poverty still existed, particularly in the more peasant-based European countries, and in the USA, but high levels of employment, and statist policies funded by growth seemed to offer all the dream of a new future. For most Western countries, the years immediately after 1945 were ones of relative stability and consensus. Against such a background, it is easy to see how Bell's 'end of ideology' thesis grew.

Given the rise of statism in the West, and growing evidence of problems – especially economic ones – in communist systems, it is easy to see why another form of 'endism' became fashionable during the 1960s and 1970s, especially on the moderate left. This was called 'convergence theory', which held that communist systems would adopt more market-oriented principles and pay greater attention to Western freedoms, while Western systems would become, if anything, more statist and welfare oriented. This argument had various forms of methodological assumption. Usually it was argued that dynamic economies needed a level of freedom not found in communist systems. On the other hand, it was argued that democratic pressures in the West required a high degree of intervention to prevent gross inequalities and abuse of 'rights' (hence the apparent success of the Civil Rights movement for blacks in the USA during the 1960s). At its most methodologically simple, the argument was a form of 'I've seen the future and it works' (to adopt a famous Western comment on the early USSR). This often involved eulogizing social democratic Sweden as a model full-employment, prosperous, participatory society.

But by the late twentieth century, Sweden's social democratic consensus had broken down, and its much vaunted polity had become characterized by features such as growing unemployment, and racism. Punitive marginal tax rates seemed to have encouraged evasion and been a disincentive to effort. Slowing economic growth helped lead to very high interest rates, which in themselves acted as a brake on investment – and thus future growth. Sweden had gone from being a model to admire, to a case study of the problem of achieving growth in a high tax and interventionist economy. Indeed, the social democrats, who dominated Swedish politics after the 1930s, lost power in the 1980s. In neighbouroughing Norway, high revenues from oil continued to fund public expenditure, but the 15 per cent of the vote obtained by the populist, anti-immigrant, Progress Party in the 1997 elections underlined that all was not well with the once much vaunted 'Scandinavian model'.

It could be argued that China has perhaps conformed to the convergence model in the economic, if not political sphere (the system remains in the late 1990s clearly a dictatorship). However, at the turn of the new millenium, the rest of the former communist bloc seems characterized by a remarkable dual process. On the one hand it has adopted free market principles and policies, such as privatization, with the promise of good times to come. On the other hand, former communist parties have often revived (usually with new names), for instance in Russia, Poland and East Germany. Moreover, ex-communist states have often been plagued by ethnic tensions. At present, the scenario-building exercises based on the last two sets of developments seem distinctly more justified than ones based of the prospect of the onset of widespread prosperity. It is hard to see how economic aspirations raised by the collapse of communism can be fulfilled in the short run, while it is easy to see how rapid economic change promotes a psychological need to achieve a sense of community through ethnicity, or reviving old collectivist ideals. (This is especially true among men who have lost, or fear losing, their 'manly' jobs, ending up unemployed, or in 'knicker jobs'.)

In economic terms, former communist states seem at times more royalist than the king, for they have adopted (albeit somewhat erratically) radical free-market policies at a time when there are growing doubts about them in the West. The Keynesian dominance of the immediate post-war years in the West gave way in the 1970s and 1980s to more *laissez-faire* policies, which had been preached most notably by Hayek and Friedman for over twenty years. This was a time when New Right economic policies, including privatization and tax cuts, seemed to offer hope for rapid new growth. However, many Western economies have failed to achieve the growth rates hoped for (certainly unemployment remained high in Western Europe during the 1990s, though the US economy boomed). Predictably, in the European countries most influenced by the New Right, for instance Britain, a reaction set in to the more radical neo-liberal economic prescriptions – although a general acceptance of the importance of markets and dangers of the big state has permeated even much of the left. Some New Right supporters argue that their policies were not really implemented in full, that administrations such as Ronald Reagan's and Margaret Thatcher's (let alone George Bush's and John Major's during the 1990s) were too influenced by pragmatism and electoral pressures. However, this raises major issues about whether a democracy could sustain the high levels of unemployment which such radial *laissez-faire* policies would almost certainly mean in the short run. It also raises questions about the acceptability of large internal differences in income and wealth. Indeed, the victory of Tony Blair in 1997 in part owed a debt to a sense of unease about growing inequalities in Conservative Britain.

THE END OF IDEOLOGY AND THE TWENTY-FIRST CENTURY

What exactly is the relationship between democracy and capitalism, and have they really triumphed? Are there not obvious contradictions between democracy and capitalism? (for instance, between the latter's concentration of power, including areas such as the media, and the former's promise of individual freedom, or between democracy's commitment to majority decisions and the more liberal concept of natural rights). And what of new radical challenges, glossed over in the above discussion, for instance from feminism, ecologism, or Islam? Islamicists point to the spiritual emptiness of a world ruled by mammon, and where democracy seems perfectly consistent with ignoring the poorest and weakest in society (the American boom during the 1990s has not eliminated a large underclass, especially among ethnic minorities). The ecologist case could be read as stating that the triumph of capitalism is likely to led to world destruction: how could mass industrialization be envisaged without destroying the world's ecosystem? (just compare the 10 million population of Britain at the time of the Industrial Revolution with the billion plus current population of China, and think about the world effects of industrialization). Radical feminists can mock how 'democrats' concern themselves with issues like falling turnouts in elections, whilst ignoring patriachy and the resulting male political domination (is there not a sense in which politics is a male game, reflecting male values?).

The last point illustrates the limitations of Fukuyama's definition of democracy, or rather his confusions about democracy. A minor example concerns the way he talks of America being a liberal democracy in the eighteenth century, and Britain being one by the mid-nineteenth century. Yet he also uses as a key defining aspect of democracy the existence of universal adult franchise (1919 in the USA; 1928 in Britain). More seriously, he fails to see that some non-Western democracies, for example in Malaysia, are committed to democracy in the sense that their governments are accountable to their subjects and must maintain constitutional rather than personal rule. But this is not *liberal* democracy. It is not founded on individualism, on the sense of rights, or on the dividing line between private and public which is central to Western liberal democratic theory, if not always practice (a conception largely missing from Islamic thought). Predictably, Fukuyama seems confused about whether countries such as Singapore, even Japan, are democracies.

Similarly, Fukuyama makes a serious mistake in using one word ('capitalism') for many forms (American, Korean, Swedish, and so on). Even within Western forms, some commentators have distinguished between 'Anglo-American' and 'Rhenish' (archetypally, German-Dutch-Swiss): the former is seen as short-term and individualist, whereas the latter stresses the community and takes a longer view. Fukuyama recognizes that there are some differences, but seems to believe that a largely American-style capitalism will be the shape of the future. However, Islamic society has resisted Western 'capitalist' and democratic modes of socio-economic organization for centuries? Possibly the ultimate lack of an apparently viably, modern, economic philosophy in Islamic thought damns it to perish in the face of globalization. But even if this is the case, it is not clear that American as against Rhenish capitalism will be the model. Certainly, in spite of the recent success of the American economy, there are some – especially those with a leaning to the left – who hold that the Rhenish model is more likely to be a model for 'export'.

There are also more complex, controversial, philosophical points about democracy and capitalism. Nietzsche's criticism of democracy, echoed by the leading Nazi intellectual, Heidegger, was that its very nature undermined a sense of 'recognition'. Was there not a levelling in democracy, in theory at least, which removed distinction and merit, which militated against leaders? Moreover, if democracy truly was an end state, would there be any goals left worth fighting for – goals which historically had helped give people a sense of 'recognition' and purpose? It is worth noting that Fukuyama adds this point in his book, inserting a note of caution about soulless, consumerist 'last men', which was missing in the original essay which launched the 'end of history' debate. Whilst not endorsing Nietzsche's radical critique of egalitarianism and democracy, Fukuyama believes that part of what it is to be human involves struggle and sacrifice. In an important sense, this Hegelian dialectic – and Nietzschian vitalism – seems to undermine the possibility of a stable end state.

Modern Western society is unlike any of the 'great' societies in history in that it stresses the individual over the holistic group. Within it, relations between men and things (especially goods) seem more important than those between men and men. This point was made by Marx, and has since been picked up by others of very different political persuasion. Michael Polanyi in *The Great Transformation* (1957) noted how exceptional the modern era is in the way that economics and the market are made sacrosanct. This raises the issue of how such a society is legitimized. The market was initially supported in the West by the Protestant ethic, with its emphasis on profit as a reward for hard work, and other legitimating aspects. However, markets are now increasingly seen essentially as efficient allocative mechanisms. The Hayekian 'epistemological' defence of the market makes little attempt to defend profit in terms of just reward; luck and other factors all play their part. Instead, the market is seen as a complex knowledge-mechanism. Attempts to 'plan' are now seen as inevitably leading to lower national income, bureaucracy, and 'unfreedom'.

This problem of legitimation is stressed by Bell in his book *The Cultural Contradictions of Capitalism* (1974), and others on both right and left have highlighted the moral void at the heart of modern liberalism. It is not necessary to be an ecologist to ask what happens if growth slows down, even stops. Will the masses be content with the formalities of political freedom, although their living standard falls? Looked at another way, it is not necessary to be fascist to ask whether the individualist-hedonist ethos makes it difficult to fight a future *major* war. Nor should it be assumed that Fukuyama's 'mastery over science' means that the West will always keep a technological lead which will avoid heavy losses in battle. Space-invader images of cruise missiles and smart weapons 'zapping' Iraqi targets in the 1990s Gulf war may have provided a technologically reassuring picture. But Saddam Hussein did not choose to launch his weapons of mass destruction. In the post-communist world, where Russia retains a high technological ability in weaponry, but notably low-paid personnel, who can be sure that nuclear and germ weapons will not increasingly be available to people and states who are willing to use them?

Clearly at this point the argument has moved away from political ideologies to a much broader view, including material and other developments. Certainly it has never been the point of this book to argue that economic, institutional and other factors are not crucial to the process of history. However, this book has sought to show that ideas are important too, and that the allegedly dominant ideology of liberal-capitalism faces many challenges – both internal and external. A major task facing the student of politics at the turn of the twenty-first century, therefore, is a careful consideration of both liberalism and other ideologies in order to understand what they have to say about the contemporary condition. This is what Chapters 2–11 have sought to provide. Collectively, they have shown that political ideologies are far from dead, that history is protean rather than linear and finite. Our children will almost certainly not – as a Soviet leader predicted at the turn of the 1960s – live under Red flags. But nor should we necessarily assume – in the way implied by many 'endists' – that the future world flag will be the McDonald's logo superimposed on the Stars and Stripes.

NOTES

1. R. Aron, *The Opium of the Intellectuals*, Norton, New York, 1962 (French edn, 1955); D. Bell, *The End of Ideology*, The Free Press, New York, 1960; S.M. Lipset, *Political Man*, Heinemann, London, 1960.
2. F. Fukuyama, *The End of History and the Last Man*, Hamish Hamilton, London, 1992.
3. For the classic statement see Z. Brzezinski and C.J. Friedrich, *Totalitarianism, Dictatorship and Autocracy*, Praeger, New York, 1961. Although subsequently much criticized on account of its cold war origins, the approach has had defenders in the 1990s. See especially G. Sartori, 'Totalitarianism, Model Mania and Learning from Error', *Journal of Theoretical Politics*, 5, 1993.
4. For Bell's response to this see, the 'Afterword' in the 1988 edition of *The End of Ideology*; and D. Bell, 'The End of Ideology Revisited', (2 articles), *Government and Opposition*, 23, 1988.
5. F. Fukuyama, 'The End of History', *The National Interest*, 16, 1989, p.3.
6. See, for instance, T. Burns (ed.), *After History? Francis Fukuyama and His Critics*, Littlefield Adams, London, 1994; *New Left Review*, no. 193, 1992, has extended left-wing reviews of Fukuyama's book by F. Halliday, M. Rustin and R. Miliband; and A Shtromas (ed.), *The End of 'Isms'*, Blackwell, Oxford, 1994.
7. S.P. Huntington, 'The Clash of Civilizations', *Foreign Affairs*, 72, 1993, p.22.
8. S.P. Huntington, *The Clash of Civilizations and the Remaking of World Order*, Simon and Schuster, London, 1997.
9. See also B. Barber, *Jihad vs McWorld: How Globalism and Tribalism Are Reshaping the World*, Ballantine, New York, 1996.
10. As the following pages mainly cover arguments raised in previous chapters, further notes have been dispensed with. There is also no 'Guide to further reading' for this chapter.

INDEX